Wyndham Lewis titles published by Black Sparrow Press

The Apes of God (novel) (1981)
BLAST 1 (journal) (1981)
BLAST 2 (journal) (1981)
The Complete Wild Body (stories) (1982)
Journey Into Barbary (travel) (1983)
Self Condemned (novel) (1983)
Snooty Baronet (novel) (1984)
BLAST 3 (journal) (1984)
Rude Assignment (autobiography) (1984)
The Vulgar Streak (novel) (1985)
Rotting Hill (stories) (1986)
The Caliph's Design (essays) (1986)
Men Without Art (essays) (1987)

Forthcoming:

The Art of Being Ruled (philosophy)
Time and Western Man (philosophy)
Tarr (novel)
The Revenge for Love (novel)

D1319269

WYNDHAM LEWIS
MEN WITHOUT ART

EDITED WITH AFTERWORD & NOTES BY SEAMUS COONEY

BLACK SPARROW PRESS • SANTA ROSA • 1987

Cover illustration: "Two Vorticist Figures" by Wyndham Lewis.
Pen and ink, gouache, 9¼ x 12½ inches, 1912. Michel 116.

LIBRARY OF CONGRESS CATALOGING-IN-PUBLICATION DATA

Lewis, Wyndham, 1882-1957.
  Men without art.

  Includes index.
1. Literature, Modern — History and criticism.
I. Title.
PN710.L45   1987   809   87-733
ISBN 0-87685-687-3
ISBN 0-87685-688-1 (deluxe cloth)
ISBN 0-87685-686-5 (pbk.)

EDITOR'S NOTE

THE TEXT FOR THIS EDITION of *Men Without Art* is that of the first edition, published by Cassell in London in 1934 (and reprinted photographically by Russell and Russell in New York in 1964). The first edition was riddled with misprints and errors, many of them Lewis's responsibility and a number of them substantive. Some three hundred and fifty of these have been corrected here, where necessary by consulting Lewis's sources. Other changes are minor: the use of quotation marks has been regularized according to current American usage (double everywhere except for quotations within quotations). Spellings have been made consistent, but in general Lewis's British spelling has been retained. Some minor typographical changes have also been made (placing long quotations as indented blocks, for instance). In principle, I have made only those corrections of Lewis's grammar and his often unconventional punctuation and syntax as were necessary for unimpeded intelligibility. All changes are recorded in the Table of Emendations. As in the original edition, Lewis's own notes are indicated by superscript numerals and printed at the foot of the page; a few editorial additions to them are indicated by square brackets.

A lengthy section of Explanatory Notes has been provided — more than most readers will need, I'm sure, but I have thought it better to err on the side of completeness (and even so not all the information that one might desire has been located). Here will be found notes on persons mentioned in the text, translations of all passages and phrases in French and other foreign languages, sources of quotations and allusions (when known), and the like. These notes are available for interested readers but are not signalled in the text in order to avoid distracting interruptions.

Finally, the Afterword offers some account of the book's reception, both public and private, its contributions to contemporary critical debate, and its enduring value.

I want to thank Paul Edwards for valuable suggestions that helped with the Notes and Afterword (though of course responsibility for their shortcomings remains mine). Thanks too to my university for a sabbatical leave which facilitated work on this project.

Seamus Cooney
Western Michigan University
Kalamazoo, Michigan

CONTENTS

MEN WITHOUT ART

INTRODUCTION

"I am going to make you a rather original proposal. Supposing we all of us take off our shoes and stockings so that we can
see in what condition are our respective feet." — GUY DE
MAUPASSANT, at a dinner given in his honour.

IN THIS BOOK I have, not for the first time, proceeded from the particular to
the general — from the concrete to the abstract — from the personal to the
theoretic. The former is so much more popular than the latter. Better, I thought,
to put on what is most popular first. So I have taken the relatively engaging
personalities of Messrs. Hemingway and Faulkner and used them as an advance-
illustration, as it were, of what I have to say. Having given the reader a good
run with the popular novelists, I pass, still on the personal plane, into a
somewhat chillier field — that of Mr. T. S. Eliot — as literary critic, not as poet.
Still, that is a figure which has come to be very well known and greatly discussed, greatly influential among the very young. After I have finished with
him, and his friend Mr. I. A. Richards, I pass over into somewhat less comfortable regions; but still Mrs. Virginia Woolf is there to provide a little firm
foothold in mere personality for those who prefer persons to ideas. But in fact
beyond a clearly defined, and quickly overtaken limit, you must be prepared
to work a little bit, to look an abstract idea in the face and mildly cudgel your
brains, if you are going to understand much about books and other products
of the artistic intelligence. By this means, at all events, namely that of progressing by easy stages from the particular to the general, it has been my object to lead on the general reader — the "plain reader" perhaps is better — to an
understanding of the absolute necessity of looking behind the work of art for
something which is not evident to the casual eye, and which yet has to be
dragged out into the light if we are to understand what any work of art is *about*.
For that it is *about* something is an axiom for me, and *art-for-art's-sake* I do
not even trouble to confute.

"But what is art about anyway?" — Plain Reader asks perhaps, on his mettle
at once: "Except the orderly registration of pleasure? I like (Plain Reader goes
on) a nice Medici Society Hobbema on my wall — it gives me a peaceful feeling: or a sporting print of a hunting scene — it makes me think of the good old
days, like singing 'Old John Peel with his coat so gay — Who lived at Troutbeck
once on a day.' Then a novel, that is *art* I suppose. I like a nice novel — I am
a youngish Plain Man and I don't mind a spot of love, but I prefer *mystery*:
give me a good gory murder all the time! When I was up at Oxford I belonged
to the Crime Club — I couldn't get on very well with Mrs. Woolf. For me a novel
is just a good yarn, or a bad one, about love, crime, romance, adventure: it
takes one out of oneself; the author, presumably, is mainly occupied with the
problem of taking us out of ourselves — he's a sort of illusionist — making us
live for a few hours a more exciting life than our own. When he has satisfactorily achieved that, and paid into his bank the cheque he gets for doing it,
his function is at an end as far as I'm concerned."

11

If you are not so Plain a Reader as all that I apologize for this "Rugger Blue" interlude (upon the model of Mr. I. A. Richards's class of sawneys): but it is just as well to be prepared for the worst!

The above is however a true account of ninety-nine novels out of a hundred, which are written, of course, especially for Rugger Blues, Cabinet Ministers, Sporting Girls, and the widows of colonial officials. One novelist in a hundred jacks up his ramshackle, mercenary piece of sensational entertainment onto a more complicated plane. Mrs. Woolf has done that, for instance — a little meretriciously; and, in fact, adapted Joyce and Proust and other such things for the salon. But still Mrs. Woolf is far too "highbrow" for the Rugger Blue, and is regarded by Sir Austen Chamberlain probably as a broth of a girl, and right over his head God bless her! As it is with the novel, so it is with the poem, the picture, the play, the film-play, statue or musical composition. All forms of art of a permanent order are intended not only to please and to excite, believe me, Plain Reader, if you are still there, but to call into play the entire human capacity — for sensation, reflection, imagination, and will. We judge a work of art, ultimately, with reference to its capacity to effect this total mobilization of our faculties. The novel is no exception to this rule. So undoubtedly a work of art, in the full-blooded intellectual sense, is no joke at all, but, from the "low-brow" standpoint, a rather grim affair; and this in spite of the fact that *Gulliver's Travels* has been a great success as a nursery story-book, because of all the gwate big men and the tiny little chappies!

Implicit in the serious work of art will be found politics, theology, philosophy — in brief all the great intellectual departments of the human consciousness; even the Plain Reader is aware of that in theory. But what is not so clear to very many people is that the most harmless piece of literary entertainment — the common crime story for instance, or the schoolboy epic of the young of the English proletariat centred around the portly figure of Bunter, "the owl of the Remove" (see *Magnet Library*, weekly 2d., of all newsagents) is at all events politically and morally influential. How often has it not been pointed out that it is useless to talk of *No more war*, of World Disarmament, while millions of children are being fed with a warlike ideology — the Church Brigade, for instance, and the literature provided for the Church Brigade, in which violence and cruelty play such an important part? And the influence upon the mind of the whole nation, adult and juvenile, of the Hollywood film-factory is terrific: for "shaping lives" it is obviously an engine comparable to the Society of Jesus. Why people find this and analogous facts so difficult to understand astonishes me. Yet a whole barbarous system of conduct, and judgements to match, is *implied* in every flick of the kinetic novelettes.

But I have not written this particular book in order to demonstrate these important truths. The principles of intellectual *detection* — the injunction to look *behind* everything, however trivial, in the art-field, as a matter of routine, and challenge all "face values" — merely have to be restated every time, for the benefit of the inattentive, and the chronically "comfortable" — the inveterately "cosy." My present essay is not even for the "Plain Reader," so much as for the "Plain Writer"; and not *too* "plain," even at that, I may as well add. But I will explain, as briefly as possible.

.   .   .   .   .   .

This book has, in fact, been written, to put it shortly, to defend Satire. But to "Satire" I have given a meaning so wide as to confound it with "Art." So this book may be said to be nothing short of a defence of art — as art is understood in the most "high-brow" quarters today. (How I have been able to identify "Satire" and "Art" I argue in Part II.) That there is some occasion to defend art, at the moment at which I write, is pretty generally conceded. Indeed a society of *Men Without Art* is not a mere dream of the future, but a matter of practical politics — many politicians and theologians envisage such a possibility with the most unruffled calm, if not with relish.

For all practical purposes, then, we may describe this book as a defence of contemporary art, most of which art is unquestionably satiric, or comic. And it is a defence against every sort of antagonist, from that deep-dyed Moralist, the public of Anglo-Saxony, down to that nationalist nuisance, which would confine art to some territorial or racial tradition; from the Marxist who would harness art to politics, up to the mystical dogmatism which would harness it to the vapours of the spirit-world.

"But what the devil is art!" somebody may call out again, "that it should be so elaborately defended as all that? Is it a Church; is it a schism; have we the makings of a political party in the studies and studios?" — But that I have not set out to define in these pages. What can be with safety affirmed, however, and at that it can be left, is that if I have here put up a defence of art, it is not for its *beaux yeux*! Anything but that — heaven defend us from the *beaux yeux* of the *beaux arts*! Art is not here defended for its own sake: *art-for-art's-sake*, of Walter Pater, is nothing to do with art — it is a spectator's doctrine, not an artist's: it teaches how to enjoy, not how to perform. I am a performer. It is as a performer that I shall speak.

As a performer, that is to say as an artist. Professor Walter Raleigh (I must quote from a newspaper article) has written about William Blake — "His work is one prolonged vindication of the cause of all the artists in the world." That was because Blake was himself a performer; it was a fine exhibition of *esprit de corps*, as well as of self-help: and he felt that this "vindication" was imposed on him, and I have no doubt it was. How much more is not that the case today?

Many books are written concerning the tricks of the performer's trade. Those are useful books (especially for performers): but here is one of a somewhat different type, and perhaps of more interest to the lay reader. It is not a book about the craft of writing or of painting, except incidentally. It is about the ethical or political status of these performances. It is as though an illusionist came forward and engaged us in argument as to his right to make men vanish, to cause rabbits to issue from their breast-pockets, to read their thoughts, and the sound reasons that he had for plunging swords into baskets, and bringing them forth dripping with innocent blood.

Here you have a notorious satirist explaining to you how it comes about that he may with impunity compose disobliging epics, or vignettes, including all and sundry — planting postiche noses, doubling the dimensions of ears, compressing and elongating anatomies *ad lib* — to confine oneself to the corporal. These pages will be eagerly read by all satirists — for though you would scarcely believe it, satirists suffer much as a class from an uneasy conscience — are always asking themselves "how far they may go" — if they may dare say this, or would it not be too brutal to say that. But it should also be read with some attention by many of the satirized. And you do not have to be of much importance today to figure in a work of satire (see later chapter). And there are a vast number of people who come in contact with art and artists who would be glad for a few hints as to how to handle the latter, and how to deliver a *mauvais coup* to the former (for art is not really popular, that is to say, modern art). But in spite of this miscellaneous audience, it is mainly for the satirist, or more generally the artist (have you noticed how today they are one — and can you wonder at it, as one man to another?) that this treatise has been written. Last but not least, it is in the nature of an *Entlastungs Offensive*, upon the *personal front*, as it might be called. For that highly ethical proverb, *God helps those who help themselves*, is more true of the satirist than of anybody. No one will exactly rush to the assistance of the satirist, when hard-pressed — he is a sort of Cain among craftsmen — so the satirist is compelled to move swiftly to his own.

.   .   .   .   .

But my opening part deals with the work of three people, two novelists and a critic. As artists, of course, all three are satirists. Mr. Hemingway, in the rôle he has chosen for himself, is, as it were, a proletarian clown; he satirizes *himself* — but a self that is not his private self at all, but rather a sort of projection of the spirit of Miss Stein into the slow-moving and slow-thinking bulk of a simple-hearted labourer — say an American lumber-jack. He is a pseudo-lumberjack, as it were (and so responds to the requirements of the *pseudo* principle of Eliot and Richards). — Mr. Faulkner I call "a satirist with a corn-cob." He is a fierce moralist, who operates upon the satiric plane, armed with corn-cobs and such like sardonic weapons of aggression, to insult the victims of his ethical rage.

Mr. T. S. Eliot, as a poet, is no exception to the rule that all art is in fact satire today. Sweeney, the enigmatical Mrs. Porter, Prufrock, Klipstein and Burbank, are authentic figures of Satire and nothing else. But as the critic he is a very different kettle of fish to what he is as poet. Where he comes in, making a valuable third in this trio of introductory studies, is that he supplies the theological factor lacking in the other two. He is preoccupied with problems of *belief*, as that applies to theologic, as well as to political and other forms, of belief. And as the moralist and the politician are the two chief enemies of the artist today, Mr. Eliot's ethical, or rather non-ethical, standpoint, and the *pseudo* principle he has received from Mr. I. A. Richards, provide suggestive devices for the better defence of the small garrison of satirist-artists, invested in their cubist citadel.

Although there is nothing written or painted today of any power which could not be brought under the head of *Satire* (if you allow a fairly wide interpretation to that term) yet I could not find a fictionist deliberately dealing in satire — either occasionally or all the time — of sufficient significance to use as one of my illustrations — except myself. Under these circumstances, I have been compelled to refer to the work in satire of Mr. Wyndham Lewis, "Personal Appearance Artist" (Part II, Chapter II).

So the three chapters of which Part I is composed — consisting of the work of Hemingway, Faulkner and Eliot (critic) respectively — are intended to supply the sort of information that is required, by a hypothetical reader of this book, about two notable "creative" writers and a celebrated literary critic. These chapters are intended to demonstrate upon the living model, selecting contemporary figures and so focussing the general argument upon the field of the day-to-day reading of the Plain Reader — *Class* A.1 (or A.2) — for I am *fairly* democratic, and in any case eschew as far as possible all that is *too* hereditary-Grand-Duke. To demonstrate *the approach* indicated in such a programme as mine, by showing that programme in operation in three independent critical studies, has been my idea.

I felt that if I did not, somewhere in the course of this study, come down to brass tacks — turn my critical hand-torch upon the inside of a book or two — the reader might only half grasp what all the argument was about. For he might quite well have said to himself: "Mr. Lewis is very concerned with ethical and political pros and cons, and certainly all that *may* apply to some writers (deliberate tract writers like Mr. Shaw) but how can it have any bearing upon such mere storytellers as the author of *Farewell to Arms* or *Sanctuary?*" That sort of misunderstanding, I think you will agree, I have cleared up at the start, in my Chapters I and II.

The third chapter of my first part, regarding the *pseudoist* enthusiasms of Mr. Eliot, is arbitrarily associated with Chapters I and II. It is intended to supply you, again, at the outset, with what appears to me the true view of Mr. Eliot, the Anglo-Saxon (and Anglo-Catholic) representative of continental *thomistic* literary criticism (this is a mouthful, but how else describe it?). The rôle of that type of criticism plays an important part in the argument of my book as a whole. And Mr. Eliot himself, in a general way, stands as it were for the marriage of "the dumb ox" and of Bloomsbury — the "dumb ox," in this instance, being Aquinas. A strange wedding! — fraught with the oddest consequences both here and in Boston: but that is not the subject of this essay, except incidentally. And I hope it is unnecessary for me to say that I do *not* identify St. Thomas Aquinas with the eminent poetic partner of Mr. I. A. Richards? The idea is this: that, as we live in a sort of lunatic asylum — or a clinic for the variously "complexed" — in which it would be quite hopeless to attempt to apply any rational principle in our vital dealings with this seething undergraduate and art-student mob who have become the only audience for the artist, and their for the most part clownish masters, it is best to discover how we can use, to the advantage of such light as is vouchsafed us, even the darkest and most fantastic solemnities — even the most inconsequent of pseudo-systems — which, whatever they might be in other times and other places, are very concrete affairs in the world in which we find ourselves.

That all standards of taste and good sense have gone by the board and vanished completely from the popular plane, is generally accepted among us. What I expounded, upon those lines, by the method of verbatim quotation from book or newspaper, demonstrating the affiliation of the sublime and the ridiculous, in my paper *The Enemy*, and in my critical books, is now being expounded by a host of people, from Mr. I. A. Richards (and his appendix the Leavises) down to every bottle-washer in Fleet Street. But it is always *the other fellow* — never Number One — who is bereft of criteria and standard-less: although it is pretty clear that if things are in a bad way upon one plane of a finely homogeneous, very thoroughly *levelled*, civilization, they are liable to be in a bad way up in the "highbrow" loft as well as down in the "lowbrow" basement. Is not however "the present writer," as are all other writers, suspect? Certainly he is! Time alone can show which of us, of all these figures engaged in this pell-mell confusion, has preserved the largest store (and at the best it must be modest) of what is rational, and the least affected with rank bogusness.

But I think I have said enough to indicate the purpose of the three monoliths — the essays upon Hemingway, Faulkner and Eliot — which embellish my first part. And now, I think, we may proceed to the business of the book.

PART ONE

CHAPTER I

ERNEST HEMINGWAY

THE "DUMB OX"

ERNEST HEMINGWAY IS a very considerable artist in prose-fiction.

Besides this, or with this, his work possesses a penetrating quality, like an animal speaking. Compared often with Hemingway, William Faulkner is an excellent, big-strong, novelist: but a conscious artist he cannot be said to be. Artists are made, not born: but he is considerably older, I believe, than Hemingway, so it is not that. But my motive for discussing these two novelists has not been to arrive at estimates of that sort.

A quality in the work of the author of *Men Without Women* suggests that we are in the presence of a writer who is not merely a conspicuous chessman in the big-business book-game of the moment, but something much finer than that. Let me attempt to isolate that quality for you, in such a way as not to damage it too much: for having set out to demonstrate the political significance of this artist's work, I shall, in the course of that demonstration, resort to a dissection of it — not the best way, I am afraid, to bring out the beauties of the finished product. This dissection is, however, necessary for my purpose here. "I have a weakness for Ernest Hemingway," as the egregious Miss Stein says:[1] it is not agreeable to me to pry into his craft, but there is no help for it if I am to reach certain important conclusions.

But *political significance!* That is surely the last thing one would expect to find in such books as *In Our Time, The Sun Also Rises, Men Without Women,* or *Farewell to Arms.* And indeed it is difficult to imagine a writer whose mind is more entirely closed to politics than is Hemingway's. I do not suppose he has ever heard of the Five-Year Plan, though I dare say he knows that artists pay no income tax in Mexico, and is quite likely to be following closely the agitation of the Mexican matadors to get themselves recognized as "artists" so that they may pay no income tax. I expect he has heard of Hitler, but thinks of him mainly, if he is acquainted with the story, as the Boche who went down into a cellar with another Boche and captured thirty Frogs and came back with an Iron Cross. He probably knows that his friend Pound writes a good many letters every week to American papers on the subject of Social Credit, but I am sure Pound has never succeeded in making him read a line of *Credit-Power and Democracy.* He is interested in the sports of death, in the sad things that happen to those engaged in the sports of love — in sand-sharks· and in Wilson-spoons — in war, but *not* in the things that cause war, or the people who

---

[1] *The Autobiography of Alice B. Toklas.*

profit by it, or in the ultimate human destinies involved in it. He lives, or affects to live, *submerged*. He is in the multitudinous ranks of *those to whom things happen*—terrible things of course, and of course stoically borne. He has never heard, or affects never to have heard, that there is another and superior element, inhabited by a type of unnatural men which preys upon that of the submerged type. Or perhaps it is not quite a submerged mankind to which he belongs, or affects to belong, but to something of the sort described in one of Faulkner's war stories: "But after twelve years," Faulkner writes, "I think of us as bugs in the surface of the water, isolant and aimless and unflagging. Not on the surface; in it, within that line of demarcation not air and not water, sometimes submerged, sometimes not."[1] (What a stupid and unpleasant word "isolant" is! Hemingway would be incapable of using such a word.) But—twelve, fifteen years afterwards—to be *submerged*, most of the time, is Hemingway's idea. It is a little bit of an *art pur* notion, but it is, I think, extremely effective, in his case. Faulkner is much less preoccupied with art for its own sake, and although he has obtained his best successes by submerging himself again (in an intoxicating and hysterical fluid) he does not like being submerged quite as well as Hemingway, and dives rather because he is compelled to dive by public opinion, I imagine, than because he feels at home in the stupid medium of the sub-world, the *bêtise* of the herd. Hemingway has really taken up his quarters there, and has mastered the medium entirely, so that he is of it and yet not of it in a very satisfactory way.

Another manner of looking at it would be to say that Ernest Hemingway is the Noble Savage of Rousseau, but a white version, the simple American man. That is at all events the rôle that he has chosen, and he plays it with an imperturbable art and grace beyond praise.

It is not perhaps necessary to say that Hemingway's art is an art of the surface—and, as I look at it, none the worse for that. It is almost purely an art of action, and of very violent action, which is another qualification. Faulkner's is that too: but violence with Hemingway is deadly matter-of-fact (as if there were only violent action and nothing else in the world): whereas with Faulkner it is an excited crescendo of psychological working-up of a sluggish and not ungentle universe, where there *might* be something else than high-explosive—if it were given a Chinaman's chance, which it is not. The latter is a far less artistic purveyor of violence. He does it well: but as to the manner, he does it in a way that any fool could do it. Hemingway, on the other hand, serves it up like the master of this form of art that he is, immeasurably more effective than Faulkner—good as he is; or than say the Irish novelist O'Flaherty—who is a *raffiné* too, or rather a two-gun man; Hemingway really banishes melodrama (except for his absurd escapes, on a Hollywood pattern, in *Farewell to Arms*).

[1] "Ad Astra." [*These Thirteen.*] William Faulkner.

To find a parallel to *In Our Time* or *Farewell to Arms* you have to go to *Colomba* or to *Chronique du règne de Charles ix*: and in one sense Prosper Mérimée supplies the historical key to these two ex-soldiers — married, in their literary craft, to a theatre of action *à outrance*. The scenes at the siege of La Rochelle in the *Chronique du règne de Charles ix* for instance: in the burning of the mill when the ensign is roasted in the window, that is the Hemingway subject-matter to perfection — a man melted in his armour like a shell-fish in its shell — melted lobster in its red armour.

S'ils tentaient de sauter par les fenêtres, ils tombaient dans les flammes, ou bien étaient reçus sur la pointe des piques. . . . Un enseigne, revêtu d'une armure complète, essaya de sauter comme les autres par une fenêtre étroite. Sa cuirasse se terminait, suivant une mode alors assez commune, par une espèce de jupon en fer qui couvrait les cuisses et le ventre, et s'élargissait comme le haut d'un entonnoir, de manière à permettre de marcher facilement. La fenêtre n'était pas assez large pour laisser passer cette partie de son armure, et l'enseigne, dans son trouble, s'y était précipité avec tant de violence, qu'il se trouva avoir la plus grande partie du corps en dehors sans pouvoir remuer, et pris comme dans un étau. Cependant les flammes montaient jusqu'à lui, échauffaient son armure, et l'y brûlaient lentement comme dans une fournaise ou dans ce fameux taureau d'airain inventé par Phalaris.[1]

Compare this with the following:

We were in a garden at Mons. Young Buckley came in with his patrol from across the river. The first German I saw climbed up over the garden wall. We waited till he got one leg over and then potted him. He had so much equipment on and looked awfully surprised and fell down into the garden. Then three more came over further down the wall. We shot them. They all came just like that.[2]

"In no century would Prosper Mérimée have been a theologian or metaphysician," and if that is true of Mérimée, it is at least equally true of his American prototype. But their "formulas" sound rather the same, "indifferent in politics . . . all the while he is feeding all his scholarly curiosity, his imagination, the very eye, with the, to him ever delightful, relieving, reassuring spectacle, of those straightforward forces in human nature, which are also matters of fact. There is the formula of Mérimée! the enthusiastic amateur of rude, crude, naked force in men and women wherever it could be found . . . there are no half-lights. . . . Sylla, the false Demetrius, Carmen, Colomba, that impassioned self within himself, have no atmosphere. Painfully distinct in outline, inevitable to sight, unrelieved, there they stand, like solitary mountain forms on some hard, perfectly transparent day. What Mérimée gets around his singularly sculpturesque creations is neither more nor less than empty space."[3]

[1] *Chronique du règne de Charles ix.* Mérimée.
[2] *In Our Time.* Hemingway.
[3] *Miscellaneous Studies.* Walter Pater.

I have quoted the whole of this passage because it gives you "the formula," equally for the author of *Carmen* and of *The Sun Also Rises* — namely *the enthusiastic amateur of rude, crude, naked force in men and women*: but it also brings out very well, subsequently, the nature of the radical and extremely significant *difference* existing between these two men, of differing nations and epochs — sharing so singularly a taste for physical violence and for fine writing, but nothing else. Between them there is this deep gulf fixed: that gifted he of today is "the man that things are done to" — even the "I" in *The Sun Also Rises* allows his Jew puppet to knock him about and "put him to sleep" with a crash on the jaw, and this first person singular covers a very aimless, will-less person, to say the least of it: whereas that *he* of the world of *Carmen* (so much admired by Nietzsche for its bright Latin violence and directness — *la gaya scienza*) or of Corsican vendetta, he was in love with *will*, as much as with violence: he did not celebrate in his stories a spirit that suffered bodily injury and mental disaster with the stoicism of an athletic clown in a particularly brutal circus — or of oxen (however robust) beneath a crushing yoke: *he*, the inventor of Colomba, belonged to a race of men for whom action meant *their* acting, with all the weight and momentum of the whole of their being: *he* of post-Napoleonic France celebrated intense spiritual energy and purpose, using physical violence as a mere means to that only half-animal ideal. *Sylla, Demetrius, Colomba*, even *de Mergy*, summon to our mind a world bursting with purpose — even if always upon the personal and very animal plane, and with no more universal ends: while Hemingway's books, on the other hand, scarcely contain a figure who is not in some way futile, clown-like, passive, and above all *purposeless.* His world of men and women (*in violent action*, certainly) is completely empty of will. His puppets are leaves, *very violently* blown hither and thither; drugged or at least deeply intoxicated phantoms of a sort of matter-of-fact shell-shock.

In *Farewell to Arms* the hero is a young American who has come over to Europe for the fun of the thing, as an alternative to baseball, to take part in the Sport of Kings. It has not occurred to him that it is no longer the sport of kings, but the turning-point in the history of the earth at which he is assisting, when men must either cease thinking like children and abandon such sports, or else lose their freedom for ever, much more effectively than any mere *king* could ever cause them to lose it. For him, it remains "war" in the old-fashioned semi-sporting sense. Throughout this ghastly event, he proves himself a thorough-going sport, makes several hairbreadth, Fenimore Cooper-like, escapes, but never from first to last betrays a spark of intelligence. Indeed, his physical stoicism, admirable as it is, is as nothing to his really heroic imperviousness to thought. This "war" — Gallipoli, Passchendaele, Caporetto — is just another "scrap." The Anglo-Saxon American — the "Doughboy" — and the Anglo-Saxon Tommy — join hands, in fact, outrival each other in a stolid determination absolutely to ignore, come what may, what all this is about. Whoever may be in the secrets of destiny — may indeed be destiny itself — *they* are not nor ever will be. They are an integral part of that world *to whom things happen*: they are not those who cause or connive at the happenings, and that is perfectly clear.

> *Pack up your troubles in your old kit bag,*
> *Smile boys, that's the style*

and *keep smiling*, what's more, from ear to ear, a *should-I-worry?* "good sport" smile, as do the Hollywood Stars when they are being photographed, as did the poor Bairnsfather "Tommy" — the "muddied oaf at the goal" — of all oafishness!

I hope this does not seem irrelevant to you: it is not, let me reassure you, but very much the contrary. The roots of all these books are in the War of 1914–1918, as much those of Faulkner as those of Hemingway: it would be ridiculous of course to say that either of these highly intelligent ex-soldiers shared the "oafish" mentality altogether: but the war-years were a democratic, a *levelling*, school, and both come from a pretty thoroughly "levelled" nation, where personality is the thing least liked. The rigid organization of the communal life as revealed in *Middletown*, for instance (or such a phenomenon as N.R.A.) is akin to the military state. So *will*, as expressed in the expansion of the individual, is not a thing we should expect to find illustrated by a deliberately typical American writer.

Those foci of passionate personal energy which we find in Mérimée, we should look for in vain in the pages of Hemingway or Faulkner: in place of Don José or of Colomba we get a pack of drugged or intoxicated marionettes. These differences are exceedingly important. But I shall be dealing with that more carefully in my next chapter.

So any attempt to identify "the formula" for Prosper Mérimée with that of Ernest Hemingway would break down. You are led at once to a realization of the critical difference between these two universes of discourse, both employing nothing but physical terms; of how an appetite for the extremity of violence exists in both, but in the one case it is personal ambition, family pride, romantic love that are at stake, and their satisfaction is violently sought and undertaken, whereas in the other case purposeless violence, for the sake of the "kick," is pursued and recorded, and the "thinking subject" is to regard himself as nothing more significant than a ripple beneath the breeze upon a pond.

If we come down to the manner, specifically to the style, in which these sensational impressions are conveyed, again most interesting discoveries await us: for, especially with Mr. Hemingway, the story is told in the tone, and with the vocabulary, of the persons described. The rhythm is the anonymous folk-rhythm of the urban proletariat. Mr. Hemingway is, self-consciously, a folk-prose-poet in the way that Robert Burns was a folk-poet. But what is curious about this is that the modified *Beach-la-mar* in which he writes, is, more or less, the speech that is proposed for everybody in the future — it is a volapük which probably will be ours tomorrow. For if the chief executive of the United States greets the Roman Catholic democratic leader (Al Smith) with the exclamation "Hallo old potato!" to-day, the English political leaders will be doing so the day after tomorrow. And the Anglo-Saxon *Beach-la-mar* of the future will not be quite the same thing as Chaucer or Dante, contrasted with the learned tongue. For the latter was the speech of a race rather than of a class, whereas our "vulgar tongue" will really be *vulgar.*

But in the case of Hemingway the folk-business is very seriously com-plicated by a really surprising fact. He has suffered an overmastering influence, which cuts his work off from any other, except that of his mistress (for his master has been a *mistress!*). So much is this the case, that their destinies (his and that of the person who so strangely hypnotized him with her repeating habits and her *faux-naif* prattle) are for ever interlocked. His receptivity was so abnormally pronounced (even as a craftsman, this capaci-ty for being *the person that things are done to* rather than the person who naturally initiates what is to be done to others, was so marked) and the affinity thus disclosed was found so powerful! I don't like speaking about this, for it is such a first-class complication, and yet it is in a way so irrele-vant to the spirit which informs his work and must have informed it had he never made this apparently overwhelming "contact." But there it is: if you ask yourself how you would be able to tell a page of Hemingway, if it were unexpectedly placed before you, you would be compelled to answer, *Because it would be like Miss Stein!* And if you were asked how you would know it was not by Miss Stein, you would say, *Because it would probably be about prize-fighting, war, or the bull-ring, and Miss Stein does not write about war, boxing or bull-fighting!*

It is very uncomfortable in real life when people become so captivated with somebody else's tricks that they become a sort of caricature or echo of the other: and it is no less embarrassing in books, at least when one entertains any respect for the victim of the fascination. But let us take a passage or two and get this over — it is very unpleasant. Let us take Krebs — the "he" in this passage is Krebs, a returned soldier in a Hemingway story:

> When he was in town their appeal to him was not very strong. He did not like them when he saw them in the Greek's ice cream parlor. He did not want them themselves really. They were too complicated. There was

something else. Vaguely he wanted a girl but he did not want to have to work to get her. He would have liked to have a girl but he did not want to have to spend a long time getting her. He did not want to get into the intrigue and the politics. He did not want to have to do any courting. He did not want to tell any more lies. It wasn't worth it.

He did not want any consequences. He did not want any consequences ever again. He wanted to live along without consequences. Besides he did not really need a girl. The army had taught him that. It was all right to pose as though you had to have a girl. Nearly everybody did that. But it wasn't true. You did not need a girl. That was the funny thing. First a fellow boasted how girls mean nothing to him, that he never thought of them, that they could not touch him. Then a fellow boasted that he could not get along without girls, that he had to have them all the time, that he could not go to sleep without them.

That was all a lie. It was all a lie both ways. You did not need a girl unless you thought about them. He learned that in the army. Then sooner or later you always got one. When you were really ripe for a girl you always got one. You did not have to think about it. Sooner or later it would come. He had learned that in the army.

Now he would have liked a girl if she had come to him and not wanted to talk. But here at home it was all too complicated. He knew he could never get through it all again. It was not worth the trouble. That was the thing about French girls and German girls. There was not all this talking. You couldn't talk much and you did not need to talk. It was simple and you were friends. He thought about France and then he began to think about Germany. On the whole he had liked Germany better. He did not want to leave Germany. He did not want to come home. Still, he had come home. He sat on the front porch.

He liked the girls that were walking along the other side of the street. He liked the look of them much better than the French girls or the German girls. But the world they were in was not the world he was in. He would like to have one of them. But it was not worth it. They were such a nice pattern. He liked the pattern. It was exciting. But he would not go through all the talking. He did not want one badly enough. He liked to look at them all, though. It was not worth it.[1]

So much for Krebs: now open Miss Stein and "meet" Melanctha.

Rose was lazy but not dirty, and Sam was careful but not fussy, and then there was Melanctha. . . .

When Rose's baby was coming to be born, Rose came to stay in the house where Melanctha Herbert lived just then, . . .

Rose went there to stay, so that she might have the doctor from the hospital. . . .

Melanctha Herbert had not made her life all simple like Rose Johnson. Melanctha had not found it easy with herself to make her wants and what she had, agree.

Melanctha Herbert was always losing what she had in wanting all the things she saw. Melanctha was always being left when she was not leaving others.

Melanctha Herbert always loved too hard and much too often. She was always full with mystery and subtle movements . . .[2]

[1] *In Our Time*, pp. 92, 94. Ernest Hemingway.
[2] *Three Lives*, p. 89. Gertrude Stein.

etc., etc., etc.

Or here is a typical bit from *Composition as Explanation*:

> There is singularly nothing that makes a difference a difference in begin-
> ning and in the middle and in ending except that each generation has something
> different at which they are all looking. By this I mean so simply that anybody
> knows it that composition is the difference which makes each and all of them
> then different from other generations and this is what makes everything
> different otherwise they are all alike and everybody knows it because
> everybody says it.[1]

There is no possibility, I am afraid, of slurring over this. It is just a thing
that you have to accept as an unfortunate handicap in an artist who is in
some respects above praise. Sometimes it is less pronounced, there are
occasions when it is *almost* absent — Krebs, for instance, is a full-blooded
example of Hemingway steining away for all he is worth. But it is never
quite absent.

How much does it matter? If we blot out Gertrude Stein, and suppose
she does not exist, does this part of Hemingway's equipment help or not?
We must answer *Yes* I think. It does seem to help a good deal: many of
his best effects are obtained by means of it. It is so much a part of his craft,
indeed, that it is difficult now to imagine Hemingway without this mannerism. He has never taken it over into a gibbering and baboonish stage
as has Miss Stein. He has kept it as a valuable oddity, even if a flagrantly
borrowed one — ever present it is true, but one to which we can easily get
used and come to like even as a delightfully clumsy engine of innocence.
I don't mind it very much.

To say that, near to communism as we all are, it cannot matter, and
is indeed praiseworthy, for a celebrated artist to take over, lock, stock and
barrel from another artist the very thing for which he is mainly known,
seems to me to be going too far in the denial of the person, or the
individual — especially as in a case of this sort, the trick is after all, in the
first instance, a *personal* trick. Such a practice must result, if universally
indulged in, in hybrid forms or monstrosities.

And my main criticism, indeed, of the *steining* of Hemingway is that
it does impose upon him an ethos — the Stein ethos, as it might be called.
With Stein's bag of tricks he also takes over a *Weltanschauung*, which may
not at all be his, and does in fact seem to contradict his major personal
quality. This infantile, dull-witted, dreamy stutter compels whoever uses
it to conform to the infantile, dull-witted type. He passes over into the
category of *those to whom things are done*, from that of those who
execute — if the latter is indeed where he originally belonged. One might
even go so far as to say that this brilliant Jewish lady had made a *clown*
of him by teaching Ernest Hemingway her baby-talk! So it is a pity. And it

---

[1] *Composition as Explanation* (p. 5). Gertrude Stein.

is very difficult to know where Hemingway proper begins and Stein leaves off as an artist. It is an uncomfortable situation for the critic, especially for one who "has a weakness" for the male member of this strange spiritual partnership, and very much prefers him to the female.

Hemingway's two principal books, *The Sun Also Rises* (for English publication called *Fiesta*) and *Farewell to Arms*, are delivered in the first person singular. What that involves may not be at once apparent to those who have not given much attention to literary composition. But it is not at all difficult to explain. Suppose you, Raymond Robinson, sit down to write a romance; subject-matter, the War. You get your "I" started off, say just before the outbreak of war, and then there is the outbreak, and then "I flew to the nearest recruiting station and joined the army" you write. Then the "I" goes off to the Western Front (or the Italian Front) and you will find yourself writing "I seized the Boche by the throat with one hand and shot him in the stomach with the other," or whatever it is you imagine your "I" as doing. But this "I," the reader will learn, does not bear the name on the title page, namely Raymond Robinson. He is called Geoffrey Jones. The reader will think, "that is only a thin disguise. It is Robinson's personal experience all right!"

Now this difficulty (if it be a difficulty) is very much enhanced if (for some reason) Geoffrey Jones is *always* doing exactly the things that Raymond Robinson is known to have done. If Raymond Robinson fought gallantly at Caporetto, for instance, then Geoffrey Jones — with the choice of a whole earth at war to choose from — is at Caporetto too. If Raymond Robinson takes to the sport of bull-fighting, sure enough Geoffrey Jones — the "I" of the novel — is there in the bull-ring too, as the night follows day. This, in fine, has been the case with Hemingway and *his* First-person-singular.

Evidently, in this situation — possessing a First-person-singular that invariably copies you in this flattering way — something must be done about it. The *First-person-singular* has to be endowed so palpably with qualities that could by no stretch of the imagination belong to its author that no confusion is possible. Upon this principle the "I" of *The Sun Also Rises* is described as sexually impotent, which is a complete alibi, of course, for Hemingway.

But there is more than this. The sort of First-person-singular that Hemingway invariably invokes is a dull-witted, bovine, monosyllabic simpleton. This lethargic and stuttering dummy he conducts, or pushes from behind, through all the scenes that interest him. This burlesque First-person-singular behaves in them like a moronesque version of his brilliant author. He *Steins* up and down the world, with the big lustreless ruminatory orbs of a

Picasso doll-woman (of the semi-classic type Picasso patented, with enormous hands and feet). It is, in short, the very dummy that is required for the literary mannerism of Miss Stein! It is the incarnation of the Stein-stutter — the male incarnation, it is understood.

But this constipated, baffled "frustrated" — yes, deeply and Freudianly "frustrated" — this wooden-headed, leaden-witted, heavy-footed, loutish and oafish marionette — peering dully out into the surrounding universe like a great big bloated five-year-old — pointing at this and pointing at that — uttering simply "CAT!" — "HAT!" — "FOOD!" — "SWEETIE!" — is, as a companion, infectious. His author has perhaps not been quite immune. Seen for ever through his nursery spectacles, the values of life accommodate themselves, even in the mind of his author, to the limitations and peculiar requirements of this highly idiosyncratic puppet.

So the political aspects of Hemingway's work (if, as I started by saying, one can employ such a word as *political* in connection with a thing that is so divorced from reality as a super-innocent, queerly-sensitive, village-idiot of a few words and fewer ideas) have to be sought, if anywhere, in the personality of this *First-person-singular*, imposed upon him largely by the Stein-manner.

.   .   .   .

We can return to the folk-prose problem now and face all the questions that the "done gones" and "sorta gonnas" present. Mr. H. L. Mencken in his well-known, extremely competent and exhaustive treatise, *The American Language* (a clasic in this field of research, first published fifteen years ago) affirmed that the American dialect had not yet come to the stage where it could be said to have acquired charm for "the purists." If used (at that time) in narrative literature it still possessed only the status of a disagreeable and socially-inferior jargon, like the cockney occurring in a Dickens novel — or as it is still mostly used in William Faulkner's novels, never outside of inverted commas; the novelist, having invoked it to convey the manner of speech of his rustic or provincial puppets, steps smartly away and resumes the narrative in the language of Macaulay or Horace Walpole, more or less.

"In so far as it is apprehended at all," Mencken wrote in 1920, "it is only in the sense that Irish-English was apprehended a generation ago — that is, as something uncouth and comic. But that is the way that new dialects always come in — through a drum-fire of cackles. Given the poet, there may suddenly come a day when our *theirns* and *would 'a hads* will take on the barbaric stateliness of the peasant locutions of old Maurya in 'Riders to the Sea.' "[1]

The reason that the dialect of the Aran Islands, or that used by Robert

---

[1] *The American Language* [3rd ed. (1923)], p. 396.

Burns, was so different from cockney or from the English educated speech was because it was a mixture of English and another language, Gaelic or lowland Scotch, and with the intermixture of foreign words went a literal translation of foreign idioms and the distortions arrived at by a tongue accustomed to another language. It was "broken-English," in other words, not "low-English," or slum-English, as is cockney.

Americans are today un-English in blood—whatever names they may bear: and in view of this it is surprising how intact the English language remains in the United States. But the *Beach-la-mar*, as he calls it, to which Mencken is referring above, is as it were the cockney of America. It has this great advantage over cockney, that it is fed with a great variety of immigrant words. It is, however, fundamentally *a class-jargon*; not a jargon resulting from difference of race, and consequently of speech. It is the *patois* of the "poor white," the negro, or the uneducated immigrant. It is not the language spoken by Mrs. Alice Roosevelt Longworth, for instance, or by Ernest Hemingway for that matter. But it is very *American*. And it is a *patois*, a fairly good rendering of which any American is competent to give. And you have read above the affectionate way Mencken refers to *our* "theirns" and "would 'a hads."

English as spoken in America is more vigorous and expressive than Oxford English, I think. It is easy to mistake a native from the wilds of Dorsetshire for an American, I have found; and were "educated" English used upon a good strong reverberant Dorsetshire basis, for instance, it would be all to the good, it is my opinion. Raleigh, Drake, and the rest of them, must have talked rather like that.

But with cockney it is not at all the same thing. There you get a degradation of English—it is *proletariat*, city-slum English, like Dublin-slum English. That is in a different category altogether to the weighty, rapid, and expressive torrent of the best Dorsetshire talk; and, as I have said, the *best* American is in the same category as the Dorsetshire—or as non-slum Irish—a good, sound accent, too. But the question to be answered is whether the *Beach-la-mar* Mr. Mencken has in mind is not too much the deteriorated pidgin tongue of the United States; and whether, if that is *affectioné* too much by the *literati*—as being the most *American* thing available, like a jazz—it is not going to be a vulgar corruption, which will vulgarize, as well as enrich, the tongue. So far it exists generally in inverted commas, as in Mr. Faulkner's books. Is it to be let out or not? A question for Americans.

For fifty years dialect-American has tended, what with negro and immigrant pressure, to simplify itself grammatically, and I suppose is still doing so at this moment.

> His [the immigrant's] linguistic habits and limitations have to be reckoned with in dealing with him, and the concessions thus made necessary have a very ponderable influence upon the general speech. Of much importance is

the support given to a native tendency by the foreigner's incapacity for employing (or even comprehending) syntax of any complexity, or words not of the simplest. This is the tendency toward succinctness and clarity, at whatever sacrifice of grace. One English observer, Sidney Low, puts the chief blame for the general explosiveness of American upon the immigrant, who must be communicated with in the plainest words available, and is not socially worthy of the suavity of circumlocution anyhow. In his turn the immigrant seizes upon these plainest words as upon a sort of convenient Lingua Franca — his quick adoption of *damn* as a universal adjective is traditional — and throws his influence upon the side of the underlying speech habit when he gets on in the vulgate. Many characteristic Americanisms of the sort to stagger lexicographers — for example, *near-silk* — have come from the Jews, whose progress in business is a good deal faster than their progress in English.

While England was a uniquely powerful empire-state, ruled by an aristocratic caste, its influence upon the speech as upon the psychology of the American ex-colonies was overwhelming. But today that ascendancy has almost entirely vanished. The aristocratic caste is nothing but a shadow of itself, the cinema has brought the American scene and the American dialect nightly into the heart of England, and the "Americanizing" process is far advanced. "Done gones," "good guys" and "buddies" sprout upon the lips of cockney children as readily as upon those to the manner born, of New York or Chicago: and there is no politically-powerful literate class any longer now, in our British "Bankers' Olympus," to confer prestige upon an exact and intelligent selective speech. Americanization — which is also for England, at least, proletarianization — is too far advanced to require underlining, even for people who fail usually to recognize anything until it has been in existence for a quarter of a century.

But if America has come to England, there has been no reciprocal movement of England into the United States: indeed, with the new American nationalism, England is deliberately kept out: and all the great influence that England exerted formally — merely by being there and speaking the same tongue and sharing the same fundamental political principles — that is today a thing of the past. So the situation is this, as far as our common language is concerned: the destiny of England and the United States of America is more than ever one. But it is now the American influence that is paramount. The tables have effectively been turned in that respect.

.   .   .   .   .   .

But there is a larger issue even than that local to the English-speaking nations. English is of all languages the simplest grammatically and the easiest to make into a *Beach-la-mar* or *pidgin* tongue. Whether this fact, combined with its "extraordinary tendency to degenerate into slang of every kind," is against it, is of some importance for the future — for it will have less and less grammar, obviously, and more and more cosmopolitan slang.

—Mr. Mencken is of opinion that a language cannot be too simple—he is all for *Beach-la-mar*. The path towards analysis and the elimination of inflection, has been trod by English so thoroughly that, in its American form, it should today win the race for a universal volapük. Indeed, as Mr. Mencken says, "the foreigner essaying it, indeed, finds his chief difficulty, not in mastering its forms, but in grasping its lack of forms. He doesn't have to learn a new and complex grammar; what he has to do is to forget grammar. Once he has done so, the rest is a mere matter of acquiring a vocabulary."

There is, it is true, the difficulty of the vowel sounds: but that is easily settled. Standard English possesses nineteen distinct vowel sounds: no other living European tongue except Portuguese, so Mr. Mencken says, possesses so many. Modern Greek, for instance, can only boast of five, we are told. "The [American] immigrant, facing all these vowels, finds some of them quite impossible; the Russian Jew, for example, cannot manage *ur*. As a result, he tends to employ a neutralized vowel in the situations which present difficulties, and this neutralized vowel, supported by the slip-shod speech-habits of the native proletariat, makes steady progress."

That that "neutralized vowel" has made great progress in America no one would deny who has been there; and, starting in the natural language-difficulties of the Central European immigrant, the above-mentioned "neutralized vowel" will make its way over here in due course, who can doubt it? These vowels must be watched. *Watch your vowels* should be our next national slogan! The fatal grammatical easiness of English is responsible, however, for such problems as these, as much as the growing impressionability of the English nation, and the proletarianization, rather than the reverse, of the American.

As long ago as 1910 an English traveller, Mr. Alexander Thompson, in a book called *Japan for a Week*, expresses himself as follows:

> It was only on reaching Italy that I began fully to realize this wonderful thing, that for nearly six weeks, on a German ship, in a journey of nearly ten thousand miles, we had heard little of any language but English!
>
> It is an amazing thing when one thinks of it.
>
> In Japan most of the tradespeople speak English. At Shanghai, at Hong-Kong, at Singapore, at Penang, at Colombo, at Suez, at Port Said—all the way home to the Italian ports, the language of all the ship's traffic, the language of such discourse as the passengers held with natives, most of the language on board ship itself, was English.
>
> The German captain of our ship spoke English more often than German. All his officers spoke English.
>
> The Chinese man-o'-war's men who conveyed the Chinese prince on board at Shanghai, received commands and exchanged commands with our German sailors in English. The Chinese mandarins in their conversations with the ships' officers invariably spoke English. They use the same ideographs in writing as the Japanese, but to talk to our Japanese passengers they had to speak English. Nay, coming as they did from various provinces of the

Empire, where the language greatly differs, they found it most convenient in conversation among themselves to speak English.

If you place side by side the unfortunate impressionability of Hemingway, which caused him to adopt integrally the half-wit simplicity of repetitive biblical diction patented by Miss Stein, and that other fact that Mr. Hemingway, being an American nationalist by temperament, is inclined to gravitate stylistically towards the national underdog dialect, in the last resort to the kind of *Beach-la-mar* I have been discussing, you have the two principal factors in Hemingway as artist in prose-fiction, to make of what you can.

Take up any book of his, again, and open it at random: you will find a page of stuff that is, considered in isolation, valueless as writing. It is not written: it is lifted out of Nature and very artfully and adroitly tumbled out upon the page: it is the brute material of every-day proletarian speech and feeling. The *matière* is cheap and coarse: but not because it is proletarian speech merely, but because it is *the prose of reality* — the prose of the street-car or the provincial newspaper or the five and ten cent store. I have just opened *Farewell to Arms* entirely at random, for instance, and this is what I find:

> "If you had any foreign bodies in your legs they would set up an inflammation and you'd have fever."
> "All right," I said. "We'll see what comes out."
> She went out of the room and came back with the old nurse of the early morning. Together they made the bed with me in it. That was new to me and an admirable proceeding.
> "Who is in charge here?"
> "Miss Van Campen."
> "How many nurses are there?"
> "Just us two."
> "Won't there be more?"
> "Some more are coming."
> "When will they get here?"
> "I don't know. You ask a great many questions for a sick boy."
> "I'm not sick." I said, "I'm wounded."
> They had finished making the bed and I lay with a clean, smooth sheet under me and another sheet over me. Mrs. Walker went out and came back with a pyjama jacket. They put that on me and I felt very clean and dressed.
> "You're awfully nice to me," I said. The nurse called Miss Gage giggled. "Could I have a drink of water?" I asked.
> "Certainly. Then you can have breakfast."
> "I don't want breakfast. Can I have the shutters opened, please?"
> The light had been dim in the room and when the shutters were opened it was bright sunlight and I looked out on a balcony and beyond were the tile roofs of houses and chimneys. I looked out over the tiled roofs and saw white clouds and the sky very blue.
> "Don't you know when the other nurses are coming?"
> "Why? Don't we take good care of you?"

"You're very nice."
"Would you like to use the bedpan?"
"I might try."
They helped me and held me up, but it was not any use. Afterward I lay
and looked out the open doors onto the balcony.
"When does the doctor come?"

It is not writing, if you like. When I read *Farewell to Arms* doubtless
I read this page as I came to it, just as I should watch scenes unfolding
on the screen in the cinema, without pictorial criticism; and it, page eighty-
three, contributed its fraction to the general effect: and when I had finished
the book I thought it a very good book. By that I meant that the cumulative
effect was impressive, as *the events themselves* would be. Or it is like
reading a newspaper, day by day, about some matter of absorbing
interest — say the reports of a divorce, murder, or libel action. If you say
anyone could write it, you are mistaken there, because, to obtain that
smooth effect, of commonplace reality, there must be no sentimental or
other heightening, the number of words expended must be proportionate
to the importance and the length of the respective phases of the action,
and any false move or overstatement would at once stand out and tell
against it. If an inferior reporter to Hemingway took up the pen, that fact
would at once be detected by a person sensitive to reality.

It is an art, then, from this standpoint, like the cinema, or like those
"modernist" still-life pictures in which, in place of *painting* a match box
upon the canvas, a piece of actual match box is stuck on. A recent example of this (I choose it because a good many people will have seen it) is
the cover design of the French periodical *Minotaure,* in which Picasso has
pasted and tacked various things together, sticking a line drawing of the
Minotaur in the middle. Hemingway's is a poster-art, in this sense: or a
cinema in words. The steining in the text of Hemingway is as it were the
hand-made part — if we are considering it as "super-realist" design: a
manipulation of the photograph if we are regarding it as a film.

If you say that this is not the way that Dante wrote, that these are not
artistically permanent creations — or not permanent in the sense of a verse
of Bishop King, or a page of Gulliver, I agree. But it is what we have got:
there is actually *bad* and *good* of this kind; and I for my part enjoy what
I regard as the good, without worrying any more about it than that.

That a particular phase in the life of humanity is implicit in this art is
certain. It is one of the first fruits of the *proletarianization* which, as a result
of the amazing revolutions in the technique of industry, we are all undergo-
ing, whether we like it or not. But this purely political, or sociological side
to the question can be brought out, I believe, with great vividness by a
quotation. Here, for instance, is a fragment of a story of a mutiny at sea:

I opened the door a little, about two inches, and saw there was a rope round the companion, which prevented the doors opening. Big Harry and Lips asked me what I wanted. I said I wanted to go down to the galley. Big Harry said: "Plenty of time between this and eight o'clock; you stop down below." I then went into the chief mate's room, which was the nearest to me. There was nobody there. I went to the second mate's room, he was not there. I went to the captain's pillow, it was standing up in his bed, and I found two revolvers loaded, one with six shots and one with four. I took possession of them and put them in my pockets. I then stood on the cabin table in the after cabin, and lifted the skylight up and tried to get out there. Renken was standing at the wheel, and he called out, "Come aft, boys, the steward is coming out of the skylight." I then closed the skylight and came down again. The after-skylight was close to the wheel, about 10 feet as near as I could guess. I could see him. The light used for the compass is in the skylight, and the wheel is in the back of it. The light is fastened to the skylight to light the compass, and the compass is just in front of the wheel. Before I could get the skylight closed I heard their steps coming aft, and I went down into the cabin and told the boy to light a fire. Shortly afterwards I heard five shots fired on deck . . . about a second afterwards the same as if somebody was running on deck. I could not judge which way they were running; the noise on the deck, and the vessel being in ballast, you could hear as well aft as forward. That was about twenty minutes after hearing the captain call out. I put the revolvers away in my locker. I then took it into my head to take the revolvers into my possession and chance it; if the men came down to me to do anything wrong, to save myself. I put them in my pockets, one on each side. About 5:30 Green, the boatswain, came down first, and French Peter, Big Harry, and all the other lot followed. The deck was left without anybody, and the wheel too, they came into the cabin; Trousillot was there as well. They did not speak at first. The first thing they did was to rub me over. They could not feel anything. I had the two revolvers with me, but they did not feel them. French Peter and Big Harry felt me over. All the others were present. Green said, "Well, steward, we have finished now." I said, "What the hell did you finish?" He said, "We have finished captain, mate and second." He said, "We got our mind made up to go to Greece; if you like to save your own life you had better take charge of the ship and bring us to Greece. You bring us to Gibraltar, we will find Greece: you bring us there you will be all right, steward. We will take the boats when we get to Greece, and take the sails and everything into the boats, and sell them ashore and divide the money between ourselves. You will have your share, the same as anybody else; the charts and sextants, and all that belongs to the navigation, you can have. Me and my cousin, Johny Moore, have got a rich uncle; he will buy everything. We will scuttle the ship. My uncle is a large owner there of some ships. We will see you right, that you will be master of one of those vessels." I said, "Well, men, come on deck and get them braces ready, and I hope you will agree and also obey my orders!" The other men said, "All right, steward, very good, very good, steward, you do right." That was all I could hear from them, from everybody. The conversation between me and Green was in English, and everybody standing round. He spoke to the other men in Greek. What he said I don't know. I said, "Where are the bodies? Where is the captain?" Green said, "Oh they are all right, they are overboard," and all the men said the same. . . .[1]

[1] *Forty Years in the Old Bailey.* F. Lamb.

That is not by Hemingway, though it quite well might be. I should not be able to tell it was not by Hemingway if it were shown me as a fragment. But this is by him:

Across the bay they found the other boat beached. Uncle George was smoking a cigar in the dark. The young Indian pulled the boat way up on the beach. Uncle George gave both the Indians cigars.

They walked up from the beach through a meadow that was soaking wet with dew, following the young Indian who carried a lantern. Then they went into the woods and followed a trail that led to the logging road that ran back into the hills. It was much lighter on the logging road as the timber was cut away on both sides. The young Indian stopped and blew out his lantern and they all walked on along the road.

They came around a bend and a dog came out barking. Ahead were the lights of the shanties where the Indian bark-peelers lived. More dogs rushed out at them. The two Indians sent them back to the shanties. In the shanty nearest the road there was a light in the window. An old woman stood in the doorway holding a lamp.

Inside on a wooden bunk lay a young Indian woman. She had been trying to have her baby for two days. All the old women in the camp had been helping her. The men had moved off up the road to sit in the dark and smoke out of range of the noise she made. She screamed just as Nick and the two Indians followed his father and Uncle George into the shanty. She lay in the lower bunk, very big under a quilt. Her head was turned to one side. In the upper bunk was her husband. He had cut his foot very badly with an axe three days before. He was smoking a pipe. The room smelled very bad.

Nick's father ordered some water to be put on the stove, and while it was heating he spoke to Nick.

"This lady is going to have a baby, Nick," he said.

"I know," said Nick.

"You don't know," said his father. "Listen to me. What she is going through is called being in labour. The baby wants to be born and she wants it to be born. All her muscles are trying to get the baby born. That is what is happening when she screams."

"I see," Nick said.

Just then the woman cried out.[1]

The first of these two passages is from a book entitled *Forty Years in the Old Bailey*. It is the account of a mutiny and murder on the high seas, the trial occurring on May 3 and 4, 1876. It was evidence verbatim of one Constant von Hoydonck, a Belgian, twenty-five years of age, who joined the vessel *Lennie* at Antwerp, as chief steward, on October 22. This is a *Querschnitt*, a slice, of "real life": and how close Hemingway is to such material as this can be seen by comparing it with the second passage out of *In Our Time*.

.   .   .   .   .   .

[1] *In Our Time.* Ernest Hemingway.

That, I think, should put you in possession of all that is essential for an understanding of the work of this very notable artist: an understanding I mean; I do not mean that, as a work of art, a book of his should be approached in this critical and anatomizing spirit. That is another matter. Where the "politics" come in I suppose by this time you will have gathered. This is the voice of the "folk," of the masses, who are the cannon-fodder, the cattle outside the slaughter-house, serenely chewing the cud — *of those to whom things are done,* in contrast to those who have executive will and intelligence. It is itself innocent of politics — one might almost add alas! That does not affect its quality as art. The expression of the soul of the dumb ox would have a penetrating beauty of its own, if it were uttered with genius — with bovine genius (and in the case of Hemingway that is what has happened): just as much as would the folk-song of the baboon, or of the "Praying Mantis." But where the politics crop up is that if we take this to be the typical art of a civilization — and there is no serious writer who stands higher in Anglo-Saxony today than does Ernest Hemingway — then we are by the same token saying something very definite about that civilization.

CHAPTER II

WILLIAM FAULKNER

THE MORALIST WITH THE CORN-COB

IF I SAID THAT WILLIAM FAULKNER was composed in equal measure of Sherwood Anderson and of Powys, I should say all that was necessary, from my standpoint. A gigantic 480-page Morality, like *Light in August*, is to me profitless and tiresome: a Calvinist moralist, delecting himself with, and turning to good library-sale's account, scenes of chopping, gashing, hacking, and slitting, is to me "abomination" if it is not "bitchery" — to use the words of one of his more typical figures, "Old Doc Hines." But his subject-matter, I agree, cannot be helped — no doubt the great rustic heart of America *is* moralist through and through, with a brand of fierce and blood-lustful sadic morality. With me, it is just that *La Terre* of Zola or the *earthy* works of Lawrence or Anderson, is not my favourite reading; just that the ranting sadism of melodrama is out of date and should be kept out of date: that the symbolical villagers of Mr. Powys are so ethically mechanized, into an abstract system as heavily centred in Sex, with the full stature of its serpentine capital-letter, as any Freudian tract, and so they, for me, become dull and empty exercises in Bunyan, which prevent me from reading far: merely that writing of the following order, from *Light in August*

Now it was still, quiet, the fecund earth now coolly suspirant[1]

is as I see it irretrievably second-rate, built out of a wordy poetic padding, and every time it occurs (every half dozen pages that is) it puts me off (I become "coolly suspirant" myself, with the best will in the world to salute the qualities I think I perceive elsewhere in William Faulkner): it is simply that I have listened to all the "Black Laughter" that I ever want to hear in the pages of Mr. Sherwood Anderson, and now, five years afterwards, find myself listening to it again in his disciple. Hemingway I can read with delight; but Faulkner fills me periodically with *White Laughter* and I do not thank him for it, I want to forget I am White for a while.

Having made this confession, and so warned you that I am not the person to come to for resounding appreciations of Faulkner's books, I can proceed. For this moralist is not an insignificant man, and, as one might expect, his books do contain a moral, which, for our purposes, we may assist him to drive home and develop.

.　　　.　　　.　　　.　　　.

---

[1] *Light in August*, p. 226.

I will begin with purely literary criticism. First of all then, Faulkner, unlike Hemingway, is a novelist of the old school — the actual texture of his prose-narrative is not at all "revolutionary" or unusual. Just occasionally (as in the opening page or two of *Sartoris* and here and there in *Sanctuary* and *Light in August*) a spurious savour of "newness" is obtained by a pretended incompetence as a narrator or from a confused distraction — a "lack of concentration" it would popularly be called if it occurred in the narrative of a police-court witness. There is, very occasionally, a clumsy slyness of this sort, of the *faux-naif* variety, but it is quite a minor thing. Just now and then — only for a page or two — he will Joyce for a bit, but merely to the extent of innocently portmanteauing a few words just to show he is on the right side, such as "shadowdappled" or "downspeaking": but he has not much luck with this, as he is apt to arrive at such a result as the following: "the rank *manodor* of his sedentary . . . flesh" — which looks too like *escupidor* to be a happy conjugation. For the most part his books might have been written by a contemporary of Trollope or the early Wells. Nothing has changed since Balzac in the following description of a great "character," full of "humours," an eccentric country doctor named Peabody.

> He crossed to an ancient roll-top desk and rummaged through the dusty littery upon it. There was litter and dust everywhere in the huge room. Its four windows gave upon the square, but the elms and sycamores ranged along the sides of the square shaded these first-floor offices, so that light entered them, but tempered, like light beneath water. In the corners of the ceiling were spider webs thick and heavy as Spanish moss and dingy as old lace, and the once-white walls were an even and unemphatic drab save for a paler rectangle here and there where an outdated calendar had hung and been removed. Besides the desk, the room contained three or four miscellaneous chairs in various stages of decrepitude, a rusty stove in a sawdust-filled box, and a leather sofa holding mutely amid its broken springs the outlines of Dr. Peabody's recumbent shape; beside it and slowly gathering successive layers of dust, was a stack of lurid, paper-covered nickel novels. This was Dr. Peabody's library, and on this sofa he passed his office hours, reading them over and over. Other books there were none.
>
> But the waste-basket beside the desk and the desk itself and the mantel above the trash-filled fireplace, and the window-ledges too, were cluttered with circular mail matter and mail order catalogues and government bulletins of all kinds. In one corner, on an up-ended packing-box, sat a water cooler of stained oxidized glass, in another corner leaned a clump of cane fishing-poles warping slowly of their own weight; and on every horizontal surface rested a collection of objects not to be found outside of a second-hand store — old garments, bottles, a kerosene lamp, a wooden box of tins of axle grease . . .[1]

There is no reason whatever why a novelist today should not use the most "straightforward" methods of narrative — the *code napoléon* was good

[1] *Sartoris*, pp. 101–102.

enough for Stendhal, and we might do far worse than model ourselves upon it — I am not at all quoting this passage to damn Mr. Faulkner for being "old-fashioned": my object is to place him technically. More than half of his text belongs, as far as the *genre* of the writing is concerned, to the "psychological" method of Conrad (or the translations of the great nineteenth century Russian authors).

> So he would trick and avoid Brown in order to reach the cabin first. He expected each time to find her waiting. When he would reach the cabin and find it empty, he would think in a kind of impotent rage of the urgency, the lying and the haste, and of her alone and idle in the house all day, with nothing to do save to decide whether to betray him at once or torture him a little longer. By ordinary he would not have minded whether Brown knew about their relations or not. He had nothing in his nature of reticence or of chivalry toward women. It was practical, material. He would have been indifferent if all Jefferson knew he was her lover.[1]

That is his way of telling a story. It is not "from the inside," nor yet "from the outside," nor anything new-fangled of that sort. It just the the very respectable method that served for a century, from Stendhal to Conrad, say.

But there is a lot of *poetry* in Faulkner. It is not at all good. And it has an in the end rather comic way of occurring at a point where, apparently, he considers that the *atmosphere* has run out, or is getting thin, by the passage of time become exhausted and requiring renewal, like the water in a zoological-garden tank for specimens of fish. So he pumps in this necessary medium, for anything from half a dozen to two dozen lines, according to the needs of the case. This sort of thing:

> Moonlight seeped into the room impalpably, refracted and sourceless; the night was without any sound. Beyond the window a cornice rose in a succession of shallow steps against the opaline and dimensionless sky.[2]

His characters demand, in order to endure for more than ten pages, apparently, an opaque atmosphere of whip-poor-wills, cicadas, lilac, "seeping" moonlight, water-oaks and jasmine — and of course the "dimensionless" sky, from which moonlight "seeps." The wherewithal to supply them with this indispensable medium is as it were stored in a *whip-poor-will tank*, as it might be called: and he pumps the stuff into his book in generous flushes at the slightest sign of fatigue or deflationary listlessness, as he thinks, upon the part of one of his characters.

To compare him with Ernest Hemingway as an artist would indeed be absurd: but actually he betrays such a deep unconsciousness in that respect as to be a little surprising. In the above passage (about the *impalpuble seeping of the moonlight*) you may have remarked a peculiar word, "sourceless." If in reading a book of his you came across this word — say upon the first page of *Sanctuary* where it occurs ("a thick growth of cane and brier, of

---

[1] *Light in August*, p. 256.
[2] *Sartoris*, p. 160.]

cypress and gum in which broken sunlight lay sourceless") and said to yourself *"sourceless* — what for mercy's sake is that!" you would soon find out. For a dozen pages farther on (where more poetic atmosphere was being pumped in, in due course) you would probably come across it again: and after you had encountered it half a dozen times or so you would see what he meant. But I will give you a few examples of *sourceless*.

Sartoris:

> p. 41: "a thin *sourceless* odour of locust drifted up."
> p. 48. "the room was filled now with a gray light, *sourceless* and chill."
> p. 145. "Moon and insects were one . . . dimensionless and *without source*."
> p. 147. "Invisible and *sourceless* among the shifting patterns of light and shade."
> p. 254. "beyond the window sunlight was . . . *sourceless* yet palpable."

Sanctuary:

> p. 111. "a rich *sourceless* voice coming out of the high darkness."

These Thirteen:

> p. 284. "a *sourceless* goat-bell."
> p. 353. "From the docks a ship's siren *unsourced* itself."

Unsourced itself is good; and "a sourceless goat-bell," too, for that matter! But if he is so innocently pleased with this little verbal toy that he uses it upon all occasions, there are other words (apart from such hackneyed ones common to all American books as *frustration*) which he uses so repeatedly that it would be a game for an idle person to count them — "timbrous," "viscid," "shard," "sibilant," etc. No one ever had less care for the *mot juste*. "Myriad," I think, is as good an illustration as any, especially as it is a word that is in itself revelatory, an obviously musical and romantic word to catch and captivate the common eye. Here are a few *myriads*:

Sartoris:

> p. 6. "flowers . . . *myriad*, odorless and unpickable."
> p. 11. "among the *myriad* candles."
> p. 55. "*myriad* with scent and with a drowsy humming of bees."
> p. 85. "The night was dark, *myriad* with drifting odors of the spring, and with insects."
> p. 112. "the heady and *myriad* odors of the waxing spring."
> p. 132. "as the horse swirled in a *myriad* flickering like fire."
> p. 322. "to his sharpened senses the silence was *myriad*."

Light in August:

> p. 78. "he seemed to hear a *myriad* sounds."
> p. 85. "Beyond the open window the steady insects pulse and beat, drowsy and *myriad*."
> p. 98. "he was hearing a *myriad* sounds of no greater volume."
> p. 101. "the intervals filled with the *myriad* voices."
> p. 246. "the peaceful *myriad* sounds of insects from beyond the summer windows."

p. 264. "the quiet dusk peopled . . . by a *myriad* ghosts."
p. 266*a*. "the dark was filled with . . . voices, *myriad*, out of all time."
p. 266*b*. "going on, *myriad*, familiar."
p. 290. "Through the open window comes the hot, *myriad* silence of the breathless night."
p. 300. "He hears now only the *myriad* and interminable insects, leaning in the window, breathing the hot still rich maculate smell of the earth."
p. 365. "Through the open window there comes now only the peaceful and *myriad* sounds of the summer night."
p. 466. "He hears above his heart the thunder increase, *myriad* and drumming."

These are only a few "myriads" picked out of two books, casually noted in passing — there are many myriads more than that! But this little word does, I am afraid, tell its tale; as do also the quotations from pp. 290 and 365 respectively, of *Light in August*. For the two passages, both beginning "Through the open windows," are almost identical, and they occur within hailing distance of each other.

There is no question here of conscious repetition. It reveals the character of this slipshod and redundant artistic machine. And as to "the open window," that is, as a matter of fact, invariably *the funnel* out of which the "myriad" insects, whip-poor-wills, fire-flies and lilac blooms pour every five or ten minutes in William Faulkner's text.

"The Spring will soon be here now in Southern Indiana!" exclaims with ecstatic monotony the hero of Hemingway's brilliant skit, *Torrents of Spring*, as he sniffs the *chinook*. And this type of writing (it was Sherwood Anderson that Hemingway was parodying in *Torrents of Spring*) is dealt with as it deserves, and once and for all, in that little critical masterpiece. It must be extremely irritating for him (as for any other American possessed of a critical sense, and desiring to see established in America a school of prose-fiction of a technically tough, non-romantic order) to find this more recent, and now immensely advertised version of Andersonism perpetuating the very type of romantic bric-à-brac which *Torrents of Spring* was composed to discourage. There is no occasion to pursue any further this analysis of the purely artistic quality of the work of Faulkner. His entire output, from that standpoint, is elementary. But it must be remembered that "the novel" does not stand or fall by its artistic excellence. The work of a certain great Russian novelist, who was a harassed bread-winner as well as a great dramatist, has demonstrated that. And there is much more to be said for Faulkner than this exposure of his technical equipment might suggest.

.   .   .   .

Faulkner is as full of "passion" — of sound and fury — as Hemingway is austerely without it. He is as hot and sticky as Hemingway is dry and without undue heat. He works up and up, in a torrent of ill-selected words, to his stormy climaxes. With Hemingway the climaxes are registered by a few discreet touches here and there. The characters in Faulkner's books are as heavily *energized* as the most energetic could wish. And if they are all futilely energized and worked-up to no purpose — all "signifying nothing" — if each and all of his stories is "a tale told by an idiot" — that does not make his Sartorises, Popeyes, Christmases, the priest in *Mistral* or Temple Drake, any the less an impressive company, in their hysterical way. All are demented: his novels are, strictly speaking, clinics. Destiny weighs heavily upon every figure which has its being in this suffocating atmosphere of whip-poor-wills, magnolias, fire-flies and water-oaks (not to mention the emanations of the *dark* and invariably *viscid* earth). And the particular form that that destiny takes is *race*. Whether it is Christmas or Sartoris, it is a matter of fatality residing in the blood. They are driven on in a crazy and headlong career by the compulsion of their ancestry. Hightower, the disgraced minister, is mystically involved with his grandfather, a Confederate cavalry officer: when he takes up his cure in Jefferson, he amazes and startles his parishioners, "up there in the pulpit with his hands flying around him and the dogma he was supposed to preach all full of galloping cavalry and defeat and glory just as when he tried to tell them on the street about the galloping horses, it in turn would get all mixed up with absolution and choirs of martial seraphim." This rapidly became a first-class village scandal. "The young minister was still excited even after six months, still talking about the Civil War and his grandfather, a cavalryman, who was killed . . . wild too in the pulpit, using religion as though it were a dream. . . . It was as if he couldn't get religion and that galloping cavalry and his dead grandfather shot from the galloping horse untangled from each other, even in the pulpit." His wife deserts him, commits suicide, leaps out of the window of a louche hotel in Memphis, Tennessee, and he is disgraced. At the end he recognizes that it is his galloping grandfather who has ruined him. He is made to say to himself: "I know that for fifty years I have not even been clay:" (he has never even come to life, he has been a dream — of a galloping grandfather — all the time): "I have been a single instant of darkness in which a horse galloped and a gun crashed. *And if I am my dead grandfather on the instant of his death*, then my wife, his grandson's wife . . . the debaucher and murderer of my grandson's wife, since I could neither let my grandson live or die. . . ."[1]

Violent death, as this indicates, is a matter of such importance in Faulkner's universe, it has such a baleful attraction, for his most ordinary puppets, in expectation or in memory, that it is able, two generations away, to so paralyze the imagination of one of them as to turn him into a dream of death-on-horseback!

[1] *Light in August*, pp. 56–57, 465. Lewis's italics.]

The Civil War, and that apparently central problem of the American soul, the Black and White (for it is rather an important issue, all said and done, whether you shall give the negro equality and a century later have a mulatto America, or on the other hand lynch him as soon as look at him) are the shadows over every life dealt with by Faulkner. The Sartoris family is literally rotten with fatality — there the *doom* becomes deliberately comic:

> It showed on John Sartoris' brow, the dark shadow of fatality and doom, that night when he sat beneath the candles in the dining-room and turned a wine-glass in his fingers while he talked to his son. . . .
> "And so," he said, "Redlaw'll kill me tomorrow, for I shall be unarmed. I'm tired of killing men. . . . Pass the wine, Bayard."
> And the next day he was dead, whereupon, as though he had but waited for that to release him of the clumsy cluttering of bones and breath, by losing the frustration on his own flesh he could now stiffen and shape that which sprang from him into the fatal semblance of his dream.[1]

Death is a bagatelle to a Sartoris — and indeed a Sartoris only becomes really effective after demise. As a ghost he is *some* ghost! But it is *de rigueur* that the death itself should be particularly *violent* — that every Sartoris exacts. And in that respect, where all his characters are concerned, Faulkner is a bit of a Sartoris himself.

The first Sartoris to whom we are introduced — "Old Bayard" — dies in a motor-car from heart-failure when it dashes down a precipice. And his aged relative, "Miss Jenny," is not at all satisfied with that. "Miss Jenny felt that old Bayard had somehow flouted them all, had committed *lèse majesté* toward his ancestors and the lusty glamour of the family doom by dying, as she put it, practically from the 'inside out.' " But it was all right really, because old Bayard hated motor-cars until he realized one day that they were engines of destruction — instruments of *violent death* — especially as driven by a Sartoris, and especially by his grandson "young Bayard" Sartoris. And so he *insisted* upon his grandson driving him about till they both fell down a precipice.

> "In the nineteenth century," John Sartoris said, "genealogy is poppycock. . . . Yet the man who professes to care nothing about his forbears is only a little less vain than the man who bases all his actions on blood precedent. And I reckon a Sartoris can have a little vanity and poppycock, if he wants it!"[2]

But a wife of "a Sartoris" gets a nasty taste at times — not of "poppycock" but of unadulterated fatality. "Bayard," she whispered, leaning against him. . . . "She took his face between her palms and drew it down, but his lips

[1 *Sartoris*, p. 23.]
[2 *Sartoris*, p. 92.]

were cold and upon them she tasted fatality and doom." And this spectacle of doom and damnation—for it is essentially a Judaic doom, based
upon Genesis and upon Exodus, a spell cast by the Old Testament
prophets—is most sardonically contemplated, and commented upon, by
women, negroes, doves and of course whip-poor-wills. Miss Jenny in the
cemetery, reviewing the "swashbuckling" tombs of the Sartorises is a good
example of this.

The war is, in a sense, a complication for a "doomed" Sartoris, because
"doom" in such a war as that of 1914–1918 becomes as cheap as dirt. One
Sartoris vulgarly succumbs, but the other goes home, and commits suicide
in an aeroplane as soon as the war is over and normal conditions of safety
restored. And yet of course a man beneath a curse, predestined to a violent
death is, in a sense, in his element in a world-war—the element of the light-
ning flash and thunder-stone. "And that's all. That's it. The courage, the
recklessness, call it what you will, is the flash, the instant of sublimation;
then flick! the old darkness again. That's why. It's too strong for steady
diet. And if it were a steady diet, it would not be a flash, a glare."[1]

A flash, a glare—that is what Faulkner's books are intended to be—a
very long flash, and a chronic glare, illuminating a "doomed," a symbolical
landscape—centred in that township of the Old Dominion symbolically
named Jefferson.

The longest flash and glare of all is Light in August—and that, I think,
is a flash in the pan. It is full of wearisome repetitions and is long-winded
to the last degree: it is hysterical and salvationist more than is necessary,
and it is comical where it is not meant to be. It contains, however, a great
deal of good observation and passages of considerable power. Christmas,
the half-negro, supplies us with all of these. He is a quite empty little figure,
like "Popeye" in Sanctuary: but he carries round a big "doom" with him
all right, and he makes it sound. His doom is of course his blood—or rather
his two bloods, the white and the black. Here is the description of his flight
and lynching:

> It was not alone all those thirty years which she did not know, but all
> those successions of thirty years before that which had put that stain either
> on his white blood or his black blood, whichever you will, and which killed
> him. But he must have run with believing for a while; anyway, with hope.
> But his blood would not be quiet, let him save it. It would not be either one
> or the other and let his body save itself. Because the black blood drove him
> first to the negro cabin. And then the white blood drove him out of there,
> as it was the black blood which snatched up the pistol and the white blood
> which would not let him fire it. And it was the white blood which sent him
> to the minister, which rising in him for the last and final time, sent him against
> all reason and all reality, into the embrace of a chimera, a blind faith in
> something read in a printed Book. Then I believe that the white blood deserted

[1] These Thirteen, p. 109.

him for the moment. Just a second, a flicker, allowing the black to rise in its final moment and make him turn upon that on which he had postulated his hope of salvation. It was the black blood which swept him by his own desire beyond the aid of any man, swept him up into that ecstasy out of a black jungle where life has already ceased before the heart stops and death is desire and fulfilment. And then the black blood failed him again, as it must have in crises all his life. He did not kill the minister. He merely struck him with the pistol and ran on and crouched behind that table and defied the black blood for the last time, as he had been defying it for thirty years. He crouched behind that overturned table and let them shoot him to death, with that loaded and unfired pistol in his hand.[1]

But the "doom" in the case of Joe Christmas is complicated by a new factor, namely, the presence of a personal fate referred to as "the Player." This personage only turns up quite at the end of this long trail, and I am bound to say does not behave at all nicely. Here he is — moving Percy Grimm, who has tracked down the fugitive negro, and run him to earth behind the kitchen-table in the disgraced pastor's house.

> "Jesus Christ!" Grimm cried, his young voice clear and outraged like that of a young priest. "Has every preacher and old maid in Jefferson taken their pants down to the yellow-bellied son of a bitch?" He flung the old man aside and ran on.
> It was as though he had been merely waiting for the Player to move him again, because with that unfailing certitude he ran straight to the kitchen and into the doorway, already firing, almost before he could have seen the table overturned and standing on its edge across the corner of the room, and the bright and glittering hands of the man who crouched behind it, resting on the upper edge. Grimm emptied the automatic's magazine into the table; later someone covered all five shots with a folded handkerchief.
> But the Player was not done yet. When the others reached the kitchen they saw the table flung aside now and Grimm stooping over the body. When they approached to see what he was about, they saw that the man was not dead yet, and when they saw what Grim was doing one of the men gave a choked cry and stumbled back into the wall and began to vomit. Then Grimm too sprang back, flinging behind him the bloody butcher knife. "Now you'll let white women alone, even in hell," he said. But the man on the floor had not moved.[2]

With this sinister Player (spelled with a capital p) we reach a further complication of Faulkner's studied amateur fatalism. We first hear of the presence of the Player while Grimm is in pursuit of Christmas before the latter reaches the shelter of the house. "He [Grimm] was moving again almost before he had stopped, with that lean, swift, blind obedience to whatever Player moved him on the Board. . . He seemed indefatigable, not flesh and blood, as if the Player who moved him for

[1 *Light in August*, pp. 424–425.]
2 *Light in August*, p. 439.

pawn likewise found him breath."[1]

The belief of W. B. Yeats that human life is a game of chess, in which beings of a supernatural intelligence, in another dimension, are engaged, lending us sometimes their wisdom and their strength, seems to be implied in this. But I should doubt if Faulkner is the master of any systematic notion of fatality. Evidently he took a great fancy at some time to the conception of a rigid destiny controlling human life, as exemplified in the Greek Drama: and it supplies the melodramatic backbone of his books. That is all, I think.

．　　　　．　　　　．　　　　．　　　　．　　　　．

There can be nothing harder to define than *melodrama* in distinction to tragedy. But a too great addiction to a notion of "fate," and a consequent loosening and slackening of the "realistic" web of "chance" or "accident," will undoubtedly lead a writer more surely than by any other path — especially if his purposes are sensational, and mainly directed to excite and to entertain — to what would probably be described as the *melodramatic*. Faulkner seems to me to be melodramatic, distinctly. All his skies are inky black. He deals in horror as in a cherished material. Coincidence, what he would call "fate," does not stand on ceremony, or seek to cover itself in any fussy "realistic" plausibility, with him. When the doomed man, at long last, is to be run to earth, there is every probability (according to the law of these *improbable* narratives) that after wandering all over the world, he will be run to earth at the very door of the cottage in which dwells, quite unknown to him, his old grandmother, who, however, has never set eyes on him until that day, and who has no idea whether such a person as he exists or not until she finds him with the rope round his neck. In short, there is *no* coincidence that this robust fatalism is not prepared to admit. This certainly makes novel-writing easier.

Of course, the intellectual morale of a destiny-crank, on the grand model, is sorely tried in any case. It is enervating for him in that respect, even as it is for men at large, in its influence upon their general outlook. The conception of an all-embracing destiny has its concomitant in an obviousness of association, and imposes at once a mechanical form upon existence: as it is pre-eminently the philosophy of the pure determinist.

A man like William Faulkner discovers fatalism, or whatever you like to call it: it at once gives him something to live for, or rather gives his characters something to live for — namely a great deal of undeserved tribulation culminating in *a violent death*. That simplifies the plot enormously — it is, in fact, the great "classical" simplification, banishing expectation. No one who knows Faulkner's work is in any doubt, in picking up a book of

[1] *Light in August*, p. 437.

his, as to what will happen to the principal character; he will unquestionably die a violent death, there is no occasion to turn to the last page. He is, in fact, as dead already upon the first page, to all intents and purposes, and bloodily dead, as is the corpse at the opening of a Van Dine crime-novel. And it takes a more powerful and subtle intelligence than Faulkner's to cope with this essentially mechanical situation in such a manner as not to make it appear over-mechanical to the reader — or to prevent it from degenerating into a flabby and artificial structure, with eventually the necessary pawns practically emerging from a trap-door, or being telepathically spirited to the spot desired, blatantly in the nick of time. And where everyone knows what is going to happen the temptation merely to moralize the mechanism into *such* a preordained pattern that the march of events is a purely *ad hoc* progression, highly unreal and unconvincing, is very great. In fact, increasingly, there will be little incentive to do anything else, for such a story-teller. His attitude will tend to become like that of the doomed man himself. Why worry? A supernatural agency is at work. Miracles are the stock in trade of a supernatural agency. — Indeed, once you have admitted the existence of a supernatural agency, the unlikely and fortuitous are more "natural" than the reverse. Indeed, it only remains a question of what quantity, if any, of non-fatalist, non-miraculous, constituents you shall include.

Since the climax is from the start in full view of *everybody*, including the figure who is destined to suffer it, the tendency must be at least to slacken the tension and conventionalize all that comes *in between*. And in *Light in August* — that last of this fatal series and the best example of its working — that is just what we find. A great deal of prosy melodramatic talk does intervene, in an interminable, sultry, marking time, until the Player shall introduce the carving-knife, and balefully point at the root of all the "abomination and bitchery," namely the sexual organs of the half-caste hero.

The advantages of the destiny-technique, where a highly-trained and intelligent audience is concerned, are obvious, as of course they have been universally accepted as a canon of European art since the time of the Athenian tragedy. If you eliminate the element of surprise (the capital source of a fevered and inartistic excitement) the tragedy can be regarded purely as a spectacle, and, relieved of all the vulgar tittivation and hysteria accompanying suspense, the individual attention of the audience can be given to the quality of the interpretation, the art factor: the actor becomes more important than the plot, subtleties of "rendition" are not lost, but may be savoured at leisure, a mood of philosophic contemplation may supervene, in place of the dream-like animal unconsciousness accompanying all violent action. The argument in favour of the *pseudo-statement*, or the *absence of belief*, advanced by Messrs. T. S. Eliot and I. A. Richards, is established upon a similar principle.

But the success of this principle, as it issues in works of creative art, must depend upon the specifically *artistic* quality of the executant. And here William Faulkner is very weak. Then it will depend upon the integrity of the taste of the epoch that has called this conception forth. The early and middle Victorian period had plenty of melodrama, upon the Greek "destiny" model. But it was very inferior stuff. And then it will also depend, for success, upon the intellectual foundations of the system which is responsible for it. And here, as I have said, in Faulkner's case I take it to be a personal fancy, merely, arising out of his experience, certainly (his war-experience, in all probability) but not of sufficient metaphysical solidity to guarantee it against irresponsible abuse. And, apart from the melodramatic "Player" (who only turns up once, as far as I know), "fate" seems to be with him a scientific notion, centred in heredity.

.   .   .   .   .   .

If you base your nomenclature upon an ethical vocabulary — call the township where your people have their being Backbite-on-Avon, make its mayor a Mr. Joseph Graft, its judge Judge Geoffrey Gallows, its local detective Ezra Lynx, and so forth, you are following a classical model, and the attention of the reader can be concentrated upon the game you have proposed to him, according to rules that have been universally accepted. The function of the "critic" in that case becomes a simple one — that is cricket, from his point of view. All is as cut and dried as could be wished, within those disciplines.

Faulkner does not do that, he does not invite such facile comparisons as does Powys. But the town with which most of his books deal is symbolically named "Jefferson"; his Sartorises all have the name of Bayard, that "preux" whose chevaleresque attitudes they emulate: his diabolical half-caste is called "Christmas," his outcast minister is named "Hightower" suggestive of a high aloofness, and so on. The christening of his *dramatis personae* tends to the quality-name. But on the whole it approximates more to Dickens than to Bunyan. Lucas Burch and Byron Bunch (children of a Dickens-like coincidence), Dr. Peabody, Brother Strother and the Snopeses, are a Dickensian company.

I have said (not in disparagement) that Faulkner is an "old-fashioned" writer compared with Hemingway, and this accounts for a good deal. He has gone back to the old conception of "the novel," or he has never emerged from it would, I suppose, be more exact. He is artistically a contemporary of Conrad or Trollope (his Hightower, for instance, is an American Mr. Crawley of Hogglestock). He is a bold and bustling romantic writer, of the "psychological" school. That is the main thing to grasp about him. It is, in short, except for a mere handful of *shadowdappleds* and *manodors*, as if Joyce had never jingled: except for *one* little shamefaced

WILLIAM FAULKNER 49

flourish, it is as if Miss Stein had never stuttered: "Memory believes before knowing remembers. Believes longer than recollects, longer than knowing even wonders. Knows remembers believes a corridor in a big, long, garbled, cold, echoing building," etc.[1] That is the lot — and it is, now I come to look at it, Joyce rather than Stein — the rhythm is the Irish sentiment, not the Jewish lack of sentiment.

Miss Jenny, in *Sartoris* and elsewhere, with her "fiddlesticks!", the racy good sense of her comic relief, and the negro chorus generally, are pure Dickens, and there are swarms of oddities, or "cards" — most of them, in their lives, blatant examples of coincidence, the victims of the minor operations of his pervasive fatality.

All this is to say that he has to be judged according to conventional standards of romantic novel-making: the question of his success or ill-success must be subordinated to the framework of a conventional and unreal pattern. Whereas Hemingway, reporter of genius that he is, fails or succeeds largely upon whether you decide he has got the facts *dead-right*, or, on the other hand, has ever so slightly shifted and conventionalized them in the process of reporting them, Faulkner neglects or ignores that criterion of "realistic" method. He must be judged according to romantic standards only — as, for that matter, is the case with most novelists. There are few people, who are professional novelists, able to do anything else, if they are to "make good," than to conform to the more conventional and romantic standards of this rather slovenly, undisciplined art. And of course it remains an open question whether such an art deserves the more exacting approach at all.

.   .   .   .   .   .

Of the books I have read of Faulkner's I like *Sanctuary* best. Its hero, "Popeye," is sexually impotent, and what is called "degenerate." As a child he cuts up live kittens with scissors; he is sent to a reformatory; and in due course, as a man, he becomes the "killer" of the sort with which we are familiarized by gangster books and films. The automatic strapped under his armpit satisfies the requirements of the sinister vacuum, of "bloodlust" and vanity, which Nature has installed at the heart of his being, to be his particular destiny. For "fate" works full-time here as well, and *Sanctuary* is a highly moral tale.

Popeye is, in this case, the instrument of fate, with his automatic and his corn-cob. The book was no doubt suggested to Faulkner by the *Faux monnayeurs*, of André Gide — that and Judge Lindsey's *Revolt of Youth*. It is, again, pure melodrama, as a gangster and bootlegging novel could

[1] *Light in August*, p. 111. [All printings give "garbled," surely an obvious misprint for "gabled."]

scarcely help being. Miss Reba, the brothel-keeper (the scene for instance where the three old cronies are drinking in Miss Reba's office after the funeral of the man killed by Popeye) is an excellent if *scabreux* Dickens. The wife of the bootlegger, Goodwin, hands on hip—her baby in a box behind the stove to prevent the rats getting at it—telling the juvenile good-timer, Temple Drake, what she thinks of her and all her kind—the corrupt little "college-girl" tribe, the daughters of the Rich—is a piece of melodramatic moralism, and as such extremely good—and of course politically very much to the point.

> "I know your sort. I've seen them. All running, but not too fast. Not so fast you cant tell a real man when you see him. Do you think you've got the only one in the world?"
> "Gowan," Temple whispered. "Gowan."
> "I have slaved for that man," the woman whispered, her lips scarce moving, in her still, dispassionate voice. It was as though she were reciting a formula for bread. "I worked night shift as a waitress so I could see him Sundays at the prison. I lived two years in a single room, cooking over a gas-jet, because I promised him. I lied to him and made money to get him out of prison, and when I told him how I made it, he beat me. And now you must come here where you're not wanted. Nobody asked you to come here. Nobody cares whether you are afraid or not. Afraid? You haven't the guts to be really afraid, any more than you have to be in love."[1]

But the essence of the book—which I think was missed in the reviews I saw—is to be sought for in the pessimism engendered in any American of intelligence by the spectacle of child-corruption conjoined and coeval with the fantastic lawlessness which came in with Prohibition, culminating in the notorious case of the Lindbergh baby, and which gave Popeye and his kind (the violent little gutter-Caesars of the Underworld) their chance. For it is not an accident that William Faulkner's gangster is one of the most insignificant and useless of men, brought to the top by the growing chaos in the heart of society—for whom human beings are flies to be dismissed from life as lightly as a troublesome insect, for the reason that he is himself a thing of the same order—that is undoubtedly the idea, and a highly moral one, you will agree.

The best way to bring out the full meaning of Faulkner's novel will be to quote a couple of pages from it, which is, as you will observe, a kind of fictional illustration of Judge Lindsey's essay.

> The waiting crowd was composed half of young men in collegiate clothes with small cryptic badges on their shirts and vests, and two girls with painted small faces and scant bright dresses like identical artificial flowers surrounded each by bright and restless bees. When the train came they pushed gaily forward, talking and laughing, shouldering aside older people with gay rudeness, clashing and slamming seats back and settling themselves, turning their faces up out of laughter, their cold faces still toothed with it, as three middle-aged women moved down the car, looking tentatively

[1] *Sanctuary*, p. 59.

left and right at the filled seats.

The two girls sat together, removing a fawn and a blue hat, lifting slender hands and preening not-quite-formless fingers about their close heads seen between the sprawled elbows and the leaning heads of two youths hanging over the back of the seat and surrounded by coloured hatbands at various heights, where the owners sat on the seat arms or stood in the aisle; and presently the conductor's cap as he thrust among them with plaintive, fretful cries, like a bird.

"Tickets. Tickets, please," he chanted. For an instant they held him there, invisible save for his cap. Then two young men slipped swiftly back and into the seat behind Horace. He could hear them breathing. Forward the conductor's punch clicked twice. He came on back. "Tickets," he chanted. "Tickets." He took Horace's and stopped where the youths sat.

"You already got mine," one said. "Up there."

"Where's your check?" the conductor said.

"You never gave us any. You got our tickets, though. Mine was number —" he repeated a number glibly, in a frank, pleasant tone. "Did you notice the number of yours, Shack?"

The second one repeated a number in a frank, pleasant tone. "Sure you got ours. Look and see." He began to whistle between his teeth, a broken dance rhythm, unmusical.

"Do you eat at Gordon hall?" the other said.

"No. I have natural halitosis." The conductor went on. The whistle reached crescendo, clapped off by his hands on his knees, ejaculating duh-duh-duh. Then he just squalled, meaningless, vertiginous; to Horace it was like sitting before a series of printed pages turned in furious snatches, leaving a series of cryptic, headless and tailless evocations on the mind.

"She's travelled a thousand miles without a ticket."

"Marge too."

"Beth too."

"Duh-duh-duh."

"Marge too."

"I'm going to punch mine Friday night."

"Eeeeyow."

"Do you like liver?"

"I cant reach that far."

"Eeeeeyow."

They whistled, clapping their heels on the floor to furious crescendo, saying duh-duh-duh. The first jolted the seat back against Horace's head. He rose. "Come on," he said. "He's done gone." Again the seat jarred into Horace and he watched them return and join the group that blocked the aisle, saw one of them lay his bold, rough hand flat upon one of the bright, soft faces uptilted to them. Beyond the group a countrywoman with an infant in her arms stood braced against a seat. From time to time she looked back at the blocked aisle and the empty seats beyond.

At Oxford he descended into a throng of them at the station, hatless, in bright dresses, now and then with books in their hands and surrounded still by swarms of coloured shirts. Impassable, swinging hands with their escorts, objects of casual and puppyish pawings, they dawdled up the hill toward the college, swinging their little hips, looking at Horace with cold, blank eyes as he stepped off the walk in order to pass them.

At the top of the hill three paths diverged through a broad grove beyond which, in green vistas, buildings in red brick or grey stone gleamed, and where a clear soprano bell began to ring. The procession became three streams, thinning rapidly upon the dawdling couples, swinging hands, strolling in erratic surges, lurching into one another with puppyish squeals, with the random intense purposelessness of children.[1]

I need not interpret this passage very much. No one is likely to accuse Faulkner, after reading it, of a weakness, I think, for these herds of nasty children, from the two female ones slammed down into their seats, "turning their faces up out of laughter, their cold faces still toothed with it," to the two male ones who played *faux-monnayeurs* with the conductor, droning "duh-duh-duh," or breaking into a "meaningless squalling"; or in general the aimless swarms "lurching into one another with puppyish squeals, with the random intense purposelessness of children." The females "swing their little hips" in the identical manner that Temple Drake swings *her* "little hips" — they are in fact her "college" companions — and any of them would behave much as Temple Drake did in the bootlegger's den, or later in the brothel, we are, I think, given to understand.

Most significant of all, however, as an indication of the attitude adopted by Faulkner to these things, is the "woman of the people," — the "countrywoman with an infant in her arms," who is compelled to stand, and "brace herself against a seat," because the aisle is blocked by these "myriad" offsprings of the vulgar bourgeoisie, who cannot even express themselves except in an uncouth jargon of "done gones" and "eeeeeyows," literally like portentous "puppies" of some common and senseless bitch!

What you are intended to see in these scenes is undoubtedly the proliferation of a spoilt, a *purposeless*, a common, an irresponsible bourgeois society, awaiting, surely, if ever a society did, its *coup de grâce*. For nothing could be more bleak and redolent of "chaos come again" than the pages of this violent morality play.

The drunken "college-girl" egging on the "killer" to do his trick, namely to kill, on the way to the dance-hall where "Red" is put on the spot, is typical of the manner of conveying this ugly lesson. — Temple Drake taunts Popeye:

> "You're scared to!"
> "I'm giving him his chance," he said, in his cold soft voice. "Come on. Make up your mind."
>
> .   .   .   .   .   .
>
> She leaned toward him, her hand on his arm. Then she got into the car. "You wont do it. You're afraid to. He's a better man than you are."
> He reached across and shut the door. "Where?" he said. "Grotto?"

[1] *Sanctuary*, pp. 167–170.

"He's a better man than you are!" Temple said shrilly. "You're not even a man! He knows it. Who does know it if he dont?" The car was in motion. She began to shriek at him. "You, a man, a bold bad man, when you can't even ——"[1]

This is the "little-hipped" doll, "toothed" with mechanical smiles, *in action* — in the great world outside school and the family circle. She is the little sensational robot pupped by the American million-dollar-drugged capitalist system. That is certainly what this particular "thriller" is intended to convey. And what Temple Drake gets is undoubtedly what has "been coming to her"! What Temple Drake actually gets is a corn-cob; and the author's message to his country is beyond question that that is what Temple Drake, and all her kind, deserves. It is a harsh piece of sardonic pedagogy, no doubt, delivered with the hysterical violence we have come to expect from its author. But is it not salutary? Could anyone in their senses look upon this book as "obscene," in any morally derogatory sense — regard it indeed as anything but a pure work of edification? None but the most stupid — or those who felt themselves involved in its purgative lessons — could do that. William Faulkner is not an artist: he is a satirist with the shears of Atropos more or less: and he is a very considerable moralist — *a moralist with a corn-cob!*

CHAPTER III

T. S. ELIOT

THE PSEUDO-BELIEVER

THERE IS NO PERSON TODAY WHO has had more influence upon the art of literature in England and America than Mr. T. S. Eliot. And what is especially remarkable is the fact that this influence has been exerted equally in the field of theory and the field of practice. If he has caused the budding poet to mind his p's and q's and bethink himself with more than usual concern about the intellectual foundations of his verse, he has also been able, in the practice of that art, to provide the beginner with a compelling model. For ten years now countless young verse-makers both here and in America have modelled themselves upon *Ara Vos Prec, The Waste Land* or *Prufrock*. At the same time, under the guidance of his critical essays, they have imbibed a criterion which, as writers, puts (in more senses perhaps than one) the fear of God into them.

This mandarin, certainly, has succeeded in instilling a salutary *fear of speech* — a terror of *the word*, into his youthful followers: they have not thought twice, but a dozen times or more, before committing themselves to paper; and when they have come to do so, have spoken, "neither loud or long." They may not always have had much to say but they have said it in the fewest possible words. Indeed the mere act of writing (I have heard some of their confessions) has been undertaken with as much trepidation as the Victorian young man experienced in "popping the question." There have been those among them who, after endless painful deliberation, have scribbled a half a dozen lines and then fled away for good and all from composition upon such austere terms.

But at last the spell has been broken. And Mr. Auden has done it (even if it was "John, son of Warner, who pulled his bell"). It is he who has really given the *coup de grâce* to Mr. Eliot's spell. Mr. Auden abounds in speech — words have no sinister terrors for him! So once more the ink is flowing freely and the paper manufacturers are taking on a few more hands. But it is still a pretty constipated "academic youth," as they call it in Germany, that is having its fling — if it can be called a "fling" — beneath this tutelage, still in the shadow of this alarming pedagogic presence — for it will take some time for the emancipatory effect of Mr. Auden's volubility to get things flowing easily again. And it is to do but the barest justice to Mr. Eliot to say that his followers might have had many a worse mentor. Indeed, if poets could be manufactured — in the way that thesis-writing in American universities turns out competent semi-experts upon this subject or that — he should have done so.

But if Mr. Eliot has caused his followers' verses to flow with an excessive caution (for the young) he has not diminished the numbers of verse-writers: indeed, oddly enough, it is quite the reverse. At first sight this must seem very odd indeed; unless it is realized (it is a thing I have not seen noted) how fundamentally democratic are Mr. Eliot's teachings. For instance, in his very interesting study of Dante, he expresses himself as follows:

> When I affirm that more can be learned about how to write poetry from Dante than from any English poet, I do not at all mean that Dante's way is the only right way, or that Dante is thereby *greater* than Shakespeare or, indeed, any other English poet. I put my meaning into other words by saying that Dante can do less *harm* to anyone trying to learn to write verse, than can Shakespeare. . . . If you follow Dante without talent, you will at worst be pedestrian and flat; if you follow Shakespeare or Pope without talent, you will make an utter fool of yourself.[1]

What could be more matey and democratic than that? Such words could not have been written by such a writer as Mr. Joyce, say, or by Mr. Yeats. Throughout the critical writing of Mr. Eliot, and it is the same with Mr. Pound, the object cannot be said to be to *diminish* the number of servants of the Muses. *The manufacture of poets and poetry* — and of *critics* of the same — *that* can be said to be what, looked at from outside, all this "critical" activity would seem to have been about. And — although it is a little strange to wish to compass such an end — this does not seem to me to be a bad thing from a certain standpoint. Mere *numbers* is of importance, especially today. Ezra Pound is to my mind, first and last, a technician: so it is this gospel of a sort of literary mechanics that was to be expected of him. He is the knowing craftsman, generously imparting the tricks of his trade. And Mr. Eliot — who as critic and poet may be regarded as the outcome of Ezra on the technical side (he stands in the same relation to the latter as does Hemingway to Miss Stein) — he too teaches a mechanism, a little automatically; for it is evident that the good Ezra hypnotizes him, as well as laying him under a deep obligation.

Ezra Pound is a figure of real importance, and the art of letters in our time owes a great deal to his intelligence. Nothing I say here must be interpreted as a lack of recognition of that fact. But one of the peculiarities of Ezra Pound is that he in the same breath will deliver himself of judgements regarding writers of very great intellectual power — say Mr. Joyce — that are discerning and just: and judgements of writers possessing no interest whatever, for man or god, which are undeniably silly. But how is this? It is extremely difficult to reconcile these two types of utterances of the author of the admirable "Cantos." He knows a good thing when he sees it, and needless to say he does first-rate things himself. But he does not know a dull thing when he sees it.

[1] *Selected Essays*, p. 238.

Having asked *How is this?* let me provide an answer. There is first Pound's fatal democratic expansiveness. He has a big heart. He would really like to see a world of Dantes, more or less — at least that is the impression that his behaviour conveys. He would teach *anybody* how to be Dante — *technically*. And if some earnest and as he would say "discipular" personage has shown himself an apt learner of tricks, he loses all self-control, throws discretion to the winds, and at the top of his voice proclaims him a super-Dante on the spot. It is magnificent, but it is not criticism.

Temperamentally, T. S. Eliot is as *close* as Ezra is exuberant. He is as arrogant as Ezra is modest — as sly as Ezra is open. He is democratic *in spite* of himself, as it were. And whereas Ezra is pure mechanism, Eliot's critical system is all about something: where Pound's system was *anybody's* system who cared to give themselves the trouble to be a poet, Eliot, working the same system, ostensibly very democratic, does impose extra-mechanical tests for those proposing to use it.

There is much more purpose, in fine, in Mr. Eliot than in Mr. Pound. There is much more personality. And he has paid a great deal of curious attention to the sanctions required for the expression of the thinking subject in verse or prose. In a sense, in spite of his democratic programme, he has made it difficult, rather than easy, for the student to participate in the creative activities about which he has written so much. Anybody with a tongue in his head, anyone certified born of woman, indeed any son of a bitch, can assume the laurel, as far as Mr. Pound is concerned — he is anything but particular on that head; but for Mr. Eliot it is a matter of some moment to know if he has politics, and *which*; and, still more, what his theology may, or may not be. He is as alive to the problems of "the background," as Mr. Pound is sublimely indifferent to them. And one feels, even, that had he his critical life to live over again he would scarcely take on Mr. Pound's fanatically technical system: he has even said somewhere (Max Eastman exults over it) that he is not quite sure that criticism is necessary at all! He might never start being a critic at all if he had his time over again! He might leave "mental inertia" where and as he found it. For: "If we wish for a population easy to control by suggestion," I quote his friend Mr. I. A. Richards, "we shall decide what repertory of suggestions it shall be susceptible to and encourage this tendency except in the few. But if we wish for a high and diffused civilization, with its attendant risks, we shall combat this form of mental inertia."[1] Mr. Eliot may have tired of the latter of these alternatives.

Of the two provinces of poetry and literary criticism respectively, in which Mr. T. S. Eliot is equally at home and somewhat *maître de séance*, it is the latter into which, in this essay, I am pursuing him. It is Mr. Eliot the critic who requires, to my mind, some serious scrutiny — not only far

---

[1] *Practical Criticism*, p. 314. I. A. Richards.

more "scrutiny" than he is ever likely to receive at the hands of his adherent Mr. Leavis, for instance (or from Mr. Leavis's master, Mr. Richards), but far more than he has, in fact, received from any of his casual critics. Mr. Stonier, for example,[1] though on the right tack, has traversed a little too heedlessly this unsubstantial but tricky system, though his chapter on Eliot is very well worth reading. There is one main subject to be studied in connection with anything that can be described as Mr. Eliot's critical system: namely the whole question of *sincerity*, in all its ramifications. That notion, with all the values attaching to an actual doctrine of *Make-Believe*, has gradually become for Mr. Eliot, as for Mr. Richards, the central affair.

The latter has been responsible for giving definition to Mr. Eliot's critical impulses, and bringing into a glaring prominence the essential muddle-headedness of this strange classicist and "revolutionary" poet — this odd "cultural" humanist and true believer. And Mr. Richards has performed this task of definition, and of *exposure*, for his partner, with a certain ruthlessness — the effects of which, seeing the closeness of the partnership, are not without their comic side. — I may add that I am not here occupied in saving Mr. Eliot from his friends. I am doing little more, really, than underlining and interpreting what Mr. Richards has already most effectively (though discreetly) performed.

> The only possible *sincere man* would in fact be God. Or to put it in another way, the only man who could conceivably qualify for the epithet "sincere" would be the perfect man. So under these circumstances all men are condemned, and that should be obvious, to varying degrees of "insincerity."
> But "sincere" is merely a popular counter, so in discussing this highly important matter it is well to keep before us all the time what popularly is meant by "sincere." We all know what we have in mind when we employ this word, and it always means, with any of us, about the same thing. When we say so-and-so is sincere, we mean he is *not* a "humbug," that he does not habitually attempt to deceive us as to his "real" feelings and intentions. The opposite of "sincere," to get at it in that way, is "spurious," "bogus," "sham," "humbugging," "spoof," etc., etc. The mere parading of these terms defines, negatively, our meaning when we make use of the term "sincere."

That perfect insincerity would qualify a man for an asylum, we may at once agree with Mr. Richards. Sincerity can only mean identity with truth. But in the popular sense the *sincerest* men are those in the asylums, for there can be no duplicity where there is absolute, and demented, *belief.* The lunatic who believed himself to be Mussolini would be entirely "sincere," as we commonly use the term. But the man who hoaxed people into believing he was Mussolini in order to rob them, would be "insincere." On the other hand the latter would be nearer to the truth than the former (since he would *know* that he was not Mussolini), and so, as the word is used by Mr. Richards, he would be more sincere. Also, we may agree with Mr.

---

[1] *Gog Magog.* G. H. Stonier.

I. A. Richards when he says that the *cleverer* you are the less "sincere" you are, as a rule, in the popular sense. But even there it is necessary to make some qualifications. "Stupid people can be very sincere" — yes, but not *all* stupid people are "sincere," and stupidity is not synonymous with *sincerity*. "Simple readers," as Mr. Richards says, incline to regard the ironist as "insincere." His solemn blarny takes them in, and when they recognize it for mockery they reflect that no man could *take them in*, even in mockery, who was not a born "dissembler." It is the "simple readers" who are most likely to be concerned about "sincerity." "Sincere" even, is essentially a word of "the simple," is it not? Yes. But what is the opposite of "the simple"? Is it not "the knowing"? (It is not "the wise.") And when these terms are being used to exert an emotional leverage, who would you rather be, a simple man or a knowing one? However unsatisfactory the "simple" rôle may be, it has more aesthetic appeal than has "the knowing."

But let us examine the fallacies residing in the simple, popular, counter "sincere." It is not difficult to see, if we reflect for a moment or two about it, that this term "sincere," as popularly used, has no value whatever except a moral one.

Popularly, what is regarded, once more, as a "sincere man" in contrast to an "insincere man"? Well, the sincere man "speaks his mind" — that is a typical description of a sincere man. There is no dissimulation about him. He just is a plain, blunt man, who on all occasions speaks up and says just what he thinks.

This is of course socially commendable on the face of it. But it has nothing to do with the *value* of what he thinks, which may be negligible or quite likely harmful. Indeed it can be argued — and for my part I have inclined to believe that it should be argued — that on the whole "sincerity" of such a low quality is not even socially or morally desirable; and that, in short, such "truthful" gentlemen should not be encouraged to "speak out" in that manner at all. I do not say that they should be taught to lie. But they should be prevented from publishing on all occasions their ill-digested, poor-quality, and crudely emotional "truth." This would bring to an end the platforms in Hyde Park on Sunday afternoon? Even so! But this is a mere opinion. I give it here to illustrate as concretely as possible my meaning, do you see.

So, as regards this man who "speaks his mind," two questions must be asked: namely, is he satisfied, or not, that his mind is a perfect instrument of truth? If he is so satisfied, he is a fool. If he is not, then in speaking it too emphatically he lays himself open to the charge of insincerity or bounce.

But since none of us can lay claim to the possession of this perfect instrument of truth — we are all only dealing in different degrees of falsity — is there to be an embargo upon all our utterances? Must neither Mr. I. A. Richards, Mr. Eliot, nor myself, be allowed to open our mouths, because what we say is certain in advance, and in the nature of the case, to be untrue? Further, since we are all three intelligent enough to know it must be untrue, we shall be behaving insincerely into the bargain. I should naturally reply *no* to this, there must be no embargo, as would (speaking for themselves) Mr. Richards and Mr. Eliot. And of course there *are* many many people whose falsity is much more flagrant than ours!

But it is at this point that Messrs. Eliot and Richards, on the one hand, and myself on the other, part company, I am afraid. For *they* desire, if I have understood them aright, more "sincerity" than I do. Or rather, their system of thinking aims at a canon of truth fundamentally less sincere in detail (qualitatively less), but more widely extended (quantitatively — greater in amount). They believe that with the wider net they can catch God — "the Path," the Good Life — or can do so better than with the more concentrated contraption.

How this comes about is as follows. At the very centre of this discussion regarding the "sincere" and the "insincere" is the problem of personality. Mr. Eliot stands for the maximum of *depersonalization*, and Mr. Richards for the maximum of *disbelief* or suspension of judgement. But let us hear Mr. Eliot and Mr. Richards. First let us hear Mr. Eliot and make some comments upon his statements, and then do the same with Mr. I. A. Richards.

Mr. T. S. Eliot.

What is to be insisted upon is that the poet must develop or procure the consciousness of the past and that he should continue to develop this consciousness throughout his career.

What happens is a continual surrender of himself as he is at the moment to something which is more valuable. The progress of an artist is a continual self-sacrifice, a continual extinction of personality.[1]

My meaning is, that the poet has, not a "personality" to express, but a particular medium, which is only a medium and not a personality. . . . Impressions and experiences which are important for the man may take no place in the poetry, and those which become important in the poetry may play quite a negligible part in the man, the personality.[2]

This is Henry James's "sense of the past": it is also Mr. Pound's sense of the past, which is the main and sole feature of Mr. Pound as an artist: and Mr. Eliot has taken that over entire and intact from his master in counterpoint. But Mr. Pound is, in his practice, a *reductio ad absurdum* of this theory of literature, a brilliant and delightful one, but nevertheless

---

[1] *Selected Essays*, p. 17. T. S. Eliot.
[2] *Op. cit.*, p. 20.

absurd. Where Mr. Eliot recommends "a feeling that the whole of the literature of Europe from Homer and within it the whole of the literature of his own country has a simultaneous existence and composes a simultaneous order," he is dutifully teaching the doctrine of Ezra Pound, and he has in his own major pieces given effect to that teaching with important variations of his own. But I think that anyone who peruses Mr. Pound's *Cantos*[1] must agree, while admiring extremely the great patches of magnificent translation, really granitic landslides from other times into our tongue, and recognizing the great technical resources displayed, that there is such a tendency to regard a scuffle in fourteenth-century Siena as fundamentally more interesting than a similar scuffle in Wigan or Detroit today, that even the historic *depersonalization* has not been achieved: since the fourteenth-century Sienese would probably regard the twentieth-century *fait-divers* as more curious and interesting than the *fait-divers* at his own front door. And I think we are compelled to conclude that romance *has* entered into this too strictly chronologic amalgam — that the *time-view* is eminently present, and that this is not the "impersonal" but the "romantic" temper. For it is easy to say "the historical sense involves a perception, not only of the pastness of the past, but of its presence."[2] But that past is, at the best, seeing its proportions, very selective, and its "presence" is at the best ideal. You cannot purge it of the glamour of strange lands. Strange times, after all, *are* strange lands, neither more nor less. And so this theory of "the presence of the past" results in a new exoticism (proper to our critical and chronological civilization) — an exoticism of exactly the same order as Baudelaire's exoticism ("*les cocotiers absents de la superbe Afrique*," etc.): of that of Monsieur Paul Morand, or that of Gauguin, Firbank or Stevenson. And so the *here and now* is diminished too much: and we desert the things that after all we stand a chance of learning something concrete about, for things that we can never know except through a glass darkly and as it were in a romantic dream.

This historical and chronological attitude would have been incomprehensible to the classical mind, as has often been pointed out: and the classical mind (that of the man who lived firmly in the present) gained in coherence and strength. But, it is argued, today we cannot do that. The Hellene of the classical age possessed no libraries, full of the material of history, whereas we do. He knew nothing of the world about him, whereas we do. We are committed, willy nilly, to an interminable historic research: this is taken for granted, though often deplored. "It is arguable," writes Mr. Richards, "that mechanical inventions, with their social effects, and a too sudden diffusion of indigestible ideas, are disturbing throughout the world the whole order of human mentality, that our minds are, as it were,

---

[1] *XXX Cantos.* Ezra Pound, 1933.
[2] *Selected Essays*, p. 14.

becoming of an inferior shape — thin, brittle and patchy, rather than controllable and coherent. It is possible that the burden of information and consciousness that a growing mind has now to carry may be too much for its natural strength. If it is not too much already, it may soon become so, for the situation is likely to grow worse before it is better."[1]

The "burden of information and consciousness" does in fact overbalance the man of today, in many instances. What with the consciousness or the "sense" of the past, and the labour of gathering "information" about it, to enable it to become an integral part of the present, those who succumbed to the theory of Mr. Pound or Mr. Eliot should scarcely expect not to lose coherence — they must expect to "sacrifice" more and more of that "self" or "personality," which is merely a living adequately at any given moment, to become an "impersonal" rendezvous for two-dimensional phantoms, and to look more or less like a bric-à-brac shop, observed from the outside.

Of course I know that such a statement as "the poet has, not 'a personality' to express, but a particular medium, which is only a medium and not a personality," fits in very well, for instance, with Bertrand Russell's account of the psyche — a rendezvous as it were for a bundle of sticks, not the *sticks* but just the rendezvous — or with the functional picture of the Behaviorist. But those are *not* the affiliations to which Mr. Eliot is most apt to give his official recognition! And of course he never misses an opportunity of showing his disapproval of Bertrand Russell. So that, it would seem, should not be invoked to help us. But what I think may be said is that in a great deal of his literary criticism Mr. Eliot has indeed tended to confuse scientific values with art values. It *might* be a good thing — I do not say it is — for an artist to have a "personality," and for a scientist not to have a personality: though here of course I am not using a "personality" in the *Ballyhoo* sense — I do not mean an individualist abortion, bellowing that it wants at all costs to "express" itself, and feverishly answering the advertisement of the quack who promises to develop such things overnight. I mean only a constancy and consistency in being, as concretely as possible, *one thing* — at peace with itself, if not with the outer world, though that is likely to follow after an interval of struggle — something like what Montaigne meant, in fact, when he wrote of his work:

> L'ouvrage eust été moins mien: et sa fin principale et perfection, c'est d'estre exactemente mien. Je corrigerois bien une erreur accidentale . . . mais les imperfections qui sont en moy ordinaires et constantes, ce serait trahison de les oster.[2]

Mr. Eliot and Mr. Richards, I have said, stand for the maximum of *depersonalization* and of *disbelief* respectively (and to a large extent interchangeably). We have heard Mr. Eliot on the subject of *depersonalization*,

[1] *Practical Criticism*, p. 320.
[2] *Montaigne*, Book III, Ch. V.

and have supplied a fairly thorough commentary upon that. Now I suggest that we hear Mr. Richards upon the subject of *disbelief.*

Mr. I. A. RICHARDS.

In the first place, immensely useful as Mr. Richards has been to Mr. Eliot, and much as the latter has been influenced by him, the outspokenness of his logic has at times a little disturbed the more cautious, muffled and circumlocutory author of *Mr. Prufrock*: and never more so, I imagine, than when, in *Science and Poetry*, he triumphantly produced Mr. Eliot as *the man with absolutely no beliefs whatever* (though of course, expediency aside, such a theoretic *depersonalizer* as Mr. Eliot could scarcely be surprised at such a *dénouement*, however disturbing he might find it). The words complained of were as follows—the italics are those of the text:

> by effecting a complete severance between his poetry and *all* beliefs, and this without any weakening of the poetry, he [Mr. Eliot] has realized what might otherwise have remained largely a speculative possibility, and has hown the way to the only solution of these difficulties. "In the destructive element immerse. That is the way."[1]

I cannot help thinking that Mr. Eliot has taken this indiscretion of his colleague's too much to heart (the more unrelievedly religious character of his subsequent verse suggests it). To be held up to the world as the guy who had *par excellence* taken to the "destructive element" as a duck does to water, and swum about in it to such purpose as to have proved, for all time, that *without a shred of true belief of any sort*, an artist can still survive intact, and write first-rate poetry—that was scarcely the kind of advertisement Mr. Eliot had plotted out for himself! All he can do, however, is to find Mr. Richards "incomprehensible," on the next occasion.—"Mr. Richards's statement (*Science and Poetry*, p. 76 footnote) that a certain writer has effected 'a complete severance between his poetry and *all* beliefs' is to me incomprehensible."[2]

Mr. Eliot is using the disbelief theory of Mr. Richards in the essay (that on *Dante*) in which—in a *Note to Section II*—the above repudiation appears: and I am afraid the presence of this *gaffe* or snag prevents him from drawing all the conclusions he otherwise would have done from his working of the *disbelief* or *pseudo-statement* theory: he has been put too much on his guard.

Mr. Richards's statement is substantially true—or so it seems to me—but this feather cannot be worn in Mr. Eliot's cap—or it is not his desire to wear it—in his lifetime: possibly it is envisaged as a posthumous ornament, a passport to the communist millennium. Mr. Eliot is no Marxist—he would probably far rather live in a capitalist society than in a Marxist:

[1] *Science and Poetry*, p. 64.
[2] *Selected Essays*. T. S. Eliot.

but he thoroughly realizes that our present world of art and letters in Anglosaxony is half Marx and half *status quo* — he is a man who is naturally on the side of the Many, he has a quantitative mind, and he imbibed more than his share of romantically "radical" values in his tender years: they show through the snobbish veneer, that is all. The "classical" *panache* and all the rest of it, that is in the nature of a disguise. Those were, in the first instance, mere gestures of a stylistic effrontery, picturesquely gallic — a bit of Cyrano — *un peu de Cocteau quoi!* — a bit of *le dandy* as inherited from Baudelaire and the French romantics — a paradoxical pirouette — a slow, a *very* slow-movement stately pirouette!

As to the *Criterion*, that is a very "catholic" canon: it is a very broad, and indeed loose-minded affair, where the politics of *la vieille France* jostle the disintegrating tenets of "super-real" psychoanalysis: it did at one time perhaps make an effort to supply the Anglosaxon intelligentsia with something as logically inflexible as the French periodicals of political *action*; but not only was that a difficult undertaking — for Anglosaxony is inveterately "liberal," and to get together a team of writers not "tainted" with liberalism would be no easy matter: but Mr. Eliot himself was not sufficiently interested. He exhibited himself as "a royalist" to an indignant whig public — he called them a lot of naughty whigs and wagged his finger — and supplied *just so much* of that comedy as was welcome to brighten up the scene, but not a scrap more than was safe and comfortable. Am I here accusing Mr. Eliot of being a "humbug" then? To that I can only answer — No: rather he is *pseudo* everything, and he has found his theorist to explain and justify him, namely Mr. I. A. Richards.

But meanwhile we have got here, in this Eliot-Richards combination, a new aesthetic of *art pur*, which has, I believe, never been intelligently examined. The *Disbelief Theory* we could label it for convenience. It is, I dare say, the most important literary theory, upon the English scene, since that of Walter Pater, and deserves all our attention. I will attempt therefore to outline this new *art-for-art's-sake* — or stylists' evangel — universal and "catholic" in the popular sense — for, *however disguised*, that is what I believe it is.

"SINCERITY" IN THE THEORIES OF RICHARDS AND ELIOT

Both Mr. Richards and Mr. Eliot are preoccupied with the problem of *sincerity*, and it has become for them I believe the central problem of all. Mr. Eliot's *Note to Section II*[1] is undeniably a tissue of contradictions, one would say an elaborate exercise in hedging were it not so *palpably* confused.

[1] *Selected Essays*, ["Dante,"] p. 255.

But that need not really detain us. It is unfortunate that, on the grounds that his "theory" was "embryonic," and on the grounds that "I confess to considerable difficulty in analysing my own feelings," we should have such a shifty quicksand upon which to work, but that cannot be helped. We shall have to guess from a colony of *embryos*, that is all, what sort of adult thought would most probably ensue.

"If you deny the theory that full poetic appreciation is possible without belief in what the poet believed, you deny the existence of 'poetry' as well as 'criticism,' " Mr. Eliot writes: and throughout his *Note* he proceeds to deny it, half-deny it, and then take back his denial: to say that "it is possible, and *sometimes* necessary, to argue that full understanding must identify itself with full belief." But all this "hangs on the meaning" — or "a good deal" — for there is *nothing* here that is not doubly and trebly qualified — "on the meaning *if any*, of this short word *full*." Clearly with such floating and vapourish material it is not possible to do very much, unless one deals with it a little roughly, and just ignores its tacking and doubling; and so, observing it attentively *as a whole*, takes its *general* sense to be its *true* sense. It starts: "The theory of poetic belief and understanding here employed for a particular study is similar to that maintained by Mr. I. A. Richards (see his *Practical Criticism*, pp. 179 ff. and pp. 271 ff.)." Similar certainly it is, and at that we can leave it for all practical purposes — merely noting that, having started by saying this, he proceeds to say that it is *not* similar — although it *is* similar — and so forth! So (armed with this caution, that anything that is said in one place will invariably be contradicted in another) let us proceed to the text of the essay on Dante.

"We can make a distinction between what Dante believes as a poet and what he believed as a man. Practically, it is hardly likely that even so great a poet as Dante could have composed the *Comedy* merely with understanding and without belief." This means, if it means anything, that the "belief" of Dante (represented by the dogmatic philosophical system of St. Thomas Aquinas) was a support with which Dante the poet certainly could not dispense, because of his natural human feebleness — had he been a little more "great" he could have done without that dogmatic belief and treated the Hell and Paradise of Christian dogma as a Punch and Judy Show. But this "private belief" by means of which he propped himself up for this enterprise "becomes a different thing in becoming poetry. It is interesting to hazard the suggestion that this is truer of Dante than of any other philosophical poet. With Goethe, for instance, I often feel too acutely 'this is what Goethe the man believed,' instead of merely entering into a world which Goethe has created. . . . That is the advantage of a coherent traditional system of dogma and morals like the Catholic: it stands apart, for understanding and assent even without belief, from the single individual who propounds it. Goethe always arouses in me a strong sentiment of disbelief in what he believes: Dante does not."

That I think is plain enough: the *sensation even of belief*—the smell of it in conjunction with the smell of a "personality"—is sufficient to put Mr. Eliot off. "This is what Goethe, the man, believed!"—that reflection precludes artistic enjoyment. In the other case, that of the Roman Catholic poet, the "belief" has been disinfected, as it were, by the mere fact of possessing general assent. (The more people believe a thing the more true it is, in other words.) It is not what one man thought, but what several millions thought—what *nobody* thought really, in a sense, but what a great multitude passively sheltered in their consciousness, "believed" and accepted. Although he probably was not (for "even so great a poet as Dante," etc.) the author of the Inferno *could* have been simulating merely an interest or belief in what he wrote about. He was "impersonal."—And so we get back to the "impersonality" of science—for not invariably, though often, men circle back to what they started with.

No *belief* can be held by a man in his own right—he can only hold beliefs in common with all other men, banded together in an organized communion of official belief: these big, impersonal, community-beliers do *not* smell: but any belief held by the individual *does*: that is the idea. And it is of course the Catholic view over against the Protestant. There *is* another "standpoint," or modification of this pretty obvious piece of common sense. The dogmatic hostility to the *individual*—so that anything whatever that can be attributed personally to him is distasteful—is a *learnt* and adopted latter-day attitude, rather than a practical one. For the fixed and unalterable dogma of a mob might, for some noses, possess an effluvium that exceeded, at times, even the private stench of a subjective fug. But on the whole we must agree to the principle that the most widely held beliefs are the most satisfactory, when they are possible at all—when, in short, they have not become so mechanical as to preclude participation without the risk of such personal impoverishment as to defeat their own ends. But this is really a mere gesture of conformity. Mr. Eliot has not been concerned in his writings with the nature of religious beliefs, but with the specific problems of literary criticism. Except in *Thoughts after Lambeth*—a rather unfortunate excursion, I venture to think—he has left divinity severely alone. "Certainly, anyone who is wholly sincere and pure in heart may seek for guidance from the Holy Spirit; but who of us is always wholly sincere . . . ?"[1] he asks on that unhappy occasion. Sincerity would be necessary there—indeed, not many steps could be taken in that type of homiletic without entry into the Roman Church, it seems to me, as the rather ridiculous feebleness of the above-mentioned paper shows. And sincerity is precisely what Mr. Eliot is afraid of—sincerity in the sense of integral belief of any sort. You may say he is too sincere to believe out and out. He has built up a great reputation as a critic of the art he has

[1] *Thoughts after Lambeth.*

successfully practised, and that system is balanced, in a feat of very peculiar equilibrium, upon a notion of *insincerity*, in essence not so dissimilar to the theory advertised by Oscar Wilde in *The Decay of Lying*. "Insincerity" and "lying" are not of course used here with any of the popular stigmas attached to them, but only as we find them employed in the works of Oscar Wilde or of Mr. I. A. Richards or of Mr. Eliot himself. The Naughty Nineties were nothing if not socially snobbish: and *all* the moral values, of "honest," or of "good," necessarily came into contempt, as belonging to a vulgar order of servant-girl superstition, as it were.

> She was poor, but she was honest,
> Victim of a rich man's crime.

— that little Ninetyish ditty sums up the attitude in question to "virtue" very well. And Oscar Wilde, when he was engaged in stealing from foreign authors, or pillaging less-known English ones, no doubt got some kick out of the "criminal" character of these acts of literary "dishonesty," on the same principle that *anything* that flew in the ugly face of vulgar, or *bourgeois*, prejudice, was to be enthusiastically indulged in. But for the exposure of all the various perversions of this romantic way of feeling, I would like to refer the reader to an excellent book, published a few months ago, namely *The Romantic Agony*.[1] Such a mass of evidence is there assembled — verbatim evidence, which is most important — as should convince anyone I think of the fact of how a satanic culture, in the literary world, substituted itself for the central religious belief, which had crashed at the time of the French Revolution. These peculiar Christians — Baudelaire, Wilde, etc., etc., there is a long gallery of them — definitely turned to the Rebel Angel of Milton and he became the hero of their disordered theology.

But to return to Mr. Eliot — who as a poet, I believe, will be recognized by and by as the last of that line of romantics, the last *agonisant* of *The Romantic Agony*, though not a satanist — it is natural that the sensitive artist-nature should experience discomfort when it feels that a poet (of all people) is not *lying* — in the Oscar Wilde sense. For as there can be no absolute truth, let us relegate "truth" to the category of "mob belief," and, as artists, have no more to do with it! In a *Dialogue on Dramatic Poetry*, an essay that might have been written in "the Nineties," one of the characters, E (Eliot?) remarks:

> "I say that the consummation of the drama . . . is to be found in the ceremony of the Mass . . . drama springs from religious liturgy. . . . But when drama has ranged as far as it has in our own day, is not the only solution to return to religious liturgy? And the only dramatic satisfaction that I find now is in a High Mass well performed."

To which E's friend B replies:

[1] *The Romantic Agony*. Mario Praz, Oxford University Press.

"Are we to say that our cravings for drama are fulfilled by the Mass? . . .
No. For I once knew a man who held the same views as you appear to hold,
E. He went to High Mass every Sunday, and was particular to find a church
where he considered the Mass efficiently performed. And as I sometimes accompanied him, I can testify that the Mass gave him extreme, I may even
say immoderate satisfaction. It was almost orgiastic. But when I came to
consider his conduct, I realized that he was guilty of a *confusion des genres*.
His attention was not on the meaning of the Mass, for he was not a believer
but a Bergsonian; it was on the Art of the Mass. His dramatic desires were
satisfied by the Mass, precisely because he was not interested in the Mass,
but in the drama of it."[1]

This is the spirit in which Mr. Eliot suggests that Dante should be read:
consider the *Inferno* and the *Paradiso* as dramas — absurd if you like, a
powerful hallucination of a diseased age — anything you will, but certainly a powerful system of symbols, which while you read, you will *believe*
in the only sense in which "belief" really has any meaning: and indeed, since
they are more compact and compelling than any other symbols, you *may*
even get the habit of this particular belief; and certainly no harm will be
done if you do.

Indeed, according to the theory of *pseudo-belief*, I cannot see that this
attitude can fail to be an advantage: for though Mr. Eliot says that were
we persuaded that Dante did not believe in his hell and heaven, that that
would interfere with our enjoyment of the poetry, I do not think that is
at all consistent; for it seems to be identifying "the man, the personality,"
with "the artist." And that is forbidden, according to the canons of the
pseudo-believer. "Experiences which are important for the man may take
no place in the poetry, and those which become important in the poetry
may play quite a negligible part in the man, the personality." But "we can
make a distinction between what Dante believes as a poet and what he
believes as a man": and "The *belief attitude* of a man reading the *Summa*
must be different from that of a man reading Dante, even when it is the
same man, and that man a Catholic."[2] The "personality" is the Catholic,
it seems, therefore: *he* has the belief-attitude of religion: but the "artist,"
ideally, has no *belief-attitude* at all, for he has no personality — he is "a
medium" merely. And it would weaken very much our view of the "self-
sacrificing" artist — for he, not the personality, is the hero of the piece — to
suppose that the mere "personality" had put him up to writing a "religious"
poem. This would not be the mediumistic account of the transaction which
this aestheticism exacts. And the more we read of this *pseudo-statement*
or *pseudo-belief* theory, the more we feel that the response of a person
to the drama of the *Inferno* would be a very different one if he in fact *believed* that his own flesh might quite well be grilling there for all eternity,

[1] *Selected Essays.*
[2] *Selected Essays*, p. 20.

in the manner described: and the more we admire the heroism of "the artist," who is coupled to a "personality" who enjoys that belief, and who yet is able to abstract himself entirely from those inartistic sensations. But to be a *pseudo-believer* you must believe anyway in this pseudo-man "the artist." There is no way out of that! And that is the difficulty. For how are you to keep *all* personality out of the purer, the "impersonal," vessel? And even a *little* personality that had crept in, in spite of every precaution, would be capable of corrupting the artist-self to such a degree as to render it thoroughly suspect and unserviceable.

> I am in agreement with Mr. Richards's statement on p. 271. . . . I agree for the reason that if you hold any contradictory theory you deny, I believe, the existence of "literature" as well as of "literary criticism."[1]

And "the statement on p. 271" is as follows:

> For it would seem evident that poetry which has been built upon firm and definite beliefs about the world, *The Divine Comedy* or *Paradise Lost*, or Donne's *Divine Poems*, or Shelley's *Prometheus Unbound*, or Hardy's *The Dynasts*, must appear differently to readers who do and readers who do not hold similar beliefs. Yet in fact most readers, and nearly all good readers, are very little disturbed by even a direct opposition between their own beliefs and the beliefs of the poet.

I may say at once that this statement sounds nonsense to me: or, shall we say, I am a *bad reader* or imperfectly *pseudo*. But that is not the point. What is important is to consider if these "good" readers of Mr. Richards are such admirable fellows as the term suggests. There are no doubt very many people today who are sublimely indifferent to what a play or poem or novel *is about*. To that extent Mr. Richards's statement is correct. But that is, I think, merely a criticism of an age which is not only tolerant and over-liberal, but, indeed, indifferent to every value whatever, except a hedonistic or pragmatical one. And because Mr. Eliot wants to continue to be a "literary critic," to enjoy the satisfactions of exercising personal influence in that way — because he would like to have his apple and eat it too — to be "a humanist" and "not a humanist" — to be free to criticize the "humanism" of Babbitt and yet to practise it on the sly, upon the basis of a theory of *pseudo-belief*, invented for him by Mr. Richards, or which he and Mr. Richards have concocted between them — that is no reason why I, or you, should endorse an *art-for-art's-sake* theory which cannot bear examination.

But let us, on the other hand, *as artists*, make use of Mr. Richards's aesthetic barrage, and let us humour Mr Eliot: we may be saved a lot of trouble. The interference of the moralist may be side-stepped by leaving these gentlemen alone — as I have done up to the present, I may point out. I only now break that silence because I am quite sure that they, and their "appendixes" of the Leavis variety, are too firmly entrenched to be easily

---

[1] *Selected Essays*, p. 255.

routed, and so they may be safely repudiated, without our ceasing to benefit by their *pseudo-believer's* protection.

.   .   .   .   .   .

MR. RICHARDS'S THEORY OF PSEUDO-STATEMENT OR PSEUDO-BELIEF

But I have still to give a brief account of Mr. Richards's theory of *pseudo-statement* or *pseudo-belief*.[1] "It is *not* the poet's business to make true statements," says Mr. Richards. What he makes are rather *pseudo-statements*. Some people — mathematicians for instance — simply cannot read poetry because of this *bogus* quality which governs it — "they find the alleged statements to be *false*," and that puts them off. "It will be agreed," Mr. Richards gravely remarks, "that their approach to poetry and their expectations from it are mistaken."

Poetry (or any form of pure art, I suppose) is emotional, not logical: "the acceptance which a pseudo-statement receives is entirely governed by its effects upon our feelings and attitudes." Again: "A pseudo-statement is 'true' if it suits and serves" some emotional attitude — which "on other grounds" is "desirable." So the "truth" of art turns out to be what we *desire*. Anything that we *desire* is *true*. Mr. Richards and Mr. Eliot, these two pseudo-believers, are, in other words, highly subjective thinkers, to say the least of it! But subjectiveness of mind is *not* a quality that the criterion of Mr. Eliot professes to applaud!

Thus the *pseudo-believer* is the perfect pragmatist. "A pseudo-statement is a form of words which is justified entirely by its effect in releasing or organizing our impulses and attitudes," to a useful and desirable end.

"Statements true and false alike do of course constantly touch off attitudes and *action*." Whether a thing is "true" or "false" matters very little, if it stimulates effective action. "Our daily *practical* existence is largely guided by them." But this, it appears, "is one of the great new dangers to which civilization is exposed. Countless *pseudo-statements* — about God, about the universe, about human nature, the relations of mind to mind . . . pseudo-statements which are pivotal points in the organization of the mind . . . have suddenly become, for sincere, honest and informal minds, impossible to believe. . . . This is the contemporary situation. The remedy . . . is to cut our pseudo-statements free from belief, and yet retain them, in this released state, as the main instruments by which we order our attitudes to one another and to the world."

There you have it: the agreeable, the life-giving, lies that we tell ourselves must be cut off from all embarrassing logical entanglements, and erected into autonomous systems — the *pseudo-belief* takes the place of *belief*.

[1] From Chap. VI, "Poetry and Beliefs," *Science and Poetry*. I. A. Richards.

And that this will be quite all right and perfectly in order is proved by poetry: *"for poetry conclusively shows that even the most important among our attitudes can be aroused and maintained without any belief entering in at all."* And then comes, in a footnote, the statement already quoted that made Mr. Eliot uncomfortable, namely that he had effected "a severance between his poetry and all beliefs."

There, I think, is the whole bag of tricks. It is the whole bag of tricks, except for the subsidiary discussion regarding *sincerity* — which grows out of the discussion of *pseudo-statements*.

"For extreme degrees of insincerity we should look in asylums," says Mr. Richards: for extreme degrees of subjectivity, that is, for extreme degrees of *pseudo-ness of belief-attitudes*. And so he identifies "sincerity" with closeness to the objective facts of science.

But of course the "facts" of science turn out usually not to be facts, except in a limited sense. And it is far more the breakdown of *scientific* beliefs than that of religious beliefs which has precipitated the present *crisis of belief*, as I suppose it would be called or, as it is also seen to be here, a *crisis of sincerity*. This aspect of the matter Mr. Richards neglects. The attacks of the Critical Philosophy upon the fundamental beliefs of physical science, and the most recent semi-Berkeleyan developments in physicist mathematical theory, is the real source of the present flabbiness of *sincerity*. But that would not in fact affect sincerity so much, if it were not for questions of self-interest or personal vanity, which personal and predatory instincts take advantage of this situation to create bogus images of "truth" suited only too much to their own highly pragmatic ends. For the sceptic or agnostic can after all be as *sincere* as the dogmatic fanatic.

Mr. Richards — whom I regard as a sincere man, in the ordinary sense — does not disguise the difficulty — he does not minimize the effort required to be sincere: indeed he overdoes it if anything: his anxiety about his own and other people's sincerity — his envy of the dog, for instance, who is without effort instinctively sincere — must tend to undermine self-confidence, and to cause people to become self-conscious. But Mr. Richards is after all a psycho-analyst: and in everything the psycho-analyst promotes self-consciousness, and tends to turn perfectly sound humdrum instinctive people into cranky and unreliable human machines. But still let us agree with him that "sincerity" is "not a quality that we can take for granted." Especially is that the case in a disorderly epoch, where irresolution is the order of the day.

> We can *feel* very sincere when, in fact, as others can see clearly, there is
> no sincerity in us. Bogus forms of the virtue waylay us — confident inner
> assurances and invasive rootless convictions. And when we doubt our own
> sincerity and ask ourselves, "Do I *really* think so; do I really feel so?" an
> honest answer is not easily come by. A direct effort to be sincere, like other
> efforts to will ourselves into action, more often than not, frustrates its inten-
> tion. For all these reasons any light that can be gained upon the nature of
> sincerity, upon possible tests for it and means for inducing and promoting
> it, is extremely serviceable. . . .[1]

Here we see it, in Mr. Richards's account, as a sort of *impotence to
believe*. These "means for inducing and promoting it" smack of specifics
for more enterprising virility, Pelmanism, or other props for the will or
fillips for the senses proper to a shell-shocked society. — But Mr. Richards
finds a "stimulating discussion" of this difficulty in *Chung Yung*. This turns
out to be precepts for successful extroversion — that is "sincerity" — to "effect
a union of the external and internal." Finally *"those who are 'most
themselves' cause others about them to become also 'more themselves.' "*

That "the being oneself" should be the fundamental difficulty hit upon
by Mr. Richards is instructive. For manifestly the *pseudo* technique must
tend to undermine the vigour of this all-important self hood to a peculiar
degree. And Mr. Eliot's insistence upon the suppression of the personality
and the creation of a privileged *play-boy alter ego* is not going to help
matters — not going to promote "sincerity" — either.

Indeed, Mr. Eliot's is an elaborate system of dogmatic insincerity: and
Mr. Richards's (in a somewhat different context, and as a matter of fact
in a rather more robust manner) is also essentially a doctrine of the insincere. For you cannot resolutely cut adrift the *pseudo* and the fanciful
from all beliefs, and in the violent subjectivism that must ensue attain
"sincerity." Indeed, however much you may profess, and even genuinely
profess, a desire to promote "sincerity," you are in fact arming yourself
with the weapons of insincerity, to gain a purely selfish and subjective
end — by *any* means, upon whatever terms.

Mr. Eliot, according to my notion, is insincere: he has allowed himself
to be robbed of his personality, such as it is, and he is condemned to an
unreal position. I see his difficulty of course, and understand that in the
first instance he was moved by a desire to effect a *total* separation between
what he regarded as fine in his personality from what he regarded as unsatisfactory. And he has always been particularly alive to the sensation
which has found a theological expression in the doctrine of original sin.
But let me quote from a well-known sceptic to bring out this point a little
more clearly — it is this particular doctrine, that of original sin, that this
sceptical Victorian is attacking.

---

[1] *Practical Criticism*, p. 283.

I, on the contrary, hold that Christ was a man, and so far have surely a higher opinion of human nature than you. I regard the character of Christ as within the range of human possibilities. . . . Why should I be forced to postulate an incarnation of deity to account for goodness . . . ? Your answer has been often given by theologians. It is, simply, that human nature is corrupt and virtue supernatural . . . man can only approximate to this (Christ) type by supernatural aid. Human nature is the residuum left when all good impulses are supposed to come from without. The heart is deceitful above all things, and desperately wicked. From ourselves come nothing but lust, hatred, and the love of darkness. Certainly, therefore, humanity cannot produce a Christ — nor even a decent member of society.[1]

Often from the opposing camp one can obtain some useful help: and the above Eminent Victorian agnostic account of the backgrounds of the doctrine of original sin — the central doctrine of Christianity — will clarify for the general reader what I have to say. It is of course the *interpretation* of this doctrine that is the trouble. A going more than half-way to meet salvation — a tendency to bedevil oneself in order to procure for the principle of salvation a super-suitable subject — has been seen to lead the more hysterical of the orthodox, or the pseudo-orthodox, into the paths of satanic romance. The *Romantic Agony* was fed upon such states of mind. Taken to its logical conclusion, it would cause a person to become the reverse of "a decent member of society": it has at all times opened the door to ill-conditioned instincts: every personal meanness or frank dishonesty may be a constant temptation to the mind desirous of substantiating this doctrine. Often an extremely untidy *morale* and faulty discipline has been the result.

When you reflect that Christianity literally stands or falls by this doctrine, that of the Fall and the Atonement, it is easy to see how great the temptation may prove to become more "sinful" than is strictly necessary — to embrace sin (even if by sin is meant nothing more than an envious and unpolished disposition, a rancorous or a hasty temper) — in fact to *prove* the Fall, as it were, and tearfully to invite the graces of the Atonement. The fact that men are mischievous and disagreeable little animals for the most part, may be accounted for in various ways: but the orthodox way is by pointing to the power of the great curse that was laid upon all mankind at the Fall.

But if we take the case of a man of intellectual attainments, this formidable doctrine may decidedly lead him astray: for may he not just leave his human nature — that "residuum left when all good impulses are removed," into a supernatural category — in an inert and untidy condition, to shift for itself, and the more vices and meannesses this merely human self arrives at displaying in a sense the better, for the greater glory of God; and meanwhile place all his pride in an hypostatized intellectual contraption,

[1] *An Agnostic's Apology*. Sir Leslie Stephen.

a super-self — to which he may sometimes refer as a litmus paper — or a filament of platinum — or sometimes as a more personal emanation, after all, but strictly inhuman and "above the law"?

Upon the one hand we have Jean-Jacques Rousseau, with his "noble savage" — his originally good, instead of fundamentally bad, human being: and on the other we have this man-under-a-curse, the "miserable sinner," of the orthodox Christian. We are perhaps too much inclined to be affected by these two conventional poles of feeling and of doctrine. Because we find Rousseau's notion provokes our laughter, we are perhaps too disposed to feel that all men are *born* gangsters, dope-fiends, treacherous and disloyal associates, envious — Wainewrights and Wildes in the making — close-fisted pimps, poisoners and cuckoos-in-the-nest. Then when the armament kings and others get up a million-dead Armageddon, we say, *Ah there is the caveman-under-a-curse coming out! Of course, there is no holding back these bloodthirsty masses!* At least the politicians murmur that, and the public acquiesces. Few people today understand what nonsense that is, for they never ask themselves how it happens they can go about the streets of a great city from year's end to year's end without seeing the slightest disturbance of the peace — without seeing a single blow or hearing so much as an angry word exchanged. Yet would this universal calm and order reign if men were indeed such bloodthirsty cavemen as they are made out to be? Of course it would not! They are, on the contrary, extremely well-trained and pacific monkeys. Their street manners are unimpeachable — their cage-etiquette above reproach.

I am not here arguing that we are not beneath a curse of some kind, and a very portentous one. I am only arguing on behalf of a less exaggerated and mediaeval view of our depravity and unlovely disposition — a little perhaps on the side of Rousseau even — not for a "noble savage," but for a pretty peaceable, humane and well-behaved creature, such as Vilhjálmar Stefánsson depicts in his Esquimaux communities, before the coming of the white trader — and not only Stefánsson but all those who have travelled in the Friendly Arctic: merely to surmise that Coronation Gulf, on the Polar Archipelago, at the time Franklin passed that way, was a more pacific and virtuous spot than New York at the same epoch.

This may seem to you a very long way round to travel to reach a solution of the *personality* problem we have been discussing here: but I believe that some such method as this is the best under the circumstances. The personality is not, I think, quite the pariah it becomes in the pages of Mr. Eliot: I do not believe in the anonymous, "impersonal," catalytic, for the very good reason that I am sure the personality is in that as much as in the other part of this double-headed oddity, however thoroughly disguised, and is more apt to be a corrupting influence in that arrangement than in the more usual one, where the artist is identified with his beliefs. If there is to be an "insincerity," I prefer it should occur in the opposite sense —

namely that "the man, the personality" should exaggerate, a little artificially perhaps, his beliefs — rather than leave a meaningless shell behind him, and go to hide in a volatilized hypostasization of his personal feelings. That may be more "insincere" in the one sense, but for the extrovert activities it is more satisfactory: the man is thus "most himself" (even if a little too much himself to be quite the perfect self, on occasion): and through being less cosmopolitan in the sense of the temporal or chronologic cosmos, he must in the end be more effective.

APPENDIX

(TO T. S. ELIOT — PSEUDOIST)

SINCE WRITING the foregoing essay upon "Mr. Eliot — *pseudoist*," a new book of his has appeared.[1] There is nothing much new in it, except that at last he shows definite signs of a resolve to wriggle out of the Richards dilemma, by hook or by crook.

Mr. I. A. Richards may be said to have been "found out," in the sense that people now recognize the weakness of his *psychological* method of literary criticism: he carries less weight, I think, with the scholastic young and the highbrow critical world, and has done Eliot, the poet, about all the good he is ever likely to do: but there remain all those vulnerable points in Mr. Eliot the critic, laid bare as a result of this lengthy association, to be somehow or other liquidated. It will not be easy, I prophecy — Mr. Eliot's ingenuity will be taxed to the utmost. Even the average review-critics who have dealt with this book, I notice, are a little shocked and indignant at its lavish inconsistencies, its studied evasiveness, and seem to be dimly aware that they are not merely in the presence of a scholar's "cautiousness," but confronted with some deep-seated equivocation. — But anyhow, here he is in these latest essays, squaring up to his old partner — not throwing "caution" to the winds, certainly, but forgetting about it, in a revelatory manner, once or twice too often.

I do not think that a breach with the arch-interpreter of the *Waste Land* is to be anticipated. But Mr. Richards *has* been mentioned in association with Matthew Arnold by Mr. Eliot! This is a very serious occurrence. "I only assert again," for Mr. Eliot asserts it several times, "that what he [Mr. Richards] is trying to do is essentially the same as what Arnold wanted to do." — This, from Mr. Eliot, is much stronger than you would think!

Mr. Eliot is *accusing* Mr. Richards of being like Arnold! Having degraded Arnold into the position of an inferior critic, to his complete satisfaction (and to that of the "academic youth" of America, I am sure, as well) it then

---

[1] *The Use of Poetry and the Use of Criticism.* T. S. Eliot, Nov. 2, 1933.

occurs to him as an excellent idea to send people he does not approve of
to join Arnold — like *sending to Coventry*, a little! Matthew Arnold becomes
a sort of purgatory to which unsatisfactory people are dispatched — and
Mr. Richards has definitely taken that road, in Mr. Eliot's pages. As I said,
there is nothing much new in this book, nothing that is not covered in the
above analysis, except that the uneasiness and discomfort caused by the
strangely clairvoyant remarks of his partner Mr. Richards is very marked —
it has greatly increased: and, to relieve this, he has committed himself to
certain further qualifications, which he might claim, indeed certainly would,
as having modified his position as laid down in the *Selected Essays*. So
I thought it better to add this postscript.

.   .   .   .   .   .

Matthew Arnold, writes Mr. Eliot, wanted "to preserve emotions without
the beliefs with which their history has been involved"[1] (desired that is,
to make use, for cultural purposes, of the religious emotions, and to have
them *without* the religion): "there is . . . danger . . . of leading the reader
to look in poetry for religious satisfactions."[2] And Maritain is freely
quoted, indeed all over the place — as follows for instance: "It is a deadly
error to expect poetry to provide the super-substantial nourishment of
man."[3]

But Matthew Arnold was guilty of that "deadly error." As Mr. Eliot has
stated elsewhere, "The total effect of Arnold's philosophy is to set up Culture
in the place of Religion."[4] And Mr. Richards foresees "a mental chaos such
as man has never experienced," and "we shall then," he informs us, "be
thrown back, as Matthew Arnold foresaw, upon poetry. Poetry is capable
of saving us." And Mr. Eliot remarks (after quoting this passage), "I should
have felt completely at a loss in this passage, had not Matthew Arnold
turned up." Matthew Arnold settled it! And with Ezra Pound and the late
Irving Babbitt, Mr. Richards and Matthew Arnold now inhabit a cultural
compound of a melancholy blue tint! "Salvation by poetry is not quite the
same thing for Mr. Richards as it was for Arnold; but so far as I am concerned these are merely different shades of blue."[5]

Mr. Eliot is precluded on account of his rôle as theologian, from pointing out the common or garden foolishness of this *salvation by poetry* of
his partner Mr. Richards (a *salvationist* reminiscent of Mr. Middleton
Murry — though Mr. Murry and all his works are anathema, whereas Mr.
Richards, fundamentally not unlike him, has been for nearly a decade Mr.

---

[1] *The Use of Poetry and the Use of Criticism* [p. 135].
[2] *Op. cit.*, p. 140.
[3] *Op. cit.* [p. 124].
[4] *Selected Essays*, p. 384.
[5] *Op. cit.*, p. 131.

Eliot's critical *alter ego*). For it is theologically "a deadly error": and so the fact that it is also *absurd* sinks into insignificance. — Entirely apart from his particular differences with Mr. Richards, with whom he has run so long in tandem, it is evident that Mr. Eliot will be forced (largely owing to the salutary action of his partner, who was not inclined evidently to have him there forever upon such very *pseudo* terms, and who clearly forced the issue by the remark previously quoted) to go into critical opposition with everybody not a certified church-goer. — Of course, there may have been pressure and heckling from many quarters of late — I do not know: but even so I believe that we owe a great deal to Mr. I. A. Richards, for sternly clarifying Mr. Eliot's position as critic, and indeed as poet, and for forbidding him from being so comfortably *pseudo* as he would have liked to have remained. In other words, Mr. Richards was *not* prepared to allow him to continue, on false pretences, to enjoy the gratifying advantages of the "rebel" in art, and simultaneously the advantages of an opposite sort in criticism: and — still less — to connive at his indefinitely mixing theory and practice up into a peculiar cocktail of his own.

Of course, Mr. Eliot is still very civil, outwardly, to his honoured colleague: but this is no longer a case of the "detachment" one has to expect in the ordinary way, as a characteristic attitude on the part of this "royalist, classicist and catholic" for all those (from that standpoint) decidedly *shady* figures by whom he is surrounded, and by whom he has been so faithfully supported: for instance, his recognition of anomaly, as proved by his uneasy attitude to Mr. Herbert Read (psychoanalyser and dutifully sex-dissector of William Wordsworth — how this scandalized Babbitt! — who asked me whether Read was *really* approved by Eliot in this romantic Freudian foray! — Read, as critic less sound than as poet, all too undiscriminating admirer of those great contemporary figures, Erich Maria Remarque, Lion Feuchtwanger, and the sham-Tolstoy, Wassermann). Mr. Eliot, as skipper of the *Criterion*, always has the air of glancing a little sardonically askance at this first mate, as though he had got on board while he wasn't looking, and was not quite a sufficiently orthodox seaman to be entrusted with the navigation of such a ship — as indeed he is not (solely from the purist standpoint — he would be an excellent mate, or for that matter skipper, of some *other* ship — and if you are to be a purist, you must at least take care a little in such matters) — at least *he* is not the man, it is pretty clear, if the *Criterion* is to fly the royal ensign, and steer according to classical canons, to a pseudo-Roman port! — But I have dealt already with that sort of central absurdity in Mr. Eliot's position in the matter of his paper — that strange organ of Tradition: and so long as his colleagues do not blow the gaff, or over-conscientiously drag out all these damaging contradictions into the light of common day, all is well, and Mr. Eliot, sardonic but decorous, goes peacefully his *pseudo* way! Indeed, stretched out in a comfortable deck-chair under his poop-awning (the latest *Crime Club* romance upon his knee), he is perfectly ready that his first mate should head the good ship *Cri* for *any* port — the most *liberal* in the world, or the *reddest*, for that matter, in the universe — he will put the telescope to his blind eye — perfectly agreeable that navigation should be conducted upon the best relativist principles, with the Einstein chronometer and the Marx sextant, or any other instruments whatever, however heterodox — providing only the boatswain *pipes* at the right time, in the true traditional fashion, and so long as the royal colours continue to float aloft and the crew touch their forelocks and say *sir* when addressing an officer!

But Mr. Eliot's most recent critical book is notable for one thing; and that is a new dismemberment of his much-discussed "personality." The present stratifications of public taste, Mr. Eliot tells us, "are perhaps a sign of social disintegration." I heartily agree of course — as I do to so much that Mr. Eliot says, paying lip-service to an ideal of Order. And individual "stratifications" — Mr. Eliot — whether temporal or other — are *likewise* "a sign of disintegration"! And Mr. Eliot has exhibited a yet further sign in this direction. For now he has disowned the Mr. Eliot of 1923 (driven to this, it is true, by the haunting dilemma of Mr. Richards and the *Waste Land* "without belief"). "In the course of time," he tells us, "a poet may become merely a reader in respect to his own works." And Mr. Eliot has become that. He reads *The Waste Land* with astonishment now — in the light of his friend Mr. Richards's account of it! He cannot *contradict* Mr. Richards, for Mr. Richards knows as much about the intentions of the Mr. Eliot who wrote it as he does himself. So "when Mr. Richards asserts that *The Waste Land* effects 'a complete severance between poetry and *all* beliefs' I am no better qualified to say No! than is any other reader."[1] Mr. 1933 Eliot picks up this much-discussed work, and, with some diffidence, gives his partner, Mr. Richards, the benefit of his opinion as regards what this fellow (bearing his name), of 1923 meant; and he "admits" that he "thinks" that his colleague and critical crony *for once*, is *wrong*. But that is a mere opinion, and he merely offers it for what it is worth, which is not much, seeing how little he knows about this poet-fellow (an American I believe!) who was responsible for this cross-word puzzle, of synthetic literary chronology, of spurious verbal algebra. Did the author of *The Waste Land* believe in God? — "How can I say?" drawls Mr. Eliot, testily. — But he confesses that it is difficult for him to believe that *anyone* bearing his name should not believe in God; and, under correction, is of opinion that *some* belief or other must have been present when the lines "She bathed her feet in soda-water" were written. Mr. I. A. Richards shakes his head dubiously

---

[1] *Use of Poetry and Use of Criticism*, p. 130.

however. He does not detect much orthodox theology, he makes it perfectly plain to his plausible partner, in *The Waste Land.* He is sorry, but there it is! And Mr. T. S. Eliot (1933) does not insist. A mere namesake has no more claim upon him than the next. It is not a question of Mr. Eliot having *forgotten*, he assures us. He has "merely" *changed*.[1]

What all this means is that, in order to escape from giving a *Yes*, or, as he says, a *No* to his trusty but incorruptible partner, and fellow-pseudoist, Mr. Richards — unable any longer to just say he "does not *understand*" Mr. Richards, and leave it comfortably at that — he is driven to the expedient of announcing a further piecemealing of his personality (already one would have thought sufficiently cut up between the private self — the believer; the poet — the unbeliever; and the literary critic — not always very flattering to the poet, though of course not without certain evident partiality for him all the same!).

It is rather an extreme device — this disintegration into a multiplicity of chronologic selves. What, however, it does effect is to exempt him from providing an authoritative answer to the no doubt more and more puzzled questions of the crowd of ardent followers of himself and Mr. Richards — on the grounds that he is no longer the *same* Mr. Eliot, but another, so cannot possibly know what *The Waste Land* Tom planned and intended. But it is not at all certain that, even if it had been written this week, he could be pinned down any more: for later on, where he is describing how a poem comes to be written, we are told that "this disturbance of our quotidian character . . . results in an incantation, *an outburst of words, which we hardly recognize as our own.*"[2] He would "hesitate to say that the experience at which I have hinted is responsible for the creation of all the most profound poetry written. . . . Some finer minds, indeed, may operate very differently; I cannot think of Shakespeare or Dante as having been dependent upon such capricious releases." But it is Mr. Eliot's way — the automatic way. Something touches a button, and out it comes. So, if you marched up to him five minutes after he had "released" some "outburst of words" in this manner, and exclaimed, "Ha ha! Got you this time my fine fellow! What did you mean when you wrote *that* — and *that*!" he would be quite capable of replying with the utmost detachment: "*Who* wrote *what*? I am sorry, I am entirely unable to answer you. I have not the least idea! It is not to *me* you must address such questions. Go rather and address yourself to my partner Mr. I. A. Richards! He is not very reliable, but he probably knows more about it than I do."

Or he might say it was incubated a twelvemonth beforehand, and that so much had happened in the meantime. Or he might retire, with infinite grace, into the shadow of a modesty as remarkable as it was sudden. "The

[1 *The Use of Poetry and the Use of Criticism*, p. 130.]
[2 *Use of Poetry and Use of Criticism*, p. 145.

essence of poetry, *if there is any*, belongs to the study of aesthetics and is no concern of the poet or of a critic with my limited qualifications."[1]

.   .   .   .   .   .

If there is one thing more than another paraded by Mr. Eliot, the literary critic, it is a supposed logical precision of statement, a fastidious carefulness in the use of words. Is it a gross self-delusion, one sometimes wonders, or a mere barefaced bluff, that causes him to level accusations against Matthew Arnold say (whom of course he a good deal resembles) of slipshod terminology, of mental vagueness and lack of consistency — of holding a doctrine that was "vague and ambiguous"?[2]

For instance: "Arnold had little gift for consistency or for definition," he blandly informs us:[3] "Nor had he the power of connected reasoning at any length: his flights are either short flights or circular flights. Nothing in his prose work, therefore, will stand very close analysis." Or again: "[Arnold] lacked the mental discipline, the passion for exactness in the use of words and for consistency and continuity of reasoning, which distinguishes the philosopher."[4]

How fatally this describes Mr. Eliot himself no one, I think, who has followed the exposure of his doctrine in the foregoing pages can fail to perceive. And that his confusions and inconsistencies are, or look like, barefaced confusions and conscious inconsistencies does not make it any better: for I dare say to some extent that was the case with Arnold too — only he had the decency to cover up his tracks a little more carefully than has Mr. Eliot. Or, if you like, he did not draw attention to his logical insecurity and sleight of hand by *plugging* those defective portions of his critical system with a tortuous padding of pretended precision. He at least left the thing alone, once he had done it, as neatly as the matter warranted.

.   .   .   .   .   .

It may of course be true, it is possible that Mr. Eliot really believes that he displays "a passion for exactness." Even if, compared with the general critical standards of the day, it may be that his critical writings *do* look, to the casual student-reader, as pretty "closely-reasoned," and characterized by "exactness." He certainly *wants* them to look like that.

No doubt with his infant-milk, he must have imbibed a great respect for the traditional scientific attributes — (1) impersonality, (2) exactness. And this survives. So perhaps, after all, it is not so much bluff as sheer self-delusion.

[1] *Op. cit.*, pp. 149–150.
[2] *Selected Essays*, p. 387.
[3] *Selected Essays*, p. 379.
[4] *Use of Poetry and Use of Criticism*, p. 122.

But philosophy and criticism stand or fall, in one sense, together. Mr. Eliot underlines this fact. "You cannot deplore criticism unless you deprecate philosophy."[1] The day of philosophic systems, however, is passed: no philosopher is allowed to claim any more, today, than what is, in fact, a systematic arrangement of his *personal* idiosyncracies. The idea is this: the *person* possessed of a philosophic bent — whether it be Kant, Hobbes, Spinoza, Spencer — *wishes* that a certain number of things were true, and, very naturally proceeds — with all the impersonal pomp of the paraphernalia of an absolute "system" — to bestow upon them the appearance of revelation. Such and such a cosmos appeals to him — say, because of the teaching of Maimonides, and the general, even racial, colour of his mind — and he proceeds to build such a cosmos, from such and such a set of axioms: that is his "system."

But why should what is denied to the philosopher be granted to the literary critic — or to the critic-mongering poet? Should not the "depersonalization" notion we have been considering, for instance, so airily thrown out, be received on the same footing as any other "system" (only there is this important difference between the two cases, namely that the literary critic is saved a lot of unnecessary trouble with his little "system" — even, when he is a poet at the same time, it can peep out as a sort of professional "tip" — he does not anyway have to build any self-consistent architecture: he can murmur, with a musing expression, that he *believes* that this that or the other should be thus and thus, and usually add that he has not *worked it out* properly yet, but perhaps may do so soon — though he is very vague about it just at present (in fact, a bit confused!) and (being by way of being a scholar and so very very *cautious*, as all true scholars must be, it is generally conceded) he does not wish to commit himself *at present*, more than just to say that, in his opinion, *it is quite on the cards*, that such and such a thing *may* be proved to be — some day — by somebody far abler than himself (for a spectacular "modesty" is very important too — it goes with "caution") *may* be shown to be of such and such an order.

(This caricature of the manner of the scholar, this caricature of the technique of the philosopher, is scarcely an exaggeration of what can be discovered in Mr. Eliot's text.)

Yet "our individual taste is poetry bears the indelible traces of our individual lives with all their experience pleasurable and painful. We are apt either to shape a theory to cover the poetry that we find most moving, or — what is less excusable — to choose the poetry which illustrates the theory we want to hold. You do not find Matthew Arnold quoting Rochester or Sedley. And it is not merely a matter of individual caprice. Each age demands different things from poetry."[2]

[1] *Use of Poetry and Use of Criticism*, p. 21.
[2] *Use of Poetry and Use of Criticism*, p. 141. T. S. Eliot.

How very true that is. And yet how it seems to contradict, somehow, Mr. Eliot's critical attitudes elsewhere. But he *will* sometimes shrink on you like that, all in a moment! and become a poor lost person, "not qualified" to pronounce upon anything to do with the subject he has just been discussing at all. — But there I must leave the matter for the present, in the hope that, faithful to the lead given us all by Mr. I. A. Richards, I have made some contribution, at all events, to this intricate question.

PART TWO

CHAPTER I

THE GREATEST SATIRE IS NON-MORAL

"The frantic rage which Dryden's satire provoked was because
of that *coolness* always to be discovered at the centre of his
scorn." — PROFESSOR SAINTSBURY.

THERE IS NO man's "shop" but must appear somewhat cynical to the outsider. To overhear two physicians conferring is enough to make the flesh
of the bravest creep. That is classical. But it is the same with every profes-
sion. (Most pure business sounds to the outsider and non-business man
like a confabulation of convicts of course, engaged in the preparation of
some novel *coup de main.*) And the craft of the satirist must perforce retain a few of the more brutal fashions of thinking that are proper to his
occupation. You know our Hogarth's face, in a nightcap? — it is like a
bulldog, in a sense — the most brutal of animals, the *matador par excellence.*

There is, again, a whole world of difference between the satirist — so
extended as to mean all artists not specifically beauty-doctors, as I have
ordained here — and the "realist." Yet the "materialism" of the matter of the
grotesque is liable to shock. We shall be committed to an examination of
all those controversial values pertaining to that naked world of the
Satyricon, of *Volpone*, of the *Médecin malgré lui.* We shall have to weigh
the dictum of Taine:[1]

> Au plus bas degré sont les types que préfèrent la littérature réaliste et le
> théatre comique, je veux dire les personnages bornés, plat, sots, égoïstes,
> faibles et communes . . ."

against the opposite dictum of Flaubert:[2]

> Il n'y a ni beaux ni vilains sujets . . . on pourrait presque établir comme
> axiome, en se posant au point de vue de l'Art pur, qu'il n'y en a aucun, le
> style étant à lui tout seul une manière absolue de voir les choses.

And then *style* is of course a magician who can convert a ragged crone
into an object of great beauty. It is *style* that checkmates subject-matter
every time, and turns to naught the beauty-doctor laws of the metaphysician. But merely to decide, upon an aristocratic principle, which, in the
view of Nietzsche, gave the *Mahomet* of Voltaire the palm over all subsequent and less "classical" compositions, will scarcely satisfy a public of today. Flaubert stands accused of more than vulgarity: he is arraigned, by
one of the masters of the catholic revival, for his turpitude in employing,

---

[1] *L'Art et la morale.* Ferdinand Brunetière.
[2] Quoted by L. J. Bondy, *Classicisme de Ferdinand Brunetière.*

in deliberate isolation, instincts that issued, certainly, in what he called "style,'" but which were intended for the service of a more elevated principle. "La faute de Flaubert est grave, aussi. L'art substitué à Dieu, cela l'engage dans une voie . . . périlleuse."[1]

It will be our duty to take into account the various motives which may decide a man to go and live among such vulgar and imbecile personages as satire, and comedy, require. In the case of Flaubert, to go no farther than he, "style" was not the whole of the story. Like any Christian martyr he went and established himself in the centre of the bourgeois body—he regarded himself as possessing "a message" of sorts—if only that of a plumber. And he dies at his post, struck down by the bourgeois, while at his unsavoury work, there is no dispute at least on that head. Hear Mauriac, his accuser:

> puisque'il ne pouvait plus se soustraire a l'étude du Prudhomme moderne, eh bien, il prendrait le taureau par les cornes; cette énorme bêtise bourgeoise deviendrait le sujet de son livre, il l'incarnerait, ce serait son chef-d'oeuvre. . . . Le Bourgeois . . . s'installe à sa table, se couche dans son lit, remplit ses journées et ses nuits, et finit par le prendre à la gorge. Le Bourgeois a eu sa peau enfin; il a, à la lettre, assassiné Flaubert. L'alchemiste de Croisset est mort victime des expériences qu'il tentait sur la créature humaine: il éliminait l'âme du composé humain, pour obtenir de la bêtise à l'état pur: elle l'a asphyxié.[2]

We shall be in these pages, as we are in real life, haunted by this BOURGEOIS of Flaubert. Like a pneumatic carnival personage, incessantly expanding as the result of the fierce puffing of the Marxist into his ideologic bladder, the Bourgeois of Flaubert has assumed portentous proportions.

We are informed by Albalat that Gautier and Flaubert when they met, upon the occasion of the latter's periodic visits to Paris, would sit down and discuss "the bourgeois" for hours together. "Flaubert detested the 'bourgeois' in overalls as much as the 'bourgeois' in plus fours. When Théophile Gautier and he addressed themselves, at one of their séances, to the declamatory abuse of the 'bourgeois,' they worked themselves up to a great pitch of lyrical rage, became as red as turkey-cocks and were obliged afterwards to change their linen (*ils . . . devenaient rouges comme des coqs et se voyaient forcés de changer de chemise*)."

They really took their "bourgeois" seriously! And these two charming and intelligent men, thundering away at each other in the past (an echo of their voices may still be caught, on a quiet afternoon) opposed to the bourgeois—but what do you suppose? It sounds absurd, in our present dispensation, but it was *the artist* that these two Frenchmen were thinking

---

[1] *Trois grands hommes.* F. Mauriac (Editions du Capitole).
[2] *L'Art et la morale.* Ferdinand Brunetière.

about, and "bourgeois" meant nothing really but the enemy of art. They were as simple as a couple of noisy peasants — in a sense: and *art* filled the whole of their minds and bodies. A passion for a concrete realization of all the mysterious energies with which they were wound up like clocks, possessed them night and day. These two French craftsmen, drenching their shirts with perspiration as they cursed for hours on end the wicked giant who was the great enemy of their craft, were far more mad than Blake, I think. And as to Blake's "prolonged vindication of the cause of all the artists in the world," they did a good deal of that, too, between them.

These will be the sort of subjects among which we shall be picking our way. We shall interrogate these great profane figures composed of "pure art" — these *hommes-plumes* compact of *mots justes* — and see what messages they may have for our even more *be-bourgeoised* period: we shall not be prevented from speculating as to what is our antithesis — with "bourgeois" where it was before, but bigger and weaker, but "artist" somehow changed, and perhaps paired off with some other abstraction. For the politician — whose art is anything but the *mot juste* — has pushed away the artist and now stands where the latter once stood, keeping all to himself the "burgess-gentleman." But if we have to range far afield before we have done with the questions which, one after the other, we shall find this critical enterprise calls up, we will now start with satire pure and simple, and join issue at once with the moralist, who regards satire as belonging pre-eminently to his domain.

There is no prejudice so inveterate, in even the educated mind, as that which sees in satire a work of edification. Indeed, for the satirist to acquire the right to hold up to contempt a fellow-mortal, he is supposed, first, to arm himself with the insignia of a sheriff or special constable. No age, for many centuries, has been so lawless as ours — nothing to compare with Capone it is said, for instance, has ever been known in America. And perhaps for this reason an unnatural sensitiveness to law and order is noticeable in all of us: and in the field of the ethical judgement, as much as in that of the civil law, is this the case. Perhaps that is the reason why, in this defence of the art of satire, I give the place of honour to the moral law, and settle accounts with that source of interference first. — As to the law of libel, the anomalies and injustices of that have often been canvassed: I do not propose here to add to that already considerable body of criticism. It is rather the subtler forms of interference, generally neglected, which I have in mind and am proposing to pass under review.

I am a satirist, I am afraid there is no use denying that. But I am not a moralist: and about that I make no bones either. And it is these two facts, taken together, which constitute my particular difficulty. It is contended, against the satirist, that since man is not autonomous — and who but will agree to that I hope? — he cannot arm himself with laughter and invective, and sally forth to satirical attacks upon his neighbour, without first acquiring the moral sanction of the community — with whose standards and canons of conduct he must be at one — and first advertising himself as a champion of some outraged Mrs. Grundy. So, with Mrs. Grundy on the one side, and Dr. Bowdler on the other, and with a big crocodile tear in his eye (at the thought of the pain he may have to inflict), he sets himself in motion. That is the popular picture. The more sophisticated picture would today only differ from this in the nature of the preparations prescribed: a short prayer for absolution regarding the blood he was about to spill, or if the god had the features of Demos, an invocation to his bloody fist — a brief class-war-dance, with a "more power to my elbow incantation!" And so forward to battle, the Geneva Bible in the breast-pocket. But, whatever else it may be, it must be represented as a salutary expedition, undertaken on behalf of something with an infallible title to the moral judgement-seat.

There is of course no question that satire of the highest order has been achieved in the name of the ethical will. Most satire, indeed, has got through upon the understanding that the satirist first and foremost was a moralist. And some of the best satirists have been that as well. But not all. So one of the things it is proposed to do in these pages is to consider the character, and the function of, non-ethical satire; and if possible to provide it with a standing, alongside the other arts and sciences, as a recognized philosophic and artistic human activity, not contingent upon judgements which are not those specifically of the artistic or philosophic mind.

·   ·   ·   ·   ·   ·

"The frantic rage which Dryden's satire provoked in his opponents" has been attributed, by Professor Saintsbury, to a *coolness* always to be discovered at the centre of his scorn. Further, Dryden dispensed with the protective moralistic machinery of the classical satire. It was, in short, not because his opponents were *naughty* that Dryden objected to them, but because they were *dull*. They had sinned against the Reason, rather than against the Mosaic Law. This it was that aroused the really "frantic rage"! For all those satirized by Juvenal, or smarting beneath the scourges of most other satirists, of the classical or modern age, have been able at a pinch to snigger and remark that "Yes, they *knew* that they were very wicked!" and to make, even, of such satire an advertisement.

But if you remove from satire its moralism, then it has no advertise-ment value whatever for the victim — then it is doubly deadly, and then also the satirist is doubly hated by those picked out for attack. And society also, the implicit ally of the moralist, is in a sense offended (though the way society takes it depends upon the society — ours luckily does not stand upon its moral dignity very much).

It could perhaps be asserted, even, that the greatest satire *cannot* be moralistic at all: if for no other reason, because no mind of the first order, expressing itself in art, has ever itself been taken in, nor consented to take in others, by the crude injunctions of any purely moral code. This does not mean that the mind in question was wanting in that consciousness of itself as a rational subject, which is never absent in an intellect of such an order: but that its abstract theory, as well as its concrete practice, of moral judgements, would differ from the common run, and that their introduction would merely confuse the issue. The artistic impulse is a more primitive one than the ethical: so much is this the case — so little is it a mere dialect of the rational language in which our human laws are formulated, but, on the contrary, an entirely independent tongue — that it is necessary for the artist to change his skin, almost, in passing from one department into the other. You cannot with the same instruments compass a work of edification and a work of beauty — and satire may be "beautiful," rather in the way that mathematics claims to be that — with a rational handsomeness peculiar to it; and even such a tub-thumper as Bunyan, being an artist, is there as witness to that fact, as has often been pointed out. With the person predestined to an artistic vocation, cheerfulness, or moods of a yet more anomalous order, *will* keep breaking in: so it is better, perhaps, to admit them at the start.

But how can satire stand without the moral sanction? you may ask. For satire can only exist *in contrast* to something else — it is a shadow, and an ugly shadow at that, of some perfection. And it is so disagreeable, and so painful (at least in the austere sense in which we appear to be defining it here) that no one would pursue it *for its own sake*, or take up the occupation of satirist unless compelled to do so, out of indignation at the spectacle of the neglect of beauty and virtue. — That is I think the sort of objection that, at this point, we should expect to have to meet.

Provisionally I will reply as follows: it is my belief that "satire" *for its own sake* — as much as anything else for its own sake — is possible: and that even the most virtuous and well-proportioned of men is only a shadow, after all, of some perfection; a shadow of an imperfect, and hence an "ugly," sort. And as to *laughter*, if you allow it in one place you must, I think, allow it in another. Laughter — humour and wit — has a function in relation to our tender consciousness; a function similar to that of art. It is the preserver much more than the destroyer. And, in a sense, *everyone* should be laughed at or else *no one* should be laughed at. It seems that ultimately that is the alternative.

When Addison introduced the word "genius," to take the place of the word used up to that time, "wit," he did us all a disservice. Wit as a generic term for all those possessed of an excellent judgement, would tend (apart from the advantages resulting from its less pretentious sound) to marshal the gifted upon the *laughing* side of the world. But that little change of a popular monosyllable made all the difference, and today *the laugh* is not wholly respectable: it requires to be explained, if not excused.

But satire is a special sort of laughter: *the laugh* alone possesses great powers of magnification. But *the laugh* that magnified Falstaff till he grew to be a giant like Pantagruel, is not the laugh of the satirist, which threw up the Maids of Honour in Brobdingnag. Now, no one resents the size of Falstaff: he is a routine figure of fun; the jolly toper. But everyone resents the scale of the Maids of Honour, and resents the sounds of the cataracts heard by Gulliver when they made use of their *pots de chambre*. But I will produce the Maids of Honour, so that our sense of what we are discussing should become first hand.

> The Maids of Honour often invited Glumdalclitch to their apartments, and desired she would bring me along with her, on purpose to have the pleasure of seeing and touching me. They would often strip me naked from top to toe and lay me at full length in their bosoms: wherewith I was much disgusted: because, to say the truth, a very offensive smell came from their skins: which I do not mention or intend to the disadvantage of those excellent ladies, for whom I have all manner of respect. . . . That which gave me most uneasiness among these Maids of Honour, when my nurse carried me to visit them, was to see them use me without any manner of ceremony, like a creature who had no sort of consequence. For they would strip themselves to the skin, and put on their smocks in my presence, while I was placed on their toilet directly before their naked bodies, which, I am sure, to me was very far from being a tempting sight, or from giving me any other motions than those of horror and disgust. Their skins appeared so coarse and uneven, so variously coloured, when I saw them near, with a mole here and there as broad as a trencher, and hairs hanging from it thicker than pack-threads, to say nothing further concerning the rest of their persons. Neither did they at all scruple, while I was by, to discharge what they had drunk, to the quantity of at least two hogsheads, in a vessel that held three tuns.

These are very painful passages. There is no question here of the mere he-man vulgarity of the egregious Scottish surgeon, Smollett. It is much more uncomfortable than that, not alone for the nice-minded but without exception for all the spokesmen of Mr. Everybody.

In this painful effect of true satire we might expect to find the main avenue of attack of the moralist — he might say that it was *ill-natured* instead of *good-natured*, as is mere burlesque. But it is not to that that we must look today, when we are taking our measures of defence, as being the spot likely to draw the fire of the ethical batteries.

The painful nature of satire was recognized by Hazlitt, but promptly misunderstood; for he was looking for something in satire which under no circumstances belongs there, and which in consequence he could not find. "Bare-faced impudence, or idiot imbecility, are his dramatic commonplaces," he writes of Ben Jonson. So, although one would have thought that Ben Jonson had acquitted himself to admiration of what is after all, in the narrowest sense, the satirist's job, the good Hazlitt finds fault with him for that very reason—because, in fact, Hazlitt did not at all like satire.

The very reasons Hazlitt finds to attack Ben Jonson, do, it seems to me, exactly describe a master of that kind of art: and actually, what Hazlitt says could be applied, with more aptness, to other writers than to Ben Jonson—writers, to my mind, even more important than the author of *Volpone*. This point is one of such significance for an understanding of satire in general, that I will quote the entire passage.

> Shakespeare's characters are men; Ben Jonson's are more like machines, governed by mere routine, or by the convenience of the poet, whose property they are. In reading the one, we are let into the minds of his characters, we see the play of their thoughts, how their humours flow and work. . . . His humour (so to speak) bubbles, sparkles, and finds its way in all directions, like a natural spring. In Ben Jonson it is, as it were, confined in a leaden cistern, where it stagnates and corrupts; or directed only through certain artificial pipes and conduits to answer a given purpose. . . . Sheer ignorance, bare-faced impudence, or idiot imbecility, are his dramatic commonplaces — things that provoke pity or disgust, instead of laughter.[1]

But why should not idiot imbecility provoke laughter? Obviously the answer is: Because, being found in a human being, it is "letting down" the species, and so to laugh at it would be unethical and *inhuman*. Physical deformity, again, is often comic. Many dwarfs are highly grotesque (superbly grotesque, one may say without offence in the case of dwarfs), and they even relish the sensation of their funniness. But most people only laugh covertly at such spectacles, or sternly repress a smile. For, they would say, these are "things" which should "provoke pity or disgust, instead of laughter." Such is the Anglo-Saxon point of view.

But the dago is different. Dwarfs, in Spain, are the object of constant mirth, on the part of their "normal" fellow-citizens. Everyone pokes fun at them, there is no hypocrisy, as with us, and the dwarf gets on very well indeed. He is treated as a pet animal, and enjoys himself very much. Also, since he has a great deal of practice, from morning till night, he often ends by being a first-class clown. In short, neither disgust nor pity is experienced by these dagos where their dwarfs are concerned. They feel perhaps that God has made them a present of these hideous oddities to be their sport: and the dwarf feels that too, and is quite puffed-up with his own importance and proud of his god-sent job.

[1] *The English Comic Writers*. Hazlitt.

And, after all, pulling long faces at the dwarf, and surrounding him with an atmosphere of inhuman pity, is bad for the dwarf. It is better to explode with laughter at the sight of him — better for all concerned. So far so good: but what of the shell-shocked man, for instance? He is often very funny, and it is very difficult not to laugh. But that is like laughing at the contortions of a dying man, and it would be too brutal a society that made a habit of laughing at its shell-shocked persons — especially as it would be to the society of the laughers to which ultimately the responsibility for these disfigurements would have to be brought home. Therefore there is no society that does not refrain from guffawing at the antics, however "screamingly funny," of its shell-shocked men and war-idiots, and its poison-gas morons, and its mutilated battle-wrecks.

But here is also a principle, of use in the analysis of the comic. *Perfect laughter*, if there could be such a thing, would be inhuman. And it would select as the objects of its mirth as much the antics dependent upon pathologic maladjustments, injury, or disease, as the antics of clumsy and imperfectly functioning healthy people. At this point it is perhaps desirable to note that in general human beings display no delicacy about spiritual or mental shortcomings in their neighbours, but only physical. To be a fool with a robust body can be no more pleasant for the person in question than being an intelligent dwarf: yet no one scruples to laugh at the former, but parades a genteel sensitiveness regarding the latter. Infinitely more pain is inflicted by laughter provoked by some non-physical cause than by that provoked by the physical. So do not let us take too much for granted that we can put our finger blindfold upon *the supreme "cad."*

Our deepest laughter is not, however, inhuman laughter. And yet it is non-personal and non-moral. And it enters fields which are commonly regarded as the preserve of more "serious" forms of reaction. There is no reason at all why we should not burst out laughing at a foetus, for instance. We should after all only be laughing *at ourselves!* — at ourselves early in our mortal career.

Returning to Hazlitt's misunderstanding; in Swift, in Dryden, in Pope, it is not the "natural," "bubbling" laughter of Shakespearean comedy that you should expect to find, any more than you would look for a jovial heartiness in a surgeon at work, or, if you like (to take a romantic illustration), in an executioner. It would decidedly be out of place. *Laughter* is the medium employed, certainly, but there is laughter and laughter. That of true satire is as it were *tragic* laughter. It is not a genial guffaw nor the tittilations provoked by a harmless entertainer. It is tragic, if a thing *can* be "tragic" without pity and terror, and it seems to me it can.

But when Hazlitt speaks of the characters "like machines, governed by mere routine," there, I think, he gives himself entirely away. For what else is a character in satire but that? Is it not just because they are such *machines, governed by routine* — or creatures that stagnate, as it were "in a leaden cistern" — that the satirist, in the first instance, has considered them suitable for satire? He who wants a jolly, carefree, bubbling, world chock-full of "charm," must not address himself to the satirist! The wind that blows through satire is as bitter as that that predominates in the pages of *Timon* or *King Lear*. Indeed, the former *is* a satire. And *Hamlet*, for instance, is very much that too — a central satire — developing now into comedy, now into tragedy.

Laughter is again an anti-toxin of the first order. As a matter of fact *no* man (as I have hinted above) — any more than the shell-shocked man — should be laughed at. It is unfair, therefore it is "caddish," to laugh at *anybody*: we all, as much as the shell-shocked man, really could cry *cad*, or have cad cried for us, at an outburst of mirth at our expense. And this does not only apply to the obviously defective. It is unnecessary to enumerate the tragic handicaps that our human conditions involve — the glaring mechanical imperfections, the nervous tics, the prodigality of ob-jectless movement — the, to other creatures, offensive smells, disagreeable moistures — the involuntary grimace, the lurch, roll, trot or stagger which we call our *walk* — it is only a matter of degree between us and the victim of locomotor-ataxy or St. Vitus's dance. . . .

By making a great deal of noise ourselves we at least drown the alarm-ing noise made by our neighbours. And the noise that, above all others, has been bestowed on us for this purpose is the bark which we describe as our *laugh*. I approve of a *barking man* myself — I find that I have less occasion, with his likes, to anticipate a really serious *bite*. So laughter is *per se* a healthy clatter — that is one of the first things to realize about it.

An illustration of this principle, in a parallel order of feeling, is furn-ished by Henry James, where he is discussing the virtue in a novelist of hard work — and the clatter and bustle which, as it were, accompanies it. Put *laughter* for *hard work*, and you will see what I mean, I think. These are the words of that great puppet-manufacturer:

> It is, as you say, because I "grind out" my men and women that I endure them. It is because I create them by the sweat of my brow that I venture to look them in the face. My *work* is my salvation. If this great army of puppets came forth at my simple bidding, then indeed I should die of their senseless clamour.

CHAPTER II

MR. WYNDHAM LEWIS

"PERSONAL-APPEARANCE" ARTIST

(The theory of the External, the Classical, approach in Art)

"Mr. Wyndham Lewis could be described as a *personal-appearance* satirist." — MONTAGU SLATER, *The Daily Telegraph.*

MAKING OUR WAY BACK to that statement of Hazlitt's with which we began: the great opportunity afforded by narrative-satire for a *visual* treatment is obvious. To let the reader "into the minds of the characters," to "see the play of their thoughts" — that is precisely the method least suited to satire. That it must deal with the *outside,* that is one of the capital advantages of this form of literary art — for those who like a resistant and finely-sculptured surface, or sheer words.

The literary art is not only on the whole less experimental than pictorial and plastic art, but it is also, in the nature of things, possessed of different canons — canons that are inherent both in the nature of the material, and in the fact that the literary art is far more directly involved in life than the pictorial or the plastic. I do not myself believe that anything in the literary field can be done that will correspond with what has been called "abstract design." But still the art of letters *is* influenced, via life, by the movements in the sister field of painting, sculpture and architecture. So it is not at all beside the point to illustrate my arguments, upon this test of Hazlitt, from parallels in painting or sculpture.

"Shakespeare's characters are men: Ben Jonson's are more like machines," Hazlitt exclaims. And I have replied — "Of course they are! — in both cases that is just what they were intended to be." But "men" are undoubtedly, to a greater or less extent, machines. And there are those amongst us who are revolted by this reflection, and there are those who are not. Men are sometimes so palpably machines, their machination is so transparent, that they are *comic,* as we say. And all we mean by that, is that our consciousness is pitched up to the very moderate altitude of relative independence at which we live — at which level we have the illusion of being autonomous and "free." But if one of us exposes too much his "works," and we start seeing him as a *thing,* then — in subconsciously referring this back to ourselves — we are astonished and shocked, and we bark at him — we *laugh* — in order to relieve our emotion.

Freedom is certainly our human goal, in the sense that all effort is directed to that end: and it is a dictate of nature that we should laugh, and laugh loudly, at those who have fallen into slavery, and still more, those who batten on it. But the artistic sensibility, that is *another* "provision of nature."

The artist steps outside this evolutionary upward march, and looking back into the evolutionary machine, he explores its pattern — or is supposed to — quite cold-bloodedly.

Without pursuing that issue any further at the moment, let us merely consider how that affects these values of Hazlitt — which are, in brief, the *humanist* values — which are starkly opposed to all the plastic and pictorial values in the ascendant today — values which, incidentally, are in general mine.

If you have ever seen and can recall the sculpture of Auguste Rodin — those flowing, structureless, lissom, wave-lined pieces of commercial marble — you will then have the best possible illustration of the in-this-sense *humanist*, the naturalist technique. They are Bergson's *élan vital* translated into marble: the whole philosophy of the Flux is palpitating and streaming in those carefully selected and cleverly dreamified stone-photographs of naked nature.

Now where Hazlitt describes Shakespeare as *"letting us into the minds of his characters,"* where we are able to observe "the play of their thoughts," the humours flowing hither and thither — the Shakespearean creation bubbling and sparkling, and finding its way "in all directions, like a natural spring," there he is placing before us a great artist of the naturalist, the *humanist* school: he is discovering the same manner of praising the art of Shakespeare that the contemporaries of Auguste Rodin found to exalt that much-overrated master of the Flux — who, it is as well to say, degraded the art of sculpture in stone to the level of confectionary in sugar or icing.

Over against this pretty picture of a happy, guileless, universe, set in the mellow naturalist setting of a not-too-formal park (which, it is implied by Hazlitt, is the bedrock truth about our human life, or "that is all ye know and all ye need to know") is placed the satiric *machinery* of "rare Ben Jonson" — *rare* perhaps because he conformed rather to the type of men-to-come, than to his somewhat happy-go-lucky humanist companions.

If you asked me what I suggest you should place over against the perverted cascades of sleek, white, machine-ground stone of the Bergsonian sculptor, well, there is a wide choice. Neither the Greeks, nor yet the Renaissance masters (except here and there) afford a quite effective contrast. The *naturalist* stream started flowing in Hellas, and it has gone on flowing in the centre of the European consciousness ever since. Only now, at last, has it begun to dry up. I should direct you to Egypt, to China or Japan, to select the monumental counterblast to this last vulgar decadence of the original Hellenic mistake. The Japanese Buddhist sculpture would be as good as any for your purpose — to confront, with its opposite principle, "The Kiss" say of Auguste Rodin — or any of the stream of vulgar ornaments that have gushed out for forty years in its wake, and which still infest the tables and mantelpieces of Kensington and Mayfair, and are to be encountered in great profusion in the shop windows of Bond Street.

At this point I believe I may legitimately make an observation, not without its bearing upon the present critical analysis. It is this: the majority of people who write books of "criticism" do not write any other books — they prefer to criticize, not to produce: whereas with me you do not have to cudgel your brains as to *why* I should sit down and reduce to some order, in a statement that is a generalization from experience, my opinion of how books of a certain class should be written. I have an obvious interest in what I am writing about! And if you should wish to retaliate upon me, there are the targets standing ready. All you need is to be a practised shot! A "deliberate theory of life, of nature, of the universe," I do not deny it, is to be found within the crypts and tissues of this criticism: and whether or not it be true that "the philosopher must ever be, more or less, a partisan," I certainly — deliberately — am that.

This book has derived in the first instance, from the notes written in defence of my satire, *The Apes of God.* That book was a fiction-satire, as you may recall, of considerable proportions — a handsome target you will agree: and because of its satiric content it provoked, not an outburst of recrimination — nothing half so frank as that, but what was intended to be a pulverizing hush. The tables were turned upon these malcontents, however, and in the end the satirist had the best of it. If this had not been the history of these notes, and if a good many people did not associate them, as they must do, with the arguments for and against regarding this particular work, I should avoid direct reference to a book of mine. But as it is there is some reason for turning to it for a moment, and that I now will do.

In another book (not a novel, but criticism) the outlook, or the philosophy, from which it derived, was described by me as "a philosophy of the EYE." But in the case of *The Apes of God* it would be far easier to demonstrate (than in the more abstract region of philosophical criticism) how *the eye* has been the organ in the ascendant there. For *The Apes of God* it could, I think quite safely, be claimed that no book has ever been written that has paid more attention to the *outside* of people. In it their shells or pelts, or the language of their bodily movements, come first, not last. And in the course of the controversy it provoked, I referred to a reader's report on a portion of this book, in which the gentleman in question described it as the work of a *visuel* (de Gourmont's expression). That definition I should certainly accept, as also where he wrote: "everything is told from the outside. To this extent it is the opposite of, say, James, who sought to narrate from the *inside* the character's mind. James, in short, was a Bergsonian where you are a Berkeleyan!" — there too I am in agreement with this sympathetic publisher's reader.

There was a newspaper article which appeared some weeks after the publication of the *Apes*, which I also quoted at the time, and which, for the light it throws upon the matter in hand, can be used with advantage here — since for an understanding of the creative literature of today and of tomorrow it is very necessary, I believe, to grasp the principles involved in this question of *outside* and of *inside*.

Mr. Montagu Slater, in an article in *The Daily Telegraph* entitled "Satire in the Novel," wrote as follows: "Posted inside the head of a person . . . the novelist informs us of everything that is being enacted upon that inaccessible stage." Thus posted *within*, the novelist lays bare, for the benefit of the reader, the "stream of consciousness of the individual." *The Apes of God* is cited, among others, as one belonging technically to that class of books which melts away the cases and envelopes of human beings, to deal wholly with their "thought-streams," etc. But such a method says Mr. Slater, "makes contemporary satiric novels inept."

I may say at once that I quite agree with this reviewer that the *inside-method* does tend to ineptitude, and that many books written during the last decade have been peculiarly inept for that reason. But the particular books he chose — the other two as much as *The Apes of God* — were not examples of that *inner* method at all, as it happened.

That the *inner method* should never be employed at all I should not be disposed to lay down. It has its uses. Nowhere is it indispensable, but can play its part, if it is decided to make use of it, as a sort of comic relief. — The first twenty pages of *The Apes of God*, for instance, is a slow-movement prelude: in the half-light of extreme decrepitude (employed as the illumination for those opening pages) the "thought-stream" of one of the principal personages, Lady Fredigonde, is revealed to the reader, like the sluggish introspective waters of a Styx. It can scarcely be said that the *outside* of this personage is neglected: but, in her case, the *inside* is there too, that is all. Fredigonde has a special rôle allotted her, however: she appears before the formal raising of the curtain upon the Apes proper. She herself is the *prelude*.

But this aged personage is half out of life, half in. The *interior* method was chosen in that instance as being particularly appropriate. Incidentally its use (for the purpose of projecting this brain-in-isolation, served only by the senses paralysed with age) is an exposure of the literary dogma of the "internal monologue," regarded as a *universal* method. Where elsewhere in another satire (with "Satters" in *Childermass*) I made use of it, I did so with that even more clearly in view.

So what I think can be laid down is this: In dealing with (1) the extremely aged; (2) young children; (3) half-wits; and (4) animals, the *internal* method can be extremely effective. In my opinion it should be entirely confined to those classes of characters. For certain comic purposes it likewise has its uses, especially when used in conjunction with a full-blooded Stein-stutter — used, pianissimo, to such good effect, as I have shown, by Ernest Hemingway.

In my criticism of *Ulysses* I laid particular stress upon the limitations of the *internal* method. As developed in *Ulysses*, it robbed Mr. Joyce's work as a whole of all linear properties whatever, considered as a plastic thing — of all contour and definition in fact. In contrast to the jelly-fish that floats in the centre of the subterranean stream of the "dark" Unconscious, I much prefer, for my part, the shield of the tortoise, or the rigid stylistic articulations of the grasshopper.

This can be put in another way. The massive sculpture of the Pharaohs is preferable to the mist of the automatic or spirit-picture. Then, the dreamy and disordered naturalism of so much European art is akin to the floating, ill-organized, vapours of the plastic of the spiritist. And just now I selected as an illustration the most anomalous of all these manifestations of extreme naturalism — the floating wave-lined images in stone of Auguste Rodin.

To put this matter in a nutshell, it is *the shell* of the animal that the plastically-minded artist will prefer. The ossature is my favourite part of a living animal organism, not its intestines. My objections to Mr. D. H. Lawrence were chiefly concerned with that regrettable habit of his incessantly to refer to the intestinal billowing of "dark" subterranean passion. In his devotion to that romantic abdominal *Within* he abandoned the sunlit pagan surface of the earth.

But to return again to Satire: Satire is *cold*, and that is good! It is easier to achieve those polished and resistant surfaces of a great *externalist* art in Satire. At least they are achieved more naturally than can be done beneath the troubled impulse of the lyrical afflatus. All the nineteenth century poetry of France, for instance, from the *Fleurs du mal* onwards, was stiffened with Satire, too. There is a stiffening of Satire in everything good, of "the grotesque," which is the same thing — the non-human outlook must be there (beneath the fluff and pulp which is all that is seen by the majority) to correct our soft conceit. This cannot be gainsaid. Satire is *good!*

But so far in these pages we have been accepting the term Satire without stopping to define it. (To define it anew, of course; for the historical definition is far too narrow for what such a definition would have to include today.) Satire in reality often is nothing else but *the truth* — the truth, in fact, of Natural Science. That objective, non-emotional truth of the scientific intelligence sometimes takes on the exuberant sensuous quality of creative art: then it is very apt to be called "Satire," for it has been bent not so much upon pleasing as upon being true.

No work of fiction, however, is likely to be only "Satire," in the sense that a short epigrammatic piece, in rhyming couplets (an Epistle of Pope) would be. For again it is necessary to return to the fact that fiction-satire is narrative: a great part of it is apt to be of a most objective nature, cast in a mould very near to the everyday aspect of things. It will only appear "grotesque," or "distorted," of course, to those accustomed to regard the things of everyday, and everyday persons, through spectacles *couleur-de-rose.*

But there is the "truth" of Satire and there is the "truth" of Romance. — The term Satire suggests off-hand some resolve on the part of the "satirist" to pick out disobligingly all that is objectionable and ill-favoured in a given system of persons and things, and to make of that a work of art. Certainly such a "satire" as *The Apes of God* is not that. Indeed often it is nothing but people's vanity that causes them to use that term at all: often they are, in what they call "satire," confronted with a description of their everyday life as close to the truth as that found in any other artistic formula. It is merely a formula based rather upon the "truth" of the intellect than upon the "truth" of the average romantic sensualism.

Must we say, then, that "Satire" is merely a representation, containing (irrespective of what else may be included in it) many of those truths that people do not care to hear?

What is "the truth" regarding any person? What is the objective truth about him? — a public and not a private truth? What is that in a person, or in a thing, that is not "satire," upon the one hand, or "romance," upon the other? Is there such a purely non-satiric, non-romantic truth, at all? Such questions may at all times with advantage be asked; but the very core of the satiric impulse is of course involved in them.

All men are *some* sort of hero to themselves: equally there is no man who is not, to *somebody or other,* a disagreeable person, as unsightly as a toad, or else a first-class figure of fun. How are we to reconcile these opposites — the seeing-of-ourselves-as-others-see-us, and the self-picture? It is difficult to see how the objective truth of much that is called "Satire" can be less true than the truth of lyrical declamation, in praise, for instance, of a lovely mistress. There is, in both cases, *another* truth, that is all. But both are upon an equal intellectual footing I think — only the humanly "agreeable" is more often false than the humanly "disagreeable." That is unavoidable, seeing what we are.

Natural Science is a disagreeable study in its way (this was acutely recognized by Leonardo da Vinci, himself a man of science, as well as, in his rôle of plastic artist, a master of vitalist illusion). What interests and delights *the individual* again, is, *sub specie aeternitatis* far less interesting, much less delightful. The values proper to the specific organism have to be accounted for, that we all know. So, to conclude, do not let us arbitrarily describe as "Satire" all that is disagreeable to ourselves. That would be a misnomer. For it may not be *satire* at all!

As well as being a satire, *The Apes of God* is a book made of the outside of things. And it is also a book of *action.* By certain critics it was described, even, as an orgy of *the externals* of this life of ours (cf. "Mr. Lewis could be described as a *personal-appearance* satirist," etc.). But that is a compliment. Its author lays great store by that *externality*, in a world that is literally inundated with sexual viscera and the "dark" gushings of the tides of *The Great Within*. Call him a "personal-appearance writer" and he is far from being displeased! You please *him* by that, even if *he* displeases so many people (it would appear) by treating of their *externals* in the way that he does — just by being so *personal-appearance!*

Hazlitt, to return to him again for a moment, must be credited with seeing that "the fault . . . of Shakespeare's comic Muse is . . . that it is too good-natured and magnanimous." That is the fault also, no doubt, of Hazlitt's *criticism*. And there were, and have been since, many satirists far more apt to bring out this fault in Hazlitt than was "rare Ben Jonson." — Shakespeare's comic muse "does not take the highest pleasure in making human nature look as mean, as ridiculous, and contemptible as possible," writes Hazlitt. "It is in this respect, chiefly, that it differs from the comedy of a later, and (what is called) a more refined period . . . vanity and affectation, in their most exorbitant and studied excesses, are the ruling principles of society, only in a highly advanced state of civilization and manners. Man can hardly be said to be a truly contemptible animal, till, from the facilities of general intercourse . . . he becomes the ape of the extravagances of other men."

There must, however, even according to this account, be some first exemplar — some *original* ape! This Rousseauesque picture of man's original perfection does, even in the statement, halt, and seems to point, in spite of itself, to the conclusion that in some form or other that original "ape" was man!

Again, if you insist, as does Hazlitt, that it is "when folly is epidemic, and vice worn as a mark of distinction, that all the malice of wit and humour is called out and justified, to detect the imposture, and prevent the contagion from spreading," the answer you must expect is as follows: At what period of history has folly *not* been epidemic (allowing for ups and downs and for more and less): when has "vice" not been an advertisement, and virtue a handicap? — Certainly Hazlitt's attitude to "man" is sentimental. The Tudor dramatists were as much surrounded by epidemics of folly as were the later Stuart writers. There was here a seesaw of opinions and of tastes — neither age was quite civilized enough.

But (in conclusion) the justification of "all the malice of wit" must be more securely grounded than this theory of human corruption succeeding upon a state of original blessedness would allow, so simply stated as that.

It is with man, and not with manners, that what we have agreed to describe as "satire" is called upon to deal. It is a *chronic* ailment (manifesting itself, it is true, in a variety of ways) not an *epidemic* state, depending upon "period," or upon the "wicked ways" of the particular smart-set of the time.

"Period" will not be entirely ruled out, doubtless: only in future it will be *world-period*. The habit of thought of this nation or of that, at a given moment of its discrete history, will sink into the insignificance it deserves. The new world-order will possess within it "periods," but itself will not be a "period." Since there is no "present" properly speaking just now, more than ever the majority of people live in the past. It is impossible in consequence to make them understand the changes that are being effected even inside themselves. Even the chronic *period-tasting* of this time serves to screen and hide away the reality.

Immense and critical revaluations are taking place — an *Umvertung aller Werte*. It is the passing of a world, as it were, not of an empire or of single nations. This will only be manifest to Mr. Everyman in the sudden light of cataclysms, exploding in the midst of his comfortable fog. The war was such a cataclysm — but Everyman has already forgotten it!

The present revaluations (operating in every corner of the earth) are of a very different order, both in scale and in kind, to those which changed the "period" of Elizabeth into the "period" of Charles II. Those were intrinsically no more important than the mutations of taste within a small German duchy. These facts are of capital importance for literature, of course: but it is quite out of the question to bring many people to an understanding of them. This does not matter: but it makes it difficult to discuss anything of first-rate importance, in literature as much as in politics, with that blind spot always there.

A serious work of art today has a much vaster stage at its disposal, and one far more weighted with fatality, than that possessed by the Elizabethan drama, with its Renaissance motives — upon which, I daresay, it was more easy to be "good-natured," to be "magnanimous" and kind. For my part, I am called a rebel, I am called a reactionary, according to which boss at the moment I am facing, or whose dogs are barking at my heels. However that may be, the "revaluations" I refer to appear to me *good*. But that our drama need be a "catastrophic" *tragedy of blood* is not true. That is *not* good. To degrade it into something savage and provincial, that cannot be good. The people who are eager to do that — to *sadify* and to ensanguine the noblest of our plots — are the same order of savages who imposed those stupid conventions of "blood" upon the great Tudor dramatists. Like their Elizabethan forerunners, on all hands artists are mixing blood and bombast, more and more, into their inventions, to satisfy this roaring Pit.

Simply in terms of quantity, however, how much more sinister are the reverberations of their thunder! How much more powerful and absolute are the forces involved! What can the artist at present hope for? Only that the gladiatorial phase will pass, and that all the novel perspectives of this universal stage at length may be utilized. An old-fangled Tragedy of Blood could be put on for the children on Sundays — as it were a Red Matinée! —

as a concession to those ferocious Peter Pans who could not grow up. A few could go up on the stage even and be slaughtered in the Roman fashion, for the delectation of the rest. That would be *good*. What has been called by Mr. Roy Campbell the "Bloomsbury game of ping-pong" will go on till the bitter end, of course: and, on the other hand, best-selling writings and paintings will never cease to be poured forth, so long as the present huge democratic societies of the West are organized by astute middlemen into *Book of the Month Clubs*, or into *Royal Academies*. But there is no being "Elizabethan," or being "Georgian," any more, for the man who is in fact an artist. All *that* is over except as a pretty period-game. An artist who is not a mere entertainer and money-maker, or self-advertising gossip-star, must today be penetrated by a sense of the great discontinuity of our destiny. At every moment he is compelled to be aware of that different scene, coming up as if by magic, behind all that has been familiar for so long to all the nations of the Aryan World. Nothing but a sort of Façade is left standing, that is the fact: before which fustian property (labelled *The Past*, a cheap parody of *Ancien Régime*, with feudal keeps in the middle-distance), the Gossip-column Class bask in enormous splashy spot-lights of publicity. It is what is behind the Façade that alone can be of any interest in such a pantomime.

For an understanding of the literature of today and of tomorrow it is very necessary, I believe, to grasp the principles involved in this question; namely, that of the respective merits of the method of *internal* and *external* approach — that statement of mine, made just now, I will return to before concluding the present chapter.

My reasons for believing that the method of *external* approach is the method which, more and more, will be adopted in the art of writing are as follows:

(1) The *external* approach to things belongs to the "classical" manner of apprehending: whereas the romantic outlook (though it may serve the turn of the "transitionists") will not, I believe, attract the best intelligences in the coming years, and will not survive the period of "transition."

(2) The *external* approach to things (relying upon evidence of the *eye* rather than of the more emotional organs of sense) can make of "the grotesque" a healthy and attractive companion. Other approaches cannot do this. The scarab can be accommodated — even a crocodile's tears can be relieved of some of their repulsiveness. For the requirements of the new world-order this is essential. And as for pure satire — there the eye is supreme.

(3) All our instinctive aesthetic reactions are, in the west of Europe, based

upon Greek naturalist canons. Of the *internal* method of approach in literature, Joyce or James are highly representative. Their art (consisting in "telling from the inside," as it is described) has for its backgrounds the naturalism (the flowing lines, the absence of linear organization, and also the inveterate humanism) of the Hellenic pictorial culture. Stein is Teutonic music, *jazzed* — Stein is just the German musical soul leering at itself in a mirror, and sticking out at itself a stuttering welt of swollen tongue, although perhaps, as she is not a pure Teuton, this is not quite fair to the Teuton either — it is the mirror that is at fault.

(4) If you consider the naturalism of the Greek plastic as a phenomenon of decadence (contrasted with the masculine formalism of the Egyptian or the Chinese) then you will regard likewise the method of the "internal monologue" (or the romantic snapshotting of the wandering stream of the Unconscious) as a phenomenon of decadence.

(5) A tumultuous stream of evocative, spell-bearing, vocables, launched at your head — or poured into your Unconscious — is, finally, a dope only. It may be an auriferous mud, but it must remain mud — not a clear but a murky picture. As a literary medium it is barbaric.

(6) If Henry James or if James Joyce were to paint pictures, it would be, you feel, a very *literary* sort of picture that would result. But also, in their *details*, these pictures would be lineal descendants of the Hellenic naturalism. Only, such details, all jumbled up and piled one against the other, would appear, at first sight, different, and, for the Western Hellenic culture, exotic. — Nevertheless, as in the pictures of most Germans, all the plastic units would be suffused with a romantic coloration. They would be overcharged with a literary symbolism; their psyche would have got the better of their Gestalt — the result a sentiment, rather than an expressive form.

(7) We know what sort of picture D. H. Lawrence would paint if he took to the brush instead of the pen. For he did so, luckily, and even held exhibitions. As one might have expected, it turned out to be incompetent Gauguin! A bit more practice, and Lawrence would have been indistinguishable from that Pacific-Parisian Pierre Loti of Paint.

(8) To turn once more to the renowned critic with whom we started, Hazlitt. In reading Shakespeare, he said, "we are let into the minds of his characters, we see the play of their thoughts. . . . His humour (so to speak) bubbles, sparkles, and finds its way in all directions, like a natural spring." — And that natural-spring-effect is the Greek *naturalism*, of course, as I have already indicated. That naturalism (whatever else may or may not happen) is bound to be superseded by something more akin to the classic of, say, the Chinese.

Shakespeare is the summit of the romantic, naturalist, European tradition. And there is a great deal more of that Rousseauish, *natural-springishness*, in much recent work in literature than is generally recognized.

But especially, in the nature of things, is this the case with the *tellers-from-the-inside* — with the masters of the "interior-monologue," with those Columbuses who have set sail towards the El Dorados of the Unconscious, or of the Great Within.

(9) Dogmatically, then, I am for the Great Without, for the method of *external* approach — for the wisdom of the eye, rather than that of the ear.

CHAPTER III

IS SATIRE REAL?

"You do not treat nature wisely by always striving to get beneath the surface." — JONATHAN SWIFT

THAT THE MORALIST — in whatever disguise — can give us as much trouble as the politician — in whatever disguise — is certain. But of course it may be as a politician that he is found to have disguised himself! Or the politician may disguise himself as a moralist — that is very bad indeed, when the politician does that! But in whatever form this interfering personage may turn up, there is one thing about which you may be perfectly certain; and that is, that the old crude humanist or humanitarian values of *good* and of *bad* will not be found in his repertory of annoyance. If that were so we should not have to bother about him very much. There is no advertisement value today — luckily for the artist (if not for other people) — in the simple-hearted *good* and *bad* of the old morality.

Now the time has come, at all events, to go over, in defence of our principle, into that other department, and examine the credentials, a little more closely than customarily is done, of the self-elected officials of the Good Life. In point of fact, the moralist could more justly be described as the votary of the Bad Life — if by *bad* we agree to understand impoverished, full of humiliations, robbed of all freedom and delight — the life, at its best, of such a man as Toussaint L'Ouverture, in which a virtue must be made out of every necessity, where *necessity* is the order of the day — and in which a code is prepared for the coolie of tomorrow, which is what these gentlemen recognize to be, in the near future, our savage lot. We are not invited to resist, but on the contrary a brisk intellectual business is done in the preparation of salves and soporifics for submission — so political are in essence our moralities!

Against this moralist exploitation of a highly immoral situation some voice has to be raised. My voice will have to serve for the present there is no other (compromised as it is by the fact that it has for some time now been the vehicle of "Satire," and although its accents have an unmistakably personal sound, since I am an artist first, and a critic afterwards) until such time as a more respectable advocate can be found. There is no time to be lost, gentlemen of the jury! That is my excuse for appearing before you, with all my sinful infractions of the moral law upon my head, in a case that is, in fact, it is common knowledge, my own, and in the interest — can I deny it? — of my many books. But at least there is this to be said — we all know where we are! I lay no claim to being a disinterested party or

107

to being a pure servant of the Law. I am a partisan. Satire, so-called, is one of my trades. And all I would do is to remind you that the functionaries of the law are often untrustworthy — or they exhibit, shall we say, a strange propensity to side with the stronger and more orthodox party: they cannot even be depended on not to betray what is ostensibly their own client. And what we must assume it is your desire to hear is not some version of the facts, manipulated always in the interests of a not very scrupulous *status quo*, but the truth and nothing but the truth. That, *foi de gentilhomme*, you shall hear from my lips, or at least that portion of the truth that is all that any individual can lay claim to. *That* you shall receive pure and unadulterated. More I cannot say, and he who lays claim to more is misleading you, whether he is conscious of doing so or not.

Our contemporary moralists are of many kinds. But there is one respect in which they remarkably resemble one another: for all, starting from the premise of our unautonomous nature, seek to rob us of artistic as of political freedom, in the name of this, that, or the other Law. But what are these moralists, and what is their actual relation to the Law they invoke?

Not only "that which humbles us upon the sensuous plane is found to elevate us upon the intellectual plane," but alas it has been found likewise *to puff us up*! And when reason speaks the language of feeling, it is liable to become a most muddled jargon, too! Contact with the high ritual of the Law can scarcely be good for those with an unsatisfied appetite for power: and when the superior person passes over from the merely social and sensual region of the genteel ambition (where today the white bows upon the backsides of his maid-servants are few and far between) into the snobbish approaches, as apprehended by him, of a paramount Authority, got up in the uniform of life-and-death, something very unpleasant happens to this interested volunteer, this befrocked laity. That is only to be expected.

As far as the Moral Law is concerned, there was little that was theoretic in the judgements upon which the Roman satirists relied, for their credentials, as ethical bullies. The stoic teaching ignored entirely the logical backgrounds: it was a pragmatical and hand-to-mouth morality. But where a high theory existed, ethical principles have in practice looked much the same everywhere — in Christendom or Pagan Rome, in India or Japan: whereas the theories, by which they were arrived at, have often been as different as possible.

As to the moralities of the moment, the real trouble about them, as I see it, is their bastard quality, and the uneasy hold their sponsors have upon them. Emerging as they do in response to growing lawlessness, and in opposition to dogmas of the Marxo-Nietzschean "beyond the law" order, they are too often found to be contaminated with the very things against which they are invoked. This is an old dilemma. Combatants infect each other, whereas non-combatants remain relatively immune.

The services rendered by tradition, in its energetic field-work against the ignorant mob, have been great. But one often is disposed to wonder if much that passes for tradition is upon the side of reason at all. Modernism, which is merely the nervous jingo exaggeration of the more futile novelties of the Zeitgeist, has enucleated it: we see it possessed of a meretricious colour more reminiscent of the revivalist or salvationist army-technique, than of a more scientific, impartial and catholic, temper, for all the prestige of the classical disciplines invoked.

In assailing, for instance, the mere "good-timer," a spurious traditionalism will be seen to take on depressing affectations. What can only be called (in contrast to what is then attacked) the *badtimer* makes his appearance. But that is to do the audience of such a display a very bad turn indeed: for that audience does not need to have thrust upon it, on top of the disciplines of famine or of straitened life, the ritual of romantic renunciation, too. To offer the other cheek is better when that cheek is not hollowed out by want.

But it is worse than that! In the desire to obtain at all costs the American "kick" even (or should we say above all?) out of religious experience, whirlwind visits are paid to the pages of the more highly-peppered mystics. Distilled into a post-slump narcotic, the religious tears crystallized in the *Dark Night of the Soul* make their appearance upon our scene. Now all steamed-up, this "dark" entertainer will howl or moan out at the astonished (and rather impressed) assemblage, of intellectual *badauds*, that this *badtimism* is the latest, most sensational, thing in truth — and so arrives at something truly American (in the worst sense, for every country possesses a nadir of its most mechanical local-coloration) — an *up-to-date* brand of intellectualist salvation. Indeed, the "kick" obtained from the flushed perusal of the confessional ecstasies of a "trunk-butcher," or the inquisitorial croonings of a Chicago "killer," contributes probably to the stimulation of the luxuries of the affected "dark night" of the *badtimer*. That is the background, after all!

The mere "goodtimer" is a distasteful spectacle I know; but *badtimism* is a hundred times less edifying. If our old friend Cocteau is the archetype, that is not to say that less flamboyant figures are not tarred with the same religious *chic*. And this order of literary monks and fakirs are closely related to the pseudo-yogi mystical charlatans — the most eminent of which has been Gurdjieff.

The salvationist afflatus, the desire to get, get, get — yes to *go-get* — religion, with a great big mystical kick in it, is dangerous for religion too. For "the pragmatic glorification of belief contains the deep poison of scepticism . . . and this like a Nessus shirt will destroy any religious belief that puts it on," as a writer who is, racially, a religious specialist has said. It is not necessarily a hedonistic ethics which promotes such a criticism as this of the *badtimer*. The badtimer is a child of his time — and it is a *bad* time. Today all of us are living at a lower material level, our standards have been pushed down, as a consequence of the war and then the slumps. That is merely to describe the proletarianization of everybody: these are the painful initiations for all of us into the conditions of the Servile State. We who were born free, see ourselves everywhere becoming serfs. Upon whichever hand we look, we discern the slaves' badge awaiting us, or if not us our children. And even the transition, the transformation into the slave, is not a pleasant process, anything but. Under these circumstances we shall be in need, shall we not, of a philosophy, or a religion. And the ideal slave-ethic is the *Stoic*; I believe I am correct in saying? The slave, Epictetus, should be brought forward again.

A particular difficulty besets the artist, if he decides to retaliate upon the moralist *badtimer*, on behalf of an art threatened with ethical proscription. The artist is regarded as the essential pleasure-man, the born hedonist. And as an American philosopher has said, mankind "rebels against regarding [pleasure] as the only good. It associates morality rather with painful efforts to achieve things worth while which are not inherently pleasurable, though there may be pleasure in achieving them. Indeed the pursuit of pleasure is generally regarded as something reserved for our leisure moments when we are not engaged in the more serious and important life-activities."

Of course quite respectable hedonist philosophers can be named: but it is impossible to imagine a time more unsuited than the present for the enunciation of such a philosophy (unless the Marxist should be included under that caption). The *opposite* of hedonism — which I have called *badtimism* — a philosophy of pain — is just as little to be recommended, although in some cases it may be highly respectable, too. But it looks as though it might stand a chance of becoming one of the official doctrines supporting our particular social consciousness — though the stoical injunctions would be far better than that.

I will postpone until subsequent chapters, where gradually my arguments upon this head will be unfolded, a consideration of the grounds upon which the satirist who is not first and foremost a moralist may establish his claim to prosecute his unpopular art. For to say, "I pen or paint (as Swift or Hogarth) these libellous pictures directed at my own kind because it has been my whim to do so," is not the answer that I should offer for your serious consideration, nor is it the answer that I would generally recommend.

I have accorded the place of honour to the problem of *law*, especially of the moral sanctions. But without a great deal of preliminary investigation, it is impossible to get down to the fundamentals of this issue, involved as it is with the question of the very nature of Satire, as we understand it here. Then again, the particular quality of the ethical criticism that is to be anticipated at the present time, is of major importance to our cause — the cause of good Satire: for as good and bad mean one thing in one place, and another in another, so is it with times, and our time has a "good" and "bad" peculiar to it. But moral judgements chop and change, and are never the same for long together: and the moralist today is installed indeed upon a veritable quicksand, as well as is the "irresponsible" laughing figure he would denounce: and he is often himself a complex of orthodox moral and "amoral" values. The great intricacy of his logical position commits him to an evasive and equivocal technique: and this technique does not lend itself, of course, to a simple treatment, if it is to be interrogated. It is the same with him as with the latterday Marxist: his values are so highly intellectualized that none of the simpler components of *good* and *evil* are to be found. Just as with the present Marxism not a trace of the original humanitarian values of Socialism remains (the "good of the greatest number," as originally defined for instance, is a doctrine that plays no part in his present scheme of salvation): so with the ethical mind, which officially confronts the orthodox Marxist on the contemporary political stage, with the weapons of tradition brandished aloft, the "good life" he points to may be a very *bad life* indeed from the standpoint of common sense, as I have just pointed out, and his values closely scrutinized, possess disquieting points of resemblance with those of his adversary, as I have suggested, too.

So today Satire can be judged *good* or *bad* upon no familiar or traditional pattern of ethical codification. The values inherent in the terms *real* and *unreal* are more likely to be of service to us, therefore, in such an investigation, than those popularly residing in *good* and *bad*. The sort of question we shall have to ask ourselves will rather be *Is Satire real?* than *Is Satire good?* confronted with the *soi-disant* moralist technique. I am sorry that it is not more simple, but these are the facts. And even the counter "real" will be seen to get itself mixed-up with all sorts of social values: we may even find it as far afield as to be engaging in a heated enquiry as to whether such and such a fictitious person is a *real* lady — or a perfect gentleman! *Vulgar* is, again — just as in the case of the anti-bourgeois front — an important counter on the ethical front. The Marxist epithet "bourgeois" is of course borrowed from those post-revolutionary French literati who ridiculed the standards of the irresponsible mercantile classes, which, in "the Bankers' Olympus" of the last century, had succeeded to the aristocratic classes. Yet it is the favourite word of opprobrium upon the lips of the class-conscious "proletarian" (taught him by his intelligentsia *souffleur*). The sneer of an aristocrat is employed by the coal-heaver (ideally) to wither his master, who is a mere vulgar money-man — a pasty and fat city-merchant, that is the idea, without any of the aristocratic virtues, without the aristocratic sense of responsibility (of "duty"), without art and without manners, a vulgar fellow, in short. And with *vulgar* another counter, *stupid*, will be found invariably to consort.

This is where the satirist finds that he has to be very careful indeed. For it is awfully difficult to satirize people who are the reverse of vulgar, and the reverse of stupid. Indeed, it would be highly unreasonable to do such a thing at all. And yet the satirist will find that, over and over again, he will be admonished for resorting to such vulgar and such stupid subjects: and the more effective his shafts have been proved to be, the more severe will be those strictures.

What we ultimately shall arrive at, of course, in the case of the critique of the ethical judgement, is a sort of Nietzschean universe, in which "good" signifies merely the values of the master-caste, and "bad" the values of the servile caste. And the moralist-critic will exhibit a fine irresponsibility in his juggling with these very ill-defined values, it will too often be found. He will even belittle morals in the interest of some esoteric higher ethos.

I hope I shall not have alarmed you by this frank confession of the intricate and difficult nature of the investigation proposed. But it was really no use my attempting to lead you on, unaware, into this maze that stretched before us. Had I done so, you would very soon have been turning on me, loudly asking how it was that, having embarked upon a defence of Satire against the moralist, we had got into a dispute about "realism" and "disembodied art": and what had realism to do with *morals* anyway!

But realism may have a good deal to do with morals, as you subsequently will discover. For the "realist" school of prose-fiction is apt to deal with people who do little credit to the highest aspirations of our human-nature, just like Satire. Theirs is not the spirit of the *Chansons de geste*, but rather of the laboratory, or even of the lavatory. Their Arthuriads tend to convert the grail into a *pot de chambre* — not of the Maids of Honour, but of the small house-drudge. But whereas Satire often deals with people socially eminent — people of gossip-column calibre — but, because it presents them in a light that is not conducive to showing off their importance, it is accused of selecting an *insignificant* material: "realism" pure and simple is apt deliberately to choose the *really* insignificant, and often merits I think the indignant protests of the snob. This would not be the case, however, if, as Satire sometimes does, it magnified the little — just as a flea, magnified, is as important an object as an elephant. For what is after all "importance" except littleness magnified, and polished up, perhaps. The subjective eye of a given epoch acts as a magnifying glass, in the way that the atmosphere has erroneously been supposed to do at sunset in the case of the departing sun, to increase the portentous proportions of a number of truly insignificant people. And so we get what is currently estimated as "important" or "great."

Satire performs much the same conjuring trick, only it selects its people to be magnified with more care—deliberately, for its own philosophic purposes. But once these figures have been so magnified—not as "realism" works, but in an heroical manner of its own—whatever they may have been to start with, they become really important, they occupy space. With this magnification they undergo also a subtle change, they develop more energy. And they have at least just as much right to so tower and so bulge as they do, as have the gigantic nobodies, the colossal midgets, who (owing to that subjective magnification performed by the popular eye, by the popular Press, to which I have referred) have come to overshadow the modern scene. So when the satirist is rebuked for the magnification conferred by him upon *his* particular nobodies, and asked why he has not selected the already artificially enlarged nobodies of the moment, he could rather pointedly reply that the latter were already big enough—that he could do nothing more with them, beyond what has already been done by their position in *the public eye*—and that no satire of his could, in any case, make them look much more foolish!

In my next chapter I shall begin a careful analysis of what is behind these closely-related modes of criticism—the criticism on the score of scale or *importance*, and the criticism on the score of *realness* (as the subjective as against the objective, that is) and I shall go on to show how they may merge in one another. I shall in the course of this lengthy analysis uncover a *moralist-in-the-making*, as it were: a moralist, that is, as understood to-day. But in my next chapter, and in those that follow it, I shall be concerned not with the ethical judgement any more, but with all the other descriptions of judgement that go to the making of that very complex flower, the intellectualist-moralist, who is the only type of moral critic who today can exert any influence, and so influence, to any serious extent, the productions of Satire, and, in a more general way, of Art.

CHAPTER IV

HENRY JAMES

THE ARCH-ENEMY OF "LOW-COMPANY"

"There is surely no principle of fictitious composition so true
as this, — that an author's paramount charge is the cure of souls,
to the subjection, and if need be to the exclusion, of the picturesque." — HENRY JAMES.

HOW CLOSELY IN SOME CASES the problems of the satirist march with those
of the fictionist (when they are not, as often happens, the same person) can
easily be demonstrated, I think: and it is a fact of no little importance. There
are two kinds of people (I have already touched upon this relationship) who,
at one time and another, have been accused of keeping low company. One
is the satirist (any satirist): the other is the fictionist of the school of "realism." In the latter case, of course, the controversy was most active and
bitter in the last century, when, with Flaubert and Balzac, militant, "scientific," *realism* first came on the scene. But the controversy still continues.

A case in point is Mr. Hemingway. He has been accused (by Mr. Eliot)
of being too literal a fellow, and of clinging to the hearty ideals of a less
enlightened age — the age of "realism," in fact. (Unnecessary to say, it is
always assumed that the present age is very superior to the immediately
preceding ages — Mr. Eliot's position is exactly the same as Mr. Strachey's
in that respect — and full of superior people, as well as peculiarly knowing
ones!) In this chapter I have decided to interrogate Henry James, who is
undoubtedly, in the Anglo-Saxon world, the great *genteel* classic, embodying better than any other single man the principles of Anglo-Saxon
"idealism," in opposition to the more rough and pagan principles which
have always obtained upon the European continent.

The "importance" value in the *humanist* canon is, for the Anglo-Saxon,
a strangely conventional thing. And Satire suffers as much as any art, in
Anglo-Saxony, from this misunderstanding — based upon notions of social
eminence (surely the most trivial of things) — as to the natural outlets for
such an intelligence. The Anglo-Saxon would confine Satire to being the
polite and "humorous" distortion of an eminent personage — the mildly scur-
rilous servant, the jester of a "free" Democracy: to being a parodist of
persons — not the titanic and critical vehicle of ideas — the *maker* of persons, of a Tartuffe or a Tristram Shandy.

A "Massacre of the Insignificants," that is what most successful and really
destructive satire is represented to be at the present time — *never* as the

115

"Massacre of the Innocents." Nobody would dare to pretend today that he is not a fit subject for the satiric art. Hence, to discomfit the satirist, the victims (or friends on their behalf) have formed the habit of shrugging their shoulders and saying: "Why doesn't X attack old So-and-So? He is only wasting his time in attacking *me* (or us). I don't mind of course, if it amuses him to beat the air—or to bludgeon a dead horse!"

There has never been a satirist of recent years, I should think, who has not been puzzled by this circumstance—that, following upon the publication of a successful satire, upon all hands he will have found people exclaiming: "But *why* waste time upon such insignificant people!"—As if (in the first place) those who gave vent to such exclamations were not themselves people of a similar order of significance to those exposed in the satire: and then as if a *satire* could be written at all about persons whom the satirist liked or admired!

When Bolingbroke was expressing admiration for the Duke of Marlborough, somebody present objected, reminding him of the well-known fondness for money of the founder of Blenheim Palace (for the bill for the construction of which Inigo Jones had to whistle—it was a meanness that ran in the family). But Bolingbroke at once retorted—"*He was so great a man, I had almost forgot he had that fault!*"—So, if you succumb to "the graces" of a Marlborough, you forget that in the matter of money he is a most un-graceful person. You see nothing but those famous "graces"—*always the graces!* understood to perfection. And you will leave it to others to be the satirist of that person.

But against Pope, and against Swift, this charge has especially been brought—that the persons they assailed were *small*. Cibber, Budgell and Settle—unworthy of notice were such people! It would have pleased humanity at large *far better* if Pope had fallen upon Swift, for instance, and if Swift had held up Pope to scorn! Yes, of course. Oh, why attack the little? That is the burden of the critic's song.

But even if that were so, and if Cibber, Budgell and Settle were *too* small, as we are told, yet the term satire comprises many forms of art. What applies to Satire in verse, of the type of the *Satires and Epistles*, does not apply to prose narrative. And, of course, no one would complain about a narrative treating of "insignificant" people, if it only made them agreeable and harmless little people—indeed upon such a task as that the greatest mind might be employed with advantage!

But the splendour of the persons involved—the moral stature, or the magnificent intellectual presence—is scarcely a measure of the importance of a work of art. I have seen pictures of peasants (to turn to the plastic arts), and even of idiots, that were certainly greater pictures than other ones of more imposing persons, depicting emperors or princesses.—So the satirist must take such aspersions upon his *dramatis personae* with a grain of his own rough salt, and only the weak-minded satirist will join in turning up the nose at his human targets.

But this was the mistake encouraged by Hazlitt: for *he* was one of the foremost of those persons who turn up their noses at the subject-matter of Satire. "In *Ben Jonson,*" Hazlitt wrote, "we find ourselves generally in low company, and we see no hope of getting out of it!"

It is a strange and paradoxical situation! Here is the satirist, at last compelled to defend his victims against the contemptuous aspersions of the rest of the world! A situation of the finest comedy.

An explanation of this paradox suggests itself. Is it not merely the revenge of the world, perhaps, taken by its spokesmen, upon its detractors? Hazlitt is a very worldly spokesman: and he appears to be wishing to identify *Ben Jonson* with those pilloried in his plays or used for his merciless sport, and to lock that satirist up for ever with his objectionable creations — as though only a *disagreeable* man would ever observe in those about him such *disagreeable* things! That seems to me, to say the least, a most imperfect psychological analysis.

"There are people who cannot taste olives — and I cannot much relish *Ben Jonson,* though I have taken some pains to do it," says Hazlitt. And what perhaps he should in fact have said (to judge from what follows) is that he could not much relish *satire* in any form.

The "realist" then (Mr. Hemingway — Balzac or Trollope) is criticized for associating with low people — either socially low, or intellectually low. And to witness the operation of this charge — preferred by a master of the opposite school — we cannot do better, as I have said, than address ourselves to Henry James. In his early attacks upon Anthony Trollope he reveals with peculiar clearness what he had, at all times, at the bottom of his mind. And to those attacks I propose first of all to turn. They are to be found in a posthumous collection of articles.[1] They are very brilliant and lucid statements, and I am using the same collection when I come to discuss what for convenience I call the art of the "soul" versus the art of the body.

James is reviewing (in 1865) Trollope's *Miss Mackenzie,* and he is very severe indeed in his expostulations regarding the vulgarity and the stupidity of the people depicted. "Mr. Trollope," he says, "may consider that he has hit the average. . . . Literally, then, [he] accomplishes his purpose of being true to common life. But in reading his pages, we were constantly induced to ask ourselves whether he is equally true to nature. . . . We are . . . compelled to doubt whether men and women of healthy intellect take life, even in its smallest manifestations, as *stupidly* as Miss Mackenzie and her friends. Mr. Trollope has, we conceive, simply wished to interest us in ordinary mortals: it has not been his intention to introduce us to a company of

[1] *Notes and Reviews,* Henry James.

imbeciles. But, seriously, we do not consider these people to be much better. . . . We do not expect from the writers of Mr. Trollope's school . . . that they shall contribute to the glory of human nature; but we may at least exact that they do not wantonly detract from it. Mr. Trollope's offence is, after all, deliberate. He has deliberately selected vulgar illustrations. . . . He is an excellent, an admirable observer. . . . But why does he not observe great things as well as little ones?"

The vulgarity and *stupidity* (put by James into horrified italics, though, to express his true feelings, *vulgarity* should at least have had them too) — the *lowness* of the company that Trollope kept, genuinely horrified this over-fastidious Bostonian, and surprised him as well. How a European — how an *Englishman* — should *deliberately* come to choose such company passed his understanding and left him dazed and indignant. — Even when Trollope has the chance of escaping from this squalid impasse, he turns his back upon it! In his next attempt (called archly *Can You Forgive Her?* also reviewed by James) he had a golden opportunity, James feels. A really "poetic" creature, as she is described by James, somehow or other got into that book, rejoicing also in the "poetic" name — and title — of Lady Glencora Palliser. What a chance for a gentleman! But what does the incorrigible Trollope do? He as it were puts her ladyship down in the servants' hall, and even then forgets all about her — quite regardless of the "sensations" of James. "Poor little Lady Glencora," sighs the susceptible Bostonian, "with her prettiness, her grace, her colossal fortune, and her sorrows, is the one really poetic figure in the novel. . . . Why not, for *her* sake, have shown a little boldness? . . . Everything forbade that Lady Glencora and her lover should be vulgarly disposed of." But no: "for Mr. Trollope anything is preferable to a sensation" — even such sensations as his intelligent but snobbish transatlantic reviewer of 1865 would have derived from hearing about the Lady Glencora Palliser. *What* a lost opportunity! James is in the worst of tempers — he evidently itches to snatch the pen out of Trollope's hand and to restore the Lady Glencora to her proper place in the scheme of things!

I have selected this particular passage — *the episode of the Lady Glencora*, as we may call it — to suggest to your mind how easy it is for those unduly sensitive to "lowness" and to "highness" to allow one sort of "lowness" to merge in another — in rather the same manner that, above this melting-pot where all the "lows" run into one, the mere old-fashioned social snob is apt to converge upon, and is often found to be interchangeable with the "superior person," whose sensitiveness is intellectual rather than social. It is as a rule not difficult, in fact, by scratching a little the intelligence-snob, to find beneath that unlovely veneer that even less commendable sentimentalist out of the *Book of Snobs*. For no one can really be today a social snob *alone*. All who in sleepier times would have been simply that, have today become intellectualist. The intellectual world, as much as the Church, provides a refuge for these homeless instincts of the uprooted "bourgeois." The American of twenty-one, of the nineteen-thirties, even the Bostonian, knows a great deal more than James about the value of the bankrupt, vulgarized "Lady Glencoras" of the modern age: but it is not so long ago, a decade or two, that the James-feeling was still possible for young Bostonians: and James is particularly useful to us in the present argument, since he does show how underlying one value may be found another; related, it is true, but not usually expected to be found in such close and compromising proximity.

The satirist, of course, escapes the obloquy of consorting with common individuals, in the way it is suggested above that Trollope had done. "It has not been his intention to introduce us to a company of imbeciles," says James of the author of *Miss Mackenzie*. But the same could not be advanced against the author of *Bouvard et Pécuchet*, since obviously "a company of imbeciles" was precisely what he had set out to depict.

That would exempt Flaubert: for of course Trollope's offence is to have attempted to have passed off these low fellows ("vulgar bachelors") and their middle-aged, middle-class, trulls, as quite nice, "well-bred" people, such as anyone might gladly "meet": or else not even that: there may have been no crafty attempt, after all, to pass this debased human coin — he may have really *believed* it to be all right. — So there is both a noteworthy similarity, and at the same time an important difference, between these two cases — that of the satirist (whose subject-matter is cried-down, so soon as his satire catches on) and the fictionist of the school of "realism" — who, ultimately, is said to be "a low fellow," because he does not "contribute to the glory of human nature," so it appears, but very much to the contrary.

The *social* difficulty is really not unlike the difficulty about *subject-matter.* These "high" and "low" values (identified by Nietzsche with "good" and "bad") are the conventional values of the herd — of the top-dog herd of course, but still *the herd.* And just as eugenics, and race-doctrines, demand "Greek gods" as the "high" and only justifiable subject-matter for art (and, that fundamentally, since the classical age, has been the European standpoint, as opposed to the Asiatic, which has indifferently glorified the bird, the jackal and the mandarin) so intelligence and grace were demanded of Mr. Trollope by Mr. James, and when he did not get it he was angry. But there is so very little true intelligence or perfect grace in the world (people grossly overestimate the amount) that it is impossible to be *true,* for what that is worth, and satisfy the requirements of the "idealist" Bostonian, who *insists* upon seeing what in fact is not there, and grows peevish when his error is exposed. — But there remains the value of "the real" to be considered, as a standard (in whatever form) in the fine arts. A great confusion reigns in this field of criticism, as can be readily seen by anybody who realizes the extremely elastic nature of these counters — "real" and "ideal" — or whatever term you decide to use to provide the contrast to "realist." And "material" and "immaterial" is another pair — except that no one calls himself or herself an "immaterialist," any more than they are very anxious to have themselves called an "idealist." And the old fundamental cleavage of "corporeal" and "spiritual" — of "body" and of "soul" — is at the back of all these disputes and critical adjustments.

To be "dogmatically for the great *Without*" — to set up the Shell as your shield, against the Dark Within, in a *parti pris* for the rigours of the sun — in favour of its *public* values, in contrast to the *private* values of the half-lighted places of the mind — to evince more interest in the actor, and in action, than about the daydreams of a dilettante scene-shifter, or the brutal trances of the mob; all this must forever compromise you with the either disguised or overt doctrinaires of a disembodied, a non-corporeal, artistic expression. You have in the most unmistakable way come down upon the side of what is material, if you have accepted in the main my contentions — over against those people who prefer the mind's eye, as an instrument, to the eye upon the outside of their head. The mind's eye I refer to is that organ which looks out equally upon the past and present, but perceives the actual scene a little dimly, at the best *peeps* out upon the contemporary scene: it is the *time-eye*, as it might be called, the eye of Proust.

Proust is the archetype of the internal traveller. Walter Pater and Marcel Proust are patently of kindred intelligence. Joyce is far more robust and spacious, at his best. But James is, for us, in the field of investigation here being opened up, more important than either. For "aestheticism," though in truth rampant and ubiquitous, is on all hands violently disowned: and although the manner of Pater is today constantly imitated, on the sly, and his teaching absorbed along with his style, he is scarcely *respectable*, in the intellectual sense. But there is nothing against James. He has played, in the Anglo-Saxon world, much the part monopolized by Flaubert upon the continent — though, in detail, with all the difference that there is between the robust culture of the French and the rather anaemic and uneasy culture of the modern Anglo-Saxon.

Going to that well-head of the doctrine against which we are contending, once more let us contrive to find ourselves in the presence of that young man just come of age, domiciled in Boston in 1864–1866, who wrote the book reviews for *The North American Review*, and *The Nation*. There is one review in particular which will be of great use. A lady-novelist of the day falls into his hands: *Azarian: an Episode*, is the name of the book, and Harriet Elizabeth Prescott the name of the author.

His treatment of this book is an attack that is richly deserved, it is sufficiently plain: and in the course of it James comes to contrast what is, in fact, the *outside* with the *inside* method. He takes his stand very deliberately upon the side of the latter doctrine — although, from the passages quoted, the lady-novelist seems to have been a very doubtful representative of the opposite method. But in spite of this, what James writes — and his own subsequent practice in fiction carries this out — can be given a more general application.

The authoress "roasted" by his fledgling pen expresses herself as follows, in speaking of the blackberry: "damasked with deepening layer and spilth of colour, brinded and barred and blotted beneath the dripping fingers of October," etc. It is evident then, if we are going to use his comments in a wider context, upon the side of the external method, we should have to find something more satisfactory — and indeed of a rather opposite nature — than this.

Is "the cure of souls" the paramount charge of the fictionist, as Henry James says that in fact it is, in the quotation at the head of this chapter? Or if it is "the cure of souls," is it that necessarily "to the exclusion" of the body — if such a choice has to be made between the inner and the outer?

There is no one who would not be ready to agree that a very little of such stuff as the above prose-poetry launched at a blackberry-bush would cause one to sigh for some other and less "picturesque" treatment. Yes, but what opposite treatment does it bring to mind, as most calculated to dispel the stifling airs of that tropical verbiage? Indeed what is mainly the matter with the passage selected by James is precisely that it is too "soulful," not that it is too sensual. The blackberries "suffused through all their veins with the shining soul of the mild and mellow season," are indeed *suffused with soul*. Surely that is the essence of their particular enormity: it is as much (it could not be *more*) the "soulful" tone, as the "colourful" profusion, that is at fault.

Henry James, fine critic that he is, supplies the answer for us. If you *must* approach things in this external manner, he says, then do so in the spirit of scientific enquiry! "*If you resolve to describe a thing, you cannot describe it too carefully*," most justly he admonishes: although that you should want to describe a thing at all, he does suggest, is a little peculiar. Still, he admits that there are such misguided people, and he refers his delinquent authoress to Balzac as the *beau idéal* of the externalist craftsman. *Eugenie Grandet*, for instance, may be said to be "equally elaborate in the painting of external objects," though he reminds the blackberry-authoress that Balzac does not *copy* objects. At this point I think that the authoress, had she been given a hearing, could have retorted (if the blackberry-picture was a fair example of her handiwork) that *she* did not copy them either. And we, had we been present, might have been tempted to tell her, of course, that it would have been better if she had!

But Balzac was "literally real," James tells her: "he presents objects as they are. The scene and persons of his drama are minutely described." Yet "our sense of the human interest of the story is never lost. Why is this?

It is because these things are all described *only in so far as they bear upon the action.*"

This meticulous Balzacian externality was, then, a part of the process of conveying *the action*: and "as the soul of a novel is its action" James tells us, this is natural enough. For to convey the maximum sensation of *action*, it is indeed indispensable to deal with *objects* — with the externality of things.

"It was a characteristic of [Balzac's] mind," James goes on to say, "enriched as it was by sensual observation, to see his figures clearly and fully *as with the eye of sense. . . .* How clearly he saw them we may judge from the minuteness of his presentations. It was clearly done because it was *scientifically* done. That word resumes our lesson."

And that is very handsome of the juvenile James: for no one can claim for him that in his own characteristic work he "did things clearly." He would have to make a certain effort to give the external approach its due, its *scientific* due, confronted with even the most praiseworthy specimen of objective treatment. It was not the bent of his mind, he did not feel at home with objects — his was a world of men and women, and it would be particularly foreign to him to see men as objects at all, as things grouped among other things. His was to a remarkable degree "a cure of souls." And in many remarks he lets fall in this early piece of journalism we detect the Henry James of the great disembodied romances.

In reading books of the sensual school, he tells us, "we have sighed for a novel with a *dramatis personae* of disembodied spirits." And these precocious sighs, of the young New Englander, were not in vain, for he stepped into the breach and supplied the antidote to the over-sensual later on himself, producing many a *dramatis personae* of disembodied spirits.

"Given an animate being, you may readily clothe it in your mind's eye with a body, a local habitation, and a name. Given, we say, an animate being: that is the point. The reader who is set face to face with a gorgeous doll will assuredly fail to inspire it with sympathetic life."

But just as there are authors, so there are readers, who experience a lack of interest, even a certain repulsion, for the inanimate. Especially have they what may amount to a horror for the inanimate, or the mechanical, as exemplified in *people*. And such certainly would be found to withhold their sympathy from any "doll" stuck up, however skilfully, in front of them. And women oddly enough — for in the mass they are far more precise and mechanical than men, as their very movements denote — harbour a particular dislike for the puppets of the satirist.

But although Satire is the art with which here we are beginning and ending, it is not the only art. And the more of the vital principle that is concentrated in the body of a man — assuming that principle for the moment to be non-material — the less a mere puppet would be able to convey everything that was there. It would indeed be one-sided and foolish to neglect the vast differences that exist in the matter of psychical, or so-called psychical, power, and spiritual volume, between people, although outwardly all of us are of much the same material dimension and structure.

But is not the opposite mistake an equally fatal one? I refer to the necessity, in depicting the human being (and that, however much you may start out from the position of a literary showman of the soul) for accepting his mortal status: for recognizing that all that you have to tell about him is deeply involved in his five senses, and the sensorium in the midst of which they function: and for understanding what a great part physical action plays — if it is only slight muscular movements in the larynx — in even the soul-picture — if there can be any "picture" of the "soul." There is no occasion to be a "behaviourist" to accept that much.

The exquisitely critical intelligence of Henry James was quite able to appreciate this. But as a creative artist he was led into the field of his predilection, which was a twilit feminine universe — of little direct action, and of no gross substance at all. Yet how much better had he relieved this mass of finicks with even an occasional *direct* gesture or an explosion of some sort (not necessarily too elemental) to dispel the stuffiness. And then the rather ponderous phantoms of his ratiocination might quite often, with advantage, have been taken out for an airing: and there is not one of them that would not have been a more compelling personage if approached from that end — the externalist end.

That James was technically capable of this who can doubt, for he had an excellent eye in his head, when he consented to use it. But as a matter of fact James did not leave North America quite soon enough: he was twenty-seven years old before he finally passed over into Europe. And for the over-delicate mind of the New Englander this meant that all his senses were confirmed in the abstractness which is such a feature of the North American continent.

One of the facts of which the "visual" intelligence is peculiarly aware is the importance of the geographic background — the *visual medium*, as it were, in which men exist. This factor is for us of critical moment. But today it is a commonplace that our European urban life is being "Americanized." It is impossible, on the other hand, to "Americanize" our countryside, short of making it into a desert. Still the "Americanization," with a difference, is there. So I think we may decide with advantage, at this point, to hold up our argument, in order to obtain a clearer notion of what "America" implies. For the romantically selected backgrounds of the Hollywood films do not supply the analytic picture we require.

Anybody who has travelled by train from New York to Boston, or from New York to Washington, will realize what I mean when I say that this part of the United States is a sort of desert. The tundra, or the dune, dotted with the eternal fir tree, comes right up to the back door of the last house in almost any Pennsylvanian or New England townlet, or small city either, for that matter. Half the houses, even today, again, are framehouses, often with a brick flue and chimney running up outside the timber: and this applies as much to a great city, like Philadelphia or Boston, as to a small township. Professor Babbitt, for instance, to take a very concrete illustration, lived in a wooden house — not a log cabin — a very fine house of wood. However good looking, these wooden buildings must be highly inflammable one would think, and convey a feeling of permanence much inferior to brick or stone. But everybody almost, in the university town of Cambridge, the Oxford of America, lives in them. The shopping quarters and college buildings are of brick, but not the residential quarters or the outskirts.

Then, as most of the wooden residential houses are not enclosed with walls or fences (if anyone attempts to fence his house he is reported to the landlord, that is the rule, I believe, and compelled to pull it down), these houses stand, where they begin to thin out upon the edges of a town, or a city, in the middle of what is more often than not a steppe.

The frequently remarked "asceticism" of the American, which we usually attribute to the shadow of the old conventicles of the early Puritan settler, is much more the immediate result of living in a desert — for even *within* the towns, or for that matter cities, there has, of necessity, always been an absence of the urbanity to which the European is accustomed: a breathless business hustle has left no room for its development. To acquire a firm understanding of such little facts as these is quite worth while: England certainly is liable to influence North America, because the same language is current on both sides of the Atlantic, but, as we were saying just now, North America *does* more than reciprocate: in volume of influence England receives back all that she bestows. And since in many ways that formidable nation, which is a mixture of all the white races, is liable to throw up, if not better, yet more enterprising brains than are to be found among us, and flavoured with a slight, rather temporal than geographical, exoticism, it is all the more important to acquire a sharply-defined image of the backgrounds that account for them, more defined at all events than as a rule the educated Englishman can claim to have.

Undeniably, the "American scene" is of the utmost barrenness, physically and socially. It is planted in the midst of a relative wilderness, beneath a surprisingly hard and penetrating light. The American is still the white settler, except for the dense swarms in the great cities, and he has not been able to furnish, except in a sketchy fashion, his slice of the great New Land. It remains very empty looking: there are no nuances on the North American continent. But equally — until, I imagine, you get to the frontiers of Latin America, that is Mexico — the hardness and the crudity is not inspiring, in the way that the barrenness of northern Africa certainly is, or the centre of Spain. The actual physical landscape has something of a Swiss frigidity and emptiness.

> Boston! And, beyond Boston, that great unendowed, unfurnished, unentertained, and unentertaining continent where one sniffed as it were the very earth of one's foundations! "I shall freeze after this sun," said Albrecht Dürer, as he turned homeward across the Alps from Italy. And where was James to turn for warmth, he whose every fibre longed for that other gracious world, that soft, harmonious, picturesque "Europe" of his imagination, that paradise of form, color, style. . . . ?[1]

This is from the pages of Mr. Van Wyck Brooks's *Pilgrimage of Henry James,* a good account of his life and work, told as far as possible in his own words, or, if not that, his jargon. In this account, in James's account, of the "American Scene," always the two elements are mingled, the physical and the mental elements. The "return of the native" was like a return into a Sahara: "One felt like a traveller in the desert, deprived of water and subject to the terrible mirage, the torment of illusion, of the thirst-fever. . . . And then this emptiness, this implacable emptiness: not a shadow, nothing but the glare of a commonplace prosperity." As to the city streets — "how deficient somehow in weight, volume, and resonance were the souls one discerned in these hurrying passers-by!" This emptiness, this implacable emptiness! It is the sense of that that I have been attempting to convey.

But I will insist no more: I have said enough to indicate the background, and James's attitude to that background: and a visit to North America today would be found by any European to confirm to some extent this account by James of the waste places of his birth. Of course, in the year 1934, there were few Americans of the type of Henry James in existence — they are as rare as the Redskin! The new United States will be a very different affair. But it will still be desertic.

In the interests of aesthetic theory I have been compelled to say all this: but before proceeding allow me to add that I have in America friends whom I respect and care for to a quite exceptional degree: and if they live in a desert, it is also true that they match the Arab in the fineness of their desert hospitality. I am writing only of North America in the aggregate, as a place to live and work in, for a specialist in one of the fine arts. I should expect him — apart from coon and gangster local colour — to be, like the Arab, better at abstract than at concrete values. And it is here the concrete values upon which I am so greatly insisting.

Having said all this, the question remains whether we in Europe today are not somewhat in the same case: the rapid changes in our cities, and in a lesser degree in our countryside, whether they are "Americanizing" us or not, are at least depriving us of the secular upholstery of our continent.

[1 *The Pilgrimage of Henry James,* p. 36.]

And the more and more disembodied character of our art is no doubt in response to this external impoverishment. Just as I think a very obstinate American could make something of the "American Scene" (even without passing over into a demented expressionism, as a desperate way out of the difficulty) so I think the intensification of the European Waste, physical and spiritual, does not preclude the possibility of artistic expression. But what I do say is that as progressively the Europeans, like a vast flock of sheep, allow their hereditary property to be pillaged, and find themselves more and more drifting into a sort of "Barrens" — and as their artists lose contact with nature, driven into the subterranean caverns of their memory and inherited imagination, that the products of the intellect will grow thinner and more shadowy, the very eyesight itself will become impaired — at the best an affair of abstract notation rather than of physical gusto. But what am I saying! Has not this physical gusto already vanished? In extreme cases it has arrived, at one imaginative jump, at that stage of the proceedings at which an algebraic expression — a heavily evocative line, picked out of some widely-known text — stands for the thing that is not written — that it is somehow no longer worth while to write.

No one, of the last hundred years, writing in English, is more worthy of serious consideration than Henry James. But from a cause as concrete — and regrettable — as a serious and crippling accident in boyhood would have been, his activities were all turned *inwards* instead of *outwards*. That is the point that I would make. He was, by force of circumstances, led to conceive of art as a disembodied statement of abstract values, rather than as a sensuous interpretation of values, participating in a surface life. "America, to James, signified failure and destruction. *It was the dark country, the sinister country, where the earth was a quicksand . . . where men were turned into machines. . . .* The American artist in the American air was a doomed man: pitfalls surrounded him on every side."[1]

And he early acquired the habit of living underground, and this habit he took with him from the "American Scene" into the "European Scene." As a pattern of life for the artist this is scarcely to be universally recommended. Is it not in fact the best way to extinguish the artistic impulse altogether, if taken to its bitter and barren, logical conclusion? Admiration for the finest of such achievements should not blind us critically to that pretty obvious fact.

As a contemporary illustration to all this, imagine Mr. T. S. Eliot's horror, just as he was doubtless congratulating himself upon his timely escape from that "dark country," that "sinister country," that country "where the earth is a quicksand," and his timely establishment in a land that is still fairly "well-furnished," where every blade of grass possesses an historic identity — in pre-war Britain in fine, to behold all this orderly little cosmos

---

[1] *The Pilgrimage of Henry James* [p. 29. Lewis's italics].

turning into ashes beneath his feet, at the blast of war, and then progressively assuming more and more, socially, the dread physiognomy of the desert
from which he was in flight! — We do not, indeed, have to look very far
for the origin of the *Waste Land.*

Before leaving this subject let me quote the father of Henry James, a very
interesting man indeed, who fully realized the dangers besetting the future
novelist (there was of course no danger for the philosopher — North America
is an admirable place for a philosopher). In 1849 he wrote to Emerson as
follows (I take this from the same excellent book by Mr. Van Wyck Brooks):

> Considering with much pity our four stout boys, who have no playroom
> within doors and import shocking bad manners from the street, we gravely
> ponder whether it wouldn't be better to go abroad for a few years with them,
> allowing them to absorb French and German, and get such a sensuous educa-
> tion as they cannot get here.[1]

That "sensuous education" which formerly Europe could be depended
upon to supply is assuming more tenuous proportions every day. But where
that sensuous education is lacking entirely, it must be very difficult to make
good the loss. And later a hatred, or at all events a distrust, of "the sensuous" is liable to develop. A great talent can make a powerful if eccentric
something out of this vacuum. But it is not an influence likely to promote
the general health of the arts, and the pagan robustness most suitable for
artistic production.

Coming back to the violently sensuous reality of "the gorgeous dolls,"
and making use of this desertic non-sensuous American background as an
object-lesson (or a lesson rather in the perishing of objects) the living dolls
today that we see, as much here as in an American city, are very drably
uniformed, to commence with. It is a natural tendency in the machine-age
(as this first century of machine life is often called) to ignore the dull and
artistically uninspiring externals, and to betake ourselves to the "disembodied." But the first great step upon the road of complete disembodiment
is to get *unclothed.*

Yes, of course: the next stage, or "period," of our civilized drabness will
be the *ensemble* — that *Nacktkultur* to which every "daring" forward step
of the sportsman and sportswoman tends. Now there is, in fact, as any
art student can tell you, nothing deliciously obscene about the naked body
of man or woman: the body has a quite spurious claim to that distinction.
Its traditional purple patches, its outstanding symbols of scandal, are useful
but not pretty — and most artist's models, whether man or woman, are just
that too. But what the naked human body can claim, is that it is at once

[1 *The Pilgrimage of Henry James,* p. 1]

soulful and abstract. A "gorgeous doll" — or a "doll" at all — suggests a *dressed* figure. A naked person is much less *a thing* than is a dressed person.

Confronted by Queen Elizabeth, for instance, "dolled-up" as she is shown us in any of her portraits, you would have much more the sensation of being in the presence of a life-size puppet than if you encountered her naked. The dressed-up, and even upholstered, doll-woman again, would at first appear far more *soul-less* than the same apparition naked. And this equally would hold if you met Frobisher or Drake fully dressed, or the same gentlemen again divested of their period-costume.

The minuet never could have been invented to be danced by naked people. If at that time people had not worn clothes, quite a different ceremonial dance would have been thought up for them. And if we want to know what that other dance would be like, we only have to turn to the specimens offered us by those people who have never deserted nature, or at most abstracted themselves from her to the extent of a loincloth.

Today the hat and coat are dropping off, for half a year; or for half the world have already done so. Stockings to some extent have gone for city-street wear: shoes and socks will give place to sandals. This in the northern summer is a good sanitary measure: if health alone were the object of the decline of body-covering, it would be sensible. But all sorts of arch moralist issues are imported into it. And, advertised for other purposes than the relief of the sweat-glands, the next step *is* the naked skin. And that, among other things, will save a great deal of money. Tomorrow the Proletariat will go practically naked (this will be for health, of course, not economy, but as I say it *will* be economical all the same), and it *will* in the end make them feel smaller, and more helpless, than they would do booted and spurred: and tomorrow practically everybody will be Proletariat. So they will be practically a naked Proletariat: and this will be very *abstract* indeed. And artists who are popularly supposed to be so fond of the jolly old *Altogether* will of course yawn their heads off — but that will be neither here nor there. And, anyway, it will only be the underdog who will have gone back to nature. The women-folk of the great ones of the earth will have finer clothes than ever.

But *today* is strictly speaking our subject (though the future as one of its two time-components is not so out of the picture as all that). Already today, however, as compared with any former times, in these parts of Europe, we look, from the outside, rather uniform and indeterminate — it will be readily conceded the proletarianization does that, science does that. All the influences in fact of the machine-age, political and intellectual, are productive of this back-to-nature, or *back-to-the-body*, movement, where our persons are concerned: an abstracting and abstracting of distinctive marks, of distinctive dress, until we get down to the puritanic bedrock of the bare body and no nonsense.

But in one sense — in the sense I am interrogating here — *back-to-the-body* means *down-to-the-soul* as well. And it is in very militant reaction against this tendency, artist that I am, that I have taken up these critical weapons, and loudly call upon you to take up yours as well — as far as that is possible, and as far as it is consonant with your duties as a good Marxist boy or girl, or a good little Camelot du Roi, or good little rationalization-robot, that is perfectly understood!

That people should have deliberately desired, at any period of the history of the human race, to have made themselves into puppets or dolls may seem strange at first sight. But such undeniably is the case. And what I am suggesting as best I can, in these pages, is just this — that there was a lot to be said for their odd infatuation.

The particular ritual that dress involves, and the dramatization of the body by dress is, I believe, the reflection of a higher culture in man than is the barren metaphysics of the Naked Body. The body, it is true, is alive and kicking, more or less: it is as slippery as an eel, and as explicit as an anatomy lesson. But it reduces the "soul," as well as the flesh, to a dead level, in practice: it spells the *"naked-truth"* all right for us! But is the naked truth exactly what we require as human beings? Many people have believed not, at one period or another, and I am of that opinion.

The nude is the native dress, as well, contrary to popular belief, of the moralist. If such and such a district were "the spiritual home" of the moralist, then *the nude* would be its national costume. (Even as regards sexual morality is this the case: for in Anatole France's parable Orbe Rose, in *L'Isle des pingouins*, by the simple expedient of draping a pink something upon her rolling hindquarters, demonstrated well enough that IT indeed resides in dress, and flies "the altogether.")

If you ask me whether human life does not bear looking at in the face, or in the flesh, I certainly could find no answer but No. Art, in the profoundest way, is the affirmation of that negative principle. And art is necessary to human existence, as clothes are necessary to our bodies. Furthermore, art consists among other things in a *mechanizing* of the natural. It bestows its delightful disciplines upon our aimless emotions: it puts its gentle order in the place of natural chaos: it substitutes for the direct image a picture. And, ultimately, and analysed far enough, it substitutes *a thing* for *a person* every time — and this is as true of the book as of the painted picture. In place of "real people," it hands you the actor and actress. And is not, even according to our present standards, the finest type of acting non-naturalist? Is it not a blemish for an actor or actress to make themselves photographically "real"? Are they not, in short, when at their best, in a sense puppets? And is not costume, a large repertoire of disguise, an essential part of their art — the theatrical wardrobe, in short? But is it our experience that when confronted with a cast of actors and actresses, who to this extent are playing the puppet, an audience is backward in extending its sympathy to these "dolls," gorgeous or otherwise? It is not, I believe I am right in saying — that is, an audience whose imagination has not been bled white. So, in that case, Henry James's assumption is not borne out by the facts of ordinary experience. "The reader who is set face to face with a gorgeous doll will assuredly fail to inspire it with sympathetic life." Put "audience" for "reader," and we are now prepared, I think, to confute that assertion.

CHAPTER V

VIRGINIA WOOLF

"MIND" AND "MATTER" ON THE PLANE OF
A LITERARY CONTROVERSY

"We must reconcile ourselves to a season of failures and fragments." — VIRGINIA WOOLF

BUT WITH SUCH A CHALLENGING capitulation as that of *Body and Soul,* or *Mind and Matter,* a misunderstanding is to be anticipated, and its action must now be forestalled. It has not been courted by me, but I have allowed the issue which might be responsible for it to remain dormant, in the margin, possibly dogging my progress, in order to deal with it at the conclusion of this phase of my argument.

The effect of what I have said so far might be to throw the reader into one camp or the other — and he might certainly have got the idea that only *two,* clearly defined, generally recognized, positions were involved: and he might in the end find himself in what, even from his own standpoint, was the wrong camp.

But *Body* and *Mind,* I need not remind the reader of such a book as this, are, philosophically, two very shadowy counters. There are, on the market today, patterns of belief extending from the extreme position, on the one hand, that there is in fact no traceable psyche, but only one stuff, out of which our world is composed, properly neither "matter" nor "mind"; to the extreme position on the other, which, as a matter of fact, is much the same as the former, only with a more strongly marked subjective flavouring. The single basic stuff is more soulful at that end that it is at the other, the deterministic end, that is all.

What, then, in the course of such an argument as this, one is compelled to anticipate, is a confusion arising from the equivocal nature of the popular counters one is bound to employ. For between the extreme positions I have indicated above there lie all the more orthodox concepts: it is in that strongly *black* and *white,* half-way region, in between, that the contests of the "materialists" and the "idealists" are fought out. For instance, the old battle of the Woolfs and the Bennetts had very little meaning outside of, or beyond, that orthodox plane.

Now there is one obvious division or opposition staring you in the face — and inviting you, on one side and the other, to drop into its pigeon-hole and be at peace — that is *the classification by gender:* the Masculine and the Feminine departments of the universe. Is it necessary for us to repeat here for the thousand and first time how illusory this division is found to be, upon inspection: to point out that many women are far more grenadiers or cave-men than they are little balls of fluff; and that, on the other hand, many men are much more fluffy and "girlish" than are their sisters: that a veneer of habit, and a little bit of hair on the chin and chest, is about all that fundamentally separates one sex from the other? — But this is not an account of the matter that would be found acceptable by militant feminism. I am afraid that a great deal of what might be termed *sex-nationalism* is to be met with, though certainly there are some very enlightened women, just as there are a handful of enlightened men, who frown on, and smile at, such working-up of hot party-feelings.

In the present chapter I am compelled, however, to traverse the thorny region of feminism, or of militant feminine feeling. I have chosen the back of Mrs. Woolf — if I can put it in this inelegant way — to transport me across it. I am sure that certain critics will instantly object that Mrs. Woolf is extremely insignificant — that she is a purely feminist phenomenon — that she is taken seriously by no one any longer today, except perhaps by Mr. and Mrs. Leavis — and that, anyway, feminism is a dead issue. But that will not deter me, any more than the other thorny obstacles, from my purpose: for while I am ready to agree that the intrinsic importance of Mrs. Woolf may be exaggerated by her friends, I cannot agree that as a symbolic landmark — a sort of party-lighthouse — she has not a very real significance. And she has crystallized for us, in her critical essays, what is in fact *the feminine* — as distinguished from the feminist — standpoint. She is especially valuable in her "clash" with what is today, in fact and in deed, a dead issue, namely nineteenth-century scientific "realism," which is the exact counterpart, of course, in letters, of French Impressionism in art (Degas, Manet, Monet).

But the photographic Degas, he is literally the end of the world, luckily — he is more than off the map; and following forty years behind the French mid-nineteenth century realists, the late Mr. Bennett was such a dead horse (dragging such a dead issue) that Mrs. Woolf was merely engaged in an undergraduate exercise in her pamphlet about him, it might be asserted. In spite of that, so long as prose-fiction continues to be written, the school of "realism" will always have its followers, in one degree or another. Mr. Hemingway is a case in point, and so is Mr. Faulkner. But in any work at all of prose-fiction, however *disembodied* in theory, there is, as an important, and indeed essential component, a great deal of the technique of "realism": further than that, it could quite well be contended that most of its technique was the realistic technique, put into the service of the depicting of the "disembodied." And, in any event, satire is a very *live* issue today, about that there can be little mistake. The most brilliant and interesting of the youngest poets, of the "new signatures," Auden, is above all a satirist. Mr. Roy Campbell, in his *Georgiad* has produced a masterpiece of the satiric art, which may be placed beside the eighteenth-century pieces without its suffering by that proximity. And what goes for prosody, goes for prose too. We are probably on the threshold, according to all the signs and portents, of a great period of imaginative satire — the times are propitious. And, establishing as I am here the theoretic foundations for such work, I have found that the criticism of "realism" is of very great use for a full illumination of my subject. And that is why I have considered it worth while to dissect in detail the Woolf-versus-the-realists controversy: and this course is, as I have said, especially indicated, owing to the part that the feminine principle plays in this debate.

Equipped with this explanation, I think we may now proceed. Well then, when Mrs. Woolf, the orthodox "idealist," tremulously squares up to the big beefy brute, Bennett,[1] plainly the very embodiment of commonplace *matter* — it is, in fact, a rather childish, that is to say an over-simple, encounter. It is a cat and dog match, right enough: but such "spiritual" values as those invoked upon Mrs. Woolf's side of the argument, are of a spiritualism which only exists upon that popular plane, as the complement of hard-and-fast matter. The one value is as tangible, popular and readily understood by the "plain reader" as the other. I doubt if, at bottom, it is very much more than a boy and girl quarrel (to change the metaphor from dog-and-cat). I believe it is just the old incompatability of the eternal feminine, on the one hand, and the rough footballing "he" principle — the eternal masculine — on the other. There is nothing more metaphysical about it than that.

"If we tried to formulate our meaning in one word we should say that these three writers [Wells, Bennett, Galsworthy] are materialists. It is because they are concerned not with the spirit but with the body that they have disappointed us," writes Mrs. Woolf. Is it so simple? Or rather, were we compelled to decide upon the respective merits of a person, of the same calibre as, say, Bennett, but who was as delicately mental as he was grossly material, and of Bennett himself, should we not have to say, that in their respective ways, their masculine and feminine ways, they were much of a muchness — indeed, *a good match*? The preoccupations of Mrs. Dalloway are after all not so far removed from the interests of Mr. Bennett's characters. One is somewhat nearer to "the Palace," the other to the "Pub." But does not that even suggest a subtle kinship, rather than an irreconcilable foreignness?

The question, indeed problem, of James is far more complicated. But still, even with him, we can I believe resolve the difficulty, in part, by making use of (without at all abusing) the categories of sex. There is a good deal of meaning in the statement that his was a "feminine" art. Before he had spent his first full year in Paris, in close contact with all the devils of "realism" in the flesh, we have surprised James suffering, at a distance, the first impact of that masculine doctrine: and, invested with that "famous realistic system which has asserted itself so largely in the fictitious writing of the last few years,"[2] we have discovered him sighing "for a novel with

[1] *Mr. Bennett and Mrs. Brown.*
[2] 1865. *Notes and Reviews.*

a *dramatis personae* of disembodied spirits": and what he subsequently did in that direction himself has become a monument, to which to refer the impatient world (which *will* not, even in England, quite take the shadow for the substance and which insists, barbarian that it is, upon its daily lump of bloodshot beef). Entrenched in the merely select regions of "difficult" authorship, we encounter many a talent which does not dispose of the necessary strength to brave the light of common day.

Again it must be remembered that even Henry James is a phenomenon exclusively of Anglo-Saxon letters. He has no such standing outside Anglo-Saxony as he has in it. He is a *good* example, it is true, of that class of non-universal intelligences, so spiritually idiomatic as to be at the best a mere curiosity for the outside world. If any meaning can be found for the term "classical," it certainly would be found to describe what James was *not*. But the sort of English writers for whom his prestige has been found useful, are exceedingly delicate plants — just as un-universal as himself and much more frail. If James proved himself unable "to stomach these ferocious companions" (namely the Flauberts, de Maupassants, de Goncourts and the rest, when he entered their vociferous circle in Paris) and if even the amiable Turgenev found that James's writing "had on the surface too many little flowers and knots of ribbon," that it was not "quite meat for men," how much more would that have been the case with these small, often portentously advertised, "misunderstood" intelligentsia, thrown up by our intellectually corrupt and dilettante society in England today? Accepted as Anglo-Saxon oddities *d'outre Manche* (with the prestige of the British banking system, rather than of British art), they would have been, in the exclusive circles of French literary craftsmanship of the Third Empire: never as fellow-artists.

In our island-controversies between the highbrows and the lowbrows, the typical British lowbrow can stand, as is to be expected, for the "creeping Saxon" right enough, or the imperial "squatter," who has dulled and degraded any part of the globe where he has "squatted" — staking out his claim to import and propagate a civilized vulgarity unheard of before the colonizing of the Anglo-Saxon began. But that is really not the point. The snobbish colonial official — the Anglo-Indian as the worst offender — is quite as vulgar as the antipodean squatter — he only looks grander and mixes yogi with his Scotch and baby "polly." But he is of the same indelibly *materialist* stock, and the yoginess does not alter that fact.

I must assume that you do not know, or I must recall to your mind, the parable of Mrs. Brown and Mr. Bennett. Mrs. Woolf tells us, in a skilful little sketch, how she enters the carriage of a suburban train, and in so doing intrudes unwittingly upon a rather passionate conversation of two people – one, *very large*, a blustering, thick-set, middle-aged bully of a *man*: the other, *very small*, a very pathetic, poor little old lady (not *quite* a lady – "I should doubt if she was an educated woman," says Mrs. Woolf – but none the less to be pitied for *that!*). The big bully had obviously been bullying the weaker vessel: and Mrs. Woolf calls the former Mr. Smith, the latter Mrs. Brown. As to make conversation before the inquisitive stranger in the other corner, or else dreaming aloud, the little old woman asks her *vis-à-vis* if he could tell her whether, after being the host for two years running of caterpillars, an oak-tree dies. And while Mr. Smith (who is a shamefaced coward, as are all big bullies come to that) is eagerly replying to this impersonal question, glad to be able to mask beneath an irrelevant stream of words his blackguardly designs upon the defenceless old lady, Mrs. Brown begins, without moving, to let fall tear after tear into her lap. Enraged at this exhibition of weakness on the part of Mrs. Brown (which he probably would refer to as "waterworks" or something brutal of that sort) the big bully, ignoring the presence of a third party, leans forward and asks Mrs. Brown point blank if she will do, yes or no, what he asked her to do just now, and poor Mrs. Brown says yes, she will. At that moment Clapham Junction presents itself, the train stops, and the big bully (probably jolly glad to escape from the eye of public opinion, as represented by Mrs. Woolf we are told – for he had little streaks of decency left perhaps) hurriedly leaves the train.

Now the point of the story is, we are told, that Mrs. Woolf, being born a novelist of course, and this episode occurring apparently before she had written any novels (1910 is the date implied) is in a quandary as to what to do. She would have *liked* to write a novel about Mrs. Brown, she tells us. But how was she to do it? For after all Wells, Galsworthy and Bennett (the only novelists apparently that, true child of her time, she knew about) had not taught her how to do it: the only tools (she apologizes for this professional word) available were those out of the tool-box of this trio. And alas! they were not suitable for the portrayal of Mrs. Brown. So what was poor little she to do?

She then enlarges upon her dilemma – which she tells us was also the dilemma of D. H. Lawrence, of E. M. Forster and the rest of the people she recognizes as the makers and shakers of the new-age (*all*, to a man, ruined by the wicked, inappropriate trio – I need not repeat the names).

Finding himself in the same compartment with Mrs. Brown, Wells would have looked out the window, with a blissful faraway Utopian smile on his face. He would have taken no interest in Mrs. Brown. Galsworthy would have written a tract round her: and Bennett would have neglected her "soul" for her patched gloves and stockings.

This was really a terrible situation for a novelist to be in, in 1910: and everything that has happened since, or to be more accurate, that has *not* happened since, is due to the shortcomings of this diabolical trio (but especially, we are led to understand, to the defective pen of the eminent Fivetowner).

And what this has meant for the novelist, it has meant also for the poet, essayist, historian and playwright. *The sins of the fathers shall be visited* — it is the old old story: it is the instinctive outcry of the war-time Sitwells and Sassoons, that is was their fathers and grandfathers who had caused the war — which, as I have been at pains to point out elsewhere (*The Great Blank of the Missing Generation*) is very much neglecting the fact that there were many other and more formidable persons in the world at the same time as the amiable and probably inoffensive old gentlemen who were responsible for this recriminating offspring: and that probably those progenitors of a "sacrificed" generation were just as powerless as their sons, or fathers, to cope with the forces, visible and invisible, which precipitated the World-War — although they no doubt deserve a curse or two, just as we do ourselves, for being so short-sighted, and so ill-equipped for defence, against all the dangers that beset a modern democracy.

What Mrs. Woolf says about the three villains of this highly artificial little piece is perfectly true, as far as it goes: "the difference perhaps is," she writes, "that both Sterne and Jane Austen were interested in things in themselves; in character in itself: in the book in itself." Of course, of course! who would not exclaim: it is not "perhaps" the difference — is as plain as the nose was on Hodge's face. Of course Sterne and Jane Austen were a different kettle of fish, both to Mrs. Woolf's three sparring partners or Aunt Sallies, and to Mrs. Woolf herself.

And then Mrs. Woolf goes on to tell us that we must not expect too much of Messrs. Eliot, Joyce, Lawrence, Forster, or Strachey either. For they all, in their way, were in the same unenviable position. All were boxed up with some Mrs. Brown or other, longing to "bag" the old girl, and yet completely impotent to do so, because no one was there on the spot to show them how, and they could not, poor dears, be expected to do it themselves! Do not complain of *us*, then, she implores her public. Show some pity for such a set of people, born to such a forlorn destiny! You will never get anything out of us except a little good stuff by fits and starts, a sketch or a fragment. Mr. Eliot, for instance, gives you a pretty line — a solitary line. But you have to hold your breath and wait a long time for the next. There are no "Passion flowers at the gate dropping a splendid tear" (cf. *A Room of One's Own*) — not in *our* time. There are just disjointed odds and ends!

"We must reconcile ourselves to a season of failures and fragments. We must reflect that where so much strength is spent on finding a way of telling the truth the truth itself is bound to reach us in rather an exhausted and chaotic condition. Ulysses, Queen Victoria, Mr. Prufrock — to give Mrs. Brown some of the names she has made famous lately — is a little pale and dishevelled by the time her rescuers reach her."[1]

[1] *Mr. Bennett and Mrs. Brown.*

There you have a typical contemporary statement of the position of letters today. Its artificiality is self-evident, if you do no more than consider
the words: for *Ulysses* however else it may have arrived at its destination,
was at least not *pale*. But here, doubtless, Mrs. Woolf is merely confusing
the becoming pallor, and certain untidiness of some of her own pretty salon
pieces with that of Joyce's masterpiece (indeed that masterpiece is implicated
and confused with her own pieces in more ways than one, and more
palpable than this, but into that it is not necessary to enter here). As to
the "strength spent in finding a way," that takes us back to the fable of
Mrs. Brown, and the fearful disadvantage under which Mrs. Woolf
laboured. Anyone would suppose from what she says that at the time in
question Trollope, Jane Austen, Flaubert, Maupassant, Dostoievsky,
Turgenev, Tolstoy, etc., etc., etc., etc., were entirely inaccessible to this
poor lost "Georgian" would-be novelist: it is as though she, Bennett, Wells
and Galsworthy had been the only people in the world at the time, and
as if there had been no books but their books, and no land but England.

The further assumption is that, prior to *Prufrock*, *Ulysses* and Mr. Lytton
Strachey's biographies, there had been either (1) no rendering of anything
so exclusive and remote as the "soul" of a person: or else (2) that the fact
that there was not much "soul" in the work of Mr. Bennett made it very
very difficult for Mr. Joyce to write *Ulysses*: and that by the time he had
succeeded in some way in banishing Mr. Bennett, he had only strength
enough left to concoct a "pale" little "fragment," namely *Ulysses*.

But, again, it is obviously the personal problems of Mrs. Woolf getting
mixed up with the problems of Mr. Joyce above all people! For it is quite
credible that Clayhanger, astride the island scene — along with his gigantic
colleagues, Forsyte and Britling — was a very real problem for the ambitious
budding pre-war novelist (especially as she was a little woman, and they
were great big burly men — great "bullies" all three, like all the men, confound them!).

But let us at once repudiate, as false and artificial, this account of the
contemporary situation in the "Mrs. Brown" fable. Joyce's *Ulysses* may be
"a disaster" — a failure — as Mrs. Woolf calls it in her Plain Reader. But it
is not a fragment. It is, of its kind, somewhat more robustly "complete"
than most of the classical examples of the novel, in our tongue certainly.
It is not the half-work in short, "pale" and "disheveled," of a crippled inter-
regnum. Nor is there anything *half-there* about D. H. Lawrence's books.
Far from being "pale," they are much too much the reverse.

If you ask: Do you mean then that there is nothing in this view at all,
of ours being a period of *Sturm und Drang*, in which new methods are
being tried out, and in which the artistic production is in consequence ten-
tative? I reply: There is nothing new in the idea at all, if you mean that
the present time differs from any other in being experimental and in
seeking new forms: or if you seek to use that argument to account for

mediocrity, or smallness of output, or any of the other individual "failures" that occur as a result of the natural inequality of men, and the certain precariousness of the creative instinct — subject, in the case of those over-susceptible to nervous shock, to intermittency of output, and, in extreme cases, to extinction.

Then why, you may enquire, is it an opinion that is so widely held? — Because — I again make answer — the people who have been most influential in literary criticism, for a number of years now, have been interested in the propagation of this account of things — just as the orthodox economists have, consciously or not, from interested motives, maintained in its place the traditional picture — that of superhuman *difficulty* — of some *absolute* obstructing the free circulation of the good things of life.

Those most influential in the literary world, as far as the "highbrow" side of the racket was concerned, have mostly been minor personalities, who were impelled to arrange a sort of bogus "time" to take the place of the real "time" — to bring into being an imaginary "time," small enough and "pale" enough to accommodate their not very robust talents. That has, consistently, been the so-called "Bloomsbury" technique, both in the field of writing and of painting, as I think is now becoming generally recognized. And, needless to say, it has been very much to the disadvantage of any vigorous manifestation in the arts; for anything above the *salon* scale is what this sort of person most dislikes and is at some pains to stifle. And also, necessarily, it brings into being a quite false picture of the true aspect of our scene.

So we have been invited, all of us, to instal ourselves in a very dim Venusberg indeed: but Venus has become an introverted matriarch, brooding over a subterranean "stream of consciousness" — a feminine phenomenon after all — and we are a pretty sorry set of knights too, it must be confessed, — at least in Mrs. Woolf's particular version of the affair.

> *I saw pale kings, and princes too,*
> *Pale warriors, death-pale were they all . . .*

It is a myopic humanity, that threads its way in and out of this "unreal city," whose objective obstacles are in theory unsubstantial, but in practice require a delicate negotiation. In our local exponents of this method there is none of the realistic vigour of Mr. Joyce, though often the incidents in the local "masterpieces" are exact and puerile copies of the scenes in his Dublin drama (cf. the Viceroy's progress through Dublin in *Ulysses* with the Queen's progress through London in *Mrs. Dalloway* — the latter is a sort of undergraduate imitation of the former, winding up with a smoke-writing in the sky, a pathetic "crib" of the firework display and the rocket

that is the culmination of Mr. Bloom's beach-ecstasy). But to appreciate
the sort of fashionable dimness to which I am referring, let us turn for a
moment to Mrs. Woolf, where she is apeeping in the half-light:[1]
"She had reached the park gates. She stood for a moment, looking at
the omnibuses in Piccadilly." She should really have written *peeping* at
the omnibuses in Piccadilly! — for "She would not say of anyone in the world
now that they were this or were that. She felt very young: at the same
time unspeakably aged. She sliced like a knife through everything: at the
same time was outside, looking on. She had a perpetual sense as she
watched the taxicabs, of being out, out, far out to sea and alone; she always
had the feeling that it was very, very dangerous to live even one day." To
live *outside*, of course that means. Outside it is terribly *dangerous* — in that
great and coarse Without, where all the he-men and he-girls "live-
dangerously" with a brutal insensibility to all the *risks* that they run, forever
in the public places. But this *dangerousness* does, after all, make it all very
thrilling, when peeped-out at, from the security of the private mind: "and
yet to her it was absolutely absorbing; all this, the cabs passing."

Those are the half-lighted places of the mind — in which, quivering with
a timid excitement, this sort of intelligence shrinks, thrilled to the mar-
row, at all the wild goings-on! A little old-maidish, are the Prousts and
sub-Prousts I think. And when two old maids — or a company of old
maids — shrink and cluster together, they titter in each other's ears and
delicately tee-hee, pointing out to each other the red-blood antics of this
or that upstanding figure, treading the perilous Without. That was the manner in which the late Lytton Strachey lived — peeping more into the past
than into the present, it is true, and it is that of most of those associated
with him. And — minus the shrinking and tittering, and with a commendable habit of standing, half-concealed, but alone — it was the way of life
of Marcel Proust.

But it has also, in one degree or another, been the way of life of many
a recent figure in our literature — as in the case of Marius the Epicurean,
"made easy by his natural Epicureanism . . . prompting him to conceive
of himself as but the passive spectator of the world around him." Some,
not content with retreating into the ambulatories of their inner consciousness, will instal there a sort of private oratory. From this fate "the
fleshly school" of the last century was saved, not much to its credit certainly, by the pagan impulses which still lingered in Europe. And it became
ultimately the "art-for-art's-sake" cult of the Naughty Nineties. Walter Pater
was, of course, the fountain-head of that cult. And he shows us his hero,
Marius — escaping from that particular trap, waiting upon the introverted —
in the following passage:

[1] *Mrs. Dalloway.* Virginia Woolf.

At this time, by his poetic and inward temper, he might have fallen a prey to the enervating mysticism, then in wait for ardent souls in many a melodramatic revival of old religion or theosophy. From all this, fascinating as it might actually be to one side of his character, he was kept by a genuine virility there, effective in him, among other results, as a hatred of what was theatrical, and the instinctive recognition that in vigorous intelligence, after all, divinity was mostly likely to be found a resident.

That is, from the horse's mouth, the rationale of the non-religious, un-theosophic, pleasure-cult, of which — in that ninetyish pocket at the end of the nineteenth century, in full, more than Stracheyish, reaction against Victorian manners — Oscar Wilde was the high-priest. And there is, of course, a very much closer connection than people suppose between the aesthetic movement presided over by Oscar Wilde, and that presided over in the first post-war decade by Mrs. Woolf and Miss Sitwell. (Miss Sitwell has recently been rather overshadowed by Mrs. Woolf, but she once played an equally important part — if it can be called important — in these events.) It has been with considerable shaking in my shoes, and a feeling of treading upon a carpet of eggs, that I have taken the cow by the horns in this chapter, and broached the subject of the part that the feminine mind has played — and minds as well, deeply feminized, not technically on the distaff side — in the erection of our present criteria. For fifteen years I have subsisted in this to me suffocating atmosphere. I have felt very much a fish out of water, very alien to all the standards that I saw being built up around me. I have defended myself as best I could against the influences of what I felt to be a tyrannical inverted orthodoxy-in-the-making. With the minimum of duplicity I have held my own: I have constantly assailed the swarms of infatuated builders. So, having found myself in a peculiarly isolated position, I had begun to take for granted that these habits of mind had come to stay, in those about me, and that I must get used to the life of the outlaw, for there was nothing else to do. But it seems that I was perhaps mistaken. There is, to judge from all the signs, a good chance that a reversal of these values — the values of decay — is at hand. So in my next chapter I make, with more likelihood of a certain, not unpowerful, support than is customary, an expedition into the *bad-lands*.

CHAPTER VI

THE BAD-LANDS

IN THE MARTYRS OF THE MARSH

"Ready to indulge in the luxury of decay, and amuse himself
with fancies of the tomb." – WALTER PATER

IN THE FIVE FOREGOING CHAPTERS I have been road-making – a Roman
occupation! And I have been driving my causeway across what is in fact
an inconvenient and insanitary bog. More and more Roman! – But I could
scarcely claim that my objective has been an imperial one. It has been even
in part private and personal. But the public spirit, the Roman spirit, has
been present as well. It has been my intention in short that *other* people,
whose business takes them in this direction, should make use of the road
I have been constructing with such care. If temperamentally they prefer
the difficult, of course that is another matter, and I know that many do.
Let them by all means continue to use the tortuous and waterlogged paths
as before. But cross this region they *must*, if they are to "get anywhere":
and we see stuck all over it, as we approach it, melancholy (and they would
have us say "tragic") figures – the figures of people with little sense of direction, of feeble will, and a probably prenatal disposition to "get stuck" and
acquire merit by sombrely wrestling with insuperable obstacles –
monuments of frustration, but also of vanity. However, all the world, or
all the intelligent, are not like that; and here is a road of sorts – I may have
too hastily referred to it as Roman, I do not know: but at least it is passably
straight, from terra firma to terra firma, by the shortest route, though I
do not claim you can pass by it under a few exacting hours of hard going:
but if you know of a shorter, make it by all means: but *cross* the beastly
stretch you must, as I have said.

What, then, is this waterlogged stretch of territory, which it is necessary
to negotiate, but which has proved a profitable trap to so many tragical
stick-in-the-muds – whose portentous torsos remain, in a distracted im-
mobility, upon all hands, as dark warnings to all and sundry not to engage
in this peculiar Slough of Despond? – at once warnings and sly invitations?
And what manner of person are they who compose this gallery of scare-
crows, waving (at rare intervals) inarticulately a drooping-arm, as a signal
of distress, and emitting unintelligible incantations?

Well, the waterlogged stretch is simply the post-war decade-and-a-half,
or rather that period as it is represented in the field of art and letters. And
the derelicts that spot it like the legless statues scattered over the landscape

of Rapa Nui, are the ladies and gentlemen who have been and are luminaries of Anglo-Saxon art and letters.

But this waterlogged stretch is coeval with the uninterrupted chain of "crises" which started as soon as the obscene saturnalia of the war came to a close. It is a purely mental bog — at least in so far as the Want-in-the-midst-of-Plenty is artificial, this "waste-land" is artificial. It is a deliberate inundation, that has become chronic. And, just as in the other case, upon the popular and political plane, a man-made famine is accepted as a visitation of the inscrutable powers of nature — there is no orthodox economist who does not set out from that premise — so in this other field of intellectual endeavour (or its opposite) the same sort of assumption is the order of the day, with only this difference, that occasionally, instead of a terrible natural visitation, it is regarded as a god-sent punishment for mortal wickedness.

Most of the protests, which, from time to time, have broken forth against this policy of despair and of do-nothing, have come from the most compromising quarter possible: some indignant "hearty" has suddenly "gone off the deep end" about all this "spinelessness" — very erect (the *spine* very much in evidence) — very red in the face (from a rush of *red-blood* to the head) — very much puffing and snorting with the he-mannish instinct to castigate all these "slackers" and "cissies"! That of course has only caused the martyrs-of-the-marsh, as they might be called, entrenched in their inaccessible bog, to titter in their sleeves. That was all excellent advertisement for them — so what we want, in order to shift them, and in order to discredit the bog, is a different approach from that. If you are to discourage these depressing exhibitionists and solemn buffoons of the bad-lands, you must think of something better to do than to puff out your masculine plastron and admonish them to "be men" or anything idiotic of that sort — or to be womanly-women or mothers of men. You must go about it rather more scientifically than that. You must, in short, analyse *the bog*, the local conditions that promote its continuance. And then, as to the *genii loci* of the bad-lands, or waste-lands, in question, you must psycho-analyse them at once and shoo them out of their pits with unpleasant laughter, rather than with respectful and hortatory wrath. For they are not by any means harmless — men are imitative and they attract a crowd of followers: on the other hand they are not to be taken as anything more serious than as jokes of the Zeitgeist.

·   ·   ·   ·   ·   ·

A book has been published recently, entitled *The Romantic Agony*, by Prof. Mario Praz.[1] Confronted with this immense mass of intelligent

[1] Oxford University Press, by whose kind permission the subsequent extracts are quoted.

erudition—the harvest of a really first-rate piece of highly selective field-work—there is no one, I believe, who would remain unconvinced, of how, *at every pore*, the post-war period has sucked in the stale and sickly airs which have been hanging over Europe for a century (the putrefaction of the *ancien régime*, guillotined but imperfectly interred) and has fed itself on the same poisons for choice, as those employed for purposes of mental stimulation by the distinguished diabolists—Lord Byron, Huysmans, Baudelaire, Wilde, De Lautréamont, and the rest of them. It is a history of a century of diabolics—of *Fleurs du mal*, of the *homme fatal* as drama-tized by Byron—in his pageant of a (satanic) heart—of *Pen, Pencil and Poison* (the exaltation of the murderer, preceded by De Quincey's), of *Dorian Gray* and the exaltation of the pederast—but the list, both of names and attributes, is endless. It is the carefully-documented historical counter-part of the *Diabolical Principle*, and the sequel to the Machiavelli chapters of *The Lion and the Fox*.

If there is one thing which stands out more clearly than another from this gigantic pile of satanic bric-a-brac, so industriously assembled, under my directions (cf. *The Diabolical Principle*, etc.), by Prof. Praz, it is the astonishing rôle which is played by *morals*—specifically, of course, the Christian, or Judaic, ethic—in all this spectacle of calculated perversity. It is in fact the disintegration of Christendom that we are witnessing in all these outbursts, and the hysteria of Swinburne as much as the hysteria of Huysmans, in their monotonous insistence upon what is "evil," is patently a consequence of the fact that they are *good* boys gone wrong. They are haunted and terrified by the minatory injunctions of the Mosaic Law. It is the release from two thousand years of suppression and from the reign of an ascetic principle of life. Byron, Wilde, Huysmans (that is to say— incest, pederasty and homicide)—what is that, at bottom, but the good old melodrama of *The Girl who took the Wrong Turning*? And, indeed, how *girlish* are all these intellectual leaders—from the vulgar showing-off propensities of the social pet, the *Childe Harold*, the *Don Juan*, to the same propensities in the yet more feminine figure, Oscar Wilde, with whom the healing gush of tears was never far away, and whose strangely disgusting spasms of religiosity matched his bravado as an "evil-doer." What would a Greek (brought up in the recognition as "natural" of what Oscar Wilde regarded as deliciously "unnatural") what would Alcibiades, as an eminent example, have made of this fat Dublin buffoon, horrifying the mob, and himself into the bargain, by his "wickedness"! He could have been little else but an object of astonished derision. And yet his silly old "vice," and the startling advertisement-value attached to it, has upset our society for three decades!

Here surely is an object-lesson, if one were needed, in the disadvantages of an excessive development of the ethical will: for by the simple expe-dient of reversing it, it can be converted into a first-class instrument of farcical self-display, with all the army of false values that marches upon the heels of such an operation.

The enormous part, however, aside from such glaring examples as the author of *De Profundis*, that the moralist-mind played in this century of diabolics can be demonstrated by a brief interrogation, from this point of view, of one or two of the conspicuous participants in the saturnalia in question. Walter Pater, "the forerunner of the Decadent Movement in England," as Prof. Mario Praz calls him, will serve our turn very well.

We must not, Mr. T. S. Eliot warns us,[1] regard Walter Pater as essentially the "aesthete": for

> Pater was . . . a moralist. . . . Even in that part of his work which can only be called literary criticism, Pater is always primarily the moralist. In his essay on Wordsworth he says: "To treat life in the spirit of art, is to make life a thing in which means and ends are identified: to encourage such treatment, the true moral significance of art and poetry." That was his notion: to find the "true moral significance of art and poetry."

Or again:

> When we read him on Leonardo or Giorgione, we feel that there is the same preoccupation, coming between him and the object as it really is. He is, in his own fashion, moralizing upon Leonardo or Giorgione, on Greek art or on modern poetry. His famous dictum: "Of this wisdom, the poetic passion, the desire of beauty, the love of art for art's sake has most: for art comes to you professing frankly to give nothing but the highest quality to your moments as they pass, and simply for those moment's sake," is itself a theory of ethics; it is concerned not with art but with life. The second half of the sentence . . . is a serious statement of morals.

And these statements of Mr. Eliot's I am sure should satisfy us as to the bona fides of Walter Pater as a moralist. Actually it was this exaggerated development of his ethical will that provided the impulse for his particular contribution to the diabolics of his time. "Pater . . . had from childhood a religious bent," Mr. Eliot tells us: "he was 'naturally Christian' ": but these happy dispositions, owing to some flaw in the theologic workmanship, caused him to be responsible for what is popularly regarded as the most "immoral" outburst of any yet in modern England — the "Naughty Nineties."

His innovations in the anti-moral line are described as follows by Prof. Mario Praz:

> Walter Pater, the forerunner of the Decadent Movement in England (particularly in his conclusion to *Studies in the Renaissance* (1873), the book from which we have quoted the famous passage where the "Medusean" type of beauty is found incarnate in La Gioconda) shows himself as being "ready to indulge in the luxury of decay, and amuse himself with fancies of the tomb"

[1] *Selected Essays.* T. S. Eliot, p. 386.

— to use a phrase from *Duke Carl of Rosenmold* — in his tales of the muffled lives of exquisitely meditative youths (see *A Child in the House*, and the characteristic fate of all these youths, Marius the Epicurean, Flavian, Watteau, Duke Carl of Rosenmold), and of beauty devastated by cruelty (Denys l'Auxerrois).

The feminine souls of Pater's "frail androgynous beings" are already open to all the influences of the Decadence; Duke Carl of Rosenmold is a sensual dilettante in the manner of Ludwig II of Bavaria or of des Esseintes. It was not therefore astonishing that Pater should have crowned with his approval the *Confessions of a Young Man* (1888), in which George Moore finally succeeded, after various unsuccessful attempts (early verse imitated from Baudelaire, *Flowers of Passion*, 1878, *Pagan Poems*, 1881; the novels *A Mere Accident*, 1887 and *Mike Fletcher*, 1889) in presenting to the younger generation in England, already saturated with Pater's aestheticism, a version — which was somewhat superficial, it is true — of the gospel of Mademoiselle de Maupin and *A rebours*.[1]

It is perhaps unnecessary to point out how tales of "the feminine souls," of "the muffled lives of exquisitely meditative youths," belong to that dim world of the essentially feminine sensibility, with which we have been so closely concerned in the foregoing chapters. The exquisite palsies or languors of decay are — at full strength, if one may so paradoxically express oneself — present in this mid-Victorian moralist aesthete. The fisticuffs of Lord Queensberry are already mobilized in the wings: and to come down to the present time, the droopings and wiltings of Mr. Prufrock, or, better, the androgynous permutations of *Orlando*, might already have been foreseen.

Next, as a mate for Pater, we can take André Gide — for as Pater stands to Oscar Wilde, so Wilde stands to Gide. So we shall have three consecutive generations of moralists — of moralists-gone-wrong. And let me go to Mr. Eliot the critic for help, for a moment, too, in the matter of Gide. Yes, Gide, is a true moralist, we find, sure enough! "Certainly, a writer may be none the less classified as a moralist," Mr. Eliot lays it down, "if his moralizing is suspect or perverse. We have today a witness in the person of M. André Gide." (No wonder Mr. Eliot desires to see "Morals put in their proper place" somewhat!)

To give you some idea of the excellent thoroughness of this book of Prof. Praz, I will quote practically intact what he has to say about André Gide:

> Gide, with his own "fond noir à contenter," came under the dominant influence of Nietzsche and Dostoievsky and the more special influence of Wilde. "Etre ondoyant et divers," du Bos has described him — and perhaps one might add without further ado, a moral hermaphrodite, suspended among various potentialities, and, in consequence, negative, sterile. . . . He has, on the one hand, a fear of committing himself, and on the other, as du Bos remarks, a violent desire to commit himself. In the former is reflected his psychological ambiguity, in the latter the sadistic pleasure of the sensation

[1] *The Romantic Agony.* [p. 341–342].

of pride in one's own humiliation, and of violating and shocking the modesty of others, such as made Dostoievsky and his heroes burst forth into devastating confessions, and caused Gide to write *Si le grain ne meurt*. (One might quote as a more immediate source Wilde's attitude to scandal, except that there is more seriousness in Gide than in Wilde.) The result of this complex psychological formation was that Gide took up the attitude of a "martyr of pederasty," thus satisfying his homosexual and his algolagnic desires at the same time. It is scarcely necessary to mention that the "Prometheus" pose and the taste of satanism, the "ricanement intérieur," which are to be found in Gide, are sadistic qualities.

Certain passages from *L'Immoraliste* may be quoted in illustration of this. Michel, when he discovers that the Arab boy Moktir is a thief, instead of being angry, is delighted, and makes the thief his favourite; he is fascinated by the corrupt peasant, Bute, and by the poachers whom he accompanies in their nocturnal expeditions; at Syracuse he delights in the "société des pires gens"; he finds pleasure — even a "savoureux bonheur" — in telling lies; he possesses Marceline after a violent struggle in which he subdues and binds a drunken coachman ("Ah! quels regards après, et quels baisers nous échangeâmes . . ."); he admires that miniature Heliogabalus, King Atalaric, who, suborned by the Goths, rejected his Latin education, gave himself up to debauchery "avec de rudes favoris de son âge," and died, after a short life "violente, voluptueuse et débridée," at the age of eighteen; he proclaims that his merit consists in "une espèce d'entêtement dans le pire." The influence of Wilde, whom Gide had met in Algeria, is obvious; Wilde is to a certain extent the character of Ménalque, the corruptor, who preaches the cult of the Greek world and insinuates the Nietzschean principle of the right of might. And like Sibyl Vane in *The Picture of Dorian Gray* — of which an echo can be discerned in this book — Marceline is sacrificed to the brutal egotism of the man. . . . The same themes recur in the *Faux-monnayeurs* (1925). Little Georges is surprised in a theft, and becomes, for this reason, of special interest to Edouard (the character who represents the author himself), and all the more exciting when he is discovered to be his nephew. The incident which gives the title to the novel — that of the schoolboys who lend themselves to the circulation of false coin — is a sign of the same idiosyncrasy: the author enjoys the contemplation of the moral corruption of these seductive youths. One of them, Ghéridanisol, sets an infernal trap for the weak, feminine Boris, with the intention of leading him to commit "un acte monstrueux": this act is the suicide of Boris under the eyes of his grandfather, who, in his desperation, develops theories of diabolical mysticism:

"Et savez-vous ce que Dieu a fait de plus horrible? . . . C'est de sacrifier son propre fils pour nous sauver. Son fils! son fils! . . . la cruauté, voilà le premier des attributs de Dieu."

In this remark old M. La Pérouse seems to speak like a character from Dostoievsky; and very much in the manner of Dostoievsky also are the characters of Armand and of Strouvilhou — Armand who, like the hero of *Letters from the Underworld*, finds a bitter pleasure in degradation, abets and at the same time denounces the prostitution of his sister Sarah, contracts a venereal disease, and refuses to have it attended to in order to "pouvoir se dire, quand on commence à se soigner: 'il est trop tard!' "; and Strouvilhou whose nihilistic ideas, instilled into the mind of his young cousin Ghéridanisol, culminate in the sacrifice of Boris. Armand commits incest with his sister by proxy; in the morning he comes into the room where Bernard has slept with Sarah with his consent, and—

"s'avance vers le lit ou sa soeur et Bernard reposent. Un drap couvre à demi leurs membres enlacés. Qu'ils sont beaux! Armand longuement les contemple. Il voudrait être leur sommeil, leur baiser. Il sourit d'abord, puis, au pied du lit, parmi les couvertures rejetées, soudain s'agenouille. Quel dieu peut-il prier ainsi, les mains jointes? Une indicible émotion l'étreint. Ses lèvres tremblent. . . . Il aperçoit sous l'oreiller un mouchoir taché de sang; il se lève, s'en empare, l'emporte et, sur la petite tache ambrée, pose ses levres en sanglotant."

Here Armand is modelled on Dostoievsky's Idiot; in another place he is possessed by that same "imp of the perverse" upon which Poe, Baudelaire and Dostoievsky had all dilated, and tortures his sister Rachel, who is going blind, by his revelation of Sarah's guilt:

"Armand avait une main sur la poignée de la porte; de l'autre, avec sa canne, il maintenait la portière soulevée. La canne entra dans un trou de la portière et l'agrandit.

" 'Explique ça comme tu pourras, dit-il, et son visage prit une expression très grave. — Rachel est, je crois bien, la seule personne de ce monde que j'aime et que je respecte. Je la respecte parce qu'elle est vertueuse. Et j'agis toujours de manière à offenser sa vertu. Pour ce qui est de Bernard et de Sarah, elle ne se doutait de rien. C'est mois qui lui ai tout raconté. . . . Et l'oculiste qui lui recommande de ne pas pleurer! C'est bouffon!' "

The women in this novel, Laura, Pauline, Rachel, sacrificed and tortured, are remote descendants of Sade's virtuous Justine. (Actually, here, not even Juliette could have escaped, for Lilian, who is by no means virtuous, ends by being barbarously murdered by her lover Vincent.) Rouveyre makes the following remark on Gide's female characters.

"Ses sacrifiées religieuses, Gide les traite con amore, et pourtant, cruel tourmenteur, il va jusqu'à refuser à la dernière et à la plus significative de ses héroïnes (Gertrude de la Symphonie) la joie même de la lumière du jour, et c'est une aveugle que l'Amour voudrait bercer dans ses bras adorables. Gide imagine que, une opération lui donnant la lumière, cette âme, étrangement défaite, en est livrée naturellement au suicide."

Although Gide's work extends to our own times, it is in the Decadent Movement that it has its roots.[1]

This extremely long extract from the book of Professor Praz will, I hope, have the result of furthering its sales and putting its invaluable synthesis of information at the disposal of more people. — But where Professor Praz remarks that the work of Gide is that of a "decadent" artist whose work is still going on, "which extends to our own times," he (perhaps deliberately — perhaps there are "romantic" friends of his whom he wishes to leave out, so has to stop short where he does!) is assuming that the spirit to whose analysis he has devoted so much time, is at an end. Of course nothing could be farther from the truth. People who were not born when André Gide was gathering experiences crystallized in Si le grain ne meurt, are today, in their own moralist fashion, producing work, not certainly

---

[1] The Romantic Agony, pp. 365–369.

as important, but at least equally "romantic," in the sense understood by Mario Praz. It was for instance remarked at the time with considerable astonishment that *Point Counter Point* bore a strange resemblance to Mr. Gide's book, which had preceded it by a few years, I think I am right in saying. But it is even unnecessary to be very specific. When the literary historian of the future comes to cast his eye over our little post-war age, he will not have to go very much to the heart of the matter to detect that he is in the presence of an ethos bearing a very close resemblance to that of the Naughty Nineties: he will see the trial of Wilde as the grand finale of the "naughty" decade — then fourteen humdrum years of Socialist tract-writing — then the war — and then *more* "naughtiness." He will perhaps meditate — "Here was a people, moralist to the core, who only possessed two modes of expression, one childishly rebellious, the other dully dutiful!"

That our bad-lands have been a different sort of bad-lands to that of the scene surveyed by Whistler and by Wilde is evident enough: our *bad* has not been quite their *bad* — it has been indelibly tinged with what I have called *badtimism* among other things: it has possessed none of the friskiness, the air of irresponsible leisure, nor for that matter the extremism. But such an event as the War, 1914–18, does knock the stuffing out of a people, and already in 1920 the shadows of proletarianization were gathering fast. But all the same, in its dull way, the last decade and a half, our *Only Yesterday*, has kept the Jolly Roger of "Romance" flying as best it could.

Neither De Quincey nor Wilde could have given us points in veneration for the violent: the headmaster of Eton (Dr. Allington) has run a "Crime Club": the murder-game has been a typical highbrow amusement like the Victorian *charade*: and an immense murder-literature has sprung up (one of our most eminent social reformers, Mr. G. D. H. Cole, spends half his time drawing up instructions for salvationist revolution, half in spinning murder-plots): one of the principal highbrow papers, Mr. Desmond MacCarthy's *Life and Letters*, for some years (the fashion now has passed) "carried" nothing but news of imaginary crimes of violence: the respective merits of this, that and the other fiction murder-expert were solemnly canvassed. Also, a significant change from Edgar Wallace, the murderer became "sympathetic" and might have the better of the argument. Then came the immense romance-of-blood of the Gangster: fifteen thousand Sicilians in Chicago demonstrated unchecked their mastery in the art of assassination, and the blood-stained annals of their star killers were greedily perused, or witnessed on the films with gulps of hysterical satisfaction. It was as much a matter of common knowledge that *Aida* was Capone's favourite opera, as with the Yellow Book criminologists it was a matter of history that the poisoner Wainewright adored the *Sogno di Polifilo*. That the second-hand violence of the dime novel, or of Adelphi Melodrama, has always attracted the mob — or in a more openly brutal time, the bear-pit and cock-fight — is true enough: but what has been really peculiar to us (for the Elizabethan man about town scorned the tragedy of blood) has been that the most educated, as well as the least educated, participated in these pleasures, almost to the exclusion of any other. The Cabinet Minister, the philosophy-don, the Harley Street Specialist, the "rebel" poet, as much as the scullery-maid and office-boy, pored over a long succession of detective-fictions and *nothing else.* This has been one of the features of our proletarianization: our pleasures have become the pleasures of the mob. You have to imagine, for example, a Chesterfield, a Pitt, or a Burke occupied in their spare moments with nothing but books of the order of the "Crime Club," or the Gem Library, to get the point of this perhaps (for the average man has to resort to artifice to regard a little impersonally his own time, and nothing seems more natural after a year or two than what has the sanction of the will of the majority).

But meanwhile our Theatre has fallen into a state of complete decay: and the commercialization of the book-trade (of publishing, that is) has organized on an unprecedented scale, among educated people, the values and tastes of the cinema-mob. And of course all these things hang together, it is a perfect co-ordination of inferior values — the values of the least gifted and the least educated.

This great decay is, however, a very recent thing: whereas the so-called "decadence" of romantic art was on the way already at the turn of the eighteenth century. But it really is surprising how few of the famous writers of the last twenty years would not fit into the "romantic" category, as conceived by Mario Praz. D. H. Lawrence and Ronald Firbank, to take a couple, are almost perfect specimens for his exotic museum. And of course it is pretty certain that the exceedingly low temperatures, the atmosphere of *pompes funèbres* of his *Waste Land,* and his still more Hollow Men, qualifies Mr. T. S. Eliot for a place in this "romantic" inferno. These hymns of capitulation breathe an air that, after journeying with Professor Praz for some time, has a somehow familiar sound. Mr. Eliot's is, I am very much afraid, a "romantic agony," after all. But everyone must pick their specimens for themselves. There is here a principle of decay, a *suicide club* effect: with all the animal pleasures of life, and borrowing from the intellect a destructive intensity, and dragging the intellect with them down into their frantic maelstrom — "In the destructive element immerse"!

Professor Praz gives us, in a long quotation, Croce's account of this *mal du siècle,* and for him it is a borderland phenomenon — occurring upon the collapse of the hereditary values, before minds have secured themselves upon the New Land, beyond the romantic agonies of the dissolution. "This malady was due," Croce's words,

> not so much to breaking away from a traditional faith, as to the difficulty of really appropriating to oneself and living the new faith, which, to be lived and put into action, demanded courage and a virile attitude, also certain renunciations of bygone causes of self-satisfaction and comfort which had now ceased to exist; . . . This may have been feasible to robust intellects and characters, who were able to trace back the genetic process of the new faith without being overthrown by it, and, through inner conflicts, to reach their haven, and was also feasible, in a different way, to simple, clear minds and straightforward natures who immediately understood, adopted and prac-tised its conclusions, captivated by the light of their goodness; but it was not within reach of feminine, impressionable, sentimental, incoherent, fickle minds, . . . which liked and sought out dangers and then perished in them.[1]

[1 *The Romantic Agony*, p. xii.]

CHAPTER VII

THE TERMS "CLASSICAL" AND "ROMANTIC"

"Classisch ist das Gesunde, Romantisch das Kranke."
— GOETHE
"The world has declared for Dido against Aeneas and Rome." — Professor GRIERSON
"In the classic it is always the light of ordinary day, never the light that never was on land or sea." — T. E. HULME, *Speculations.*

WE HAVE SEEN, in the last chapter, the term "romantic" endowed with a special, and a little strained, significance. For, although all those exceedingly emotional sectaries of "the diabolical principle," were, to a man, literati of the so-called romantic school, yet not quite everybody belonging to that school can be described as a diabolist. And there is, I think, a different definition, from that implied by Professor Praz, of the term "romantic," and one of considerable use to us in critical controversy.

The obstacles to any rigid definition of these terms are many and powerful. In Professor Grierson's very interesting lecture, *Classical and Romantic*, they manifest their full force, and I think they triumph. To commence with, he points out how Heine and De Musset both, for instance, identified the romantic spirit with Christianity. That narrows it down a good deal — or widens it out. For the former Romanticism was a "passion-flower which sprung from the blood of Christ." For the latter, Romanticism was "a reactionary movement dating from the Restoration of the Bourbons, a sentimental revival of mediaeval Catholicism." It will be seen that Heine's account was nearer to that of Professor Praz than is De Musset's — for at least a blood-stained passion-flower brings us within hailing distance of the Marquis de Sade, André Gide, Lord Byron and the rest of them, more than does the frigid version of De Musset.

Heine, however, had a lot to say on the subject of Christianity it seems (I will quote from Professor Grierson): Christianity "in whose primary doctrine is contained a condemnation of all flesh; which not only gives to the spirit the control over the flesh but will destroy the flesh in order to exalt the spirit"; and from this he deduces historically all the characteristics of mediaeval art and poetry.

In the analysis of the terms "romantic" and "classical" Christianity seems then to be an important factor. But is the term "classical" to be identified with the Hellene, as the term "romantic" is to be identified with mediaeval Christianity? I suggest we pursue the latter term into its alleged religious background for a moment. For this purpose I will recall the arguments of the Nietzschean anti-Christian offensive.

The essence of the Nietzsche criticism of Christianity was as follows: With his Power doctrine, he saw in Christianity nothing but a slave-ethic, as he called it. Historically, was it not a "dope" provided for the great masses of Roman slaves, among whom it first established a foothold? As the mithraic cult was the popular religion of the Roman soldier, so Christianity was that of the Roman slave: for this "other worldliness" was obviously the only sort of thing that could meet the case of a class of men who had nothing to get out of *this* world. The slave would eagerly grasp at a promise of *another* life than ours, in which *he* would be the top-dog. And, for a person whose lot was so cast as to condemn him forever to a perpetual renunciation of every impulse of pride or will, certain injunctions of mildness, of "offering the other cheek," and so forth, were perfectly suited and might provide some consolation for the spectacle of his powerful masters enjoying what he might never hope himself to enjoy. That is, I think, a fair paraphrase of Nietzsche's account of Christianity.

That if the Christian religion does not begin and end with the Sermon on the Mount I need not remark I suppose: nor that Christianity has taken many forms. But that in the first centuries of Christianity it must have looked, to an intelligent Roman, very much what Nietzsche describes, is clear enough. And at the present juncture — which has very much the appearance of a final break-up of the Western nations as they took shape on the dissolution of the Roman power — when the European is submitting to the progressive deterioration of his standards, it would be as well for those who are influential in the Christian churches *not* to "move with the times" too much, in the sense of invoking *all* the disciplines most suitable for a meagre and slavish life; just as exhortations to ECONOMY addressed to a man living in a more and more straitened manner, an existence of "want-in-the-midst-of-plenty," are apt not to be well received. I venture to express this opinion as I feel that the theological mind is not at its best in deciding what is appropriate and what inappropriate. And there are some provisions that might seem too pat. Thus, if ever there were a time for keeping discreetly in the background all the asceticism, which is an integral part of the pure doctrine of Christianity, it is today.

The "destruction of the flesh in order to exalt the spirit" was a characteristic of the romantic mind, which it derived from the primary doctrine of Christianity, that was Heine's view. And of course there is a good deal of destruction in even the most "fleshly" flights of a Marquis de Sade, and a great insistence upon *pain* in all the long line of sensualist doctrinaires of the extremist wing of Romanticism (those who supply Professor Praz with his quarry). — Would it be possible to say, I wonder, merely as a means of reaching some concrete understanding upon the correct application of these terms, that (without at all involving any religious issue) the term *classical* should stand *rather than not* for the body, and the term "romantic" stand *rather than not* for "the soul"? — Or instead of flesh and spirit, let us put concrete and psychical (matter and mind) — rather in the way that the Roman Catholic religion is always described by the theosophist as "such a *material* religion" — "material" used in some such connotation as that?

At all events, I always think of something very *solid*, and I believe it is a sensation I share with many people, when the term "*classic*" is employed, and of something very dishevelled, ethereal and misty, when the term "romantic" is made use of. — All compact of common sense, built squarely upon Aristotelian premises that make for permanence — something of such a public nature that all eyes may see it equally — something of such a universal nature, that to all times it would appear equal and the same — such is what the word *classic* conjures up. But at *romantic* all that falls to pieces. There is nothing but a drifting dust, a kaleidoscope of undirected particles, which no logical pattern holds together, or only a very feeble one.

What we start from — in any attempt to place before us these two things — is the conception of an order on the one side, of a chaos on the other. And this is only "material," after all, in the sense that order signifies the same material as chaos, but that material logically co-ordinated: and the "immaterial," what is that except a concentrated something disintegrated, and scattered? Concrete does not mean a thing you cannot put your finger through, so much as a thing your mind can contain and compass. The romantically "mental" is thus merely something that no longer ends when the intellect ends, and the classically "material" is merely, on this plane, a cosmos, not a chaos. And that idea of something *solid* is just an effect of that geometric quality, belonging to all that is recognizably Classic, or even a distant cousin of that, in contrast to the gaseous and nebulous explosion of an intellect losing itself in the black vault of the sky, having blown a hole through the ceiling.

If you wish, a couplet of Molière, a bird-chorus of Aristophanes, a fragment of Sophocles, can figure upon the one side, and upon the other a "soupir étouffé de Weber," the "Fire, Light and Speed," of J. M. W. Turner, or the *De Profundis* of Oscar Wilde. But any selection of this sort is misleading. Far better just to think of some highly-organized visual entity — a tiger, say: and then, over against it, a dark red splash of paint upon a white-washed wall: something organic, and full of purpose, against something inorganic and purposeless.

But I will return to Grierson; he gives us the name of the *first* "romantic," which should be useful. "I feel disposed," he writes, "to claim Plato as the first great Romantic . . . it is to Plato the greatest Romantics have always turned to find philosophical expression for their mood. . . ." Finally, through the Neo-Platonists his (Plato's) influence was felt in "the great romantic movement or ferment which we know as the Christian religion, for the next great Romantic after Plato is St. Paul."

But if Plato is to be the "romantic" prototype, Aristotle is then the "classical." And that distribution of attributes is at least hallowed by custom.

But the "classical" is never the personal: that is the next thing to put down as one of the major qualifications for "classical" honours. The much-abused word "impersonal" qualifies what is to be recognized as classical as much as does the word public (in contradiction to private). "Literature at such a period," Professor Grierson writes — such a period as we agree to describe as classic, "literature at such a period *is not personal* — at least in quite the same sense or to the same degree as it is, say, in Rousseau or Byron or Carlyle or Ibsen, because there is, as it were, a common consciousness throbbing in the mind and heart of each individual representative of the age, or member of the circle for which he writes, for one must admit, and this is significant, that a classical literature has generally been the product of a relatively small society — Athens, Rome, Paris, London."[1]

But in such enormous, sprawling, proletarianized societies as ours, is it possible to have anything "classical" at all: or rather, will not the "common consciousness" upon which classical expression, with us, has to rest, be of so diffused and ill-defined a nature as to be productive of a type of expression to which there is no longer any meaning in applying the term "classical"? No "highbrow" set, in a great metropolis like London or Paris, can for a moment supply the same order of framework that was forthcoming for the artist of the Augustan age, or the homogeneous, compact society behind Dryden, Pope and Swift, or the Paris court-world for whom Racine and Molière wrote.

And then there is Brunetière, who insists that classical literature is above all didactic, is *moral*. "No writer," he says, "of such a period separates the idea of art from the idea of a definite social function or purpose." And he quotes John Addington Symonds to show the Renaissance — the unmoral age *par excellence* — in its full worthlessness — that age of the diffusion of the artistic sensibility throughout a nation, all of whose enthusiasms that could be called sincere were aesthetic, and nothing but aesthetic. The age of art-for-art's-sake, in a word.

But of course is that true altogether? Art-for-art's-sake you can have, in a hole-and-corner "movement," a little group affair such as the decade of the Yellow Book: but can an entire nation put its "soul" into a great outbreak of artistic inventiveness — build, paint and write, *as a community* — for preference, rather than anything else, because particularly prone to that sort of expression: and can we treat the results of all this magnificent activity in the same slighting way that we are accustomed to think of some *art pur* enterprise of a handful of aesthetes? There is, obviously, "definite social function and purpose" in such an art as that stretching, in fact, from

[1] *Classical and Romantic.*

Cimabue to Magnasco. But the Renaissance comes in for the sourest strictures of the moralist criticism: for it is the great obstacle: — with all its Michelangelos, Leonardos and Titians, it stands in the way of the moralist, an immense contradiction, it would seem, of his mechanical standpoint.

The "classical" has a physiognomy of sorts, then: it has a solid aspect rather than a gaseous: it is liable to incline rather to the side of Aristotle than to the side of Plato: to be of a public rather than of a private character: to be objective rather than subjective: to incline to action rather than to dream: to belong to the sensuous side rather than to the ascetic: to be redolent of common sense rather than of metaphysic: to be universal rather than idiomatic: to lean upon the intellect rather than upon the bowels and nerves.

But "classic" expression, in an unimpeachable form, is to be found nowhere in such a period as ours, for the audience is lacking — just as it takes two to make a quarrel, so it takes two to make a "classic" work of art: the artist alone is not enough. But that is true, to some extent, of every variety of artistic expression. There is a greater audience today for art than in any period we could label "classic," but it is far less select. So the more components an artist may possess of those qualities described as "classic," the more isolated he is likely to be, and the more he will have to supplement the sparseness of the audience with what is *personal* — like an auditorium for an unpopular play "packed" by friends of the company! Still, he might argue, better one good man over and over again, than a houseful of third-rate ones. And by this process of reasoning you would arrive at the seeming paradox that in a romantic age the most classically-minded artist would also be the most *personal*.

Then, last of all, in the "classic" and "romantic" opposition, it is not paganism and Christianity that are confronted. "Le paganisme," says Brunetière,[1] "ce n'est pas ceci ou cela . . . mais bien, et en trois mots, l'adoration des energies de la nature." The rational animal, man, *against* the forces of nature: such is the dramatic rôle of the classical consciousness.

And to put with this, and in appearance to contradict it, there is the general dictum that the "classical" is *the natural*. — Ben Jonson, in his complaint against the Romanticism of his age,[2] declaims as follows: "But now nothing is good that is natural: right and natural language seems to have least of the wit in it; that which is writhed and tortured, is counted the more exquisite. Cloth of bodkin, or tissue, must be embroidered; as if no face were fair, that were not powdered or painted: no beauty to be had, but

[1] *L'Art et la morale*. Brunetière.
[2] *Discoveries*. Ben Jonson.

in wresting and writhing our own tongue? Nothing is fashionable, till it be deformed: and this is to write like a gentleman. All must be as affected and preposterous as our gallants' clothes, sweet-bags and night-dressings: in which you would think our men lay in: like ladies, it is so curious."

.   .   .   .   .   .

"*Like ladies* — it is so curious!" how typical of this ruffian, so lacking in "sympathy, or intuitive perception": he who, in his *Volpone*, boggled at nothing, however incongruous — indeed "the more it advances . . . to an incredible catastrophe, the more he seems to dwell upon it with complacency and a sort of wilful exaggeration, as if it were a logical discovery or corollary from well-known premises."

We now remain with the moral problem on our hands. I approach it in anything but an aggressive spirit: a *modus vivendi* may I hope be established between the most fanatical of artists and the most fanatical of moralists. But I am such an indifferent moralist myself, and so naturally an artist, that I daresay a final settlement could only be arrived at in consultation; for I feel that the moralist's claims, and even the professional religionist's, may not be advanced by me with sufficient force, any more than the artist's would be by the latter.

It is the priority of two principles that is in dispute, no doubt — though why should such questions of priority be found at all in such connection? "The Church has no place in its scheme of life for secular literature," Professor Grierson tells us: "When Boccaccio and Chaucer are afflicted with a fit of remorse, their first thought is to burn *all* their secular writings."[1] Well, it is to come to some arrangement by which something may be saved from such a possible *auto-da-fé* that we have undertaken this long analysis of the principles at stake.

Something of the same order as the principle of dictatorship is perhaps involved, in the first place (a one-man dictatorship I mean): for what do we mean by "the artist" after all, using this expression in a manner to cut it off from the society of which ultimately the artist must be the servant, and to whose will, ethical or otherwise, he must give expression? We, the society, pay the piper, so we call the tune, I suppose: we give out to the artist the notions we wish expressed, we dictate the task, and all he has to trouble about is the adequate execution. But who are "we," and what are *our* credentials? The artist, it is as well to remember, is a very sensitive and intelligent man, in touch with natural forces of a very considerable voltage. His responsibility is therefore very great.

[1] *Classical and Romantic.* Prof. Grierson.

One of the pre-eminently "classical" attributes is *an indifference to originality*. Indeed, in the classical artist, originality would be a fault. He is given, he is served out, with all he is supposed to require for his task: not his to reason why, but to "get on with the job." "[The classical artist's] preoccupation with form is not, as with those whom Bacon describes, due to disregard of weight of matter and worth of subject, but to the fact that *the matter is given to him by his age*, has for him the weight and worth it possesses for his audience." He is tied hand and foot therefore to the values of his patrons. Their morals are his morals; it is the *Weltanschauung* that perforce he holds in common with them that is his subject-matter.

Now, no artist today recognizes this duty, for the very good reason that it is extremely difficult for him to share the values of his audience, if he is a good artist, and he probably feels that he will be accomplishing a better work by imposing a few of his own values upon *them*, rather than by translating into a delectable art-form their pernicious and unsatisfactory principles of conduct. That is why artists like Tolstoy, or our own Mr. Lawrence, turn themselves into preachers, and become insufferable moralists into the bargain: and it is also why "originality" is rife.

But the artist, left to his own resources, is not left for long in this unsatisfactory independence. Tradition and salvationist reform, upon one hand and the other, begin organizing themselves for a war to the knife: and both attempt to impose their disciplines, their ethos, their *church*, upon the artist. There is no *one* society standing ready at his back to feed him with its system of contemporary law, but two, or half a dozen. And the first part of this book deals with the problem of the artist and the traditional canon, and the second with the artist's status over against the Marxist, the most powerful of the "new." For that the "natural forces" within the artist's keeping make him necessary to both sides there is no question.

To be impersonal, rather than personal; universal rather than provincial; rational rather than a mere creature of feeling — those, and the rest of the attributes of a so-called "classical" expression, are very fine things indeed: but who possesses more than a tincture of them today? It would be mere effrontery, or buffoonery, in an artist of any power, among us, to lay claim to them — to say, "as an artist I am a classicist." With all of us — and to this there is no exception — there are merely *degrees* of the opposite tendency, at present labelled "romantic." Just as Sir John Simon states, "We are all Socialists today," so in matters of art it could be said, "We are all romantics today," with at least equal truth. Or just as with the parties in the French Chamber, there are none but are heavily tinctured with "radicalism" — most of them indeed merely an extreme left party of yesterday, or of the day before yesterday, or of the day before that —

revolutionary parties in retrospect, arranged in chronological order from left to right — a one-sided entity — so with our literary schools. All are "romantic": we are all "revolutionary": some of us possess a modicum of *das Gesunde*, but, as with Goethe, that does not make us "classic": some have escaped the contamination of an hysterical gloom (the reflection of Marx's catastrophic doctrine, or the torment of Byzantine asceticism, reflected from Russia) and in consequence have escaped one of the most pernicious of the "romantic" attributes: some of us are by nature sufficiently "extroverted" (to use a term of romantic pathology) to be fitted for public utterance, rather than condemned to the obscurities of a private and personal jargon: some of us possess such humility as to enable us to sacrifice ourselves to what we regard as the public good — well knowing that our advocacy of unpopular beliefs must destroy us economically, and raise up every sort of obstacle in our path: there are some among us whose nervous reactions are sufficiently under control to rescue us from merely fashionable mob-hypnotism: but when all is said and done, that does not make us "classical" artists. The most that can be said for the current use and abuse of this term is that did we not pay lip-service to the classical virtues — taking extremely good care however not to practise them — then even that tincture of the "classical" remaining with us would no doubt vanish out of our works.

So much for us. But what are we to say about the authentic "classics" of the past? Is it at bottom nothing but the Periclean canon? Is it possible to point to any body of literary works, since the Augustan age, answering to the description "classical," satisfying all the conditions enumerated above? And, if so, are their authors the greatest artists — or only the most "classical" artists? But I will postpone the answer to this question for a short while.

If I pay a good deal of attention to Brunetière, it is not because I regard his ideas as of greater intrinsic interest, but because the "classical" position taken up, in so unbending a fashion, by him, in the France of the Nineties, is not dissimilar to that occupied by one or two of our literary critics in the Anglo-Saxon world today — all due allowance made, of course, for the interpretation of such a standpoint into Anglo-Saxon terms. And Brunetière was not, as a matter of fact, without parts: cold, certainly, even to the point of being repellent, and at once exceedingly combative and uncommonly touchy; challenging science, but affecting himself to dispose of a more than scientific rigour in his critical operations; bringing the intense pessimism of his unregenerate days to confer an unorthodox shape, displeasing to the Roman hierarchy, upon his very personal Catholicism, he was an earnest figure of some pathos, and (which is more than can perhaps be said for his congenors in our day) a man of considerable sincerity.

Anatole France and Emile Zola were the sort of "romantic" antagonists provided for him. But practically everybody was on the other side, as it happened: his unpopularity was very marked — no one wanted a Boileau, or a Bossuet, to be let loose among the *cris de coeur* of Verlaine, and the cheap Voltairianism of Anatole France, or the brutish naturalism of Zola. He was far worse off than is the "classicist" in our own time. But there was some analogy in the late Professor Irving Babbitt's position in the United States, perhaps; for because of the latter's doctrinaire opposition to the activities of naturalist romancers of the type of Sinclair Lewis and Theodore Dreiser, he was regarded as dangerous and obstructive by practically everybody, in the book-world of New York, and a ring was made round him, and his friend Elmer More, in consequence. Professor L. J. Bondy points to this parallel, by relating the "humanism" of Brunetière with the "humanism" of Babbitt.[1]

To compare Brunetière's successive definitions of "classicism" is instructive, for they roundly contradict each other, and reveal the extreme insecurity of the foundations available for any strict doctrine of that order. His "classics" were Molière, Boileau, La Fontaine, Racine — in prose, Bossuet and La Bruyère. He held in the first place that all these illustrious men-of-letters were mere artists, nothing more. They themselves assigned to their productions, so he said, an aesthetic value, and that was all.

> L'art est pour eux un ornement de la vie commune, tout ainsi que la littérature; et l'artiste et le poète sont des hommes qui concourent, chacun pour sa part, à la diversité de l'existence, par consequent à son embellissement, et nullement des maîtres qui du haut de leur supériorité fassent la leçon à leur temps.

The sort of arrogant "masters" whom Brunetière has in mind are Flaubert and Gautier, of course, those vociferous art-for-art's-sake doctrinaires: Gautier, for instance, asserting "tout artiste qui se propose autre chose que le beau n'est pas un artiste": though why men who were capable of such achievements in the art of letters as *Bouvard et Pécuchet* or *Emaux et camées* should be disqualified by that very fact from intervening in the formative sense in the intellectual world about them — and "faisant la leçon à leur temps," as Brunetière himself pretended to do — it is a little difficult to see. They had much more justification for the assumption of the rôle of teacher than had Brunetière.

In thinking this over, as Professor Bondy shows, Brunetière came to feel that the above account of the status of the "classical" man of letters would

---

[1] *Le Classicisme de Ferdinand Brunetière.* L. J. Bondy, 1930.

scarcely describe Pascal and Bossuet. So he dropped it. It was, in fact, quite a worthless generalization.

On the matter of the *freedom* to be permitted to the "artist," again — on the best classicist principles — Brunetière wrote as follows, in 1883:

> Ce que La Fontaine et Molière nous enseignent de plus élevé comme morale, c'est l'art de gouverner notre vie au mieux de nos intérêts et de notre tranquillité. Dans les conseils qu'ils nous donnent, on ne voit place ni pour sacrifice ni pour le dévouement. On n'y voit peut-être pas non plus assez de place pour le devoir. Qui suivrait religieusement les avis de Molière et les moralités de La Fontaine risquerait fort de devinir un modèle du parfait égoïste. Remarquez que comme artistes, je ne les blâme pas. Au contraire! Car je crois fermement qu'en art et en littérature c'est une erreur que de vouloir prêcher la morale. Ou plutôt, avant tout et par-dessus tout, l'artiste a besoin de liberté, c'est à dire de ne se voir opposer aucuns principes que ceux qui gouvernent son art même.[1]

This very handsome allowance of licence, a *carte blanche* in fact to say what he liked, was later on withdrawn by Brunetière: on second thoughts, it was impossible, he reflected, to allow them to be as free as all that! But to the last, and at the expense of self-consistency, he would not bind the artists hand and foot. No. Provided they were "classic" (and no other had a right to express themselves at all) they must be left a modicum of elbow room, he stoutly contended — against himself, in the teeth of M. Brunetière!

But what are we to think of the revelations of flagrant materialism incidentally revealed in this passage? These "classical" paragons, for every true Frenchman, come off badly beneath the moralists' microscope! They teach us, it is admitted, nothing more elevated than the grossest self-interest, doctrines drawn from the comfortable bourgeois standards of the time, of grab and keep and may the devil take the hindmost — in which there is no place for "sacrifice," nor for "devotion" to cause or to person: "duty" plays no very conspicuous part in their works — the mouth-pieces of rich burghers and the privileged goodtimers of the court (though who would have expected them to be anything else?): and he who should follow their counsels would become "a perfect egoist." — In short, these particular artists intervened *too little*, it seems, in the affairs of their time: they accepted too submissively and respectfully the contemptible bourgeois morals of the French society they illustrated. But — had they not done so they would not have been "classics"!

The "classicist," furthermore, must, it seems, be a worldling, that is the fact of the matter! The sort of "wisdom" that Henry James assimilates to such worldly good sense as is possessed by the typical "man of the world" — and which he assigns characteristically to R. L. Stevenson[2] — is the measure of the ethical judgement proper to the perfect "classicist." It is this

---

[1] *Études critiques*, Vol. I, Brunetière (quoted Bondy).

[2] *Notes on Novelists*. Henry James.

"bourgeois" quality in the classical authors—this blind acceptance of the not very elevated standards of the average man amongst whom they lived, which has often been objected against them: and it is this that causes them to be "classic." So it will be seen that Brunetière does not really help us to a satisfactory admiration for the type of art he supports.

But stop: this is not the last word on the typical "classical" man-of-letters, as that controversial personage takes shape in the pages of Brunetière. There *is* something that the eminent French classicist has discovered that is at once true and somewhat more encouraging than the above passages would convey. It is this: the heroes of classicism are presented to us as essentially *men-of-action*. That is better, is it not? And that is yet another quality appropriate to the perfect "classic"—omitted in my catalogue above, but which we now must note.

> Ce que leurs oeuvres à tout [those of the great writers of the seventeenth century in France] nous enseignent, c'est l'action, et leur prose ou leurs vers nous sont des sources d'énergie. Ils n'ont pas écrit pour écrire, ni pour réaliser un rêve de beauté solitaire, mais pour agir. . . . Ils ont cru que la parole nous avait été donnée pour exprimer des idées, et les idées pour servir de lumière ou de guide à la conduite.[1]

Of course, a "rêve de beauté solitaire" might be of as much dynamic value, we feel, as an "idée"—in becoming a motive-power issuing in exemplary conduct: attractive spectacles can influence us as much as hortatory remarks. But we will leave that out of it, and attach ourselves to the description of the "classicist" as a "source of energy." And it will at once be apparent how, in this respect, he must come to be regarded as a competitor of the "romantic." For is not the "romantic" artist a confirmed tapper of the energies of the dark "powers of nature"? Say *energy* and you say "romantic"!

Leaving the Nineties in France for the moment, and coming down to the present day, let us compare two contemporary statements dealing with this troublesome antithesis, and see what light they throw upon the subject. "The difference [between Classicism and Romanticism] seems to me rather the difference between the complete and the fragmentary, the adult and the immature, the orderly and the chaotic "[2] That is Mr. T. S. Eliot's account of the matter. (We have here, you will observe, a chronological interpretation: "classical" or "romantic" are merely names for the same thing (or person) at different stages of its (or his) career. It is, as it were, the conventional reaction to these words that is instinctively selected. First there

---

[1] *Discours de combat.* Brunetière.
[2] *Selected Essays,* p. 26.

is a wilderness; but gradually man puts it in order. First, there is a "romantic" young man: but he becomes "mature" — and "classical").

But in my search for light upon this subject, I encountered on the same day (September 24, 1933) the above passages in Mr. Eliot's collected essays, and the following lines in a review by Mr. Humbert Wolfe,[1] in which the *Thirty Cantos* of Mr. Ezra Pound, and some poems by two other poets, are considered and contrasted; one of the latter gentlemen, Mr. Wolfe is using to beat Mr. Pound with, in fact, and he says:

> [Mr. S.] does not claim to be born deaf, he does not regard words as his natural enemies, and meaning as a notifiable disorder. He believes that the world is a chaos and that the creating mind imposes order and does not accept the infection of disorder, proudly exhibiting the acquired sores as honourable scars.

So, for Mr. Wolfe, the author of the *Thirty Cantos* is a person who leaves chaos as he finds it (shovelling it into his Cantos higgledy piggledy is I suppose the idea) and the disfigurements, the sore places, that result from this unhealthy exercise he complacently exhibits to the public. That is Mr. Wolfe's account. But the Cantos are presented to the public under the aegis of Mr. T. S. Eliot principally, that self-styled "classicist": who, indeed, technically is a writer who owes much to the author of the Cantos: and Mr. Eliot would be compelled to allow, I imagine, a fair share of the attributes of a "classicist" to Mr. Ezra Pound, or else risk to have it said of the latter that he was "fragmentary, immature and chaotic"!

Do not let us despair of the terms "classic" and "romantic," however, till we have gone back for enlightenment to Mr. T. E. Hulme (and, incidentally, it is he who is mainly responsible for the critical standpoint we associate today with the name of Mr. T. S. Eliot and his school, and so we have here a natural transition). The abruptness of Mr. Hulme's style is very marked, by the way. But what he has to say is worth listening to.

"I want to maintain that after a hundred years of romanticism we are in for a classical revival," Mr. Hulme pugnaciously starts off. But as it turns out "a hundred years" is too short: Romanticism began with the Renaissance, and "Romanticism" is to be identified with "Humanism." In "romantic" and "classic" two opposite conceptions of the nature of man are involved. On p. 50 in an essay entitled *Humanism*,[2] we encounter the following passage: "The first of these historical periods is that of the Middle Ages in Europe — from Augustine, say, to the Renaissance; the second from the Renaissance to now." With the Renaissance — the upthrust of the bourgeois Italian

---

[1] *The Observer*, Sept. 24, 1933.
[2] *Speculations*. T. E. Hulme. Kegan Paul.

city-republics, came in the bourgeois, the secular, values: and likewise "Romanticism" was born.

This is a very different story to that of Ferdinand Brunetière: here we have a sweeping generalization that promises to provide a wider, but also a much more actual, significance for these two battered terms. We are dealing with something as fundamental as a conception of the very nature of man. But it is after all not quite such plain-sailing as all that: for on p. 54 we have been told that "The Renaissance period corresponds very nearly both in its conception of man and in its art to the classical." And here "classical" is equated with "humanistic." But confining ourselves strictly to the essay with the title that we want, "Romanticism and Classicism,"[1] some sort of working definition can be extracted. And at the root of this definition in aesthetics is the theological dogma of original sin (as any reader familiar with the criticism of Mr. Eliot and his followers will be aware). But Hulme is trebly valuable, for in his definition can be found not only a rendezvous for aesthetics and theology, but also for politics.

"Classic" has become a political catchword, belonging principally to the *Action Française* he tells us: "It has become a party symbol. If you asked a man of a certain set whether he preferred the classics or the romantics, you could deduce from that what his politics were." And this is just the same in 1934 as it was in 1914. The politics would be *royalist*, of course, if the aesthetics were "classic" — at all events there would be no "whiggery" about them. And you would also know more or less that your "royalist" believed in the theological doctrine of original sin, that is the idea. To the French partisans of M. Maurras, "the classical ideal is a living thing. . . . They regard romanticism as an awful disease from which France had just recovered. The thing is complicated in their case by the fact that it was romanticism that made the revolution. They hate the revolution, so they hate romanticism. — I make no apology," Hulme adds, "for dragging in politics here; romanticism both in England and France is associated with certain political views, and it is in taking a concrete example of the working out of a principle in action that you can get its best definition."

To that I, for my part, heartily assent: and the "working out" cannot be pursued too far, if the definition is to be sound. — In this essay he stops his definition at the French Revolution — the period he covers is the same as that covered by Mario Praz in *The Romantic Agony*, and his conclusions are the same. And in a stocktaking of the past fifteen years, the influence of these essays of Hulme's, as one comes back to them, is seen to have been very great, in the only part of the critical world that has attempted any serious revaluation, upon the English scene. Mr. Eliot seems to have orientated himself entirely from them.

---

[1] *Speculations*, p. 113. T. E. Hulme.

Put shortly, these are the two views, then. One, that man is intrinsically good, spoilt by circumstance; and the other that he is intrinsically limited, but disciplined by order and tradition to something fairly decent. To the one party man's nature is like a well, to the other like a bucket. The view which regards man as a well, a reservoir full of possibilities, I call the romantic; the one which regards him as a very finite and fixed creature, I call the classical.

One may note here that the Church has always taken the classical view since the defeat of the Pelagian heresy and the adoption of the sane classical dogma of original sin.[1]

Rousseau, as in the teaching of Professor Babbitt, is indicated as the source of the noxious "romantic" principle of *liberty*, which inspired the French Revolution. The men of that time "had been taught by Rousseau that man was by nature good, that it was only bad laws and customs that had suppressed him. Remove all these and the infinite possibilities of man would have a chance. This is what made them think that something positive could come out of disorder, this is what created the religious enthusiasm. Here is the root of all romanticism: that man, the individual, is an infinite reservoir of possibilities; and if you can so rearrange society by the destruction of oppressive order then these possibilities will have a chance and you will get Progress.

"One can define the classical quite clearly as the exact opposite to this. Man is an extraordinarily fixed and limited animal whose nature is absolutely constant. It is only by tradition and organisation that anything decent can be got out of him."[2]

Having cut Christendom in two — into the sacred and profane periods, the mediaeval, the age of faith, and the subsequent age of sceptical enquiry; and having laid down the dividing line at the opening of the Renaissance, on the hither side of which line there are ups and downs, but a "romantic" spirit is forever present, and influential — Hulme proceeds to confuse things somewhat — as far as that applies to detail — by trotting out Nietzsche's characteristic distinction between the *classical-static* and the *classical-dynamic*. Thus Racine is on "the extreme classical side" — he is a *static* classic: but Shakespeare, he is a much more bustling and mercurial one, but a classic nevertheless. Very very "dynamic," but *classical!*

So the moment we get down to brass tacks, in the matter of these terms classic and romantic, even with such an intelligent critic as Hulme, back we are once more, upon the instant, among the confusions à la Brunetière. There is no avoiding that, it seems. The terms are strictly unusable.

---

[1] *Speculations* [p. 117]. T. E. Hulme.
[2] *Op. cit.* [p. 116.]

"After a hundred years, we are in for a classical revival," Hulme exclaimed in 1914. Well, I suppose we have had it, or are having it. By its *works* it is none too easy to tell it for such. By the words of its critical and apologetic utterances we know it is "classical," certainly, but not by what it does by way of illustration. But Hulme foresaw this difficulty, for he wrote: "When it [the classical revival] does come we may not even recognize it as classical. Although it will be classical it will be different because it has passed through a romantic period." But here we are surely in the very realm of nonsense once again. I agree with Hulme that in "cubism" the "classical" spirit was awakening once more — *if you avoid employing the term "classical"* and confine yourself to a recapitulation merely of the qualities generally alleged to belong to that type of artistic expression. But you would not be prevented from recognizing a "cubist" picture as classical because it was marked from its birth in the literally hysterical womb of Romance — indeed many a cubist picture betrayed no compromising trace whatever of this base parentage: you would be prevented from recognizing it as such because it was not "classical," any more than it was "romantic." It was something else. "Romantic" and "classical" are terms applicable only to an historical see-saw of influences in our formerly watertight Western World. And during this century we have slowly but surely left this world behind, in the sense that it is no longer necessary or possible to refer everything that happens to its narrowly-contrasted pagan and Christian — religious and secular — values.

Just as (I agree) we are, undoubtedly, on all hands slipping back into the old narrowly European grooves, under the straitening pressures of the Slump, into economic and political nationalism: and, in the bosom of nationalism, into the old Tory-Whig, Catholic and Protestant antagonisms: so we are bandying about these words "classical" and "romantic." But it is all extremely artificial — as artificial, for instance, as the Erse names in which the Irish at present masquerade. Soon we shall be expected to yodel in middle English, and then the man of the Danegelt will be incomprehensible to the man of the Saxon-south. All these things hang together — it is the end of history, and the beginning of historical pageant and play. But we are all compelled, to some extent, to enter into the spirit of the comedy — that is the humble message of this book.

There was one respect in which T. E. Hulme was a better "classic" than those that have followed him, however, and that was in his insistence upon "das Gesunde," and the robust mental attributes of health. He was not a health-snob (as tiresome as a sickness-snob, I think) but he was actually himself a person of very considerable vitality. And he possessed in that simple fact the first requisite for a "classical" standpoint. But, as we are doing a certain amount of stocktaking, and as Hulme stands in this very intimate relation to so much that has been influential in Anglo-Saxony since the war, let us hear from him again, for his language should be salutary.

With romanticism, because there "is always the bitter contrast between what you think you ought to be able to do and what man actually can, it always tends, in its later stages at any rate, *to be gloomy.*"

Ah! How abominably true! Again: "I object even to the best of the romantics. . . . I object to the sloppiness which doesn't consider that a poem is a poem unless it is moaning or whining about something or other. I always think in this connection of the last line of a poem of John Webster's which ends with a request I cordially endorse:

End your moan and come away.

The thing has got so bad now that a poem which is all dry and hard, a properly classical poem, would not be considered poetry at all." Or again: "But the particular verse we are going to get will be cheerful, dry and sophisticated." Such was Hulme's forecast. In the sequel we have seen much that is "dry" but little that is "cheerful!" And *gloom* has surely been an outstanding attribute of this strange "classicism," or neo-Anglo-classicism, that we have got.

Let us now return to the question with which this chapter opened: "Are the artists belonging to a so-called 'classical' period the greatest artists, or only the most classical?" My reply is — "Decidedly the latter!" Racine is not such a great artist as Shakespeare: but, as I see it, by no stretch of the imagination, or glove-stretching of the term, can Shakespeare be described as "classical." In painting, Nicholas Poussin is a "classical" painter. But who would desire to pretend that he matched in importance Leonardo or Titian — both individualistic, strictly "bourgeois" painters, of the wild, bad, anti-classical Renaissance — that Renaissance of which Brunetière wrote: "Le premier trait de ce nouvel esprit, c'est le développement de l'individualisme. On va vouloir maintenant être 'soi-même' avant tout; on va vouloir l'être 'le plus possible'; et, conséquement, on va vouloir l'être 'à tout prix.' " This bête noire of a period for all good classicists is not my own personal favourite, I may as well remark. I go farther afield: in a day of air-liners Pekin is nearer than formerly was Siena. So the Renaissance is not my pidgin, but it produced an uncommon number of excellent artists, many of whom were much more than craftsmen.

"If you stick to a literary judgment," says Mr. T. S. Eliot, "you cannot say that Shakespeare is inferior to any poet who has ever written, unless you are prepared to substantiate your opinion by detailed analysis; and if you depreciate Shakespeare for his lower view of life, then you have issued out of literary criticism into social criticism; you are criticising not so much the man but the age. I prefer the culture which produced Dante to the culture which produced Shakespeare; but I would not say that Dante

was the greater poet, or even that he had the profounder mind. . . ."[1]
That is very justly said, but Dante is a very solitary figure. By a count
of heads, I believe the inferior times (from that pseudo-orthodox standpoint) have produced more fine artists than the superior times. And at least
we may, by pointing out that fact, encourage those a little over-gloomy
at finding themselves in a "bad" time, and according to Mr. Eliot, bound
as sincere men (though *not*, I am thankful to be told, as "a duty") to
reproduce its lineaments. It is too much to hope that Mr. Eliot may himself
be encouraged in this way: but some poor devils may be. I should add
that I disagree with this judgement *by the age* — this *period-judgement* as
it might be described. Mr. Eliot is, I believe, too fashionable: he regards
the individual (cf. Part I) too much askance, as a sort of bogey. It is my
belief, as I have indicated, that artists are not the mere mouthpieces of a
time in quite that absolute way. And then what is "a time" after all? Time,
for Mr. Eliot, seems too much to assume the aspect of an automatically-
progressing evolutionist machine. How often does he not appeal, in the
course of his *Selected Essays* (instinctively, apparently) to some vague principle of *up-to-dateness*? The best "time" that ever was, would it not be found
to amount, on examination, to the reflexion — the organized
vulgarization — of the intellects of a handful of men, or perhaps mainly
that of one person (I have not quite Mr. Eliot's faith in the works of organized society, I am not so much a man of the world).

With Hulme I am in complete agreement regarding which of those two
conceptions — namely, the conception of man as a static animal, needing
a great deal of polishing up to appear at his best, on the one hand, and
the conception of man as a god-like and infinitely "progressive" animal on
the other — is to be preferred: just as I am in agreement with Professor Praz
in his valuation of the *Romantic Agony*. But I think that the flux of
Bergson — *l'élan vital* — had got badly into Hulme's blood — I look upon that
as a very inferior thing: he was disposed in consequence to insist on com-
petitive contest overmuch — "The ultimate reality is the hurly-burly, the
struggle." And then why must "sin" play, although in the European past
it has, such a predominant rôle? It does not matter very much. But the
dogma of original sin happened to play that humbling part at that moment, he tells us; nevertheless, it is possible to feel the same humility, with
less dogma than that requires. "What is the difference between modern art
since the Renaissance, and the Byzantine mosaic?" he asks, . . . "these two
arts correspond exactly to the thought of their respective periods. Byzantine art to the ideology which looks on man and all existing things as imperfect and sinful in comparison with certain abstract values and *perfec-
tions*. The other art corresponds to the humanist ideology, which looks
on man and life as good. . . ." This passage would be better if you deleted

---

[1] "Second Thoughts about Humanism," [*Selected Essays*]. T. S. Eliot.

the word "sinful." It does not matter, of course. But it would be better in two thousand years, if it were still in existence, as a sentence.

"Part of the fixed nature of man is the belief in the Deity. . . . It is parallel to appetite, the instinct of sex, and all the other fixed qualities." I would not argue with that; but I would say that the dogma of original sin is not as deep an instinct as that of self-preservation, or as God. In fact, is it an instinct at all? I hope not, for I have not got it.

So we have been led back to the moral issue now. The foregoing prolonged analysis should be found of service in our handling of that.

As you are no doubt aware, there are various schools that have attempted to run some system of ethics of their own, without that system being tied to a religion. And a vast amount of controversy, about it and about, has first and last occurred, all bearing upon the question of whether it was possible successfully to operate an ethical system without the theological hook-up. Poor Babbitt, with his "inner-check," was attacked from two sides at once, and it was fairly easy to show that his "inner-check" — which he claimed all men possessed, restraining them automatically from unsuitable lines of conduct — was in fact, as it was explained, a gadget that was there in his head all right, for the simple reason that his good mother put it there when she taught him to pray at night before going to bed as a small middlewest Puritan pullet: and it had worked very well! "Thus his opposition between Quality and Quantity was verbal too; it was Quantity versus Quantity, presided over by rootless Restraint, the referee who checked nothing but coherent thought." (Allen Tate.)

> Is [humanism] a derivative of religion which will work only for a short time in history, and only for a few highly cultivated persons like Mr. Babbitt — whose ancestral traditions, furthermore, are Christian, and who is, like many people, at the distance of a generation or so from definite Christian belief? Is it, in other words, durable beyond one or two generations?[1]

If religious training were superseded by "humanistic" training, would there, after a generation or two, be any of this fortuitous or post-chapel "inner-check" left? Probably not, most of his critics were of opinion, to whatever party they belonged.

Three years ago I spent a month in Harvard, and met Professor Babbitt. I found this highly controversial professor a very wise and gentle creature indeed: if all our kind were made at all upon his model, life would certainly be less eventful, but we should have little need for extraneous "checks," I think. His philosophy was, I was in agreement with his critics, a private one however, and not fitted for the world at large — for that large

[1] [T. S. Eliot, "The Humanism of Irving Babbitt," *Selected Essays.*]

rough *muchedumbre* for whom the big fierce proselytising religions are mainly manufactured — and when the "check" won't work it has been found that the rack will, with whatever sect. So I think he was extremely ill-advised to advance his enlightened scholarship as a substitute for religion, of all things, for there so obviously is no substitute. *Unto Caesar the things that are Caesar's,* and so forth. As a great critic of political and moral tendencies in modern literature he should have been content to remain. Humanism — a religion of culture — was a curious mistake, for which the American Scene again was no doubt responsible.

An ethical system must, to have any meaning today, be tied to a theological system. The great chaos of values into which we have fallen makes this necessary. And, as there must be an ethical system, it is better to tie it to the theological system whose catechism we have been taught as children and leave it there. The spectacle of an ethical system adrift, wandering helplessly about in search of Authority, of a God, is not edifying: and it is absurd. And it is still more absurd to see it masquerading as a religion.

There are people, I know, who feel that the theological system which dug itself in at the heart of the Roman Empire two millenniums ago, an archaic compound of Messianic Judaism and Hellenistic beliefs, as they put it, must at all costs be got rid of. They regard the dogmas of revealed religion as an archaic encumbrance, which can only produce over and over again "Schoolmen" to deafen us for ever with their nonsensical disputes about fantastic particulars of their primitive creed. For Charles Maurras, Christianity was "an hysterical oriental cult," to start with. But he has steered a different course to the militant anti-Christians. But let me quote an anti-humanist's account of this affair — I have never wished to appear, when I could possibly avoid it, in the rôle of historian.

> A patriot, and a royalist, but also an agnostic, M. Maurras comes to embrace Catholicism for purely political reasons. As a political credo he adheres to "the learned cortège of councils, of popes, and of all the great men of the modern élite," nor will he turn from these to place his confidence "in the gospels of four obscure Jews." His religious affiliations on these terms have been embarrassing to the Church, and in 1926 Rome called believers away from any allegiance to this dangerous and brilliant man.

As what Church would not, you will be inclined to exclaim! Or of course this way of conducting a conversion may appeal to you. Or you may hold to the other view I have outlined — out and out for a *tabula rasa* of beliefs which correspond, you think, to the nursery days of the human intellect. But such are not my views of the matter. Here is after all a serviceable framework, upon which to hang your ethic — you must have one. It seems to me stupid not to use it. After a great war, it has been said, Christianity invariably tends to swing to the Judaic end of its dogmatic container. This, I think, has happened now: though I may be mistaken. If so, the "righteousness" which was such a remarkable characteristic — as Arnold pointed out — of the people of Israel, would intensify the Puritan ethic. That is what we would suppose would happen. And do not let us be deceived by portents of an opposite sort. But one ethic is much the same as another, provided you have the machinery to instruct people that they shall not annoy their neighbours — steal, lie, and kill (except when a public dispensation is given them, as in war time), that should satisfy the most orderly.

The contempt into which morals have fallen is a rather strange thing. It is parallel (cf. Chap. III) with the enucleation of the communist doctrine of every vestige of humanitarian ethic (the very principle with which it started). The humanitarian is equally *conspué* today by the Marxist and the advanced theological doctrinaire. Both of these sectaries cold-shoulder the merely social virtues — those of tolerance and a humane good-nature, for reasons that it is unnecessary to go into here (but such dispositions of tolerance, of humaneness, plainly are *not* the stuff of which good revolutionary gunmen are made: and, on the other hand, if people live exemplary lives, they are apt to believe they can do without God, and, as I have said, they cannot).

It is not difficult to understand, I think, in such a time of harsh discomfort, of perpetual "crisis," as ours, that the religionist should look a little sourly upon the picture of the Deity as a sort of beaming Father Christmas!

Already one of the bulwarks of the Faith I have had occasion to quote has been seen to look askance at morals; he has expressed the wish to see them kept in their place. But that is anything but an original attitude. If, after all, you have "come through romanticism," are acquainted with German and French pessimism, have perused *Beyond Good and Evil*, and have taken shelter at last beneath the wing of an archangel, your Christianity, like Brunetière's — or your "classicism," as Hulme specifically foresaw — will scarcely look quite as it would have done under more orthodox circumstances. The case is an exact parallel to that of the late Professor Babbitt with his "inner-check": an impressionable adolescence of Bergsonian flux — the Relativity of yesterday — of pessimism and the rest of it, must leave behind it a machinery, of an apposite order to the ex-Christian's "inner-check."

If, again, you regard man as a perfectly fixed and "static" — corrupt, evil, untidy, incomplete — animal, as I do, as Mr. Hulme did, it is pretty evident that a kindly, tolerant and humanitarian attitude is the last thing to expect of us. But the ethical will, as generally understood, is inspired and sustained (is it not?) by such bland and kindly sentiments.

Prior to accepting Catholicism, Brunetière had for a period embraced the pessimism of Schopenhauer. He was not a misanthrope we are told by Bourget, but "il ne croyait pas à la vie. Il la considérait comme foncièrement mauvaise et douleureuse." But here are the words of the pessimist himself (I am quoting him from M. Bondy): "Croyons fermement . . . que la vie est mauvaise. . . . Croyons que l'homme est mauvais; et, en conséquence, proposons-nous, pour principal objet de notre activité, de travailler à détruire en nous, si nous le pouvons, ou en tout cas d'y mortifier cette 'volonté de vivre' dont les manifestations égoistes font une autre moitié des maux qui rendent la vie si laborieuse à vivre."[1]

This ascetic self-mortification of the "pessimist" is extremely easily translated into the terms of Christian mysticism. And in the case of Hulme's "classicist" — of necessity orthodox theologically — who has "passed through romanticism," this is what you must expect to get — as it were an arrogant asceticism, and an overmastering contempt for human life. All those powerful human blood ties of family, of race, or of sex, will in the nature of things be treated with the same hostile severity they would have encountered at the hands of a contemporary of St. Augustine — for whom the Millennium was still a thing of one day to the next.

[1] *Essais sur la littérature contemporaine.* F. Brunetière.

CHAPTER VIII

THE MATERIALISM OF THE ARTIST

"Leonardo was so delighted when he saw curious heads, whether bearded or hairy, that he would follow about anyone who thus attracted his attention for a whole day. . . . Among them is . . . the head of Scaramuccia, the gipsy captain."— VASARI's *Lives of the Painters.*

SOME PEOPLE SUFFER FOOLS GLADLY, some frown and sneer upon them, or turn loftily away. I respond to the fool after the former fashion, I take the fool for granted, I suffer easily the fool. If I were a great teacher I should probably boom at my disciples: "Suffer all fools to come unto me," and should sit for hours listening to the prattle of a fool, or gazing into his opaque and empty eyes, and watching for his dumb tongue to stammer forth some choice inanity! — But this is extremely unusual.

All these sensations to which we have been giving emphasis in the preceding chapter — the sensations of a dwarfed and almost meaningless humanity, so idiotic is it — regarding whose "history" the great historian Gibbon expressed himself in a famous passage with such resounding disrespect — have been put on record once and for all by Arthur Balfour. There is a purple passage in his famous book, *The Foundations of Belief,* which must have been more often quoted than any writing of that order in English, so near to us in time. It is possible, all the same, that it may be unfamiliar to some readers, so I will make use of it here. It is where he is dealing with "the *emotional* adequacy of the ends prescribed by the Naturalistic Ethics." He goes on, "I will suppose that in the perfection and felicity of the sentient creation we may find the all-inclusive object prescribed by morality for human endeavour. Does this, then, or does it not, supply us with all that is needed to satisfy our ethical imagination?" And he then proceeds to show us what this "perfection and felicity" looks like, employing the eye of the evolutionist for that purpose. Here is the often-quoted passage.

> For what is man looked at from this point of view? Time was when his tribe and its fortunes were enough to exhaust the energies and to hound the imagination of the primitive sage. . . These ideas represent no early or rudimentary stage in human thought, yet have we left them far behind. The family, the tribe, the nation, are no longer enough to absorb our interests. Man — past, present, and future — lays claim to our devotion. What, then, can we say of him? Man, so far as natural science by itself is able to teach us, is no longer the final cause of the universe, the Heaven-descended heir of all the ages. His very existence is an accident, his story a brief and

173

transitory episode in the life of one of the meanest of the planets. Of the combination of causes which first converted a dead organic compound into the living progenitors of humanity, science, indeed, as yet knows nothing. It is enough that from such beginnings famine, disease, and mutual slaughter, fit nurses of the future lords of creation, have gradually evolved, after infinite travail, a race with conscience enough to feel that it is vile, and intelligence enough to know that it is insignificant. We survey the past, and see that its history is of blood and tears, of helpless blundering, of wild revolt, of stupid acquiescence, of empty aspirations. We sound the future, and learn that after a period, long compared with the individual life, but short indeed compared with the divisions of time open to our investigation, the energies of our system will decay, the glory of the sun will be dimmed, and the earth, tideless and inert, will no longer tolerate the race which has for a moment disturbed its solitude. Man will go down into the pit, and all his thoughts will perish. The uneasy consciousness, which in this obscure corner has for a brief space broken the contented silence of the universe, will be at rest. . . .[1]

That the Moral Law should suffer no change, confronted with such a picture as that, is, he asserts, absurd. For

It is no reply to say that the substance of the Moral Law need suffer no change through any modification of our views of man's place in the universe. This may be true, but it is irrelevant. We desire, and desire most passionately when we are most ourselves, to give our service to that which is Universal, and to that which is Abiding. Of what moment is it then (from this point of view), to be assured of the fixity of the moral law when it and the sentient world, where alone it has any significance, are alike destined to vanish utterly away within periods trifling beside those with which the geologist and the astronomer lightly deal in the course of their habitual speculations? . . . It cannot, therefore, be a matter to us of small moment that, as we learn to survey the material world with a wider vision, as we more clearly measure the true proportions which man and his performances bear to the ordered Whole, our practical ideal gets relatively dwarfed and beggared till we may well feel inclined to ask whether so transitory and so unimportant an accident in the general scheme of things as the fortunes of the human race can any longer satisfy aspirations and emotions nourished upon beliefs in the Everlasting and the Divine."[2]

That such a generalization as this is of great use in fixing the backgrounds which we require to have constantly before us in this investigation is evident. That Lord Balfour's view of the human race was just what he described it as being, in the above words, who can doubt? The *more* dwarfed and ridiculous is man and all his works, indeed, the more does God stand out — more necessary too to men than ever before! "To give our service to that which is Universal and to that which is Abiding!" And when we turn in the direction of Man, with such aspirations in our minds, what we find

[1] *The Foundations of Belief.* By kind permission of Messrs Longmans, Green & Co.
[2] *Op. cit.*

can only call forth a contemptuous laugh — that is what this book of the late Lord Balfour teaches.

Of course, what ensues from such a view will differ a great deal according to the quality of the mind. The more conventional and arrogant mind will draw different conclusions from the mind of a higher and more independent order.

However, the complete dehumanization of religious principles, as of reformist political principles (and that these two activities have reacted upon each other, who can doubt?) has now been achieved — or at all events in such quarters (theological or political) as pique themselves upon any logical precision. Take as an example of this a phase of the anti-humanist controversy in America. It is by verbatim quotation that the best results in such work as I am attempting here can be obtained. In what I have selected next as evidence, of a very different order, the foundations of Elmer More's highly "individualist" religion is being attacked:

> He [More] has written a good deal on religion, but it is not easy to put one's finger on his idea of it. . . . And yet he does have definite ideas. Their most significant expression is in incidental remarks, when he is off his guard. About twenty years ago he took to task an interpreter of the Forest Philosophers for trying "to convert into hard intellectualism what was at bottom a religious and thoroughly human experience."
> Is intellectualism hard (or soft) incompatible with religion? If the experience was thoroughly human, was it also religious? Mr. More thinks that it was. If intellectualism has no place in religion where does it belong?[1]

Mr. Tate, in short, who is responsible for the above passage, feels that he has caught Professor More out: he has surprised that gentleman in an attitude towards religion that would degrade it to the level of a merely visionary or moral experience. "Shall [religion] be contented with visions? I think that Mr. More would say no; but he could not rationally say it." — It is obvious that Mr. More regarded "hard intellectualism" as one thing (a severe and inhuman discipline — "hard," as he says): and that he regarded religious experience (*mere* religious experience, we might almost say) as quite another — a dreamy and yielding, human, all-too-human, affair: almost a weakness, an intellectual apostasy to which our emotional nature is subject. "If intellectualism has no place in religion, where does it belong?" cries Mr. Tate. The *Summa* has not been popularized for nothing! Maritain and Fernandez have not lived in vain!

But what I am attempting to make as clear to you as I can by all this miscellaneous quotation is the divorce that has occurred in the minds of all the averagely educated, of recent years, between morality and religion: how, as a reflection of the catholic intellectual disciplines in part, the kind

[1] *The Critique of Humanism, A Symposium.* [Ed. C. Hartley Grattan. New York, 1930.]

of debased, easy-going, ethical-religion, of the liberalizing English "low" church of the Nineteenth Century (attempting painfully to adapt itself to the principles of Evolution) has come into complete contempt — with anybody who knows what's what, I mean — and we are all fairly knowing today: how religion has been seen to be "respectable," intellectually, by all the intellect-snobs all at once: and how it has become common knowledge that religion is not ultimately an affair of the heart at all, but of the more august machinery of the intellect. And how far this *dehumanizing* process has gone, can best be seen from the extremely cavalier attitude towards *morals* and all their works, which today has become fashionable.

I am not here concerned, as you know, with the religious, much less with the moral, side of this question. How it may result in a flowering of all the arrogant "amoral" Nietzschean, or Al Capone-like, characteristics of our kind — how, in short, "religion" may become the rendezvous of persons with powerful power-complexes out of a job, of social and intellectual snobs seeking an "authority" outside their little "individualist" selves for the most disagreeable forms of "individualism" possible — and how the (well-merited) contempt into which morals and moralists have fallen may provide a religious sanction for every inhumanity — and how the nadir that has been reached by the stocks of the "humanitarian" (at which word we all have learnt to spit, I hope, from Moscow to New York) — with all this I am not at all concerned. Strictly, it is the business of the moralist. I wish him joy of it, poor devil!

No, what I am meditating in the face of such a promising set of circumstances, as I have been at pains to exhibit above, is simply how the artist may benefit from them to the full: I think it is pretty plain that he may turn all this to his profit, in more ways than one. How this may be, I will now proceed to explain. The moralist is, it is generally conceded, one of the most troublesome enemies the artist has at normal times (it was the moralist closed down the theatres and brought to an abrupt end the Tudor drama — the stock historic illustration): and here we have in the up-to-date religionist (I refer to the sham and flashy, the propagandist type), an enemy of the moralist, just as the latter is of the artist. It is desired to keep the moralist in his place! But *we* want to do that too. Here is a situation of which some use surely can be made. Every support should be forthcoming for these chilly, snobbish, anti-human sectaries. For *their* pidgin is ours as well!

I will agree that the culture-technician who has, profiting by the mistakes of his predecessors, taken to "leaning heavily on religious values," is not a bird who seems to promise much for the advancement of a living art. Nor is he liable to love art too well. But it is our business not to be deceived by appearances. Of course we must not forget, either, that some sort of "a dirty little Protestant moralist" is in all probability concealed beneath however loftily labelled an intellectual envelope, with the arms of Aquinas heavy upon every pompous seal: we must be prepared for some backslidings into the manners of the Conventicle, and never forget that our "graven images" are likely to appear to the man-beneath-the-domino as "idolatries." But that does not matter — we can easily frighten the Puritan back into his hole, merely by threatening to denounce him! We hold this snob in the hollow of our hand. In the name of the Intellect we can cow the Covenanter or Universalist in the flick of an eyelash or make him blush by a passing reference to *the five points of Calvinism!* We have here a lever at our disposal which is as powerful as that of social snobbery, and indeed whose operation is very reminiscent of that. The terror of not being on the side of the Intellect, the terror of being out of date, the terror of everything and everybody — these are three great terrors which secure this guy to us and make him our man. And let us make a "ruthless" use of them. For we must not allow morals so much as to put their nose outside their dens again, in these quarters at all events! With a good solid religious backing (and I have made clear the sense in which I am using "religious") we can deal with the "irresponsible" ethical nuisance, as never before.

For a moment I would ask you to consider the difficulties in the path of the militant moralist today. What are the principal situations with which "morals" deal? Let us take them one by one, and see how they can accommodate themselves to the spirit of the times — for make no mistake, the, as it were, *professional* lay-religionist today is as busy trimming his religion to the prevailing ideologies, as was the nineteenth-century Anglican ecclesiastic (of the "new" type recorded for us by Trollope, for instance) to the evolutionist avalanche.

Let us take sex morals — they have mostly been directed to the maintenance of the family-principle, inviolate and intact. But no one today but has grown resigned to the eventual extinction of the Family — as the Machine-age develops, it will become economically impossible, everyone has begun to see. That little isolated patriarchal unit already begins to look archaic.

The "seduction" of a girl — merely by the use of that word what I am about to say has said itself — is in the nature of an altruistic act today! It is so obviously for the good of the species that suitable people should mate, that a male who — in the teeth of the short-sighted opposition of the old birds, and in spite of the "inhibitions" they have taught their offspring — a public-spirited young man *interested* enough to rape his way into a stuffy family circle, is scarcely a moral reprobate in the modern eye: he is as respectable as a sanitary inspector.

Or take the moral injunctions that tended to protect, on the sexual plane, the high-class family from the low-class one. There is a great deal of money-snobbery at present, but even that is a little disguised. And you would scarcely find a moralist who would be so tactless as to protect the poor-little-rich-girl against her own will against a Chatterley gamekeeper — if such a thing as an attractive gamekeeper could be found, but they are rare outside the pages of Romance.

As to the "eternal triangle," the moralist is as out of place in a triangle, chasing a cuckoo in a nest, as he would be pursuing a breaker-up of homes who had made the breach by way of the person of the daughter of the house, rather than that of the wife of the bosom.

Upon the sex plane, Marxist morality is in practice much the same, it seems, as American sex-ethics. Both are eminently proletarian and pro-miscuous, of course. It is an animal romance — a "boy and girl affair," as James describes even early Boston. Upon the starkly animal plane of mating everything is worked out. And no ethic can stand up against that — no bourgeois ethic. The other ethic is the natural ethic, and that is merely another word for instinct — Nature's "good" and Nature's "bad."

Thou shalt not steal — let us see how that is getting on. All the great group of ethical safeguards that accompany that central notion are today in the most intimate manner in disarray. For as everyone knows, "individualism" is a *far* greater sin than stealing from an *individual* — from your neighbour (though if you take it into your head to rob an Insurance Company or a Bank, even the Marxist will frown at you or rather shoot you against a wall). If, for instance, to take a vivid illustration, a woman writer were shown this manuscript before I got it published, and supposing she took a fancy to anything she saw there — rather envied me the way I had dealt with Mrs. Woolf's Mrs. Brown, for instance: and supposing she took it into her head to *steal* it, lock stock and barrel! What redress have I? The Law Courts? My dear sir, those are places for richer men than I am — I should soon find myself in a debtor's prison if I took such matters there, however good my case. I have a pen, you say — I could protest against the theft in spite of that. But the judgement of the public would be this — "That was a smart old girl who stole that fellow-author's idea, that was"! And of course a "brain-picker" is one of the most popular of criminals, for "brains" are rather a rare and aristocratic sort of possession.

Scarcely any *moral* stigma attaches today to house-breaking or forgery any more than to murder. There is only the question of being found out — and the real problem involved by prison and loss of social security. The enormous crime-fiction output has been partly the cause of that. But the exploitation of the criminal by the Press, the working up of romantic colour, has done its share.

The notion of *Property* however — or the anti-property ideology — is the central fact that must, in the nature of things, unpick all the tissues of that particular commandment.

Thou shalt not kill! Really, to say anything on that head seems particularly superfluous. There was the war. But there has been a great deal of killing of a more intimate and sensational order since then — killing with a real "kick" in it. All the star-killers, George "machine-gun" Kelly, the "smoke-screen" assassin; Dion O'Bannion, the diabolical florist; Legs Diamond, the sympathetic daredevil Catholic thug; Capone, the sleek cave-man, a character from a chapter of the Sicilian Vespers, record-holder in the matter of corpses — is it necessary to recapitulate them and the heroic literature and film-epic that has grown up around them? And neither nationalist war nor class-war fans are going to be too squeamish about homicide. The stage is set for *big kills.* The subconscious must have its way — no one is *responsible!* And what is human life anyway? The oriental peoples, we are always reminded, have never regarded human life in the way that, for some reason, the West has come to do: but that old-maidishness is at an end, thank God! So much for the chief plank of the humanitarian moral platform — so much for the Ten Commandments.

But I do not think it necessary for me to pursue this demonstration any farther. You will agree, I'm sure, that I have made out my case. Sweeping our searchlight a little, here and there, over the social horizon, you will concede that it has been a sensible move on the part of the theologian (the sort of theologian I am talking about) to cold-shoulder morals as he has — to insist a little less upon all that may be marshalled under the head of ethics — if not actually to take to loathing the damned things root and branch — for where would "morals" lead him in such a world as ours? — yes, to turn from this peculiarly unpromising scene of human-all-too-human bickering, sneaking, boycott, adultery, stabbing-in-the-back, pilfering, passing of stumer cheques, scrounging, back-biting, socking-on-the-nose, petting, necking, fumbling, ear-biting — the monkey-house repertoire at its most expansive (or the "mad house," as it is preferred by Mr. Shaw) to more serious and elevated matters, which have as little connection with human life as possible — to dissociate those monkey-house matters from religion, in order not to look too silly. There is my explanation, for what it is worth, of how that sort of situation has come about. It is under correction, naturally, that I advance such an iconoclastic explanation. But I beg you not to allow yourself to be driven away from it before you have given it some of your attention, and tested it a little here and there, circumstantially, upon the concrete things within your reach.

Turning now to my fellow-artists — two or three, we are a small band — I shall have little difficulty, as you may guess, in making them see the many advantages accruing from the *demoralization* of the time. The Marxist, overbearing as he is, at least presents no difficulties on the sex-plane: at all stealing he winks (except the theft of pens from post-offices, and soap from the lavatories of trains): and he positively coos over homicide! Our difficulties do not lie *there* with him. But from the side of ethics (that term most widely interpreted) the artist must expect (with cowardly indirectness, it is true, and with an obliquity that calls for a special technique, if it is to be adequately met) some damaging aspersions upon his calling — and that even from quarters which would sooner die than admit that there was anything moralistic in their censure: such persons as will approach us in the way that the Federal Government approached Signor Al Capone — not like a man, blurting out "Hands up! You're a mass-murderer — I shall handcuff you, you fiend incarnate!" but sending him a notice to the effect that the Income Tax authorities were not satisfied that he had made out correct returns, and would he please step round and explain. *That* is the sort of attack you must expect from your moralist of today. Every form of indirect technique has been perfected. Be prepared even to find yourself wrestling with a middle-west unitarian disguised as thomistic kings-man, boulevard-born-and-bred — do not be surprised to find a simple-hearted obsession about good-and-evil masquerading as an intellectual passion as coldly remote as the astronomers' most distant constellations: for if you are *not* prepared in this way you will be able to make neither head nor tail of most that transpires upon this confused and distracted, this nightmare and bogus stage.

.   .   .   .   .   .

That the Catholic Church has never been silly is because its methods have been masculine: it has been spared the vulgarity of the Protestant technique, resulting from the latter's competition with the more idiotic amusements of the democracy. Consider the Buchman "Group Movement" — pass for a moment into the Mansion House with me, where the Lord Mayor is presiding at a "Group Movement" meeting. Here are some passages from an account of what occurred:[1]

A SIMPLE RELIGION

Commander Sir William Windham said that he was brought up in the influence of a religion which he came to hate and for a number of years he never went inside a church. Now he thanked God that there was such a man as Frank Buchman. He had brought into people's lives a practical religion which they could all accept. He (Sir William) did not mind what was said in *The Times* or other newspapers about Dr. Buchman: he was a real friend, one of the best, and no matter to what Church a person might belong, Dr.

[1] *Times*, Sept. 26, 1933.

Buchman was always willing to help him in every possible way, and never asked for funds. Some newspapers had asked why Dr. Buchman did not issue certain accounts. But why should he? Money was given to him, he did not hand round the plate. It was simply given to him to carry on his work. He had helped people to find a simple religion. . . .

Testimonials were also given by undergraduates from Oxford and Cambridge. One said that he was challenged by the movement to face the moral standards of Jesus Christ, and since surrendering himself life had been full of adventure and purpose. One young woman from Oxford said that she used to go to cocktail parties at Oxford and try and have a "good time," but when she gave her life to Jesus Christ and began living under His guidance she found that God had a plan which did away with boredom. Now life for her was full of real fun and every day was a new thrill. The adventure of life was in passing on the message to other people.

Mr. George Becker, a London business man, said that he used to think a person could not be really religious and in business. Now he had found through the Group Movement that it was possible to work out Christ's will in business. . . . A miner from Fife said that the challenge of Jesus Christ was to a revolution by consent.

This alarming outbreak of maudlin lunacy is not an isolated thing, as we know: it is just the ordinary routine stuff of evangelical Christianity, irradiated with the unwholesome doctrine of the Inner Light: the "young woman from Oxford": who found, after she had given her life to Jesus, that "new thrills" were provided for her every hour or so — that life was "full of real fun" all day long, and was indeed an "adventure" with a real kick in it — she is not a *rara avis*, but as common as sparrows here, and (with more convulsions and authentic epileptic "kick" of course) might stand for half America. And Mr. Becker "working out Christ's will in business"! — it is extremely alarming, but it is an everyday occurrence, all over Anglo-Saxony.

The service of some inscrutable Power, postulated in the functions of a proper Church — to be approached, if at all, it is evident, with some hushing of the world's robot cackle — is thus burlesqued in the amateur suburban theatricals of a jolly passion-play, with all the bad acting of the English, today the worst actors in the world (with one of the greatest body of plays!). These vulgar performances cannot be stopped. Art is a thing of the same order as manners: and the Anglo-Saxon is particularly artless — more than any race they require some mediation, someone to *act* for them. It is no business of mine, nor I hope of yours, for there is little to be done about it. This "crude anthropomorphism" can alone be dealt with by the Roman steam-roller, to borrow a phrase from the journalese of the war.

However, the very voice of the "moralist" is to be heard in the utterances of the Buchmanites: and no wonder our theologian has to fight shy of that sort of thing: but we must not forget that, endowed with a little less intelligence, our theologian, whoever he may be, would be liable to be bawling at the Mansion House as one of Buchman's flock. The fortuitous disposal

of an extra voltage or two up aloft, in the "intellectual" regions, has probably saved the wretched man from that fate. But quite likely he has a
brother or two: and if that is so, we should, I expect, upon enquiry, learn
that one or other of them was handing round the plate at a chapel-meeting
at Wigan, or Blavatskyville, Tennessee. In short, scrape off the thomistic
varnish and we should find the bloodshot Covenanter underneath or
something like it: such fellows may yet, in the name of a highly respectable notion of a Prime Mover, be seeking to impose on us compulsions
secured by the lynch law, as interpreted by the Anglo-Saxon barbarian
who has got Jesus, and who regards *art* as the most immoral thing on earth,
bracketted with "seduction" and "likker." So we must beware, ultimately,
in this maze of indirectness, as much of the "theologian" as of the "moralist,"
since in spite of all protestations to the contrary, these *may* after all turn
out to be one and the same person.

· · · · · ·

There is nothing about which people show so much equanimity as the
possible perishing of art, under the mechanical pressures of the machine-
age or of social revolution. "Art may have to go! There may be no art any
more, it can't be helped!" cheerfully they will exclaim. They do not like
to think of people terrestrially happy or comfortable, and the very existence
of *art* spells for them a *little* leisure, *some* high-spirits, a modicum of peace-
of-mind! And if they are "artists" they will be even *more* cheerful about
it, for they are probably not very good ones (or if they had a little bolt
they have shot it). How well I know this reaction — at the prospect of the
death of art! And what an exotic word "artist" must seem to the majority
of people!

But of *art* there are distinctly two sorts or classes: and the exotic one
is the bogus one. No one should worry about *that* going: and that is about
all you get in the European provinces — as where we live could be called.
The "art" about which Walter Pater philosophized — or, Mr. Eliot informs
us, *moralized* — that "art" is the sort of thing that the true artist has as much
to fight shy of as has the "theologian" where the "moralist" is concerned.
Then *art-for-art's-sake*, as conceived by Walter Pater, is something extremely foreign to such artists as *did* the art about which Pater spilled his
sentiment.

But do not let us, as artists, whatever we do, get into the uncomfortable
position of our new theologian, dogged by the disgraceful banality of his
ethical *alter ego*, the egregious moralist! Let us say once and for all —
ceremoniously spitting as we utter his name — that we regard Walter Pater,
the patentee of art-for-art's-sake, as a mere parasitic litterateur, a promoter
of unreal values, bringing into disrepute the crafts he swooned over, in his

slow-motion rhapsodies — in a time and place that knew not art, however — which had more than a little to do with the prominence of his stupid theory. But we are today reacting against greater disabilities than art guessed of in Pater's time. So we have to make it very clear that we are not — to force the claims of a neglected function — claiming that art should come between the dug and the famished offspring's lips. Art will die, perhaps. It can, however, before doing so, paint us a picture of what life looks like without art. That will be, of course, a *satiric* picture. Indeed it *is* one.

But supposing you interrogate such an artist as Pablo Picasso — he is handy, he is a great artist, he is not far away. What change do you imagine you would get out of him by telling him he should not regard his pictures as the work of an artist, but as productions established upon thomistic or Marxian principles? Or put Ingres, Giotto, Leonardo in Picasso's place. If they consented to argue with you, they might point out that you were merely a parrot-robot of some sort, strayed from your time — which must be a pretty absurd one — who evidently had been put up to asking a string of empty questions, in a shrill and menacing voice: but as to "art-for-art's-sake," such a formula would mean nothing to them. Regard us as madmen, they might say to escape — our career is an involuntary one. In the meantime leave us alone. — There is indeed the classic description by Hokusai of himself — *The old man mad about drawing*. These activities are peculiar (that is why they are looked at askance by some), they cannot be carried on upon the basis of carpentry or photography. But you must stop short of regarding them as natural magic.

The very word "artist" is unfortunate. It has become silly, like every word that is a lot used: the very sort of classification that is suggested by it is a false one. But to come back to the satirist, whose case seemed at first sight a particularly difficult one. If he were to avoid degrading his satire by giving it an obvious moralist sanction, and crudely labelling all his people *good* and *bad* (to the great delight of the latter, and embarrassment of the former — who can wonder, when we refer to Buchmanism to enlighten us as to the popular conception of such values) it seemed he was in a dilemma. Well the solution for him has been found. It will be his task, in the dispensation we have sketched above, like science, to bring human life more into contempt each day. Upon the side of the ascetic, in the interests of other-worldliness, it will carry on the good work of such pioneers as Swift. It will, by illustrating the discoveries of science, demonstrate the futility and absurdity of human life. That will be its ostensible function. And a very tolerable one it is. And should it encounter the moralist — on the war-path as ever, and smelling round the bookshops and the theatres to find something about which to raise a stink — why Satire will then simply refer this ill-bred individual to the theologian! — to the sort of theologian, of course, that here we have in mind. "I must really refer you, sir, to my friend the theologian!" That is all that Satire need say, and with that can turn upon its heel.

There is *Satire* pretty comfortably fixed up, I think you will concede — with all its passports in order, and with a great big *carte blanche* to execute all and sundry at sight! But, my dear sir, *this* — our epoch — is the satirist's paradise! — How will things stand though with the other arts? For some arts are calculated to make people look more repulsive than they in fact are — whether for the glory of God or not: other arts have for their object a heightening of the more agreeable effects, and show their subjects in a rather noble, or graceful light; again, whether for the glory of God or not, as the case may be. What will become of the latter, in an age of introverted mysticism — an age that loathes the sight, smell and touch of all that is sensuous, and would turn a blind eye, a deaf ear, or an unsmelling nostril, to any blandishment — of either picture, melody, or *Quelques Fleurs*? If the ascetic is to be paramount, what is to happen to this glorified beauty-doctor, whose very calling will be anathema to the intellectual master of the day?

Well, I see I must be very frank — or rather, I must *again* be very frank. For a long time already, then, any artist in the least resembling a beauty-doctor has disappeared from the scene altogether — or he plays such a discredited and paltry part upon it that he may be regarded as no longer present, for all practical purposes. Do not look for *that* sort of art — you will not find it today, anywhere except in the museums. There it remains, a record of the personal vanity of the animal, man. This is as it should be. An art of *illusion* — an art which aids and abets Nature, in fooling us poor weak-brained half-animals, is an art that any self-respecting Christian man should be ashamed to practise. No, it is as Mr. Frank Rutter says — all the bright boys of the brush and chisel discovered long ago that beauty-doctors were at a discount — that no flattersome fellows were wanted. They knew that they had stepped into a *serious* age. They shaped their plastic and pictorial policy accordingly.[1]

The latest productions of Picasso — the sculpture in *Minotaure*[2] — of women with little simpering sex-appeal liplets and huge snouts, or more-than-Lenglen heads, with bulging tennis balls for eyes — is at least as "cruel" a commentary upon our kind, if "cruel" were the word, as is to be found in Gulliver. It is as much detached from beauty-specialities. And Picasso started life as a beauty-doctor, it is interesting to note. At the outset he

[1] *Sunday Times.*
[2] *Minotaure*, No. 2, 1933.

showed a posivitely *sickly* disposition to be sentimentally "beautiful." But he soon gave that up. It did not take him long to see that *beauty* was the last thing his contemporaries demanded of the artist. And since then he has never looked back — a long succession of novel brands of idiocy, acromegalic sluggishness, hysteria and abortion have continually poured from his brush. He has gone perhaps a shade too far in discrediting our faces and our figures, and disintegrating our fleshly envelope in general. But who can blame him? The "sentient world" is dross. It is ugly dross, as well; contorted throughout its length and breadth by the foolish grimaces into which the vulgar soul within the flesh churns it up, in yahoo laughter, or creases it, with a sly grin or simper. And for those who — to quote from that celebrated passage, conveying so well the inwardness of our time (not its mere outward, mercenary, hypocrisies), for those desiring to give their service "to that which is Universal, and to that which is Abiding," what better way can they find to go about it than to take a powerful hold upon the *externals* of our life, and so manipulate that objective reality as to make the unsightly truth stare out at us, in images that are not, and that were never intended to be, advertisements for "*homo* the wise"?

But I can see you making ready to object. I anticipate that you will tell me that the artistic partisans of the *internal* — of the dim places of the half-submerged consciousness — the "ascetic" enemies of the materialist school — turn out in reality to be upon the same side as myself. But if you think that, you have not understood me. We so called "satirists," or today just "artists," or whatever we are, must be great experts in the objective and material world in order to do our work properly: and so we must, paradoxically perhaps, relish our task. We must possess *an appetite* for what you regard as "the horrors" that we "perpetrate." But when I said "what you regard" — it was there that the essentials of this statement are to be looked for. What you regard as hideous has the same claims on us even as your ravishing self. We are the reverse of squeamish. Nay, there is no doubt about it, from the standpoint of the sentimental lady-reviewer, we are "coarse." Picasso's hands are caked with paint and clay — my own are never free of paint or ink. This *matière* which composes itself into what you regard I daresay as abortions, is delightful to us, *for itself.* However regrettable that may be, it is the price of success in an art. Materialist to that extent the artist *must* be. No artist yet has experienced any personal repulsion for a grotesque that spring up beneath his hand. On the contrary. He is on the side of "the ugly" as much as "the beautiful," as far as subject-matter is concerned. Such a policy of understanding, and alliance even, with our "theologian," as I have outlined in the foregoing pages, is one thing: but to share the aesthetic renunications of the dogmatic mystic is quite another. On the other hand, of course, the illusionist side of external phenomena means as little to us as to the most hardened saint — we are immune against Nature, since we are in her secrets. But there is more than this.

Beauty-doctors we are not, and have no intention of being: but we have a notion of beauty which is all our own — it is our secret, and it is strictly no one's business but ours. From *your* standpoint, no doubt — and from that of the average mystic, the ascetic of any order or degree — our work is a horrible one. Here we are supposed to be busy with concocting shapes and patterns to frighten even the most hardened of libertines off their vomit. That is what we look like to you. But all the time we are as happy as sand-boys: we do not feel that way about it in the least. *Our* metaphysic tells us that all the time there is a subtle mistake. What you regard as "beautiful" — the most ethereal among you, too — is often an illusion of your *sensuality*. Yes, indeed, ladies and gentlemen, your sensuality, odd as that may sound. Your *Diana-of-the-Crossways* standards you derive as a reflection from the appetites of hearty young hunting-men-husbands of the mid-Victorian age, in no way less material than the contemporary policeman or rugger-blue materialist — whose standards you deride! This is most unfortunate: but such is obviously the case, if you come to consider it a little closely at all!

Take again the many refined and fastidious reasons that are given, and the flattering conclusions that are drawn by innocent admirers of same, for a withdrawal *within* the self — in a shrinking alarm at the spectacle or the contact of all great big whopping objects of the external world of sense. That is plainly founded upon a sentimental delusion, of a quite vulgar variety. The senses are treated like great gas-taps, that pour out asphyxiating stenches. Certainly regarded as exhalations, these external qualities are *strong*. Many, even, are highly unpleasant. But can no composition have significance which possesses components that are harsh? Who possessing what would be regarded as a refined palate would desire his senses to administer to him nothing but tastes and odours of a consistent, and in the end a sickly, *sweetness*? The rough peasant cuisine is much more apt to be *nice*, than is the civilized cuisine, which, looked at from the standpoint of the champion of the "immaterial" — of the "spiritual" — values, is exceedingly nasty!

It is a fault of the modern Anglo-Saxon mind, that it is too *nice*. That is, I believe, incontestable: it has incessantly been pointed out by horrid foreigners, as well as by Anglo-Saxons themselves. In reality, the in-appearance-ascetic values enjoying such a great ascendancy in Anglo-Saxon criticism — literary, social and religious — are themselves *material* values. For what is this squeamish revulsion, at bottom, but a taste for the physically *pretty*? The poetry of Lord Tennyson, the debased pictorial standards of Burlington House, the feeble and unimaginative respectability of *Punch* — these typical modern English things (not English in the Elizabethan or cavalier sense, it is understood — just Hanoverian English — how shall we explain or describe it?) are by no means absent from this emotional and intellectual make-up of the highbrow critic, or for that matter from many artists seemingly unorthodox. The *prettiness* has not been rooted out, only overlaid. There has, as a fact, been no external agency powerful enough to accomplish any such radical operation. There is, for instance, much more of Burne-Jones in Miss Sitwell than you would suspect — much more of Lord Leighton in Mrs. Woolf: that there is much Frith in Priestley may also be true — but how much less objectionable is "The Derby Day" than the dreaminess of that Hall Caine of paint who kept Ruskin company at Winnington Hall? Now Jones would undoubtedly have regarded Frith as a dull materialist, but, seen in perspective, is Frith not the better man of the two?

A taste for the pretty (a material appetite, I assume) is the cause of a certain order of "spiritual" refinement. The three stages of this experience are as follows. First, there is the chocolate-box. Secondly, the chocolate-box image fades, it loses its roses: it becomes etherealized — but it is still "pretty." Thirdly, and lastly, it becomes a pathetic little spirit-picture face — the shadow of a rose-bud: its cheeks are wan and hollow. It is a Burne-Jones mask out of a debased Arthuriad.

But to return to the robustest artist: the intellect athletically enjoys itself in the midst of matter, and is not afraid of objective things because it has the power to model them and compose a world of its own out of objective substance. None of the painting or sculpture of the Orient would pass the canons of our beauty-doctors. It was not however anthropomorphic — it saw a bird or a frog as a bird or frog would see it, with the appropriate eye. — But the *artist is older than the fish,* as I have remarked in another connection: by this meaning the same as the statement that the intellect at its purest does not function in a specifically *human* way.

Why I have used Henry James so extensively in my earlier chapters, in preparation for these conclusions, will now, I hope, be evident. He was the modern Anglo-Saxon *par excellence* — a moralist, an "introvert"; although himself a large bull-like person, a man of timid mind; chary of embarking without a thousand precautions amid the menacing objects of the external world, as introduced, gingerly, into his world of art; as frightened to commit himself as the most cautious peasant; a social-snob, that is a believer in mob-values; a beauty-doctor in words — hence his style of an elaborate German *friseur*, which was an elephantine attempt at being verbally seductive — for he actually believed it to be "beautiful"; and withal, of course, *the best* of his order, a *petit maître* on a portentous scale.

There I will leave the matter until I come to the concluding pages of my book. The two most weighty figures in the world today (I do not say tomorrow) are the Pope and the Marxist Dictator; they alone are consistent, they alone are ubiquitous, and mean the same thing in one place as in another. As artists we shall not, however, be dealing with the Pope, nor with the Marxist caliph. The avowed and official Communist may have less to say than some semi-heretical usurper: the same will apply to the Catholic hierarchy. Never mind: those are the two fountain-heads, whether you like them or not. An artist can have no personal antipathies. In any case, *act*, I say to the artist, as the perfect opportunist, and let truth take care of itself, as it is fully competent to do. I have shown you in this part of my book how art — in the narrow sense I have in mind — may repose upon the contemporary mode of the most "enlightened," intellectualist theology, and so keep at a distance the worst of the moralists. In the next part of my book I shall show how it is possible to compact with the Marxist ideologist: all that is "inhuman" in the contemporary theologist will be of great use — all that is most "inhuman" in the Marxist doctrinaire will be of great use. Out-vying one another in "inhumanity," they will approach — they even con-sciously propose that to themselves — deliberately approach — the "inhuman" ideal of the artist.

PART THREE

FOREWORD

"Pauvre France, qui ne se dégagera jamais du moyen âge! qui se traîne encore sur l'idée gothique de la commune, qui n'est autre que le municipe romain!" — GUSTAVE FLAUBERT, letter to George Sand, 1871.

THE REFLECTIONS FROM THE POLITICAL LIFE of our time which you will discern in this part of my book will be doubly unorthodox: for you will not meet with any orthodox doctrine of either Left or Right finding a footing within these criticisms. In my essay on Shakespeare, *The Lion and the Fox,* I wrote: "far from being the feudal poet, the Shakespeare that *Troilus and Cressida, The Tempest,* or even *Coriolanus,* shows us, is much more a bolshevik (using this little word popularly) than a figure of conservative romance." So the Lewis you will be going along with here will be starting out from what is a fundamental scepticism regarding every institution of Western Democracy, as that obtains today, a scepticism at least as profound as that of the orthodox Marxist. Yet, at one as to the "destructive element," the principles that are to govern *the building,* the other side of the pulling down, are approached by me from "the standpoint of genius," as I have described it elsewhere, and also from the standpoint of my trade. That, I find, makes a great difference in what I arrive at, when I picture the state-beautiful. The cosmos of Marx is too mechanical for me. And English liberalism, or Jeffersonian democracy, is too undisciplined and based upon false sentiment.

As to the great question which divides humanity today, namely the status of the free subject — whether the free subject should be turned into a party slave, with, as alternative, the fate of an outlaw: or whether he should stop as he is, free to formulate, and vote in, any motion, however subversive or irrational: what would the official spokesman representing the interest of "genius" have to say to that? He would of course have pondered that all government in the name of Demos must today be a machine-minded cabal: that mediocrity is merely organizing itself better; and whether it be to the faction of the Left or the faction of the Right that the day goes, it must be a bad business for the intelligent few; just as *at present* it is a bad business — just as at most times it has always been a thoroughly *sale affaire.*

Why favour change (you may ask) under these conditions? Because (I answer) the old cabal is on its last legs: it is liable, at any moment, to indulge in some convulsive kick, which is likely to be as "catastrophic" as even Marx's most violent prescription: and meanwhile life is at a standstill, and the routine of customary change held up. In short, the trash-bins

191

are no longer taken away by the dustmen. The plague bacillus lifts its head. Again, it is time that mankind once more at least pretended to move on a bit—a *jump* is due, there has been a good spell of reculation—a long sag has taken place. The architects are handicapped, the painters are depressed, the writers don't know what to write about, the stage is barred against talent, and science is forbidden to go full steam ahead—lest *no* work should be found for *anyone* any more! "Genius" is in danger! *La patrie est en danger*—the "patrie" of the intelligent, industrious, unassuming minority. But I will at this point make use of the form of question and answer, and stage a debate, between the deputy of *the party of genius* on the one hand, and Citizen X. on the other.

QUESTION AND ANSWER

CITIZEN X. What I understand you to do then is to dissociate yourself from any political system whatever—any actual, or possible, system of the past, present or future?

THE DEPUTY OF THE PARTY OF GENIUS. Of course.

CITIZEN X. You dissociate yourself from human life?

DEPUTY. From all mass-organization, whether aristocratic or demotic: not from human life, but from quarrels and organized adjustments of the majority.

X. You believe in splendid isolation?

DEPUTY. No, I do not "believe in it." A certain isolation is imposed upon us, that is all. I am not unfriendly or arrogant. I merely cannot regard the impure and pragmatical art of politics equal in interest to the pure arts and sciences, which I regard as the highest manifestations of human life.

X. So you consider all régimes of equal worth?

DEPUTY. Oh no. The régime that appears to promise the best conditions for the prosecution of the highest activities of man, as I understand them, is, for me, the best.

X. But my interests are not your interests.

DEPUTY. Perhaps not. But there must be some common ground, upon which we can come to an understanding.

X. I am only an ordinary man— How can I take any interest in what you term the affairs of "genius"? That is much too high and mighty for me.

DEPUTY. It is your word, not mine. "Genius," like "highbrow," is the term to which you have given currency.

X. Yes, but you speak for a minority so small, when you employ such a word as "genius," that all that you say loses interest for the great majority of men.

DEPUTY. Not so, if you are wise: for, first and last, you have owed a great deal to that minority, and cannot do without it, unless you wish to run back to a lower form of life.

X. If we owe your sort everything, — you mean our civilization — why do
you stand apart from our political troubles at this moment, when we
should presumably need your assistance most?

DEPUTY. Our activities precede yours: your politics today are the result
of the private work of the chemists, philosophers, engineers and pure
technicians. It is not our business to intervene, except to the extent
to point out to you that in this or that circumstance you have misinter-
preted us.

X. Ah then, you *would* express an opinion — if, say, the rabid nationalist
betrayed the interests of what you regard as the Intelligence?

DEPUTY. With your permission, I should in that case certainly advance an
opinion: but especially I should be bound to do so, if not prevented,
with regard to internationalist, or any other, techniques.

X. A sort of god-almighty attitude, what?

DEPUTY. Not at all. There must exist among us some unpartisan principle. And the most obvious way of securing that is to accept and keep
intact what, to make myself readily understood, I have called the party
of "genius": *that* partisan will — yes, even the more militantly partisan
he is — provide the nearest approach to an impartial, non-partisan, principle that it is possible to have, in our human society.

X. But how shall we ordinary mortals be able to tell the authentic representative of your "party of genius" from the bogus one?

DEPUTY. That, as with all other mortal things, must be a matter of luck.
If you will allow me to say so, you must use your common sense a
little bit. There is nothing for it but that!

Politics, of one sort and another — though this is involved with ethics
too — are certainly a first-class difficulty. "I do not quite like politics," Robert
Louis Stevenson wrote in his letters: "I am too aristocratic, I fear, for that."
The fellow would find he liked them still less today — they would make
him feel still more "class-conscious." But, willy-nilly, we have very carefully
to attend to them.

In Anglo-Saxony, where for a long time we have enjoyed a very great
measure of political liberty, we scarcely begin to understand what Marxist and fascist politics are all about: but of the two — as *very free* men — we
incline rather to the Marxist than the fascist extreme. Our liberalism dic-
tates that attitude — although I believe it is a misunderstanding, a mistake
of an emotional order; I do not think most influential people here have
thought it out. — In a letter of a French royalist refugee, written to William
Windham,[1] discussing the attitude of the respective American States to the

---

[1] *The Windham Papers.*

French Revolution, he expresses astonishment that the "aristocratic" and slave-owning South should have been more boisterously pleased at those melancholy events, than the middle-class and slaveless North. "The Western States, which are comprehended between the Southern part of Maryland to Georgia, have approved openly the conspiracy against the King and the Monarchy. And it is very remarkable that the States which admit slavery were all more in favour of equality and licentiousness."

It was of course a shortcoming in psychology that caused this emigré to be surprised at that. Why, in Russia itself it was the more idle and intellectually-conceited portion of the "ruling class" that made their own overthrow possible. And the extreme lack of sentiment — of "impartiality," "fairness," "detachment" and all the rest of it — on the part of the Soviet authorities is what makes one feel most strongly that they are there for good, and will still be there when all our "fair-playing" playboys (paralysed with that chronic indecision which is the result of the liberal delusion) are in the dust.

M. Paul Valéry has described our general situation so well, that I cannot do better than quote him:

> L'Europe avait en soi de quoi se soumettre, et régir, et ordonner à des fins européennes le reste du monde. Elle avait des moyens invincibles et les hommes qui les avaient créés. Fort au-dessous de ceux-ci étaient ceux qui disposaient d'elle. Ils étaient nourris du passé: ils n'ont su faire que du passé. L'occasion aussi est passée. Son histoire et ses traditions politiques; ses querelles de villages, de clochers et de boutiques; ses jalousies et rancunes de voisins; et en somme le manque de vues, le petit esprit hérité de l'époque où elle était aussi ignorante et non plus puissante que les autres régions du globe, ont fait perdre à l'Europe cette immense occasion dont elle ne s'est même pas douté en temps utile qu'elle existât. . . .
>
> Les miserables Européens ont mieux aimé jouer aux Armagnacs et aux Bourguignons, que de prendre sur toute la terre le grand rôle que les Romains surent prendre et tenir pendant des siècles dans le monde de leur temps. Leur nombre et leurs moyens n'étaient rien auprès des nôtres: mais ils trouvaient dans les entrailles de leurs poulets plus d'idées justes et consequentes que toutes nos sciences politiques n'en contiennent. . . . L'Europe sera punie de sa politique: elle sera privée de vins et de bière et de liqueurs. Et d'autres choses . . .[1]

We have already had a good part of our beer and skittles removed from out our reach. But for Europe, for all of us, "*l'occasion est passée*," in any case. It is exceedingly important that, as individuals, we should rivet this into our heads. To be a "royalist" today, for instance, may be a good — or a bad — advertisement, for the little "royalist," but otherwise it means nothing. If those countries who, in "the Balkanization of Europe," or earlier, had lost their kings, recalled them, they would only be betrayed (literally, *right and left*) by their bourgeois governments — for these people have now

---

[1] *Regards sur le monde actuel.* Paul Valéry.

become more bourgeois than the bourgeois. The King of Spain thinks and acts — indeed I think he looks — very like Douglas Fairbanks. No, even Romanization could not do anything about "the divine right," which began, and ended, with Charlemagne.

As a mere performer, I apologize for this political dissertation. But it *is* of some importance to the artisan to know whether he should aim at being so-and-so *By Appointment* or not; whether the royal arms over his shop would be for business purposes good, bad or indifferent. In the abstract (and I am making no reflection upon the reigning family, with which everyone here is most right and properly satisfied) — in the abstract, "royalism" must be labelled "indifferent," and can even be bad. So much for the royal arms: and I have said what I think regarding those who "set the sign of the cross over their outer doors." That is no place for the cross.

I hope I have been moderately plain, and not like those who improve in obscurity and mysteriousness with every fresh piece that they write; which always makes me think that they must either have a great deal to hide, or else nothing whatever to say. But finally, is my view of the calling to which I belong too serious, and do I treat problems of public performance too much as though they were affairs of State? — Mr. Ford Madox Ford, in an *autocriticism,* supplies me perhaps with the answer that I need to that not uncommon question. He is describing the business of the novelist, and he tells us that these workmen "try to render . . . their times without *parti pris.* . . . They say: Given such and such characters, public events of the day being so and so, and the set of circumstances being so and so, what will eventuate? The main point is that public events play a principal part in the scheme as they do in our lives."[1]

That public events play a great part in our lives — however small a part we may play in public events — is certain enough. So public events are bound to "play a principal part" in the routine of many of the arts. Under these circumstances it is but natural that public events should play a considerable part in any critical books like this, which is not of course meant to be an entertainment, but a fairly searching scrutiny of the values that all the arts may use, to their advantage as arts.

[1] *Week End Review,* Sept. 9, 1933.

CHAPTER I

THE ARTIST AND THE NEW GOTHIC

"Quelle barbarie! Quelle reculade! . . . Cette guerre pour de l'argent, ces civilisés sauvages me font plus horreur que des cannibales." — FLAUBERT to George Sand, letter dated March 11, 1871.

I BELIEVE THAT I SHOULD BE wasting my time if I discussed the "security pacts" that have been repeatedly mentioned in the Press — in order, who can doubt it, to prepare the Englishman for something or other (it is uncertain whether it will turn out to be the obligation, at a moment's notice, to die alongside the Senegalese, for the swollen reserves of the Bank of France; to teach Germany not to wish to be treated on a footing of equality; or, on the other hand, to be bombed to pieces in defence of Hitler's toothbrush moustache — or perhaps to save Communist Russia from the Japanese "peril" — it is immaterial which). Whatever shapes these chains of alliances may eventually be given — whether that of an armed ring round the German Reich (with what is left of Great Britain after you have sawed off Ireland and probably Scotland assisting on the side of the Teutonic black sheep): or of a more daring arabesque, namely that of a general mix-up too complex to allow of any formula being minted which could be of the faintest use to the untrained intellect (or shall we say the damned fool — with the emphasis of course on the damned); whatever may be arrived at as a result of the diplomatic goings and comings at present in full swing, it is quite certain that that "next war" will do the trick. There will be no problem of Crumbling Industry any more, of the insane burden of taxes and international debts, of the chaos of currencies, and so forth. Europe will emerge from its much-discussed "next war" of no more political consequence than the present provincial governments of China. All the various governments have to do, therefore, is to make the necessary arrangements for this war, in mutual consultation at Geneva or Lausanne, and the European Man will make his exit once and for all, and whatever power, or powers, that are left intact, and all the more powerful for our overthrow, elsewhere, will deal with that not-so-long-ago most conceited gentleman in any way they choose. And, considering the tyrannic rôle he has played as White Conqueror, for a long time now, I do not see how he can look forward to a very gentle treatment.

But why say all this? we are all spell-bound — the Old Order awaiting the *coup de grâce*, without dignity but without any particular alarm (having signed its own death warrant every morning for the last ten years and still finding itself alive and much the same, thank you, a sullen and puzzled fatalism enables it to get along in an uncomfortable sort of comfort, *en attendant*: whereas the "proletariat" is enjoying the last years of Democracy, in a sort of comfortable discomfort, too — since the "proletariat" after all is only humanity-in-general, and it dimly guesses that it will never have such easy-going, vacillating, frightened, alternately conscience-stricken and tipsily truculent old masters again — that the Five Year Plan, or Hundred Year Plan — on the principle of the Hundred Years' War — with which it will be confronted once it is its own "Dictator," will not be so jolly as all that, and it will have no one to grumble at except itself). But it really *is* wasting time to make these remarks — in the mass, it has always been noticed, men have extremely little initiative. Those who are "resolved to do good that evil may come," or *vice versa*, are few and far between. The philosopher among men is, in the most exact particulars, like a person by himself upon an ocean. Life is but a day, as has been remarked before somewhere, and sometimes the ocean is orderly and sometimes it is not. Just at present a first-class hurricane is due. — But there is no use telling *the water* that!

.   .   .   .   .   .

Would it be the least use (I ask the question well knowing the only answer it can elicit) for us to discuss the deliberations of the Labour Party at its periodic conclaves? There are three parties in England at present, (1) the Nationalist, (2) the Labour, and (3) the Communist. The Labour Party sees (at last) quite clearly that if you entertain in your midst overwhelmingly powerful, irresponsible institutions, such as are the Banks — and a big international Casino (called Bourse, or Exchange) in which private citizens, for their personal gain, are sanctioned daily to gamble away the life and work of practically everybody alive — except themselves and the groups of money-bosses — why then of course you must expect things to look a little cockeyed after a bit. But the other two parties — the Nationalists and the Communists — do not at all agree with the party of Constituted Labour. How could they? The first is paid by the gamblers to keep quiet and very slowly and in great comfort commit hara-kiri: whereas the Communists, they perfectly well see what Labour sees, they recognize what is the matter (it does not require much intelligence after all). But *they* do not wish to mend things — to bring up to date an antiquated financial system and so forth — and precipitate a terrestrial paradise (for that is what it would mean, with our mechanical resources): but, on the contrary, to smash them, and then have the supreme salvationist job of building them up again, and pocketing all the power (same thing as money) resulting from this stupendous operation. Labour says (in the person of Lansbury or Cripps) that they do not agree that out of enhanced powers of production should come want and human disaster. "Quite so!" says the Communist: "yet it does, apparently, doesn't it! Prevent it from doing so *if you can* — if you have the power!" Both know that eggs, bacon, bread, port wine — tailored suits and motor-cars galore — billions of tons of fruit and vegetables, would burst out and immediately be available — if it weren't for the antiquated financial system. Both know that it is all moonshine to talk about the atavistic brutality of human nature, which mystically compels the peoples to arm and slaughter one another. But the one says, "we can expose this criminal nonsense and bring the machinery of government up to date by means of the democratic vote." And then the Communist replies, "you have been a long time about it!" Meanwhile Industry, and indeed life altogether, is at a standstill, and recruiting has commenced again. Has the Labour Party a Chinaman's chance of suppressing Mr. Montagu Norman, much less the Joint Stock Banks? If it has, a Golden Age would be at hand. But this is not a question of right and wrong, but of *force majeure*. That is why it is a pure waste of time to discuss solemnly the rights and wrongs of the matter. Nature (aided by science) is *too* bountiful: but the human power-complex (aided by science) is *too* powerful! So there you are. Most economists talk as if it were a purely mechanical problem with which they were confronted — as if, in fact, it were always the same dear old Nature that was in front of them. But of course it is just the opposite. It is nature all right — but it is *human* nature this time. And it is because it is a purely human problem that it is so hopeless. It is best therefore never to discuss these matters.

Such a disclaimer as this was necessary: the drawing in of this *background* at the start cannot be baulked — for everyone now knows that anything that we may say regarding the various civilized arts is contingent upon this very precarious political truce of the world continuing. Had my notes commenced, for instance, with some remarks upon a work of fiction, undoubtedly my readers would have said: "Mr. Lewis has no sense of proportion! When matters of world-shaking importance like that of *The Banks versus the People* are there to be dealt with, or the Revolution in Germany, or the Franco-Russo-Tcheko defenso-offensive pacts, or the new Roosevelt dictatorship under a 'brain-trust,' why talk about a work of art — or an artist, or an art-critic, when you have such tremendous giants as Von Papen, Neville Chamberlain, Zamora, Baruch, to write about?"

This hideous political framework, within which anything at all of a contemporary nature that we may decide to discuss, must be circumscribed and locked (and to which every particular thing must, of necessity, be referred back) is a very great handicap, not only to the artist, but to the critic of art. He usually ignores it, or if he refers to it, a little self-consciously, minimizes it — takes a leaf perhaps out of the historian's book, remarks that at the time of the Corn Laws things were much the same, and after the Civil Wars far worse, and leaves it at that. But that *everyone* does in truth either very imperfectly grasp, or quite underrate, the nature of the world-danger that is at hand, is quite certain: and, so, much of the critic's historical airs are genuine enough.

I will here quote a brief passage from the *Evening Standard*, just to establish contact, in the reader's mind, with a reality, which otherwise he would seek to forget. For is not *The Desire to Forget* the dominant passion (if one may describe the habit of mind of the drug-addict as a passion) of the majority of people by whom we are surrounded?

The passage I am quoting occurred in the pre-Roosevelt stage of the American catastrophe. It gives an insight into the conditions into which the United States had sunk upon the eve of the Presidential Election. The paragraph is headed UNEMPLOYED WANDERERS:

> Reports from Denver, San Francisco, Los Angeles and other cities throughout the country tell of small bands of homeless unemployed, many of whom are ex-soldiers, wandering disconsolately everywhere, eking out a precarious existence from the country-side.
>
> Most cities of any size have encampments of these helpless victims of economic conditions, who are supplied with tents where possible and given what food can be spared. Many are accompanied by their wives and children.
>
> Relief organizations, as well as private citizens, provide soup and vegetables wherever they can, but their existence is precarious and dreary. No city likes to drive the campers away, but they present a formidable problem as regards policing and sanitation.
>
> With the coming of winter their ranks are being augmented, and it is feared they will present an almost insurmountable problem when winter arrives, exposing them to the bitter cold in inadequate shacks and tents.
>
> The Southern States will probably bear the brunt of this strange economic burden, since the trek towards the warmer parts of the country has already started.

.   .   .   .   .   .

The horde of wandering men, and their families, who yesterday were industrious farmers, clerks or factory workers (cannot the same conditions, with local variants, be paralleled in every great Western country?), are *our* victims, the victims of our collective stupidity, lack of character, vanity, love of money, treachery, and, in short, all the other desirable qualities that make it possible for these things to continue to happen — instead of our insisting that our mad bosses should release their stores of food and clothing, and adjust the credit system in such a manner as to give these brothers and sisters of ours *work*. And tomorrow it will be we who will follow in their footsteps! There is not one of us who has not been warned, over and over again, who does not, every day, feel the pinch. And it is only by means of the gigantic smoke-screens of Lotteries and Sweepstakes, Football Matches, Beauty Contests, Cross-Word Puzzles, Sensational Crimes — the Smoke-screen put up by the Daily and Nightly Press, that this unattractive future is hidden from us.

How all this immediately affects the trade which is particularly mine, is of course as follows. The "author" is asked to write nice, kind, cheerful, empty books, full of the opiate of forgetfulness. As a fictionist he must deal *par excellence* in the Happy-ending, and so contradict reality and throttle fact — just when he knows that, as never before, *no* ending can possibly be a happy-ending. In short, just as in the War the soldier and civilian were exhorted to "keep smiling" (and it was easier for the latter than the former to do that, but nevertheless even the Trenches were, more or less, between the massacres, wreathed in wry and muddy smiles): and just as, when a particularly foolish grin was conjured up, the poor Tom Thumb was patted cordially on the back, so now, the disasters of the peace (would not Goya today do a *Desastres de la Paz*?) are required to call forth their Bairnsfathers — their "keep-smiling," cheery novelists!

Well, I do not wish to be offensive, but I do not see how situations such as these (Peace-situations, just as much as war-situations) can be treated in fiction, or in drama, or in anything else, without some degree of "coarseness" as it is called. Some are born "coarse," and some have "coarseness" thrust upon us. It is only by "coarseness" that we can paint our picture truly. As with the War-novel, so (only more so) with the Peace-novel (if it is to be the genuine article), a good measure of coarseness must be allowed.

In the same issue of a morning paper, of a recent book-season, the following two items appeared which were beautifully in apposition, fitting each other like a glove. One was the opening of the main article upon the Book-page, the other was a report of a lecture at Harrow School. Here is the first:

> A return to the old kindness of creator to creature is indicated in the first two of these novels. Both are clever, Miss Lehmann's indeed is brilliantly clever, but the cleverness in each case is used to create sympathy between the reader and the characters displayed, not, as in so many recent novels, repulsion. *Invitation to the Waltz*, is a study of a young girl at her first ball. It is tender, witty, charming. Olivia is seventeen, and not quite sure yet whether she is or isn't pretty. . . .

That is a pretty story, of the *Desire to Forget* school, evidently designed for schoolgirl reading. Meanwhile, at the same moment that the Debutantes were being interviewed by Miss Lehmann in one place, the Schoolboys were being differently entertained by Sir Philip Gibbs in another. Here is what occurred further on in that same newspaper:

YOUTH MENACED

War Danger through Trade Barriers

The Youth of Harrow crowded Harrow School speech-room last night at a rally organized by the League of Nations Union.

Sir Philip Gibbs said that when he looked at pictures of bright young things in newspapers he wished some of them would not remain young so long. After reaching the age of reason it was about time, he said, that they sat up and took notice of the world and of the things around them.

If matters went wrong it would be their bodies and their spirits that would be offered for sacrifice in any catastrophe.

The greatest threat of future war, he continued, is this intense economic nationalism by which the countries of Europe are shut up behind their own frontiers. There is no noble or splendid patriotism in that. It is the spirit of the bandit, the apache and the bullet.

Well, if you draw a parallel between the Peace (*this* Peace) and the War, there is one matter common to both perhaps worth noting. During the War the high-spirited bellicosity of the general run of women (not to mention the "goodtimer" state of mind that they went "all out" to promote) made in the long run a very painful impression upon Mr. Everyman. It gave the poor little Tom Thumb under sentence of death in the Trenches a lot to think about. It was like a condemned man in his cell (condemned for a particularly unpleasant crime that some other man had committed) reading daily reports of the "plucky" cheerfulness exhibited by his stout-hearted wife, who had turned their home into a centre for nightly saturnalia — or else reading splendid accounts of the "pluck" shown by his best girl, who, it seemed, absolutely refused to be cast down by his unhappy fate, and went out to a dance every night with a fresh boy-friend, and had a most "hectic" time of it (how the term "hectic" is historic — what a tale told by an idiot it tells!) just to show she was "worthy" of her man, in not being at all "down-hearted" not she, at what was going to happen to *him* — and would "keep the home fires burning," even as Ivor Novello tunefully suggested! Much that has happened since the War has been attributed to this attitude of "the Women" during that "great adventure." And of course the Churches suffered in the same way, owing to the fact that, in spite of a certain prayerfulness, cheerfulness would keep breaking through. For what ever were the Christian Churches doing during the agonies of this most un-Christian massacre, many soldiers enquired, both during and after the event, if they survived it, as many did (in spite of the "missing-generation" stunt).

So much for the War; but what about the Peace? (The Peace is not quite so spectacular as the War, but it need not be sniffed at on that account.) The "goodtimers" have all faded away, it is true. No one has any money left to "goodtime" with. A sort of bastard puritanical gloom has settled down over the world. But in place of the saturnalia there is a sort of smug and listless dreaminess, mimicking peace, which must be even more irritating for those who are suffering, in increasing numbers, from the "economic blizzard" (in spite of the highly unreliable announcements, from time to time, to the effect that more men are back at work). It is not after all a blizzard provoked by nature — it is not *snow*, is it, of which it is composed! It is just an absence of the paper and metal tokens of exchange — it is not so much a blizzard as a drought.

A week before the World War started everything was sluggish and humdrum — a hundred times more so than now. Yet a little sentimental gossip about Soviet Russia seems to be enough to salve the conscience of the minority in a position to do something. They will *do* nothing, here and now: but *some day* they wish it to be understood they would not be averse perhaps to having something done *to* them.

Such is the situation, very roughly indeed, and yes, hurriedly stated. Yet what those great moralists who censure us for our "coarseness," our "venom," our "vitriol," our lack of "kindliness," exhort us to do, is to go back into the *Alice in Wonderland* world of Jane Austen and Trollope. But it is to an imitation Trollope and Austen that they turn — they wish for a spurious, sugared interpretation: for even Trollope is much too severe for them, for he went out of his way to show "modernism" disintegrating the state religion, and Mrs. Proudie is distinctly a figure of "venom" and unquiet. So lovely Royal Academy pictures-of-the-year (when they are *books* we call them "best-sellers") of young girls of the middle-class at their first ball — of blushing debutantes who are in a bewitching uncertainty as to "whether they are pretty or whether they aren't," is the sort of thing that cunningly supplies this demand.

But meanwhile these two natural divisions of the human race, the male and the female, draw further apart. People are engaged to lecture the schoolboys, segregated upon a hill near London, who inform these budding straw-hatted adolescents that they are being locked and clamped into their respective countries of origin as if they were felons ("See England first" is a command, not an exhortation), and that quite soon, after a longer or shorter period of such savage segregation (isolated entirely from the world without their national frontiers) they will be invited to be blown to pieces by bombs and Big Berthas, in an effort to storm the tariff walls and bastions set up by neighbouring states. But surely this prospect is not likely to make them more, but rather less, interested in the melting vignettes of all the lovely little Olivias, just seventeen, unable to make up their minds whether they are *really* pretty or not! And of course, vice versa, these budding Olivias, instructed to be little Victorians, living under the sheltering shadow of the Prince Consort, are scarcely likely to be prepared, when the time comes, for all the things that are in store for them. For many of them must be blown to pieces, too, once the button is pressed, and the dogs of war, and the wolves of revolution, are released!

Really I cannot see that we "coarse" ones — "venomous" prophets that we are — are entirely in the wrong, and these great "keep-smiling" moralists are always right! *Commercially* sound perhaps — the pretty picture is the better seller — but ethically sound, no! Certainly our writings are violent, but is that any fault of ours? As I was writing the rough draft of this particular chapter a sort of minor revolution had broken out in Belfast. The major one to follow cannot be long delayed. That once prosperous port is now idle and impoverished, its shipping rotting in its docks, its maritime commerce at a standstill, and crowds of active men are out of work and at their wits' end what to do. Come to them, no doubt, with arms in their hands, agitators from the South! What can these people do but band together against those discredited masters of theirs, who cannot even manage their own affairs, let alone other people's!

And now, as I am finishing these notes for my book, we are reading of the landing of cargoes of machine-guns for the I.R.A., of the establishment by de Valera of an "Ogpu" (the happy possessor of "a hooded terror") and of preparations for the outlawry of "the Blue Shirts," their antagonists.

In concluding these introductory notes — in which I have mixed up, hoping to make a pattern that may stick in your mind, books and bombs, Bonus Marchers and Booksellers, "Hooded Terrors" and "Crime Clubs," Magazines of Kiss-stuff stories and Magazines of small-arms and Lewis guns — I can only ask you to forgive me if I have been an uncomfortable companion. It is not, I assure you, because I am a *bad* companion — a black-hearted, "venomous," person, replete with "hatred," or anything of that sort at all. I shall not mind, however, what is said about me if I have succeeded in leaving upon your retina a stain of blood, for the frou-frou vignettes of the next novel of the "nice" school that you read; or if I have caused you to associate a little more than before the Crime-yarn with your own entrails, *not* your next-door neighbours' or those of your neighbour next-door-but-one.

CHAPTER II

FENELON AND HIS VALET

"Vous écrasez d'un ineffable dédain tout honnête commerçant
qui préfère un couplet de vaudeville à un tercet de Dante.
. . . Cependant il est de ces bourgeois dont l'âme (ils en ont)
est riche de poésie, qui sont capables d'amour et de dévouement,
et qui éprouvent des émotions dont vous êtes incapables, vous,
dont la cervelle a anéanti le coeur." — THÉOPHILE GAUTIER.

THE POLITICS OF BREAD-AND-BUTTER have been intervolved, in the foregoing section, with the politics of the intellect. How the former underlie the
latter I have sought to bring out, leaving it a little uncertain at any moment as to which was on top, in my well-shuffled statement — flinging the
components of bread-and-butter in among the components of the intellect
pell-mell, and leaving it to be guessed how to potboil today must be to
bring to the boil a political pot. Now I propose to reverse my scrutiny of
this pair of politics, and to show how the latter underlies the former, being, however, so closely in apposition that it is in fact mixed with it. So
here too I shall be suggesting, by my treatment of the subject, how it is
daily more difficult to draw a hard and fast line — to say here the one ends
and the other begins.

.   .   .   .   .   .

If "the palace of the illustrious Archbishop of Cambray" were in flames,
and if it were impossible to save both Fénelon and his valet, which of the
two would you leave to be burnt to death? That was the question asked
by William Godwin. And in his view "there are few of us who would
hesitate to pronounce." It is safe to say, I think, that there are no longer
so few of us who would hesitate as in Godwin's day. There would be a
quite respectable volume of hesitation actually. And at the present time
there are even a great many persons (and that of a kind quite able to appreciate the claims to survival of Fénelon, and who have deigned to be
trained in a world of learning where his name is a notable landmark) who
would plump for the valet. They would rescue the valet because he was
a valet. He might, of course, be a valet of exceptional parts — he might happen to be a great poet or a remarkable philosopher, the equal in intellect
of a Fénelon. But that would be neither here nor there — except that it would
tell heavily against him, and indeed might cost him his life. Fénelon might
be saved instead! If, however, there were a charlady at the time down on
her humble housemaid's-knees scrubbing the episcopal parlour, then it

205

would undoubtedly be *the char* who would be saved, rather even than the valet, in consideration of the fact that a char is if anything nearer to "a beast" (to employ Godwin's careless and snobbish manner of referring to the animal kingdom, or all of it that does not go upright).

"A man is of more worth than a beast" says Godwin, with an easy effrontery — than "a mere animal." And arguing from this narrow-minded premise, he arrives at a hierarchy in which "the valet" (with a soul susceptible to the niceties of abstract "justice") would, if he were a conscientious valet, immolate himself without hesitation to the fame of Fénelon (for here of course it was not the palace that mattered, nor a prince of the Church, but was a question of a great man of letters who was in danger of being roasted). Godwin lays it down that "that life ought to be preferred which will be most conducive to the general good. In saving the life of Fénelon," he writes, "suppose at the moment he conceived the project of his immortal *Telemachus*, I should have been promoting the benefit of thousands, who have been cured by the perusal of that work, of some error, vice and consequent unhappiness."

That has a far-off sound — "His immortal Telemachus." How that "most conducive to the general good" just turns its back in a lordly fashion upon the real world of "what the public wants," and bothers no more about it! Anyone would think that there were only a few thousand authentic non-animals in the universe, too. Who on earth can these "thousands" have ever been who are "cured," we are confidently told, by a reading of Fénelon? Cured of what? Hysteria, or the gout? But these privileged "thousands," Godwin informs us, shed a comforting glow in their turn over the toiling millions beneath them. "Nay," he cries, "my benefit would extend further than this; for every individual, thus cured, has . . . contributed in his turn to the happiness, information, and improvement of others." *Some cure!* the legendary transatlantic slangster would exclaim. But these sorts of cures have come to be luxuries, and to be "conducive to the general good" cannot be claimed for them; and even if it could, how utilitarian is that particular "general good!"

Accustomed as we are to every disequilibrium — of war, artificial famine, pestilence, social revolution — where, in short, the burning of a bishop in his palace can be little else than a trivial Fifth of November joke — and where men of letters have become merely "authors," pawns in the exciting Big Business game-of-chance of the buying and selling of books (and where Fénelon would be treated exactly on the same footing as Elinor Glyn or Vicki Baum) this attitude of mind with regard to the "immortal" Fénelon, which was typical of the nineteenth century (and indeed of every century before this one, more or less) is almost incomprehensible. Fénelon was "immortal" because the not very numerous class who possessed a monopoly of learning or information regarded the system to which they belonged as permanent. No man of any political system today believes that what is "the system," for him, has a long lease of life; tomorrow's system, he recognizes, will repudiate the values of that of today, reverse them indeed. As a consequence, the books of Fénelon, in his eyes, are neither more nor less ephemeral than the loves and sorrows, dreams and indigestions of Fénelon's valet: and this has a considerable bearing upon the question of whether, when the house is on fire, any particular trouble should be taken to preserve the carcase of this mere "author."

A culture as great as the Hellenic today, confronted with a Dark Age, would stand far less chance of surviving, and being dug up at some future time, than did the Greek. There is a more pernicious fanaticism at large than ever before in the world, for the very good reason that the means of destruction at its disposal are so enormously enhanced by the conditions of the Machine Age. Hence a Fénelon is apt to diminish to the span of his personal life, and his personal self. He is not magnified by the telescopic effects of a distant "immortality," nor is he regarded as a portion of the heritage of a given society — for that society tomorrow may not be there. He is not seen through the temporal medium of an immutable posterity. There is no posterity. He stands for no tradition. Every impulse of the time strikes at tradition. There is no tradition. He is not in short greater than himself, he is just himself — just as the valet, on his side, is himself. It would be absurd to ask the meanest of valets, therefore, to sacrifice himself for even the most illustrious of masters in Homer's or in Dante's line of business: just as it would be absurd today to expect a Mayfair servant to regard the violent demise of the vulgar persons by whom he is employed (with no other backgrounds than he possesses himself, reading the same detective fiction, with identical passions and instincts) than much more than the death of a dog. Whereas a family servant of the century of Fénelon was less material, he would be differently moved at the passing of the domestic sun, of which he was a satellite.

It is rapidly becoming out-of-date for a captain to go down with his ship. They are saved by the nearest Soviet tanker, and quite right too. For what, after all, does the ship contain except a herd of chattering morons if it is a big liner full of people? Where there is only a crew and no passengers, he is rather awkwardly placed, for then he is the most influential person on board, the representative of the *bourgeois* classes, and rather in the position of a modern Fénelon. He, anyhow, under such circumstances, would have to leave the ship last, if possible. But as far as the valet is concerned, the greatest incentive to sacrifice is absent today — namely, public opinion. If Sir Jack Squire were consumed by fire tomorrow (Heaven avert the omen) in his North London mansion, or Mr. Aldous Huxley, in his mansion in the South of France, no one would reproach their respective valets for abandoning their masters to their fate. A valet observed lowering one of these gentlemen out of a third-storey window, and himself succumbing to the flames, would strike the world as a very odd sort of valet, if not a little objectionably queer. On the other hand, any of the ten million "Crime Club" readers – or readers of Mr. and Mrs. Cole, say – would be gently and agreeably "intrigued" to read in the morning paper of an incendiary valet who had burnt up a contemporary Fénelon, or one of the two gentlmen I have just named, first having insured his life for a substantial sum. In that, they would take a sleepy, genial interest. Whereas a valet who had followed Godwin's advice: "Suppose I had been myself the valet; I ought to have chosen to die, rather than Fénelon should have died!" – that sort of domestic would definitely make them sit up – they would at once proceed to invent some disobliging story to account for his eccentricity.

The "quandary" of the Valet and the Archbishop is a political quandary, of course. But that of the Valet and the Saint, or Hero, of what nature is that? And, of course, in our Western Civilization such men as Fénelon have been our saints or prophets. Shakespeare is the greatest Englishman, there is no religious teacher of comparable popular stature (and Science, in its present metaphysical and aesthetic mood, would not be inclined to dispute the place that Shakespeare occupies in the history of the English People).

Well, today it is a political quandary, too, I think. Of course, Shakespeare had no valet, as far as we know. But the figure of the valet is unnecessary. Substitute "a friend" – substitute week-end cottage, or tenement, for "palace" – it would be just the same thing. "In a loose and general view I and my neighbour are both of us men; and of consequence entitled to equal attention. But, in reality, it is probable that one of us, is a being of more worth and importance than the other." What has changed so much is not that people are disposed to insist that all men are brothers and equals (there is in a sense less of that than in Godwin's time), but that they are apt to base their valuations, as to what entitles a person to be regarded as of more "worth and importance than another," upon a different system of values. Materialist or "power" values have taken the place of the religious un-material values. The jealousy of the religionist has never been surpassed, if it has been equalled by that of the anti-religionist politician who so swarms and seethes today – the priest of everything that is *anti* any spiritual value whatever, as opposed to plainly corporeal, and starkly "economic," ones. A condition of purely artificial Want – which no man or group of men of the old system has the courage, intelligence or honesty to attack and dissipate – a paralysis of industry which is as fictitious as American "Prohibition" was – provides the necessary stormy background of world-distress for a legion of vociferous salvationists.

Every value that is not a political value (and "political" with the vast armies of Unemployed created by the above-mentioned artificial Want, signifies exclusively "economic") is taboo. The horrors of the Peace operate in the same manner as the horrors of War – there is perpetual crisis. To the cry of "national emergency," any measure, however oppressive, may be safely launched, as if beneath the shadow of martial law. No value that is not an economic value (a value in some breathless "plan" to rescue the world or the nation from the incurable results of Tariff, of currency shibboleths, or of Debt) is permitted.

But the jealousy of the purist political-economist, the "catastrophic" sectary, is more furiously aroused by the spectacle of what has been up till now that lay-saint of the pagan West, the "great Man," or "genius," than by any other figure upon our chaotic stage. This is a compliment to that sort of leader—but it is one that he would, for the most part, gladly dispense with. Any tradition that there is, aside from the Church of Rome, is embodied in these figures. Such names as (in England) Dickens, Darwin, Ruskin, Carlyle, are names that, more than those of statesmen or soldiers, personify an ethos. Hence the violence of the assaults that are made upon "the intellectuals," and upon the "irresponsible" artist-principle.

CHAPTER III

GUSTAVE FLAUBERT

THE IVORY TOWER

"Plus que jamais, je sens le besoin de vivre dans un monde
à part, en haut d'une tour d'ivoire." — FLAUBERT.

THAT SOMETHING RESEMBLING a Mohammedan "justice" (beneath the
shadow of the Sword) has substituted itself, or is in the course of doing
so — for a Christian "justice," in Western Democracy is, I think, evident.
And I think we have to reckon with that changed standpoint very much
more than customarily is done, if we are to understand what is occurring
in the province of Art and Letters.

In the world at large to start with, the old simple-hearted shopkeeper
money-worship (a very ugly religion) is disappearing, if for no other reason
because money as a stable thing is everywhere in process of liquefaction —
or, to make use of the Marxist's pet word, of liquidation. In place of it
is coming into being a worship of power (an ugly cult as well) and possibly
of what people would interpret as *luck*: a religion of fate, a "fatalism."

The West, in fact, can never have been so "oriental," so fatalist, as now.
And just as what you can *do to* other people (your function, or position)
is being substituted, as a standard, for what you can *do with* yourself, or
for the number and splendour of your goods and belongings (money), so
what you *are* has gone out in favour of what fate has decided you shall
represent at the moment. You are, in fine, symbolic rather than real.

You hold an office, you stand for a collectivity: you do not stand for
anything *personal* at all, that is the idea. "What magic is there in the pro-
noun 'my' to overturn the decisions of impartial truth?" And that "impartial truth" is, of course, the stealing of the power of the Many, and the
vesting it in the One — instead of merely stealing the tokens of their labour,
and hoarding them in iron safes.

A visit, even the briefest tour of inspection, to the oriental civilization
still to be seen in full flower in French North Africa, is highly to be recommended. And such a visit is sufficient to convince anyone how rapidly
Europe is not only "Balkanizing" itself, as Mr. Douglas describes it, but
also orientalizing itself. And as to the New World, America, that is already
half-oriental. It is almost as bandit-ridden and corrupt as China. (And now
it is going to have the great flocks of beggars apparently, as well, which
are such a great feature of the life of the East.)

It was the Napoleonic Wars which made it possible to transform France

211

into a "Bankers' Republic," and to introduce a host of far-reaching innovations which nothing but a mass-effort imposed on the nation by prolonged large-scale war could have done. But our wars and revolutions of 1914–1918 were infinitely more closely organized, and far greater in extent. Also, a government today does not have to wait for another war in order to organize and dragoon. Such a Peace as ours answers the purpose just as well! So it is small wonder that the changes effected in the last two decades have been even more surprising than those for which the great bandit-epic of Napoleon was responsible, and that a collectivist and fatalist society has taken the place almost of an individualist and democratically optimistic one. And in that society, at a not very distant date, there will be no money, probably, by the acquisition of which the individual can mechanically assure his freedom. Having regard to the fact that ability to get hold of money at all times has been the knack of the worst, or at all events least interesting, type of person, this should be a great benefit, on the face of it.

On the face of it, this must be so. But in spite of that, it must not be lost sight of that in some cases money has actually been a factor of personal freedom. These sacrosanct tokens – of gold, silver, copper or paper – are not so bad as they are painted if you consider the more pervasive and oppressive obligations, and the type of tokens, which might take their place. In the past, the man of parts has often made use of money he has made to eliminate human interference, and to produce work ultimately of a useful character. And I suppose it is as well to remember, too, that that ugly knack of piling up the shekels, and all the unlovely qualities of which it is composed, will pass over intact into a "power" system. It will be seen that the same sort of *Untermensch* who is good at getting money will be good at getting power. And in a "power" system (such as a rigidly bureaucratic, salvationist, revolutionary system would no doubt be) it might quite well happen that the artist or philosopher would lack even that small margin of independence that, while it lasts, a five-pound note may give. But this is a defence "of money," you may indignantly exclaim. Certainly not, I should reply, not of money (of great aggregates of unproductive capital, put out at interest and compound interest, for ever and ever): it is merely turning up, and having a look at, the reverse side of the other medal, of that phantom coin of a moneyless universe – the "power" currency, in short. It is a taking thought for the traps which the impartial, the scientific intellect may encounter when relieved of the nightmare of Mammon. It is a mere reminder that Mammon is not likely to commit suicide, but only to disguise itself and change its name. But that is rather a specialist problem, distinctly one for the political mind. And I am not here starting a quarrel with the salvationist – and I do not love money. I only love freedom.

Today we stand, of course, midway between the old "individualist" society, based on L.S.D., and the new collectivist society, based upon an armed terrorist central authority. Both probably possess enormous disadvantages. But for my part I am unable to imagine any human system of law and government that would not be bad. The "impartial truth" of Science and Art must, like Mammon, pass over into the new dispensation, however — and that as intact as possible, if we are to be civilized at all. I write purely from the standpoint of the artist and scientist (to parody my old chum Jolas). I see upon all sides the standards in the arts of which I am a practitioner getting worse and worse — the gang-mind taking the place of the individual mind, and the books and pictures not improving in the process. The business-mind more and more imposes its box-office and library-subscription standards upon the production of the intellect — that requires no pointing out. For a century this deterioration has been under way, however. It has been coeval with "the march of mind," as it was called when Thomas Love Peacock lived. This deterioration was recognized and violently commented upon by Ruskin, Samuel Butler, Thomas Carlyle, by Love Peacock, by Matthew Arnold — and, in short, by all the most clear-sighted people of the nineteenth century (the century of the Industrial Revolution), whose lot was cast in the midst of this universal collapse of taste (especially when it was a novel enough event to shock them very much). Let us continue today to comment upon it. It is the best way of securing some small redress, and of keeping a limited area clear for the operations of the "impartial truth" of art and of science. And especially as a new order is taking shape it is essential to petition it to repudiate the vulgarity of the *bourgeois*, as well as his wickedness.

I believe I am alone among writers today in advocating no partisanship in the political field. Most adopt one of the two conventional extremes — Marxism or royalism. But I am neither a King's Man nor a Collectivist. I am sure that no royalist's king today can be anything but a dangerous and mercenary puppet — that is as far as I go. Bad as Marxism may be (and it is now openly proclaimed — and lauded by those who sponsor it — as the terrorist absolutism of a Ghenghiz Khan), it cannot be much worse than the feudal and post-feudal monarchies of Europe. *Human life had better, here and now, and once and for all, be accepted as a very bad business indeed.* And such people as you (and by you I mean You) must not waste our time in predilections or beliefs of an illusory nature, pitting this system against that. All are apt to be equally bad. We must not only abandon the sort of comfortable hope which President Hoover's "Prosperity is just around the corner" pronouncement (which has since caused so many people who were its dupes to grind their teeth and to curse the statesman who was responsible for it) aimed at stimulating. We must reach far beyond that, and understand that there is no such thing as a just, humane, and enlightened régime "just around the corner" either, or anywhere in the universe at all. It is simply the part of a fool, and a pathetically conceited fool at that, to suppose that it is *pour nos beaux yeux* that any salvationist is ever going to be bustling and busy. And, of course, today the salvationist does not even pretend as much—he is relatively honest. He says: "I am Ghenghis Khan! Be on the winning side! I will save you from yourself! Leave all and follow me!" That is a distinct improvement upon the humanitarian, the sugar-tongued shark. At this moment no one has any excuse for not knowing exactly where he is!

Our position in Anglo-Saxony today, on the lendemain of our great victory in war, is very much what the French experienced in the last century after the Franco-Prussian War—after a great defeat. But the intellectual leaders of France in the last century did not, from all accounts, quite realize where they were—they were under the spell of the old European optimism. They still stormed against this régime and that, as if there were a better one, somewhere or other—perhaps "just around the corner," who could tell?

After the Paris Commune, Théophile Gautier mournfully promenaded the ruins: but at least he had the sense to see that it was no use abandoning Paris and selecting some other city to be the capital of France, for all cities are liable to Communes.

> Il y a sous toutes les grandes villes des fosses aux lions [as he says], des cavernes fermées d'épais barreaux où l'on parque les bêtes feroces, les bêtes puantes, les bêtes venimeuses, toutes les perversités réfractaires que la civilisation n'a pu apprivoiser, ceux qui aiment le sang, ceux que l'incendie amuse comme un feu d'artifice, ceux que le vol délecte . . . population immonde, inconnue au jour, et qui grouille sinistrement dans les profondeurs des ténèbres souterraines. Un jour, il advient ceci, que le belluaire distrait oublie ses clefs aux portes de la ménagerie, et les animaux féroces se répandent par la ville épouvantée avec des hurlements sauvages. Des cages ouverts s'élancent les hyènes de 93 et les gorilles de la Commune. Mais ce n'est pas la faute de Paris.

It is not the fault of Paris. No, indeed: but not only all the other cities, but all other countries and times must be situated for ever above just such a chaos of unintelligent passions, and there will always be a party (more, or less, powerful) no less vindictive and ambitious than the old ones, who will blackmail the little ordered cosmos above with the threat of this eruption, and conspire to precipitate it. No man can control these events, and they must always recur. It is better to take them for granted.

Flaubert was all that he was, not as an artist but as a great civilizing influence, because all these hostile currents of a world in dissolution met in him with a greater bitterness and with a more dramatic impact than in any other European of the nineteenth century, unless it was Dostoievsky. "*Gardons notre coeur et notre esprit*," he writes to the Princesse Mathilde (September 5, 1871)—this was the period of the Paris Commune—

Veillons sur la flamme, pour que le feu sacré brûle toujours. Plus que jamais, je sens le besoin de vivre dans un monde à part, en haut d'une tour d'ivoire, bien au-dessus de la fange où barbote le commun des hommes.

Two days after that he is writing to George Sand, with reference to the same events:

Pourquoi êtes-vous si triste? L'humanité n'offre rien de nouveau. Son irrémédiable misère m'a empli d'amertume, dès ma jeunesse. Aussi, maintenant, n'ai-je aucune désillusion. Je crois que la foule, le troupeau sera toujours haïssable. Il n'y a d'important qu'un petit groupe d'esprits, toujours les mêmes, et qui se repassent le flambeau.

Or in another letter:

Ne t'occupe de rien que de toi [he advises a friend]. Laissons l'Empire marcher, fermons notre porte, montons au plus haut de notre tour d'ivoire, sur la dernière marche, le plus près du ciel. Il y fait froid quelquefois, n'est-ce pas? Mais qu'importe? On voit les étoiles briller clair et l'on n'entend plus les dindons.

"Let the Empire go its own way—let us bolt our door and go up to the summit of our Ivory Tower." In that statement and in the letter to the Princesse Mathilde, "the Ivory Tower" makes its appearance—an important historical landmark. But for that statement of Flaubert's to be a complete record of his attitude, after "Empire," should follow the words "Republic," "Commune," and a long catalogue of words that stand for all other imaginable forms of government. He did not ever, in fact, quite reach the point at which he became conscious of this desolating inclusiveness, although that he was spasmodically aware of it there is evidence enough.

In his "political" letter, as he called it, to George Sand, of September 8, 1871, he expressed himself again as follows—which proves sufficiently how little he was either a royalist or a republican:

Les mots république et monarchie la feront rire [à la postérité]. . . . Car je défie qu'on me montre une différence essentielle entre ces deux termes. Une république moderne et une monarchie constitutionelle sont identiques.

A modern republic and a constitutional monarchy are identical—so much for royalism and republicanism, in the eyes of Flaubert: and as to Communism, the "Gothic notion of a Commune" pleased him just as little. His was a complete political nihilism, or at first sight it seems to be that. "Pauvre France!" he cries, "qui ne se dégagera jamais du moyen âge! qui se traîne encore sur *l'idée gothique de la commune*, qui n'est autre que le municipe romain!"

Mr. Edmund Wilson, who contributed a series of ingenious articles called *Critics of the Middle Class* to the *Herald Tribune*, selected *L'Education sentimentale* of Gustave Flaubert as the great par excellence anti-bourgeois book of books. (Mr. Wilson is a recent convert to Communism.) "The most remarkable of Flaubert's novels from the point of view of social criticism is *L'Education sentimentale*." Flaubert was bracketed in these articles with Karl Marx as the greatest guy of all in the anti-bourgeois racket; with some skill and many omissions he made out quite a good case:

> *L'Education Sentimentale*, though we may rebel against it and become angry at it when we first read it, still sticks in our minds and plants deep there an idea which we can never get rid of – the idea that our middle-class society of business men, manufacturers and people who live on or deal in investments, so far from being redeemed by the culture and idealism which have come out of it, has ended by cheapening and invalidating culture in all its branches – politics, science, and art – and not only these, but the ordinary human relations, love, friendship and loyalty to cause – till the whole civilization has become suspect.

What has been done to art and to pure science under Capitalism has at all times been one of the main sticks with which to beat the latter. So it is important to consider how the organization that seeks to overthrow it is likely to make good its claim to revive culture and rescue it from the cheapening effects of the contamination of the Capitalist mind.

And you have in me a person who is as nearly impartial as it is humanly possible to be – and, further, one who takes it as axiomatic that the present type of Western Democracy cannot and should not survive.

Flaubert having been rudely wrenched out of his French nineteenth century context ("bourgeois" bursting from his lips as if in a political print) by the ingenious Mr. Wilson, let us take up that challenge, and interrogate Flaubert rather more closely than Mr. Wilson has cared to do. But first I wish to put upon a proper footing a little matter that concerns me *personally*. So you will perhaps excuse me if at this point I draw your attention to what the *Zeitgenossen* of Boz archly referred to as Number One.

Here is what I have to say: if Gustave Flaubert is going to be run as a rival to Marx as the enemy of the *bourgeoisie*, I think I should like to advance my own claims as a bourgeois-baiter – they are not mean ones I believe! I know that at some future date I shall have my niche in the Bolshevist pantheon, as a great enemy of the middle-class idea. Keats said: "I shall be among the English poets after my death." I say: "I shall be among the bolshie prophets." My "bourgeois-bohemians" in *Tarr*, and oh my *Apes of God* – will provide "selected passages" for the school children in the Communist or semi-Communist State, of that I am convinced, to show how repulsive unbridled individualism can be. – But this will not be yet. I refer to these books of mine not out of vainglory by any means, but in order to demonstrate the complete absence of bias with which, in view of the special honours in store for me, I am able to approach these topics.

But (at the risk of spoiling my chances in the matter of the above-mentioned honours) I must point out – or I had better say I must humbly hint — to Mr. Wilson that Flaubert had not in mind, when he was drawing up his damaging pictures of nineteenth-century society, any other society in particular to set up against it. It is one thing to be turned sick by the spectacle of the organized vulgarity of a given social group: but it is quite another thing to accept just any ideology that happens to be opposed to it. Because B is not A, that does not say that B is better: nor does it say that B is not somewhat like A, in many important respects, and liable to produce the same effects in the sensitive observer. Nor does it say that C, different to both, would not be far better than either: or that M or N might not be the best of the lot. — But decisions regarding that we must leave to the politicans *de métier*.

As regards the Marxist creed at least there is no trouble about human *inequality*. On that head, in private conversation, any intelligent Marxist is quite as positive as the member of the most doctrinaire oligarchy. But what are the values he employs to decide who shall benefit in this hierarchical framework? That the Marxist values are dogmatically materialist values I need not mention. But it is unnecessary to press this point farther home at present.

In the case of Flaubert it is much more serious, however, even than that, for Mr. Wilson's case. Flaubert has left on record what he thought of the Paris Commune. A few more quotations from Flaubert's letters will settle that point, I think. Writing to George Sand (October 18, 1871) he says:

> Je trouve qu'on aurait dû condamner aux galères toute la Commune et forcer ces sanglants imbéciles à déblayer les ruines de Paris, la chaîne au cou, en simples forçats. Mais cela aurait blessé l'*humanité*. On est tendre pour les chiens enragés et point pour ceux qu'ils ont mordus.

To treat Communists as "simple convicts" and wish to see them working "in chains," or to call them "mad dogs," is distinctly bad. Or again:

> Je comptais revenir directement à Paris. Mais "la nouvelle Athènes" me semble dépasser la Dahomey en férocité et en bêtise. . . . En aura-t'on fini avec la métaphysique creuse et les idées reçues? Tout le mal vient de notre gigantesque ignorance. Ce qui devrait être étudié est cru sans discussion. Au lieu de regarder, on affirme. Il faut que la Révolution Française cesse d'être un dogme et qu'elle rentre dans la Science, comme le reste des choses humaines.

To take away from the great Revolution made by his countrymen and its "dogmatic" character, to empty it of its mystical content, and wish to see it enter the chilly domain of historical fact, was surely not helpful from the Marxist standpoint. Or again:

> Nous pataugeons dans l'arrière-faix de la Révolution, qui a été un avortement, une chose ratée. . . . Et cela parce qu'elle procédait du moyen âge et

du christianisme. L'idée d'égalité (qui est toute la démocratie moderne) est
une idée essentiellement chrétienne et qui s'oppose à celle de justice.

But although these quotations do seem, at first sight, to dispose of Mr.
Wilson's case, the position of Flaubert was, in fact, very far away from
anything that could be described as "reactionary" today. It was because
the Revolution "came out of mediaevalism and Christianity" that Flaubert
objected to it. No anti-God Bolshevist of today could be more hostile to
Christianity than was Flaubert; he was a match for Nietzsche in that respect.
His opposition above of the Judaic, or Old Testament, principle — the God
of Justice — to the Christian principle — the God of Mercy and of Love — is
significant. Indeed, the Russian Revolution he might not have regarded as
so *ratée* as all that; it is not certain that he would not have found the
Bolshevist as in some respects congenial: for "the idea of equality" is not
the strong point of the Communist party; and though they still make use
of the emotional machinery of Western Democracy, when it serves their
purpose, no one could be more opposed to it in spirit.

But Flaubert's disciple, Guy de Maupassant, can provide us with even
more striking evidence: the state of mind to which Flaubert's teaching led
was extremely un-conservative, even if it was not orthodoxly Communist.
"Like father, like son," and this is what the son wrote to the father, on
December 10, 1877:

> La politique!!! . . . La politique m'empêche de travailler, de sortir, de penser,
> d'écrire. . . . Je demande la suppression des classes dirigeantes; de ce ramassis
> de beaux messieurs stupides qui batifolent dans les jupes de cette vieille traînée
> dévote et bête qu'on appelle la bonne Société. . . . Eh bien, je trouve mainte-
> nant que 93 a été doux; que les Septembriseurs ont été cléments: que Marat
> est un agneau, Danton un lapin blanc, et Robespierre un tourtereau. Puis-
> que les vieilles classes dirigeantes sont aussi inintelligentes aujourd'hui qu'alors,
> il faut supprimer les classes dirigeantes d'aujourd'hui comme alors, et noyer
> les beaux messieurs crétins avec les belles dames catins.

But I will terminate this series of quotations with one from a letter, written
on the occasion of the death of Gautier (the "poor Theo" who had died
of the *charognerie moderne*). "The Fourth of September" — that is the Paris
Commune — "killed him," Flaubert exclaims:

> Ce jour-là, en effet, qui est le plus maudit de l'histoire de France, a inauguré
> un ordre de choses où les gens comme lui n'ont plus rien à faire dans le
> monde. . . . Il a eu deux haines: la haine des épiciers dans sa jeunesse, celle-
> là lui a donné du talent, la haine du voyou dans son âge mur: cette dernière
> l'a tué. . . . Je ne le plains pas; *je l'envie.*

All this evidence, taken from the private correspondence of Flaubert,
is too complex, if not contradictory, for Mr. Wilson to make much of.
For the purposes of a newspaper article such a neat theory as Mr. Wilson's
is well enough. But when a little evidence is brought against it, it looks

thin, and of too two-dimensional, popular-democratic, an order.

It is certainly true that in a general way Flaubert did possess a very healthy appetite for destruction precisely in those directions where also the Marxist thunder-bolts most commonly fall. To him almost everything and everybody are suspect, except the artist, or what Mr. Shaw has called "the philosophic man." (At the mere sight of a politician he would turn aside and violently spit. There are no doubt politicians and politicians. But we are justified in supposing that Flaubert would not have distinguished much between those of the Right and Left. And the horror experienced not only by Flaubert but by all his great contemporaries at the contact of the political animal seems at least to me to indicate a reasonably intelligent instinct.) Flaubert, that is the fact of the matter, was " 'las de l'ignoble ouvrier, de l'inepte bourgeois, du stupide paysan et de l'odieux ecclésiastique' . . . la République lui parait dépasser l'Empire en bêtise," M. Ferrère, I think, remarks (I borrow this quotation, and am not clear as to whether it is from M. Louis Bertrand or M. E-L. Ferrère).

The paradox in the Marxist standpoint today is, of course, its fiercely anti-democratic tone. For what can "democracy" mean (unless it is used in a very special sense), except the Rule of the Many? And is not the Bolshevist salvationism based upon that principle? But all the great Frenchmen of the last century, or almost all, in so far as they possessed any political bias, were anti-democrat. And it is not (in view of the above paradox) so strange as it otherwise might seem to find the Communist of today quoting them in support of Marxist doctrine. And that should give all Socialists something to think about.

Please do not jump to the conclusion that my foregoing statement is regarded by me as closing the discussion, or making an end of the matter. No political difficulty of that magnitude can be disposed of by any statement, however elaborate: and my statement here is nothing but rough pioneer work after all. It is only too well understood by me that it is not enough to say, "I am not a voter — I am not a party-man," to be left alone. As to my artist-calling I am aware that that is regarded as justified by works of edification alone, of one order or another. "Artist" *tout court* is, I know, a term of contempt. You must be labelled — as red artist, white artist, or black artist. It is obligatory. And I agree that, as things are, this intolerance is to be expected. "Show your colours!" vociferate the sellers of light and dark blue rosettes on the day of the Oxford and Cambridge Boat Race. And are not politics of as much importance as an academic sporting event? Further, I am prepared to concede that an artist in words (the novelist for instance) is more vulnerable on the political side than the artist in paint or stone, than the philosopher or mathematician. That the novelist should take sides to the extent of inclining rather to this political camp than to that is perhaps to be expected. But it is quite another matter to insist that he should conform to all the arbitrary stipulations in turn of a militant doctrine, or that he should only be measured in terms of his destructive efficacy, or his salvationist *verve*. He need even not be militant at all. And conformity of that exacting sort would in nine cases out of ten spell the extinction of his talent.

But is there such a thing as "an artist"? Or to what degree is there such a thing? Am I not, when I employ that term, just using an empty theoretic counter, to which no particular meaning can be attached? If there is no pure art, can there be any "artist" *tout court*? For artistic expression must express *something*: — some vitalist impulse drives a man to fiddle or scribble to attract attention — or more obscurely to express an ethos — is not that it? If it is the famous "personality of the artist" to which expression is given, in the art-form, why then that precious "personality" has been built up out of a number of components, has it not: which, closely enough inspected, would be found to betray a political complexion. For is the art-instinct so entirely detached from mundane affairs as the art-for-art's-sake theorist would have us believe? "*Les nuages — les merveilleux nuages!*" ah yes! that was the reply of Baudelaire to these sorts of questions I know — from the economic world of bread-and-butter the poet was estranged from-birth-up, that was the idea. He was a cloud-man. And Flaubert, was not he "*un homme-plume*"? — So let us, ere we turn our backs formally upon this most controversial region — through which every critic today is compelled to pass, before he is free to exercise his specific functions — attempt to dispel a little more the confusion, promoted by the various sectaries, which makes it so difficult for us to get on with our work.

The materialist dialectic of Marx would have seemed, to a contemporary, far enough removed from the preoccupations of the religionist. But to us it is a different matter — experience has taught us to detect religiosity in soap and margarine: it is definitely upon an intolerant religious impulse, of considerable virulence, that Marxism is floated and given momentum. The class-war is a holy war: and *la haine créatrice*, as Jaurès called it, is akin to a theologic rage. There is indeed a distinct line, beyond which it leaves the region of bread-and-butter and crude self-interest; it is later observed to have circled round and to have entered a mystical field, not so far removed from some of the great non-temporal institutions which have been the first objects of its attack.

It is "anti-God" and nihilist. God is overthrown. But soon the features of another divinity, this time pantheist and Spinozistic, are seen to emerge. Tomorrow we shall see sprouting a naturalist theology.

So undeniably it is religionists with whom you are dealing, in the persons of the Communist doctrinaires: and national-Socialism, that too, as has often been remarked, has taken on all the salvationist trappings of a religious revival — that is inevitable: religion can only be fought with religion, history has demonstrated that. We should not need the armed Nestorian bishops of today, with their bearded jaws thrust out towards the Kurd, or need to recollect the martial prowess of the Benedictine fraternity of Calatrava, to prove to us how even the sectaries of a God of Mercy can go armed from head to foot, and how near is mystical excitement to the military ideal. Economics, armed *de cap à pied*, and with a gaze that is mystic and Mohammedan, is a new invention certainly. But it belongs to a well-authenticated historical class.

The best way, to make clear the nature of our dilemma, will be, however, by analysis of the obstructions which, hailing from quite another quarter, must engage our attention. And who better than poor Flaubert, again, to supply us with the best illustration! We have just been overtaken by the French problems of fifty years ago as has already been remarked. In reading the letters of Flaubert, George Sand, Gautier, de Maupassant, one sees that at once.

There are still other religionists then — religionists I confess much more to my taste — than the materialist-religionists of the Marxian-front: namely those of the Roman Catholic Church. And one of the most brilliant of that communion, a most respectable story-teller himself, has made an admirable onslaught upon the author of Bouvard and Pécuchet, on the score that the latter stole the tears of St. Theresa and the sensations of St. John of the Cross in the service of his godless art.

In *Trois grands hommes* (Editions du Capitole) M. François Mauriac tracks down very ably the shortcomings of his great fellow-countryman, from the standpoint of the Catholic. And it is not — any more than is the Marxist — a criticism that can be lightly brushed aside. For this *homme-plume* that was Flaubert, in his Thébaïde at Le Croisset, was in his way a religionist too. His was the religion of literature. And his technician's religion — symbolized in his famous passion for *le mot juste* — has rather the same drawbacks as the economic religion of the Marxist. It was a little dry and empty: simply regarded as *verbe*, his *mot juste* was a fevered magic, and, *en tant que religion*, cannot support the scrutiny of the (more or less) lynx-eyed thomist. This "penman's" study was too like an oratory; and his occupations smacked at times of the black-mass. After hearing Mauriac, however little we accept finally his rebukes, nevertheless we feel that Flaubert had introduced a passion into his "penmanship" which did not belong there, even if we are not of opinion that it necessarily belonged elsewhere. Penmanship should be made of sterner stuff — at least that much we may concede.

Mauriac in the first place blames him for the diabolical "profundity" of his immense puppets, on the ground that they were forged in the smithy of intellectual intolerance, rather than being bitter flowers of a roundabout love. Here we cannot help feeling, as we read, that, since they were "profound," they are not of necessity diabolical: and that many of the things which aroused Flaubert's (intellectual) hatred, were after all detrimental to M. Mauriac's god. But the very thoroughness of Flaubert outrages his latest critic. His very appetite for learning is sinful—he is misappropriating a spiritual arsenal.

"Flaubert," he protests, "engouffre tout ce qui touche à la philosophie, à la religion, à l'histoire, à la mécanique, aux arts appliqués, non pour apprendre quoi que ce soit . . . mais pour transformer cet immense acquis en cauchemars et en idées fausses. . . . L'effort des siècles aboutit à ces profondes caricatures."

But it is in his accounts of the intimate emotional life of the artist, suffering and exulting over the adventures of his private *verbe*—his "just word" that became for him a thing of importance commensurate with a just God—that M. Mauriac finds most cause for censure: and that an element of scandal does in fact attach to the particular type of tears described in the following passage, we would most of us I believe be prepared to agree. But I will quote from M. Mauriac's book:

> La faute de Flaubert est grave, aussi. L'art substitué à Dieu, cela l'engage dans une voie plus périlleuse que n'eût pu faire l'art bafoué et meprisé. Ce n'est pas sans dessein qu'il use, pour peindre sa vie consacré au travail littéraire, d'un langage mystique. Il usurpe en plein conscience la place de l'Etre infini. . . . Car s'il connait les combats douleureux d'un saint, il connait mieux encore les jouissances qui singent le plaisir des chrétiens.

And then M. Mauriac proceeds to describe how Flaubert had to go and get his handkerchief, to have a good cry—or a bad cry, rather! He quotes the culprit verbatim, revealing him in the act of "lifting" one of the beatitudes reserved for works of a very different order to those merely inky ones upon which he was engaged. These are the words of the misguided master:

> J'ai été obligé de me lever pour aller chercher mon mouchoir de poche; les larmes me coulaient sur la figure. . . . Je jouissais délicieusement, et de l'émotion de mon idée, et de la phrase qui la rendait, et de la satisfaction de l'avoir trouvée.

And then M. Mauriac at this point comments upon all this, with some severity, as you will see:

> Ici Flaubert nous oblige de penser a ces contentements dont sainte Thérèse écrit; qu'ils font couler des larms de douleur qu'on dirait nées de quelque passion.

All that the religionist can object to in art pursued for its own sake —
after the manner, say, of the Sung artist, or of the Athenian sculptor — is
crystallized in the above words of Mauriac:

> La faute de Flaubert est grave . . . *L'art substitué à Dieu!* cela l'engage dans
> une voie plus périlleuse que n'eût pu faire l'art bafoué et méprisé.

It is the notion of the graven image at bottom perhaps. But at all events,
what is quite clear, is that to despise and insult art is a peccadillo beside
reverencing art overmuch. Absorbing elsewhere an emotional commodity
which is the monopoly of the priest is a great sin. For the religionist, all
great emotion must be religious. Flow it must in dogmatic channels. If it
does not, there is something the matter.

Of course the Catholic artists of the cinquecento who bickered and hag-
gled with the popes and cardinals were men of a different temper to the
self-conscious, Sunday School type of Protestant convert to be met with
today, who takes over with him into the Roman fold all the ugly habits
he derives from kirk and from conventicle. To "get" religion is a different
thing from just having one by inheritance. Still, making due allowance for
that exasperating present-day adherent of the great traditional Church, there
does remain a considerable problem for our consideration. There is the
"problem," if such a thing may be described in such a manner, of God,
apart from the dogma of any Church.

For the rest, and putting aside those artists living in the outer darkness
of the Orient, we must either assert that those heathens Homer, Lucretius,
Sophocles and the rest were bad artists: or else we must allow that a great
deal of first-rate art has been performed by persons who have not had the
advantage of being Christian salvationists.

So whether you are a libertine, or devout, you can still be an artist —
indeed, you cannot help being that if so you are made. And it is still probably the best manner of kowtowing to the supreme engineer who thought-
up the toy, to work well, to function properly: and if you are prone to
believe in the miraculous, and suppose that you, a fully-wound-up-toy,
got there *out of nothing* — if you are also *a nihilist* — that simply can't be
helped. You were in that case so *made*, as to function as a nihilist. And
I suppose if you are homicidal, or homosexual, it is the same thing, it is
all for the best or worst in the best or worst of all possible worlds.

CHAPTER IV

ANTI-ARTIST

"Genuine justice seems to demand . . . that the natural aristocract . . . should receive his due reward." — IRVING BABBITT.

NO ART SEEKS TO COMPETE with religion, it is not a way of life. It may be a way of life, a system of "salvation," for the professional critic, as we see in the case of Mr. I. A. Richards. But it cannot be that for the artist. The artist, unlike the critic, must also be a living person, and he is not likely ever to understand that sort of "salvation."

Art is by definition a mere expressive projection of something that is there. But it is not, for that reason, dependent upon one religion, or upon one way of life, more than another, or upon one political system more than another, provided the artist is allowed a reasonable freedom. Its datum is everything. It sorts out, and arranges, as science sorts out and arranges, and, at its best, is not dissimilar in function: it can be used even as a perfectly good litmus paper for many an acid test, without involving a pretentious "depersonalization" of the artist, for after all this "litmus" or this "catalyst" is only a picturesque figure of speech, and "the artist" remains just Mr. This or Mr. That — and we observe that *he* is a seething mass of highly *personal* fine-feelings — on that head he would find it impossible to deceive us!

But that, from the point of view of the jealous sectary, is the danger about an art. And that is why it is sought today arbitrarily to limit its function. And, in order to maintain itself in independence, upon the same footing as science, it must combat interference as never before: hence this book, of course. But dogmatic religion has not proved itself in the past an enemy of art, that is, upon the European scene. In the ancient East, the home-land and the fount of religious intolerance, yes; but not among the Western nations. And today it is far more from politics, usurping the place of religion, and from the "morals" surviving its overthrow or decay, that the anti-artist currents come, than from the theologian proper. (Whether of the spoof order or the real thing.) Hence the necessity, not to combat Marxism, but to counter-criticize the Marxist position, as that affects the interest of all the arts, and to deal very firmly indeed with the irresponsible moralist, possessed of no religious sanction, and as ignorant of politics as a baby in arms.

The Marxist would hotly repudiate the charge of being a religionist. In Anglo-Saxony, more often than not, he would even deny that he was a Marxist at all. But for all practical purposes, such critics as Middleton Murry, Max Eastman, Edmund Wilson, Prince Mirsky — to name a few of the more prominent — can be taken as the authoritative spokesmen of Marxism.

I have a much higher opinion of many of the dogmas of Russian Communism than I have of its spokesmen. No combination of words would convey, for instance, my sensation of being in the presence of something indescribably *unnecessary* when the name of the best known of these crops up — to take the above gentlemen. I am sorry — it's very unfortunate. Some of these personalities are liable to produce a slight discoloration, as of animus or disgust with the thing they advocate, in the critic who is answering them in their rôle of spokesmen. Whereas in reality it is only *they* who are responsible for this unmannerly blemish.

Now a great deal of the disagreeable matter discharged at the head of the artist, much of the nagging and threatening that goes on, is to be accounted for by the simple fact that the horde of Marxist or semi-Marxist scribblers are themselves artists — artists *manqués*, of course. The volume of dogmatic abuse directed more generally at the "intellectual," again, is, in the nature of things, a volume of bitter words issuing from the pens and typewriting machines of "intellectuals" — but of "intellectuals" who have a grudge against the intellect, because the intellect has not served them as well as it should, and has brought them neither fame nor money. — But a great deal of this abuse is deserved — if you allow the term "artist," or "intellectual," a wide and popular enough interpretation. These gentlemen are in fact drawing upon their wide and intimate knowledge, and merely abusing *themselves.* There is no target so good for a bull's-eye as that inside one's own breast.

Most "artists" and most "intellectuals" I, for my part, cannot pretend to very greatly esteem and love. Literally ninety-nine out of a hundred persons who live on their wits (or on their "intellects") who are labelled "artists," because they have never done a week's solid work in their lives, do in fact constitute a fraternity against which nothing too harsh can be said by the moralist, or the salvationist-politician or anybody else with the breath to spare, and the ink-pot handy. And the vocation of Art has indeed been the excuse for the existence of this army of persons who are among the most worthless specimens of our, in the mass, not very valuable kind.

In any generation the number of "artists" who are worth anything at all can be counted on the fingers of your hand — the slightest acquaintance with the history of art will show you that. And if you double or treble that number, you arrive at about the quantity of persons whom it would be legitimate to continue in that calling — in the actual composition, that is, of works of art. (The care of books — the task of the librarian, and the various branches of scholarship, would account for a few hundreds more of "intellectuals" that it is really incumbent upon any State to maintain.)

"It was Thorstein Veblen who first observed the *class distinction* involved in the conflict between science and the humanities," we are informed by

Mr. Eastman. (It *would* be Thorstein Veblen—what a name to go about with!) And this antiquated piece of academic snobbery (the social standing of the science teacher said to be inferior to that of the professor of humanities, at the time that T. V. wrote his tract)—thus dragged out and refurbished to be used as an argument against those (happening to be "professors") who expose the unreliability of the philosophy of the technician!

Yet Professor Irving Babbitt *was* a very easy man to get change out of. His "gentleman" theorising was often a little absurd: and Max Eastman or anybody else had no difficulty in picking out passages from his "constructive" theorizing for the purposes of attack and ridicule. For instance, here are a couple of illustrations from the article from which I have just quoted:

"Economic and other conditions are more favourable in this country than elsewhere for the achievement of a truly liberal conception of education with the idea of leisure enshrined at its very centre." (These are Babbitt's words.) But "leisure," with all its unfortunate associations, is surely the wrong word—and "enshrined" is not a very happily chosen word either.

"Genuine justice seems to demand . . . that . . . the natural aristocrat, as Burke terms him, should receive his due reward": again a quotation from Babbitt. But a person is either an aristocrat, or he isn't—just as a Soviet citizen is a high "commissar," or he isn't. You can call yourself a "natural aristocrat" if it amuses you to do so—just as a man on a bread-queue in Moscow could call himself a "natural commissar," if it gave him a nice feeling to do so. But when you begin to clamour for your "due reward" on that account—in the Moscow queue, clamour for the A.1. type of provisions, for instance—you arouse a great deal of unnecessary animosity. At the best you convict yourself of being rather a stupid fellow.

These terms have a very restricted meaning. If you are a gangster of the Dark Age, and at the head of your gang you occupy an important crossroads, build yourself a large stone house, call it a "castle," and prosper, you will find yourself (in common with other ruffians of the same type) an "aristocrat," sooner or later. Your liege lord will give you a patent, defining the limits of your field of brigandage—you will be the "lord" of such and such a district. But these pleasant things have always been compassed by *armed force*—just as the commissar-caste reposes upon armed force, is watched over by a terrorist police, and was born in a veritable bath of blood. And you cannot reach this social eminence by sitting in your chair in your study and proposing that you should be ennobled—because it is your "right." You must do it with arms in your hand—the typewriting machine is no substitute for the machine-gun in that little matter.

There is nothing essentially ridiculous about a "professor," until he begins laying claim (as his "due reward") to the status of "an aristocrat" or something incongruous of that sort. —In America anyhow, the only sort of "aristocrat" you are ever likely to get will be a caste of Commissars, if eventually a "Dictatorship of the Proletariat" is established there. If you put your money on that, and fancy yourself as a Robespierre, you know what to do, if you are an American.

But to return to "the artist," if there is such a thing: and there is such a thing as an exceedingly hard-working person who is engaged upon a type of work (which is certainly *work* and not *sport*, if we may judge from the labour involved) which is popularly referred to as art, for I have encountered him. Now if all that this artist asks is to be allowed to exist as an artist, and to trade his wares—if he does not want you to call him an "aristocrat" or anything exciting of that sort, but is quite content to be a workman—properly paid of course: may not this be allowed him? That is the question I should like to ask. Must he be lectured and coerced into being a politician? Is not that just as absurd as if he himself should propose to regard himself as an "aristocrat"?

But "artist" is a term that covers the poet, the novelist, the essayist, the musician, and the painter, and all the varieties of output that each of these sub-headings includes. There in fact lies the difficulty. For the busy political tout is quick to perceive that at least some of these activities are susceptible of a certain political treatment. And some, indeed, do involve the artist in a political partnership.

But the artist is vulgarly regarded as a luxurious kind of fellow, overfond of the fleshpots of Egypt, and addicted, when he gets the chance, to the company of the "aristocrat." In the proletarian textbook he is suspect from the start, on these grounds. And this is another difficulty.

How the Marxist critic must in some cases be allowed a certain foundation for his misgivings, and some reason for his strictures, may be seen from the works of Henry James, whose words again we may quote in this connection:

> It takes so many things . . . it takes such an accumulation of history and custom, such a complexity of manners and types, to form a fund of suggestion for a novelist. . . . The negative side of the spectacle on which Hawthorne looked out, in his contemplative saunterings and reveries, might, indeed, with a little ingenuity, be made almost ludicrous; one might ennumerate the items of high civilization, as it exists in other countries, which are absent from the texture of American life, until it should become a wonder to know what was left. No State, in the European sense of the word, and indeed barely a specific national name. No sovereign, no court, no personal loyalty, no aristocracy, no church, no clergy, no army, no diplomatic service, no country gentlemen, no palaces, no castles, nor manors, nor old country-houses, nor parsonages, nor thatched cottages, nor ivied ruins; no cathedrals, nor abbeys, nor little Norman churches, nor great universities, nor public schools—no Oxford, nor Eton, nor Harrow; no literature, no novels, no museums, no pictures, no political society, no sporting class—nor Epsom nor Ascot! Some such list as that might be drawn up of the absent things in American life—especially in the American life of forty years ago, the effect of which upon an English or a French imagination, would probably, as a general thing, be appalling. The natural remark, in the almost lurid light

of such an indictment, would be that if these things are left out, everything is left out.[1]

But it is perfectly obvious that the scene which, at the opening of this passage, James remarked, "might, indeed, with a little ingenuity be made almost ludicrous," was nothing like so ludicrous as that other scene (as described by James) which he offered as a contrast to it — as the minimal essential for the really first-class novelist.

All that baronial scenery catalogued by Henry James is today in England either non-existent, or so shrunken, unimportant and discredited that we may say it would be a handicap, instead of an asset, to have it behind one at the moment of writing. The American *alter ego* of "The Jolly Corner" would still have to have his face of horror. But it is questionable whether the disappointed features of the Anglicized James of today would not be just as capable of administering a shock to the self he left behind him, as would the latter's visage, when uncovered by the hands, to the exile come back to haunt New York. — The proletarianization of our background is now, as I pointed out in Part II of this book, for better or for worse, almost complete. If Mr. Max Eastman, or Mr. Edmund Wilson were able to write a "worth-while" novel (and the latter, with his *Daisy*, has definitely demonstrated that he is not) they would possess scenery or background neither more nor less proletarian than an Englishman or Frenchman. However partial the latter gentlemen might be to "high-life," the castles, the rookeries and rockeries, the scarlet-coated John Peels, the downland "ivied cottages," would be found to have grown so blurred and blotched as to be quite unusable.

From that point of view we are therefore all in the same boat. There are exceedingly few of us, however bitter a pill that may be to Messrs. Wilson and Eastman, who have not been to Princeton, Oxford or Yale (I am one of the few exceptions) — whether our politics are bolshie or bourgeois: and there are still fewer who can claim to come from the *labouring class*. Mr. Eastman's father may have been for all I know a tailor, but that doesn't count. — There is no occasion for high-hatting on that score. A tailor is a gentleman beside a true-blue stoker or miner. There is for instance a young Communist over here who is reported really to have done manual work in his teens. He is enormously looked up to in consequence. He no longer does manual work — like Mr. Eastman and myself, he now rattles a type machine. But he announced one day in the review where he at that time pontificated that he could not imagine Mr. Wyndham Lewis milking a cow. I have done much dirtier things than milking a cow (I have, for instance, as a non-commissioned officer, attended to a howitzer, a much dirtier creature than a cow — I am not proud of this association, I merely mention it to show what a handy-man I can be and how dirty I can get).

[1 Quoted in *The Pilgrimage of Henry James*, pp. 39–40.]

Cows are *not* in my line, that's a fact. But to return to the cross-legged tailor — who is a proletarian all right — are they any more in his line than in mine? — And in any case, perhaps Mr. Eastman's father was a schoolmaster after all. In which case he has a most compromising ancestry, and has no right at all to sniff at "professors" as he does!

I have heard every sort of person, from clergymen to ex-society women (who are too old to be social butterflies any longer and have "embraced" Communism, as they can no longer embrace or be embraced by anything more corporeal and satisfactory) hold forth for hours to the effect that no person should be tolerated who does not "work with his hands" — and their listeners have always been too gentlemanly or ladylike to exclaim, "But hold on old girl (or old boy) when did *you* ever lie on your belly in a mine, or do any machine-minding except punishing a typewriter — bought with twelve good guineas you had not earned yourself, but which came to you in dividends inherited from some hard-fisted old skinflint or other!"

But to expose the bluff of all the "proletarian" ink-slingers and talking-machines is not my object here — no more than is strictly necessary to establish my arguments upon a concrete emplacement and not to leave quite unanswered any source of interference which (owing to the superior funds at its disposal, and unlimited publicity space) is able to influence the mind of the student of these subjects.

Returning to Mr. Eastman's article, he quotes Paul Elmer More, Professor Babbitt's lifelong associate, as follows: "Literature may not presumptuously be cherished as the final end of existence." It will, I hope, be obvious enough that the dogmatic assumptions behind both M. Mauriac's attack upon Gustave Flaubert, and Mr. Eastman's upon the so-called "humanist" professors, give them a significant likeness. But how can this be? How can a Marxian journalist, and a Roman Catholic novelist, both be moved to make an almost identical attack upon heroes of abstract letters — of notorious upholders of the principle that *Literature is an end in itself*? Well it is so, anyway: and the reason is that in both cases we are dealing with attacks by religionists upon a *secular* principle. But whereas I respect the high abstraction of the religious principle involved in the case of the Roman Catholic sectary, I do not respect so much the antiquated materialist dialectic of the Marxian, all those false issues of manual labour, of plebeian consciousness and the rest.

CONCLUSION

THE FUNCTION OF THIS CONCLUSION is that of a brief review — something like a book-review — of my argument, rather than anything in the nature of a solution of what has gone before. In the field of art certain major difficulties arise, periodically. Obstacles to the free exercise of the artistic faculty are found to have gone on expanding and increasing in volume, from year to year. A major obstruction at length stands revealed. There comes a time, that is all, when those whose interests are mortally affected have to take action. What with the "economic blizzard," what with the encroachments of economic materialism, and of mathematical mysticism, and of moralist utilitarianism — what with nationalism, commanding you not only to "see your own country first," but as an artist to cut your garment according to some arbitrary homespun; and what with internationalism commanding you to benigger yourself and become a fantastic exotic — in brief, what with *everything* composing this framework within which the contemporary artist is compelled to work — such a moment has arrived, as to compel him to take action or succumb. A policy of "muddling through," an opportunist "marching with the times" and may the devil take the hindmost, will not help him. He must, I believe, proceed to the taking of his bearings anew, unless he is to be entirely derelict or missing a few years from now. If we are not to wake up one morning and find that, the first among civilized men, we have become the Men Without Art, we must give some attention at once to this not insignificant problem.

There is nothing mysterious about the Fine Arts, I take it: there is nothing up the artist's sleeve I hope. Art is as transparent and straightforward a proceeding as is animal life itself. Singing, dancing, acting and building are all indulged in by animals of one kind or another. The pretentions of art, I take it, do not point to anything beyond the thresholds of life, or aspire to transcend the well-defined limits of man's animal status. An animal in every respect upon the same footing as a rat or an elephant, I imagine you will agree — man, except for what the behaviourist terms his word-habit, is that and no more, except for his paradoxical "reason." So really *the word* — in contrast to the sound or image — is the thing most proper and peculiar to him (the word, and laughter perhaps). That we are merely *talking* monkeys — rats, elephants, bullocks or geese — is obvious. It is a very peculiar situation! But it is only a peculiar situation, *not* at all because it is strange that great people like ourselves should be at the same time "animals": not that. But because it is a little odd that animals like ourselves should be enabled — by means of our "word-habits" to *know* that we are

231

animals and to be compelled, or indeed *to be able* — to go on being animals and behaving as such, and yet perfectly realizing what we are.

But when we say *realizing what we are*, what, it is advisable to ask, do we exactly mean? All that we mean is, I believe, that we are able to recognize our animal limitations — our enormous physical and intellectual handicaps. Those handicaps, those drastic limitations — of gestation, metabolism, hunger and thirst, courtship, reproduction, and all the rest of it — appear to us *absurd*, as we call it — or ridiculous (laughter-provoking). *Homo animal ridens*, that is it — that is our true description.

Laughter is, however, as has been remarked very often, our "god-like" attribute. The limitations referred to above are only "ridiculous" viewed from the angle of our above-mentioned attribute, our apparatus of reason. And we must not encourage the god in us to laugh too much. This transcendental viewpoint which is explicit in laughter, must be in one sense, sparingly employed. It must rather light up *everything* we handle as artists, with its unearthly light, than blast and stunt the objects necessary to our craft. Even *a game* cannot be proceeded with to an accompaniment of *too* Homeric a guffaw! Laughter must just tip and gild as it were the wings of *all* our philosophies: and only sometimes be quarried in great blocks, by some of our most steady and scrupulous workmen. "Satire," as I have suggested that word should be used in this essay (applying to *all* the art of the present time of any force at all) refers to an "expressionist" universe which is reeling a little, a little drunken with an overdose of the "ridiculous" — where everything is not only tipped but *steeped* in a philosophic solution of the material, not of mirth, but of the intense and even painful sense of the absurd. It is a time, evidently, in which *homo animal ridens* is accentuating — for his deep purposes no doubt, and in response to adverse conditions — his dangerous, philosophic, "god-like" prerogative — that wild nihilism that is a function of reason and of which his laughter is the characteristic expression. And a bird-woman plaster-mask of Picasso — or, following Picasso, in a weightier substance, a pin-headed giantess of Mr. Henry Moore, with a little crease in the stone to show the position of the face, but with great fruity bulges for her dugs — are, as much as Mr. Joyce's Leopold Bloom, or Cissy Caffrey, or Mr. Eliot's Klipstein and Krumpacker, expressions of this tendency. And that is why, by stretching a point, no more, we can without exaggeration write *satire* for *art* — not the moralist satire directed at a given society, but a metaphysical satire occupied with mankind.

But in the contemplation of this "peculiar situation" (to return to the general, from the particular) there is a fairly simple alternative proposed to us. We may employ, it can be stated in a general way, this verbal machinery, this dialectic, to *humanize* ourselves, or to *dehumanize* ourselves as we should say still further (it is equally good for either purpose) — by that meaning to outdo in monstrosity the terrestrial monsters of the evolutionist circus by which we are surrounded, and whose destinies we share. And there is, of course, only this alternative, for beings so very oddly placed: either to accept what we call our "rational" equipment as a refinement, merely, of the mechanical animal condition — regard it as a "word-habit," which we certainly should have been better without: or else to look upon it as a *gift*, as we say in common speech.

Regarded as great herds of performing animals (the *behaviourist* view) — small, mischievous, physically insignificant and mentally extremely prone to endless imitation, very susceptible to hypnosis — as individuals and in the aggregate — regarded in that manner our *tricks* — and our "fine arts" are only part of our repertoire of tricks, not necessarily our *finest* tricks, even — are indeed too unimportant a matter to detain us for so much as the twinkling of any eye. A good dinner, accompanied by as good wine as we can get hold of; a pleasant spin in the fresh air in as satisfactory a petrol wagon as we can afford; a nice digestive round of golf; a flirtation accompanied by the rhythmical movements prompted by a nigger drum, purging us of the secretions of sex — a nice detective volume, which purges us pleasantly of the secretions proper to us in our capacity of "killers" and hunting-dogs (our lynching, arsenic-administering, and throat-cutting and policemanesque proclivities all rolled into one); all these things are far more *important* than anything that can be described as "art" — art, that is, in any *highbrow* sense (to use the clownish democratic jargon to supply the requisite gutter-picture, of what we wish to describe) — the noblest intellectual exercises of The Animal, Man — exercises which to the vivid and vulgar folk-eye of the Tom Thumb of the Bowery slum, which has none of the purity and beauty of the peasant-vision — are symbolized by *a high forehead*, the sign of a "brainy" chap.

It is regarding the *values* attaching to these tricks that we are liable to differ: for some of us attribute no significance to them at all. But all that I am arguing here is that they are *only* tricks, in the first place (we may consider the fine arts as the very fine manners of the mind) and, in the second place, that if they possess no value whatever, then *à plus forte raison*, life possesses absolutely no value either. In other words, I am taking their values for granted in this essay, I am not proceeding to their proof.

What should be said, then, it seems to me, first and last, about art (whether of the eye, ear, hand or what not) is that it is a pure game — a game, in its different forms, directly arising out of our functions of sight, hearing and so forth, and our functions as trained social animals, as political animals, of course, and as religious animals. And further, as I see it, there is no "progressive" principle at work in life. This would "class" the arts at once — to call them "a game" — if it were not that life itself, the whole of the "peculiar situation" in which we find ourselves, should also be considered purely as a game—a game in the sense that no value can attach to it *for itself*, but only in so far as it is well-played or badly-played. Art in this respect is in the same class as ritual, as civilized behaviour, and all ceremonial forms and observances—a discipline, a symbolic discipline.

It is at this point that we make contact with the moralist-at-large, having referred to *good* play and to *bad* play. With his humanist metre-stick our lay moralist (assenting, very grudgingly, to the above definition—for "game" is a word that suggests something altogether too trivial and light-hearted to him) would approach these judgements—of "good" and of "bad" play. "Very well!" he would perhaps exclaim, "have it that way if you must. Call a good action a good piece of *playing* if you like. But the *good* in the good piece of acting is my province, anyway!" And it is, of course, just there that one is compelled to discourage him, very firmly indeed. For his idea of a *good play*—to narrow down for the moment this "well-played" game in question to a theatrical performance—would always be a play of edification, which exhibited some ethical principle at work, triumphing in the face of considerable odds: just as the pure politician's idea of a "good play" would be a play throwing into prominence a party-principle—*his* party's in fact.

In a word, the moralist's, or the politician's "good," is not universal enough, but is too deeply embrued respectively with the pragmatical values of the mere animal, Man, or the values of the parish-pump.

In conclusion, if then our arts are of no value, except as pretty ornaments to an otherwise futile life—of bread-and-butter and as far as possible beer-and-skittles, upon a dogmatically animal plane—then this and all other discussions are futile too. However this may be, the valuing of our arts is bound up with the valuing of our life, and vice versa. All I have done here has been, starting from the assumption that a non-material system of values attaches to the exercises of the artist, to denounce the various interferences, by the agency of which, at present, his activities are impaired. That has been the extent of what I have here proposed. And I do not think that, within this framework, I can usefully add anything to what I have already said, and so will leave the matter in your hands, hoping that at least I may have directed your attention to a question of great moment—namely, whether the society of the immediate future should be composed, for the first time in civilized history, of *Men without art*.

APPENDIX

THE TAXI – CAB DRIVER TEST FOR "FICTION"

APPENDIX

THROUGHOUT THESE PAGES we have been considering the objects of Satire: and then we proceeded to interrogate the term "Satire" itself. But there is another term that we have been using, which equally is in need of examination. "Fiction" is a term applied, for want of a better, to a field of literature as crowded today as the most overcrowded megapolitan slum on the face of this overcrowded earth. As more space has been devoted, in this book, to works of fiction than to any other form of art, it occurred to me that it would not be amiss to include, as an appendix, these pages (which I have entitled *The Taxi-cab-Driver Test*) from an essay of mine published some years ago, in defence of *The Apes of God*.

The term "fiction" as used to describe all prose narrative, would be unobjectionable, if "fiction" had not a significance of a special order at the present time. But what it is used to describe upon the contemporary Scene makes it inadmissible where any serious work of literary art is concerned. No work of fiction is, I believe, in the fullest sense, also a work of art, which could not pass the following simple test. I believe that you should be able to request a taxi-cab driver to step into your house, and (just as you might ask him to cut a pack of cards) invite him to open a given work of fiction, which you had placed in readiness for this experiment upon your table; and that then *at whatever page he happened to open it*, it should be, in its texture, something more than, and something different from, the usual thing that such an operation would reveal. In fact, allowing for the difference in scale and of technical approach, a work of "fiction" should be as amenable to this test as would be a play by Molière or Racine, or any page taken at random in, say, the Collected Works of Donne or of Dryden. The "fiction" selected need not, of course, possess the genius of those great writers, but it should be, as it were, *an intellectual object* of a similar order to their works.

Yet upon any terms, that would be a critical scrutiny that few people would admit as decisive, in the case of their favourite "fiction." No, for them, "fiction" is, *in places*, "literature"; in other places (and in most places) it is just a slovenly blah, that (since it amuses — since it is a sort of folkprose of the Middle-Classes of Western Democracy) must be tenderly handled by the critic. No implements of precision may be used against it; in some mysterious, some most ill-defined, manner, it is *the whole* that counts. Any given page of it may, as a specimen of the literary art, be beneath contempt. Far from being an *intellectual object*, it need not be an object at all, or at the most it need only be an object that recalls a sprawling jelly of the vulgarest sentiment.

And there you have, no doubt, the sufficient reason for the phenomenon we must all have noticed, namely, that a hundred books of "fiction" every month are referred to by eminent critics in language of such superlative praise that, were it the work of Dante that was in question, it would be adequate, though a little fulsome: but, when used to describe the legion of lady-novelists, and gentlemen fictionists too, it must seem either bereft of reason, or else peculiarly dishonest and mercenary.

If you had to name one thing more than another as accountable for the immense decay in all our serious critical standards in literature, it is to be found in this acceptance of "fiction" as a serious art. That the usual commercial article that is stocked by the great Libraries and Book of the Month Clubs should be recommended to the public as a good, a bad, or an indifferent specimen of the stuff they want, would be sensible and salesmanlike. That highly paid experts should (with gloves on and heavily masked) examine these masses of written matter weekly, and appropriately report upon them in a newspaper no one could object to: if they said "This is the goods, you will like *this*," all would be well. It is when people possessing, rightly or wrongly, a great position in the literature of their very important country, are employed, at portentous salaries, to write weekly about these products in the way they do — lavishing upon them all the resources of their critical vocabularies — a vocabulary acquired for the appraisement of such tremendous works as *War and Peace*, or *L'Education sentimentale* — that there is something that stinks horribly in the State of Denmark, and that it is more than time to call a halt!

If we imagine for a moment what the contemporaries of Boileau, of Congreve, of Chapman, of Dryden, or those of so late a day as that of Verlaine, or of Jane Austen, would have thought of the frantic and incessant critical pronouncements of our most celebrated critics, then at once we perceive the extent of the degradation, from the high and fastidious standard, that the art of letters has suffered in England — seeing that we tolerate, without a single voice venturing to oppose it, this travesty of the critical function.

In some cases the dishonesty and betrayal involved are patent, for there are among the people who, for money or for social power, perform these offices those who must be conscious of what they are doing. With others, of course, that is not the case.

But lest I should be suspected of exaggeration, let me quote from the utterances of two people highly qualified to speak upon this subject. I will first quote from an article by Mr. Hugh Walpole which appeared in the *Week End Review* of August 2, 1930. This is a long time ago — the cutting was used for my *Satire and Fiction* pamphlet — but nothing has changed in the interval. The proposed drop in the prices of books was the occasion of the article. In the following extract Mr. Walpole carries out, a little surprisingly, what I have just been saying:

It is upon the question of time that the literary situation in this country now hangs. (Can a literary situation hang? In England it is hanging by the neck.) As thus. Readers have no time to read. Critics have no time to read. Publishers have no time to think. Booksellers have no time to stock. Masterpieces have no time to get settled. . . .

As things now are, history, philosophy (except the popular one that deals with sex), poetry, essay have practically no sales at all. The money earned by these books would be less money and not more if the books were published more cheaply. . . . The reduction in price concerns at present, therefore, fiction and fiction only. There are 4,440,000 novels published in England every year. (The publishers' advertisement makes it look like that.) Of this great number about twenty live longer than two months. And this is where the Time factor comes in.

Miss Gracie Smith spends a year of her splendid life in writing "Apples and Oranges." It is very clever and is accepted by a publisher. (Everyone, absolutely everyone, can today write a clever novel.) The book appears and has a number of splendid reviews. (Every novel today has splendid reviews.) Arnold Bennett says that it has merit. I myself say that it is "superb." Mr. Gerald Gould calls it "noble." These remarks are printed in huge black type in the *Observer* on two successive Sundays. Miss Gracie Smith is enchanted. Everyone seems to be talking about her. She is made for ever. A fortnight later her book is dead. Why? Because there has been no Time. Within a fortnight six other novels just as clever (*really* clever . . .) have appeared. Arnold Bennett, myself, Mr. Gould *und so weiter* have applauded all these six.

Next let us turn for evidence to the late Mr. Arnold Bennett. It was he who set the fashion of employing all the resources of the critical vocabulary to "puff" every week, for years together, a batch of goodish, baddish, and exceedingly indifferent works — and remaining silent about most that were of any moment, it might be added. And that he knew perfectly well what he was about, and practised this deception with his eyes open, can be proved by his occasional utterances, in which he came out and displayed himself as his own perfect cynic, no doubt; though of course in a sense he did himself too much honour — for, though he knew what was good when he saw it, he no doubt *liked* what was vulgar and second-rate, and so was true to his private taste, if not to his public calling. The harm he did, in my opinion, to English letters was so great that nothing one can say would be severe enough in condemnation of the bad example that he set. The tone of Mr. Bennett is different to that of Mr. Walpole — a touch perhaps of the sturdy-sanctimonious occurs. But he tells the same story in this frank interlude in his weekly puff-practice. The following passages are from an article upon "Mediocre Writers," in the *Evening Standard*, August 21, 1930:

The literary critic, especially if he is in large practice, lives a continuous martyrdom. He has to deal with vastly more new books than old, and with vastly more mediocre or bad books than good. It takes much longer to read a book than to listen to a symphony. . . . He (the literary critic) is bound to swallow what he tastes. Willy-nilly it gets into his system, producing effects sinister and unavoidable. In this respect the literary critic is in the same box as the old lead-workers in earthenware manufactories. Critics have been known to contract mortal "occupational diseases" of the mind from a steady diet of bad books.

. . . Now the chief business and pleasure of the literary critic should be to uphold the highest standards of literature. In other words, he should be the foe of mediocrity. There are a hundred reasons why he should treat honest mediocrity with the respect which it deserves; but one can fight a foe while respecting him, and the critic who wishes to find himself on the safe side on the Day of Judgment should fight the foe all the time. Does he?

The majority do not. They yield insensibly to the terrible, the insinuating, the enervating, the septic influences of the "pabulum" which they are daily compelled to swallow for a livelihood. They make more and more compromises, until they compromise themselves so far that in the end they actually prefer mediocrity to original excellence. They eat and drink mediocrity until they become mediocrity, with all mediocrity's detestation of original excellence. Thus mediocrity triumphs over them. . . . Ah! The sweet but cankerous ease of compromise! Herein is the reason why the bulk of book-reviewing is too benevolent. And, you know, almost all reviews really are too benevolent.

The late Mr. Arnold Bennett here omitted to point out that there are such things as critics who are mediocrities; who, as a consequence, do not require to "become mediocrity," and for whom to eat and drink "mediocrity" is not such a "martyrdom" as all that! It seems to be taken for granted, even, in the article in question, that *all* critics are persons of fastidious literary susceptibilities, suffering in the cause of money! But my purpose is served if I have succeeded, by enlisting these two great authorities upon the matter in hand (both, though one is dead, typical of their calling), to show that I am not alone in what I believe, but that the most illustrious experts are oddly enough of the same opinion as myself.

Now my contention is only this: that making due allowance for the fact that under any circumstances "the highest standards of literature" could not have been "upheld" satisfactorily in such a time as the present, nevertheless it is the confusion of what is known as "fiction" with the formal arts, that is responsible for the evil plight of letters. Or rather, shall we say, if "fiction" were removed into another category and recognized for what it is, there would be an immediate alleviation of those vile conditions that obtain, and which make it so difficult for a serious work of art to be regarded as anything but a kind of freak today, a kind of scandal to be as far as possible hushed up.

But if this is so, it is certainly worth while to scrutinize this term "fiction," wherever you find it applied to a type of book which obviously does not fit into the scheme of things implied by that trade-term at all.

I would go so far upon that purist road myself as to say that *no* book that could be possibly made to fit into the scheme of things suggested by the word "fiction," could possibly be a work of the least importance. No book that would not pass my taxi-cab-driver test, that is, would be anything but highly suspect as art — though it might be an awfully good aphrodisiac, or a first-rate "thriller."

But I will at once proceed to a demonstration of how my fiction-test would work.

The *taxi-cab-driver test* can be applied, in the absence of a taxi-cab driver — though not so effectively — by merely opening any book of "fiction," at the first page, and seeing what you find. I will now give a hasty demonstration of that method, selecting, for the purpose, two of the only "fiction" books I have within easy reach. Here displayed intact upon the next page, is *first-page* No. 1.

SPECIMEN A (First page of a work of Fiction)

CHAPTER I

'You won't be late'? There was anxiety in Marjorie Carling's voice, there was something like entreaty.

'No, I won't be late,' said Walter, unhappily and guiltily certain that he would be. Her voice annoyed him. It drawled a little, it was too refined — even in misery.

'Not later than midnight.' She might have reminded him of the time when he never went out in the evenings without her. She might have done so; but she wouldn't; it was against her principles; she didn't want to force his love in any way.

'Well, call it one. You know what these parties are.' But as a matter of fact, she didn't know, for the good reason that, not being his wife, she wasn't invited to them. She had left her husband to live with Walter Bidlake; and Carling, who had Christian scruples, was feebly a sadist and wanted to take his revenge, refused to divorce her. It was two years now since they had begun to live together. Only two years; and now, already, he had ceased to love her, he had begun to love someone else. The sin was losing its only excuse, the social discomfort its sole palliation. And she was with child.

'Half-past twelve,' she implored, though she knew that her importunity would only annoy him, only make him love her the less. But she could not prevent herself from speaking; she loved him too much, she was too agonizingly jealous. The words broke out in spite of her principles. It would have been better for her, and perhaps for Walter too, if she had had fewer prin-

A

That is the first page of the most important work of "fiction" of a very famous author, published in 1928, and regarded as one of the landmarks in English literature of the last decade. There is no occasion to name the author, as it is only my purpose here to show you my taxi-cab-driver test in operation, and to indicate what results may be expected. This single tell-tale page appears to me to be terribly decisive: for no book opening upon this tone of vulgar complicity with the dreariest of suburban library readers could, from my point of view, change its skin, in the course of its six hundred long pages, and become anything but a dull and vulgar book.

" 'You won't be late?' There was anxiety in Marjorie Carling's voice." That is surely so much the very accent of the newspaper serial (even down to the cosy sound of the name of the heroine) that the sort of person who would be at home in such an atmosphere is not a person likely to clamour for the "highest standards in literature." The "only two years; and now already he had ceased to love her!" — the sentimental repetitive in the "she knew that her importunity would only annoy him, only make him love her the less" — the "she loved him too much, she was too agonizingly jealous" — all this is the very voice of "Fiction," as practised by the most characteristic of lady-novelists. Whatever else may be true of such a production, it is safe to say that out of such material a serious work of art decidedly cannot be manufactured.

I next deliberately select, from the other volumes of "fiction" I have to my hand, one that will serve to illustrate my argument — namely, that "fiction" is not always "fiction": and that when it is not "fiction," in the way that my first specimen only too obviously was, then some other word should be found to describe it.

SPECIMEN B (First page of a work of Fiction)

BOOK FIRST

I

IT was but a question of leaving their own contracted "grounds," of crossing the Avenue and proceeding then to Mr. Betterman's gate, which even with the deliberate step of a truly massive young person she could reach in three or four minutes. So, making no other preparation than to open a vast pale-green parasol, a portable pavilion from which there fluttered fringes, frills and ribbons that made it resemble the roof of some Burmese palanquin or perhaps even pagoda, she took her way while these accessories fluttered in the August air, the morning freshness, and the soft sea-light. Her other draperies, white and voluminous, yielded to the mild breeze in the manner of those of a ship held back from speed yet with its canvas expanded; they conformed to their usual law of suggestion that the large loose ponderous girl, mistress as she might have been of the most expensive modern aids to the constituion of a "figure," lived, as they said about her,

A   I

As before, I open it at page number one, and this is what I find (displayed by itself upon the page facing this one): —

That is rather a different kettle of fish, the most unobservant must detect. But in any library catalogue it would appear cheek by jowl with Mr. Walpole's *Miss Gracie Smith*, as a work of FICTION. It would likewise have to consort with our specimen A.

I think that I will change my mind, and (for the sake of effect and because that may promote a more immediate understanding) reveal the name of the book whose first-page I reproduced, as my specimen A. It is *Point Counter Point*! If you do not believe me, you may turn to that work, and you will find that I have indeed placed before you the first page of that famous piece of super-fiction.

Specimen B is the first-page of *The Ivory Tower*, by Henry James.

EDITORIAL MATTER

Table of Emendations

Explanatory Notes

List of Books

Afterword

Index

TABLE OF EMENDATIONS

THE FOLLOWING TABLE lists all departures, however minor, from the text of the first edition. They include corrections of misprints (some obvious, some not-so-obvious); corrections of Lewis's frequently inaccurate quotations (the inaccuracies being usually minor, but occasionally changing the meaning of what is being quoted, sometimes comically; thus, a "martyr of pederasty" becomes in the first edition a "master of pederasty"!); corrections of Lewis's (or his printer's) errors of French orthography; and a small number of editorial emendations. This last category includes a very few corrections of grammar and punctuation when needed for intelligibility. Lewis's often irregular and unconventional syntax and punctuation have generally been left unchanged.

Several textual changes have been made throughout the book and are not noted individually below. The use of quotation marks has been regularized according to current American conventions, double quotes being used first for all quoted matter, with single quotes only for quotations within quotations. Lengthy passages which the first edition placed in quotation marks without indentation have been indented without quotation marks in this printing. Italics added by Lewis to passages he quoted have usually been left without comment; the context is a reliable indicator that they are his emphases. Ellipses in original quoted material have not been distinguished from those representing omissions. (But in the Table of Emendations, the editor's ellipses are placed within square brackets.) Verb forms and derivatives which the first edition spelled variously as -is- or -iz- have been regularized as -iz-, but otherwise British spelling has been retained. Explanatory matter that Lewis interpolated into quotations and enclosed in parentheses has here been enclosed in square brackets. A few other emendations that occur repeatedly have been listed only on their first appearance below, with the additional notation, "[and passim]." Line numbering begins with the first line of text on each page, ignoring titles and headings.

First Edition			This Edition		
Page/Line			*Page/Line*		
7	3	(*Guy* [. . .] *honour*).	11	3	GUY [. . .] honour.
8	23	Richards'	12	2	Richards's
8	30	on to a	12	8	onto a
11	32	a *mauvis coup* to	14	21	a *mauvais coup* to
11	38	*offensive*	14	26	*Offensive*
12	23	Prufock	15	3	Prufrock

249

First Edition			This Edition		
Page/Line			Page/Line		
13	12	Class A.1	15	27	Class A.1
13	26	or Sanctuary? That	15	39	or Sanctuary?" That
17	24	In our Time, The Sun also	19	21	In Our Time, The Sun
[and passim]					Also
			[and passim]		
18	n	Ad Astra.	20	n	"Ad Astra,"
19	4	bêtise	20	21	bêtise
19	27	O'Flagherty	20	40	O'Flaherty
19	34	Merimée	21	3	Mérimée
[and passim]			[and passim]		
19	35	à l'outrance	21	4	à outrance
19	36	Chronique du Règne	21	5	Chronique du règne
20	1	subjects-matter	21	7	subject-matter
22	20	Paschendaele	22	42	Passchendaele
24	3	volapuk	24	6	volapük
25	6	ice-cream	24	40	ice cream
26	1	he liked Germany	25	26	he had liked Germany
26	15	Melanctha. . . . When	25	38	Melanctha. . . . [New paragraph] When
26	17	then, . . . Rose	25	40	then, . . . [New paragraph] Rose
26	19	hospital. . . . Melanctha	25	41	hospital. . . . [New paragraph] Melanctha
27	32	Weltanshauung	26	35	Weltanschauung
30	22	peasant locution	28	37	peasant locutions
30	24	Arran	28	39	Aran
30	25	were so different	29	1	was so different
31	35	with him and	29	43	with him, and
32	1	the native	30	1	a native
32	3	towards	30	3	toward
32	27	Banker's	30	23	Bankers'
33	12	from Jews	30	14	from the Jews
33	17	volapuk	31	4	volapük
33	20	lack of form.	31	6	lack of forms.
33	29	impossible:	31	15	impossible;
36	5	sunlight, and	32	43	sunlight and
36	6	the tiled roofs of houses and chimneys and the sky	32	44	the tile roofs of houses and chimneys. I looked out over the tiled roofs and saw white clouds and the sky
36	14	doors on to the	33	5	doors onto the
37	23	at sea?	33	43	at sea:
39	15	way up the beach	35	5	way up on the beach

First Edition			This Edition		
Page/Line			Page/Line		
39	16	cigars. They	35	6	cigars. [New paragraph] They
39	n	*Years at the Old*	34	n	*Years in the Old*
40	2	very bad. Nick's	35	25	very bad. [New paragraph] Nick's
40	3	stove, while	35	26	stove, and while
40	4	Nick. 'This	35	27	Nick. [New paragraph] "This
40	5	said. 'I know,' said Nick. You don' know	35	28	said. [New paragraph] "I know," said Nick. [New paragraph] "You don't know
40	9	screams.' 'I see,' Nick said. Just then.	35	33	screams." [New paragraph] "I see," Nick said. [New paragraph] Just then
42	20	*in August.* [New paragraph]	37	18	*in August*
43	34	roll-topped	38	19	roll-top
44	18	and mail-order	38	36	and mail order
45	3	alone in the house	39	10	alone and idle in the house
46	26	*These XIII.:*	40	15	*These Thirteen:*
47	8	"the night	40	31	"The night
47	10	"The heady	40	33	"the heady
47	18	no great volume	40	40	no greater volume
47	23	with voices	41	2	with . . . voices
47	29	the hot, still, rich, maculate	41	7	the hot still rich maculate
49	36	clay": (he	42	32	clay:" (he
50	2	grandfather's wife	42	36	grandson's wife
51	13	his forebears	43	33	his forbears
52	22	anyway with	44	35	anyway, with
52	31	book	44	43	Book
58	13	building, etc."	49	4	building," etc.
59	13	the *Faux-monnayeux*	49	36	the *Faux-monnayeurs*
59	13	Lindsay	49	37	Lindsey
59	26	you can't	50	11	you cant
60	9	Lindberg	50	27	Lindbergh
60	20	Lindsay	50	37	Lindsey
60	24	painted, small faces and scant, bright	50	40	painted small faces and scant bright
60	33	hands, and	51	3	hands and
60	34	heads, seen	51	3	heads seen
61	1	aisle: and	51	6	aisle; and

First Edition			This Edition		
Page/Line			Page/Line		
61	11	cheque	51	15	check
61	13	He repeated	51	17	he repeated
61	22	duh-duh, duh.	51	24	duh-duh-duh.
61	23	vertiginous: to	51	25	vertiginous; to
61	34	can't reach	51	36	cant reach
61	37	duh-duh, duh	51	39	duh-duh-duh
61	38	He rose [New paragraph]	51	39	He rose. [No new paragraph]
62	27	*faux-monnayeux*	52	12	*faux-monnayeurs*
63	11	*coup de grace*	52	29	*coup de grâce*
63	21	towards him	52	38	toward him
63	22	won't do	52	39	wont do
63	25	"Grotto? He's	52	40	"Grotto?" [New paragraph] "He's
63	27	if he don't	53	2	if he dont
66	3	*coup de grace*	55	26	*coup de grâce*
66	27	greater	56	9	*greater*
69	36	We all known	58	27	We all know
69	n	L. H. Stonier	58	n	G. H. Stonier
70	10	Insincerity can only	58	35	Sincerity can only
72	23	career. What	60	25	career. [New paragraph] What
73	33	*cocottiers*	61	25	*cocotiers*
73	34	Firbanks	61	26	Firbank
76	6	*dénoûement*	63	11	*dénouement*
76	17	suggest	63	20	suggests
76	26	p. 76, footnote	63	27	p. 76 footnote
77	19	*la vieille France*	64	12	*la vieille France*
78	19	full appreciation	65	7	full poetic appreciation
79	2	pp. 17 ff.	65	20	pp. 179 ff.
82	1	last agonisant	67	28	last *agonisant*
82	18	to hold, E	68	3	to hold, *E*
82	26	the art of the Mass	68	9	the Art of the Mass
84	4	Richards' statement on p. 271. I	69	10	Richards's statement on p. 271. . . . I
84	6	'literature' as well as of literary criticism."	69	12	"literature" as well as of "literary criticism."
84	11	*Comedy*, or	69	15	*Comedy* or
85	10	Richards' Theory	70	3	Richards's Theory
85	n	*Poetry and Beliefs*,	70	n	"Poetry and Beliefs,"
86	10	believe. – This	70	32	believe. . . . This
86	23	he had affected	71	5	he had effected
87	6	sincerirty	71	21	sincerity
87	26	feel	72	1	*feel*

First Edition			This Edition		
Page/Line			Page/Line		
87	30	think so, do I	72	4	think so; do I
87	33	its intentions.	72	6	its intention.
88	6	*Chung Lung*	72	14	*Chung Yung*
89	11	comes nothing	73	9	come nothing
89	n	Sir Leslie Stevens	73	n	Sir Leslie Stephen
90	26	Wainwrights	74	11	Wainewrights
93	19	danger of leading	76	15	danger . . . of leading
96	14	So when 'Mr. [. . .] effects "a complete [. . .] beliefs I am [. . .] reader."	78	24	So "when Mr. [. . .] effects 'a complete [. . .] beliefs' I am [. . .] reader."
96	37	*changed*[1] [Same number used twice to refer to same source.]	79	5	*changed.*[1] [Second identical note supplied.]
97	23	He "would hesitate [. . .] that this	79	25	He would "hesitate [. . .] that the
97	27	release."	79	29	releases."
97	34	detachment? *"Who*	79	34	detachment: *"Who*
97	n	p. 130	79	n	p. 145
98	17	consistency and	80	10	consistency or for
98	n1	p. 145.	80	n1	pp. 149–150.
98	n2	p. 87	80	n2	p. 387
98	n3	p. 79	80	n3	p. 379
99	16	depreciate	81	2	deprecate
103	21	*malgré Lui*	85	18	*malgré lui*
103	22	Taine?	85	19	Taine:
103	n	*L'art et la Morale*	85	n	*L'Art et la morale*
104	3	Flaubert?	85	23	Flaubert:
104	4	ni beaux, ni	85	24	ni beaux ni
104	5	de l'art pur	85	25	de l'Art pur
104	6	manière de voir	85	26	manière absolue de voir
104	n	I. J. Bondy	85	n	L. J. Bondy
105	14	Theophile	86	32	Théophile
105	n	*L'art et la Morale*	86	n	*L'Art et la morale*
110	19	other emotions	90	27	other motions
111	5	impudence, an idiot	91	4	impudence, or idiot
115	2	Montague Slater	95	2	Montagu Slater
116	31	*élan vitale*	96	11	*élan vital*
119	12	Montague Slater	98	4	Montagu Slater
119	13	posted inside	98	5	Posted inside
121	2	*du Mal*	99	24	*du mal*
123	26	more refined, period	101	15	more refined period
124	1	mask of distinction	101	27	mark of distinction
124	2	called out, and	101	28	called out and
125	25	who impose those	102	35	who imposed those

First Edition			This Edition		
Page/Line			Page/Line		
125	25	who impose those	102	35	who imposed those
132	32	architype	109	36	archetype
132	36	Gujuieff	109	40	Gurdjieff
134	23	to day	111	8	today
134	32	remain	111	17	remains
138	3	as this — that	115	2	as this, — that
141	22	Antony Trollope	117	25	Anthony Trollope
142	10	nature: but [. . .] offence is after all deliberate. [. . .] admirable, observer	118	3	nature; but [. . .] offence is, after all, deliberate. [. . .] admirable observer
142	34	novel. Why	118	24	novel. . . . Why
145	5	*parti-pris*	120	9	*parti pris*
146	16	October, etc."	121	8	October," etc.
147	5	he does, suggest,	121	32	he does suggest,
147	24	*action*, is indeed	122	6	*action*, it is indeed
150	1	films does	123	39	films do
151	21	continent, where	125	5	continent where
151	23	Durer	125	6	Dürer
153	16	America to James	126	26	America, to James
153	18	*earth is a*	126	27	*earth was a*
153	19	the American artist, in the American air, was	126	28	The American artist in the American air was
154	8	Brooks)	127	9	Brooks):
154	35	*Nakt Kultur*	127	33	*Nacktkultur*
156	14	intellectual, is	128	39	intellectual, are
157	8	*L'Isle des Pingouins*	129	23	*L'Isle des pingouins*
157	26	'real?'	129	39	"real"?
158	25	as this one is	131	23	as this, one is
160	5	in fact and indeed	132	23	in fact and in deed
161	17	"If we try to	133	22	"If we tried to
162	28	ribbon, that it was not quite	134	20	ribbon," that it was not "quite
165	38	the truth, the truth	136	40	the truth the truth
167	33	inflential	138	13	influential
168	23	in Mrs. Dalloway	138	37	in *Mrs. Dalloway*
168	32	"She reached	139	4	"She had reached
168	34	for "she	139	6	for "She
169	3	everything: and at	139	8	everything: at
169	6	alone: she	139	10	alone; she
169	13	absorbing: all	139	17	absorbing; all
169	38	art-for-arts-sake	139	38	art-for-art's-sake
174	13	the *genuii loci*	142	31	the *genii loci*
174	32	*du Mal*	143	9	*du mal*
174	34	de Quincey's) of	143	11	De Quincey's), of

First Edition			This Edition		
Page/Line			Page/Line		
174	n	Oxford University Press	142	n	Oxford University Press
176	18	[New paragraph] "That	144	15	[No new paragraph] That
176	20	"Or again:	144	17	Or again:
176	n	Collected Essays	144	n	Selected Essays
177	1	"Pater had	144	30	"Pater . . . had
177	12	the 'Medusan' type	144	39	the "Medusean" type
177	21	Decadence:	145	7	Decadence;
177	26	(a few early lines imitated	145	11	(early verse imitated
177	31	A Rebours	145	16	À rebours
178	22	et diver	145	40	et divers
178	36	a 'master of pederasty,'	146	6	a "martyr of pederasty,"
179	2	interieur,'	146	9	intérieur,"
179	14	Heliogabalus, Atalaric,	146	19	Heliogabalus, King Atalaric,
179	16	rudes favouris	146	21	rudes favoris
179	17	life, 'Violente, voluptueuse et debridée	146	22	life "violente, voluptueuse et débridée
179	21	Menalque,	146	25	Ménalque,
179	32	idiosyncrasy;	146	34	idiosyncrasy:
179	34	Gheridanisol,	146	36	Ghéridanisol,
179	36	monstrueux';	146	37	monstrueux":
180	3	voila	146	41	voilà
180	4	Perouse	146	43	Pérouse
180	10	to in order 'pouvoir	146	48	to in order to "pouvoir
180	11	"Il est	146	49	'il est
180	13	Gheridanisol, culminated in	146	50	Ghéridanisol, culminate in
180	15	proxy: in	147	2	proxy; in
180	22	l'etreint	147	8	l'étreint
180	23	levres	147	8	lèvres
180	32	l'âutre	147	15	l'autre
180	33	portiére	147	16	portière
181	29	ne neurt	147	46	ne meurt
182	22	de Quincey	148	23	De Quincey
182	30	Desmond Macarthy	148	29	Desmond MacCarthy
183	3	annals . . . was	148	37	annals . . . were
183	7	Wainwright	148	41	Wainewright
184	11	an air that . . . have	149	32	an air that . . . has
184	23	from traditional	150	3	from a traditional
184	31	feasible in	150	10	feasible, in
185	1	Classische	151	1	Classisch
186	23	mithraditic cult	152	7	mithraic cult
187	12	straightened	152	29	straitened

First Edition			This Edition		
Page/Line			Page/Line		
188	11	From what we start— [. . .] —is from the	153	17	What we start from— [. . .] —is the
188	35	soupire étouffée	153	33	soupir étouffé
189	2	mood. . . . Finally	153	42	mood. . . ." Finally
189	3	felt in the	153	43	felt in "the
189	17	Carlyle, or Ibsen	154	11	Carlyle or Ibsen
189	17	is as it were a common	154	11	is, as it were, a common
189	19	individual member of the age, or of the circle	154	12	individual representative of the age, or member of the circle
189	20	must admit it, and	154	13	must admit, and
190	14	some 'art-pur'	154	41	some *art pur*
190	16	Manjasco	155	1	Magnasco
191	14	paganism	155	28	paganisme
191	22	to have the least	155	35	to have least
191	29	gallant's [. . .] on which	156	3	gallants' [. . .] in which
191	34	the more it advances to	156	7	the more it advances . . . to
192	15	secular literature . . ." Professor	156	21	secular literature," Professor
192	19	*auto-da-fe*	156	25	*auto-da-fé*
193	4	"The (classical artist's) preoccupation	157	4	"[The classical artist's] preoccupation
195	28	*cris de coeurs*	159	4	*cris de coeur*
196	9	la Bruyère	159	19	La Bruyère
196	15	littèrature	159	24	littérature
196	17	mâitres	159	26	maîtres
196	18	supèriorité	159	26	supériorité
196	32	*Emaux et Camailles*	159	33	*Emaux et camées*
196	n	*Le classicisme de*	159	n	*Le Classicisme de*
197	n	*Etudes Critiques*, Vol. I, Brunetiére	160	n	*Etudes critiques*, Vol. I, Brunetière
198	n	*Discourse de Combat*	161	n	*Discours de combat*
199	24	essays,[1] and [. . .] Wolfe, in	162	5	essays, and [. . .] Wolfe,[1] in
199	27	gentlemen, Mr. Wolfe,	162	7	gentlemen, Mr. Wolfe
199	29	he does regard	162	9	he does not regard
200	20	Romanticism	162	30	romanticism
200	28	Europe from Augustine	162	36	Europe—from Augustine
201	19	the classics to the	163	19	the classics or the
201	25	French partisan of	163	25	French partisans of
201	26	They regard Romanticism	163	26	They regard romanticism
201	28	it was Romanticism . . . the Revolution. They hate the Revolution so they hate Romanticism.	163	28	it was romanticism . . . the revolution. They hate the revolution so they hate romanticism.

First Edition			This Edition		
Page/Line			Page/Line		
201	31	Romanticism	163	30	romanticism
202	9	circumstances: and	164	2	circumstance; and
202	12	The views which	164	4	The view which
202	14	romantic: the	164	5	romantic; the
202	27	all Romanticism	164	17	all romanticism
202	28	possibilities: and	164	18	possibilities; and
202	30	chance, and	164	19	chance and
202	31	One can define	164	21	"One can define
202	n	*Op cit.*	164	n	*Op. cit.*
204	9	political naturalism	165	26	political nationalism
205	4	[new paragraph] 'The thing	166	10	[no new paragraph] The thing
205	25	l'être 'lê	166	27	l'être 'le
205	27	prix."	166	28	prix.' "
205	27	bête noir	166	28	bête noire
205	33	judgement	166	34	judgment
205	34	who has, ever	166	35	who has ever
206	1	analysis: and	166	36	analysis; and
206	3	criticism: you	166	38	criticism; you
206	5	Shakespeare: but	166	40	Shakespeare; but
206	n	*Second Thoughts about Humanism*	167	n	"Second Thoughts about Humanism,"
207	1	*vitale*	167	29	*vital*
208	10	Quantity versus Quality	168	22	Quantity versus Quantity
208	11	Tait	168	24	Tate
208	14	Babbitt, whose	168	27	Babbitt — whose
208	28	*muchadumbre*	169	1	*muchedumbre*
208	n	*Against Humanism*	168	n	[T. S. Eliot, "The Humanism of Irving Babbitt," *Selected Essays.*]
209	26	cortege	169	31	cortège
211	17	Bondy) "Croyons	171	3	Bondy): "Croyons
211	n	la Littérature	171	n	la littérature
212	3	Among them is the	173	3	Among them is . . . the
212	18	disrespect have	173	17	disrespect — have
212	24	emotional	173	22	*emotional*
213	29	investigations	174	11	investigation
214	8	view) to	174	24	view), to
214	17	ideals get	174	36	ideal gets
215	26	Shall religion	175	28	Shall [religion]
215	27	no: but he cannot	175	29	no; but he could not
215	n	*Humanism*, A Symposium	175	n	*Humanism, A Symposium*
218	32	Chatterly	178	6	Chatterley
219	32	to day	178	38	today
226	3	Hokuzai	183	21	Hokusai
226	5	some) they	183	22	some), they

First Edition			This Edition		
Page/Line			Page/Line		
228	14	hypocrisies) for	185	13	hypocrisies), for
228	20	the wise?'	185	18	the wise"?
230	29	Burne Jones	187	4	Burne-Jones
232	18	Outvieing	188	10	Outvying
235	2	se trâine	191	2	se traîne
235	3	autre chose que romain.	191	3	autre que romain!
235	10	being the feudal poet	191	9	being a feudal poet
235	11	shows us is much	191	10	shows us, is much
236	10	thoroughly *sâle*	191	37	thoroughly *sale*
239	22	Européenes	194	20	européennes
239	24	audessous	194	21	au-dessous
239	25	su que faire du	194	22	su faire que du
239	29	herité de l'epoque ou	194	25	hérité de l'époque où
239	32	existat. . . . [No paragraph break] Les	194	28	existât. . . . [New paragraph] Les
239	35	siecles	194	31	siècles
239	36	auprés	194	32	auprès
240	36	Maddox	195	19	Madox
241	3	*parti-pris.* . . . They say — Given	195	23	*parti pris.* . . . They say: Given
241	5	and the circumstances	195	24	and the set of circumstances
241	n	*Week-End Review*	195	n	*Week End Review*
243	2	me font plus d'horreur	197	2	me font plus horreur
244	15	*grace*	197	36	*grâce*
244	27	it's own	198	9	its own
245	17	hari-kiri	198	31	hara-kiri
246	31	write about?	199	36	write about?"
248	33	*Disastros del Paz*	201	17	*Desastres de la Paz*
249	26	newspaper?	201	44	newspaper:
255	32	immortal Telemachus	206	14	immortal *Telemachus*
256	7	than this, for	206	27	than this; for
256	30	indeed? as	207	2	indeed. As
258	8	genial interest,	208	6	genial interest.
258	27	view, I	208	23	view I
258	28	of a consequence	208	24	of consequence
258	29	But in reality it [. . .] one of us is	208	25	But, in reality, it [. . .] one of us, is
260	18	can do to other	211	16	can *do to* other
262	16	Banker's	212	1	Bankers'
263	9	century if the	213	17	century of the
264	24	ou l'on	214	19	où l'on
264	26	refractaires	214	20	réfractaires
264	32	se repandant . . .	214	25	se répandent . . .

First Edition			This Edition		
Page/Line			Page/Line		
264	32	epouvantée	214	26	épouvantée
265	12	car le feu	215	1	pour que le feu
265	15	le commune des hommes	215	3	le commun des hommes
265	19	d'amertume dès	215	7	d'amertume, dès
265	20	n'aï'je	215	8	n'ai-je
265	20	le troupeau, sera	215	8	le troupeau sera
265	21	haissable	215	9	haïssable
265	26	la plus près	215	14	le plus près
265	27	n'est-ce, pas? mais	215	14	n'est-ce pas? Mais
266	13	rire (á la	215	29	rire [à la
266	23	se traine	215	36	se traîne
266	24	autre chose que	215	37	autre que
266	28	*L'Education Sentimentale*	216	3	*L'Education sentimentale*
268	6	out of vain glory	216	40	out of vainglory
269	4	les ruins	217	24	les ruines
269	6	*l'humanité*	217	25	*l'humanité*
269	11	directment	217	29	directement
269	13	la metrophysique	217	31	la métaphysique
269	14	recues	217	31	reçues
269	16	on affirme. [. . .] Française	217	33	on affirme! [. . .] française
269	23	l'arrière-faire	217	39	l'arrière-faix
269	24	a été avortement	217	39	a été un avortement
270	17	dirigeantes: de ce ramassis	218	23	dirigeantes; de ce ramassis
270	18	cette vielle trâinee	218	24	cette vieille traînée
270	19	la bonne société	218	25	la bonne Société
270	22	les vielles classes	218	28	les vieilles classes
270	23	unintelligentes	218	28	inintelligentes
270	33	deux haines! la haine	218	37	deux haines: la haine
270	34	jeunesse:	218	37	jeunesse,
270	35	talent:	218	38	talent,
270	35	mur: cette dernier	218	38	mûr, cette dernière
270	36	je l'envie.	218	39	*je l'envie.*
271	19	was "las de [. . .] ecclésiastique . . . la	219	13	" 'las de [. . .] ecclésiastique' . . . la
271	22	Mr. Ferrère	219	15	M. Ferrère
271	24	M. E. D. Ferrère	219	16	M. E-L. Ferrère
272	15	as of much importance	219	38	of as much importance
273	3	*les merveilleuses nuages*	220	19	*les merveilleux nuages*
273	19	*creatrice,* as Jaurés	220	33	*créatrice,* as Jaurès
274	25	(*Editions du Capitole*)	221	27	(Editions du Capitole)
274	30	Thébaide	221	31	Thébaïde
274	34	*verb*	221	35	*verbe*
275	20	aboutit a ces	222	12	aboutit à ces
275	23	*verb*	222	15	*verbe*

First Edition			This Edition		
Page/Line			Page/Line		
275	29	a Dieu	222	21	à Dieu
275	30	perilleuse	222	22	périlleuse
275	32	litteraire	222	23	littéraire
276	6	poche:	222	32	poche;
276	7	délieusement et	222	33	délicieusement, et
276	12	Therese	222	38	Thérèse
276	18	perilleuse	223	5	périlleuse
276	19	meprisé	223	5	méprisé
281	15	that the natural aristocrat	227	17	that . . . the natural aristocrat
283	22	of absent	228	43	of the absent
284	22	Princetown	229	28	Princeton
285	37	Mr. Mauriac	230	25	M. Mauriac
295	28	Racine, of any page	237	24	Racine, or any page
297	2	*L'Education Sentimentale*	238	23	*L'Education sentimentale*
297	35	essay, have	239	7	essay have
297	36	by these would	239	8	by these books, would
298	6	*Apples and Oranges*	239	14	"Apples and Oranges"
298	10	'Observer'	239	19	*Observer*
299	5	symphony. He	239	46	symphony. . . . He
299	15	deserves: but	240	8	deserves; but
299	17	Judgement	240	10	Judgment
299	20	papulum	240	12	pabulum
299	21	livelihood; they	240	13	livelihood. They
299	25	triumphs over them. Ah!	240	17	triumphs over them. . . . Ah!

EXPLANATORY NOTES

11   **de Maupassant:**   Guy de Maupassant (1850–93), realist short story writer
and novelist, disciple of Flaubert.

Medici Society Hobbema: The Medici Society, founded in 1908, published reproduction prints of famous works of art. Hobbema
(1638–1709), Dutch landscape artist popular among English collectors
of the 18th and 19th centuries.

Old John Peel: The popular early Victorian song, beginning "D'ye ken
John Peel with his coat so gray?" Troutbeck is a village in what was
formerly called Westmorland, now Cumbria, near Lake Windemere.

the Crime Club: An imprint of the publisher William Collins, initiated
in 1930 and still continuing.

12   **Rugger Blue:**   One chosen to represent his school or university in the game
of Rugby, so called because Eton and Harrow schools and Oxford and
Cambridge universities use shades of blue as their official colors.

Mr. I. A. Richards's class of sawneys: Some of the quoted "protocols"
(comments on poems anonymously distributed to students) which are
analyzed in Richards's *Practical Criticism* (London, 1929) make their
authors look foolish. "Sawney" (derived from the name "Alexander,"
abbreviated to "Sandy") means "a Scotsman," and hence, by anti-
Scottish prejudice, "a fool or simpleton."

Sir Austen Chamberlain: (1863–1937) Conservative politician and
Foreign Secretary (1924–1929).

Bunter, "the owl of the Remove":   The fat schoolboy in the stories of
Greyfriars School by Frank Richards (1875–1961), published in such
cheap weekly boys' papers as *The Gem* and *The Magnet.* "2d." (two
pence or "tuppence") was equivalent to about 5¢. "The young of the
English proletariat" were, of course, the consumers, not the heroes,
of these stories.

the Church Brigade: A youth movement in the Church of England.

13   **beaux yeux ... beaux arts:**   Beautiful eyes . . . fine arts.

art-for-art's-sake: A reference to the famous "Conclusion" to Pater's *Studies
in the History of the Renaissance* (1873), which included the following sentence:

> Of such wisdom, the poetic passion, the desire for beauty, the love of
> art for art's sake has most; for art comes to you professing frankly to
> give nothing but the highest quality to your moments as they pass, and
> simply for those moments' sake.

The "Conclusion" has been called the manifesto of a generation.

261

13   **Professor Walter Raleigh ... about William Blake:** The remark is
      actually found in the essay "William Blake" in Raleigh's *Some Authors*
      (Oxford: Clarendon Press, 1923), an essay identified as having appeared
      as the introduction to the 1905 Oxford edition of *Lyrical Poems of
      William Blake*. Several of the other essays in Raleigh's book, however,
      are reprinted from periodicals, though none from a newspaper.

14   **a *mauvais coup*:** A low blow.

      ***Entlastungs Offensive*:** Diversionary attack (German).

      the *pseudo* principle of Eliot and Richards: See below, Part I, chapter
      3, passim.

      satirist with a corn-cob: See note to p. 53 below.

15   **Mrs. Porter:** See *The Waste Land*, lines 198–201.

      Prufrock: See Eliot's "The Love Song of J. Alfred Prufrock."

      Klipstein: See Eliot's *Sweeney Agonistes* (1932).

      Burbank: See Eliot's poem "Burbank with a Baedeker: Bleistein with a
      Cigar."

      tract writers like Mr. Shaw: For Lewis's attack on George Bernard Shaw
      (1856–1950), the dramatist and polemicist, see *The Art of Being Ruled*,
      pp. 52–64.

16   **the "dumb ox" ... Aquinas:** St. Thomas Aquinas was called the Dumb
      Ox by his fellow students because he was big and taciturn. G. K.
      Chesterton's *St. Thomas Aquinas: The Dumb Ox* was published in
      1933.

      my paper *The Enemy*: Lewis edited — and wrote most of the contributions
      to — this short-lived periodical, two issues of which were published in
      1927 and the third and final issue in 1929.

      the Leavises: Q. D. Leavis's *Fiction and the Reading Public* had been
      published in 1932; F. R. Leavis's *New Bearings in English Poetry* in
      1933. Together with others they had founded *Scrutiny* in 1932. Their
      indebtedness to the critical practices of I. A. Richards was clear (Mrs.
      Leavis's book began as a thesis under his supervision), but they soon
      began to criticize him in *Scrutiny*. *Scrutiny*'s critique of contemporary
      culture agreed with much that Lewis had been saying, e.g. about stan-
      dards of reviewing (see, for example, F. R. Leavis's "The Literary
      Racket" [Sept. 1932], rpt. in *A Selection from Scrutiny* [Cambridge
      Univ. Press, 1968], 1:160–62).

19   **Hemingway is a very considerable artist:** Cp. Lewis writing in
      1946–1947: "I have always had a great respect for Hemingway . . .
      [H]e is the greatest writer in America and (odd coincidence) one of
      the most successful." (*Rude Assignment*, p. 218).

      ***Men Without Women*:** Published in New York by Scribner's in 1927.

      ***Autobiography of Alice B. Toklas*:** Published by the Literary Guild in
      New York in 1933. Stein as Toklas writes about herself: "She always
      says, yes sure I have a weakness for Hemingway" (p. 265).

      Five-Year Plan: The first Soviet Five-Year Plan of national economic
      development, expanding industry and ruthlessly collectivizing
      agriculture, began in October 1928.

19 **Iron Cross:** Hitler's bravery in World War I won him the Iron Cross, Second Class, in 1914 and the Iron Cross, First Class in 1918 — "an uncommon decoration for a corporal," says Alan Bullock (*Hitler: A Study in Tyranny*, rev. ed. [New York: Harper and Row, 1962], p. 52).

Credit-Power and Democracy: By Major C. H. Douglas (London: Stanley Nott, 1920; rev. ed. 1934).

sand-sharks and Wilson-spoons: Sand sharks have two dorsal fins. I have not been able to find "Wilson-spoon" but it may be a type of fishing lure or spoon-bait.

20 **art pur:** pure art; art for art's sake.

"Ad Astra": *These Thirteen* (the American edition was *These 13*) was published in London by Chatto and Windus in 1933.

bêtise: stupidity.

Noble Savage of Rousseau: The primitivist myth of the original goodness of man is older than Jean-Jacques Rousseau (1712–1778), as the origin of the phrase "noble savage" attests: it is from a play by Dryden (1631–1700), *The Conquest of Granada*: "I am as free as nature first made man, / Ere the base laws of servitude began, / When wild in woods the noble savage ran." But the myth was given great emotional power in Rousseau's writings.

O'Flaherty: Liam O'Flaherty (1896–1984), author of such novels as *The Informer* (1925) and *The Assassin* (1928).

raffiné: refined.

21 **Prosper Mérimée:** Author (1803–1870) of *Colomba* (1841), *Carmen* (1845), and the *Chronique du règne de Charles ix* (first published in 1829 as *1572. Chronique du temps de Charles ix*).

à outrance: To the utmost, to excess.

S'ils tentaient de sauter: "If they attempted to jump out of the windows, they fell into the flames or else were spitted on the points of the pikes. . . . An ensign, dressed in full armor, tried to jump like the others through a narrow window. His breastplate, according to a fashion then quite common, ended in a sort of iron skirt which covered his thighs and belly and which flared out like the mouth of a funnel so as to allow the wearer to walk more easily. The window was not wide enough for this part of his armor to pass through, and in his agitation the ensign had thrown himself through it so forcefully that he found himself with most of his body outside but unable to move, held as if in a vice. Meanwhile the flames reached him, heated his armor, and roasted him in it slowly as if in a furnace or in the famous brass bull invented by Phalaris."

In no century: From Walter Pater, *Miscellaneous Studies* (London: Macmillan, 1895), pp. 13, 14, 15.

Sylla, the false Demetrius: All characters from works by Mérimée. Sylla is characterized in the *Essai sur la guerre sociale* (1841, 1844); "the false Demetrius," pretended son of Ivan the Terrible, is portrayed in the closet drama *Les Débuts d'un aventurier* (1852) and in the historical work *Episode de l'histoire de Russie, Les Faux Demetrius* (1853);

and Bernard de Mergy is the hero of the *Chroniques du règne de Charles ix*.

22   **Carmen . . . la gaya scienza:** "The gay science," the subtitle (in Italian) to the second edition (1887) of Nietzsche's *Die fröhliche Wissenschaft* (first published 1882), whose basic pronouncement was that "God is dead"; the subtitle signals Nietzsche's assumption of a Latin gaiety in the face of this belief. Nietzsche's admiration for Bizet's *Carmen* (and Mérimée's) may be found expressed in *The Case of Wagner* (1888), sections 1 and 2.

Fenimore Cooper: James Fenimore Cooper (1789–1851), author of *The Last of the Mohicans* (1826) and others in the series of Leatherstocking Tales. Memorably mocked for his implausibilities by Mark Twain in "Fenimore Cooper's Literary Offenses."

Gallipoli, Passchendaele, Caporetto: Locations of major and costly battles of World War I.

23   **Pack up your troubles:** Popular song of World War I.

Bairnsfather "Tommy": That is, the regular British soldier as portrayed in the wartime cartoons of Bruce Bairnsfather (1886–1959), cartoons which, Lewis felt, "seduced [the common soldier] into *joining in the insane laughter.* Living in hysterical hordes – of mud-caked, ravenous, little savages – all these millions of Europeans had their legs pulled – their swaddled in mud-coloured puttees – their legs drawn by Bairnsfather – and of course their legs shot off!" (from *The Old Gang and the New Gang*, pp. 54–55).

"muddied oaf at the goal": Lewis is alluding to the well-known lines from Kipling's "The Islanders":

> Then ye returned to your trinkets; then ye contented your souls
> With the flannelled fools at the wicket or the muddied oafs at the goals.

Middletown: Robert S. Lynd and Helen Merrell Lynd, *Middletown: A Study in American Culture* (New York: Harcourt Brace, 1929), was a celebrated social study of a middlewestern American city (Muncie, Indiana).

the N.R.A.: The National Recovery Administration, one of President Roosevelt's instruments for state control of business, ruled unconstitutional by the Supreme Court in 1935.

Don José: Carmen's lover.

24   **Beach-la-mar:** A pidgin language of the South Seas, mentioned by H. L. Mencken in his *The American Language*, 3rd ed. (New York: Knopf, 1923), p. 393.

volapük: A universal language invented by Johann Martin Schleyer (1831–1912); it reached its greatest popularity in the 1880s.

Al Smith: Democratic Party candidate for President in the U.S. elections of 1928. Roosevelt was inaugurated to succeed Hoover on 4 March 1933. Smith's visit to the White House on 14 November 1933 was newsworthy; the *New York Times* subhead was "One 'Frank,' Other 'Al.'"

24   **faux-naif:** Falsely naive.

Krebs: The protagonist in Hemingway's story "Soldiers Home."

26   **Weltanschauung:** World view.

28   **The American Language:** The first edition was published in 1919. The third edition of 1923, the one used by Lewis, was reprinted many times before being superseded by a fourth edition in 1936.

Macaulay: (1800–1859) Whig historian, notable for his declamatory style.

Horace Walpole: (1717–1797) Novelist (*The Castle of Otranto*, 1764), but chiefly remembered for his voluminous correspondence.

Riders to the Sea: One act tragedy (1904) by the Irish playwright, John Millington Synge (1871–1909).

29   **patois:** Provincial or local dialect.

Raleigh, Drake: Sir Walter Raleigh (?1554–1618), explorer, colonizer, and poet, was born in Devonshire, as was Admiral Sir Francis Drake (?1540–1596).

affectioné: Loved, liked.

His [the immigrant's]: The passage is from *The American Language*, 3rd ed. (1923), p. 212.

30   **Bankers' Olympus:** A phrase registering the critique of the undue power of banks and bankers, probably originating with the French left in the 1930s. (See Bankers' Republic, below, p. 212 and note.)

tendency to degenerate into slang: From "Is English Destined to Become the Universal Language?" (1868), by W. Brackebusch; quoted in *The American Language*, p. 386.

31   **as Mr. Mencken says:** From *The American Language*, p. 387.

"The [American] immigrant: From *The American Language*, p. 324.

Alexander Thompson: Author of *Japan for a Week (Britain for Ever)*, published in London by John Lane in 1911.

32   **matière:** Matter, raw material.

33   **Minotaure:** Surrealist review, published 1933–1939. The cover in question is reproduced in the Skira book, *Picasso: The Artist of the Century* (New York: Viking, 1971), p. 244, where Brassai is quoted as follows about its genesis:

> . . . I found him at work on the composition of the first cover for *Minotaure*. . . . On a wooden plank he had thumbtacked a section of crushed and pleated pasteboard similar to those he often used for his sculptures. On top of this he placed one of his engravings, representing the monster, and then grouped around it some lengths of ribbon, bits of silver paper lace, and also some rather faded artificial flowers. . . . When this montage was reproduced, he insisted strenuously that the thumbtacks must not be neglected.

Bishop King: Henry King (1592–1669), the Metaphysical poet, author of "The Exequy."

Gulliver: Swift's *Gulliver's Travels*.

34   **Forty Years in the Old Bailey:** Frederick Lamb is identified in the British Museum catalogue as a shorthand reporter. His book was published in 1913.

35   *Querschnitt*:   Cross section (German).

37   **Zola:**   Emile Zola (1840–1902), French naturalist novelist. *La Terre* ("the land") was published in 1887.

        Powys: T. F. Powys (1875–1953). The full identification is given in the version of this section published in *Satire and Fiction*, so we know Lewis was not thinking of the other Powys brothers, John Cowper Powys or Llewelyn Powys. T. F. Powys was the author of *Mr. Weston's Good Wine* (1927) and other novels of rural life in which the influence of Bunyan's allegorical fiction is apparent.

        Black Laughter: Sherwood Anderson's *Dark Laughter* (1925) makes frequent celebratory mention of the rich instinctual life of the Negroes, manifested in their laughter. Lewis derided this side of Anderson in *Paleface* (1929).

38   *escupidor*:   Spitoon (Spanish).

        The code napoléon was good enough for Stendhal: Lewis is thinking of the famous letter to Balzac in which Stendhal defends his style and writes: "En composant *la Chart[reuse]*, pour prendre le ton, je lisais de temps en temps quelques pages du Code civil" ("While I was writing *The Charterhouse*, I would from time to time read a few pages of the Civil Code in order to catch the tone") — *Correspondence de Stendhal* (Pléiade ed.), vol. 3, p. 399.

41   **Hemingway's brilliant skit:**   *The Torrents of Spring: A Romantic Novel in Honor of the Passing of a Great Race* (New York: Scribner's, 1926) was a satire directed at Sherwood Anderson's romantic glamorizing of the Negro. It is reprinted in Charles Poor's *Hemingway Reader*. Lewis wrote Hemingway on its publication to congratulate him on it, and in *Rude Assignment* he prints Hemingway's reply (p. 218).

        a certain great Russian novelist: "Dostoievsky, in some respects the greatest Russian novelist, had no money: in order to get it he wrote with feverish haste" (*Rude Assignment*, p. 113).

42   *Mistral*:   A story in Faulkner's *These Thirteen*.

46   **W. B. Yeats:**   Yeats's interest in the occult was life-long. His personal system of symbols had been published in *A Vision* (1925).

47   **a Van Dine crime-novel:**   S. S. Van Dine (1888–1939), American author of *The Benson Murder Case* (1926) and several other detective novels featuring Philo Vance as investigator.

48   **Bayard, that "preux":**   The French knight, the Chevalier de Bayard (1476–1524), was the original "chevalier sans peur et sans reproche" ("fearless and irreproachable knight"). "Preux" means "warrior."

        Mr. Crawley of Hogglestock: Rev. Josiah Crawley, incumbent of Hogglestock in Trollope's *Framley Parsonage*.

        as if Joyce had never jingled: Pt. 12, ch. 6, of Lewis's *The Art of Being Ruled* (1927) is entitled "Mr. Jingle and Mr. Bloom" and argues for the similarity of parts of Joyce's stream-of-consciousness rendering of Bloom's thoughts to the conversation of Dickens's Mr. Jingle in *Pickwick Papers*. The argument is repeated in *Time and Western Man*, bk. 1, ch. 16, "An Analysis of the Mind of Mr. James Joyce."

49   the *Faux-monnayeurs* ... **Judge Lindsey:** André Gide's *Les Faux-monnayeurs* (1925), translated as *The Counterfeiters* (1927). Judge Ben Lindsey's *The Revolt of Modern Youth* was published in 1925.

50   *scabreux:*   Scabrous, indecent.

Prohibition: The period from 1920 to 1933 when the sale of alcoholic beverages was illegal in the United States.

Lindbergh Baby: The baby son of Charles Lindbergh (1902–1974), who in 1927 had become world famous for making the first non-stop solo flight across the Atlantic, was kidnapped and killed in 1932. Bruno Hauptman was executed for the crime in 1936.

little gutter-Caesars: The Warner Brothers film *Little Caesar* of 1931, directed by Mervyn Leroy, starred Edward G. Robinson as a ruthless gangster.

53   *a corn-cob:*   In *Sanctuary*, Temple Drake is deflowered by the impotent Popeye by means of this phallic substitute.

Atropos: In Greek mythology, the Fate who cuts the thread of life.

55   *Ara Vos Prec:*   London: The Ovid Press, 1920.

The Waste Land: New York: Boni and Liveright, 1922 and London: Hogarth Press, 1923.

Prufrock: *Prufrock and Other Observations*, London: The Egoist, 1917.

"neither loud or long":   Cf. "Sweet Thames, run softly till I end my song, / Sweet Thames, run softly, for I speak not loud or long." — *The Waste Land*, lines 182–83.

"John, son of Warner":   The fourth of the "Six Odes" that comprise Book III of W. H. Auden's *The Orators* (London: Faber and Faber, 1932; 2nd ed. 1934) is dedicated "To John Warner, son of Rex and Frances Warner." It includes the lines "I cannot state it too clearly, I shall not refrain, / It is John, son of Warner, has pulled my chain."

56   **the knowing craftsman:**   Cf. Eliot's dedication of *The Waste Land* to Pound as "il miglior fabbro," the superior craftsman.

57   **magnificent, but it is not criticism:**   Cf. "C'est magnifique, mais ce n'est pas la guerre" ("It's magnificent, but it's not war"), the famous remark of Pierre Bosquet (1810–1861) about the charge of the Light Brigade at Balaclava, 1854.

Max Eastman exults: In "The Resurrection of the Scholar-Gentleman," (*Scribner's Magazine*, 90 [Nov. 1931]: 475–85; reprinted in *The Literary Mind* [New York: Scribner's, 1931], pp. 31–53), we find Eastman writing as follows:

> In my opinion the knell of this whole cultural incident — this little wild-goose chase into history of the demoted men-of-letters — is sounded in the recent confession of T. S. Eliot that he is dissatisfied with the meaning of his own "statements in criticism," dissatisfied also with "the terminology of the Humanists," and disposed to ask himself, "whether there is still any justification for literary criticism at all, or whether we should not merely allow the subject to be absorbed gently into exacter sciences." He has travelled far. . . But he has at least pronounced the words which may ring the curtain down upon this whole gentlemanly anti-scientific interlude.

Eastman is quoting from T. S. Eliot's article, "Experiment in Criticism," *The Bookman* (70 [Nov. 1929]: 225–33), but how far Lewis's paraphrase of Eastman's selective quoting distorts Eliot's view may be judged from the following remarks, also from the same article: "I think that the answer is clear [i.e., when we ask ourselves the question Eastman quotes]: that so long as literature is literature, so long will there be a place for criticism of it"; and further: ". . . there is good cause for believing . . . that literary criticism, far from being exhausted, has only begun its work."

57   **maître de séance:** Master of ceremonies, presiding officer.

58   **Leavis's master:** Leavis attended the I. A. Richards lectures that later resulted in *Practical Criticism*, and it is reported that some of his critical comments are incorporated among the "protocols" of that book. Leavis's early work has many appreciative comments on Richards's criticism, though he was soon to condemn strongly its utilitarian basis. In later years, Leavis made some severely qualifying judgments on Eliot's criticism also.

The only possible *sincere man*: This passage, the first paragraph of which, at least, sounds very like I. A. Richards, is not to be found in *Practical Criticism, Principles of Criticism, Science and Poetry,* or *The Meaning of Meaning.* Its source is untraced. (Paul Edwards suggests plausibly that the second paragraph may be by Lewis himself, erroneously placed in quotation marks.)

Sincerity can only mean identity with truth: The first edition reads "Insincerity," but this must be a slip. The paragraph is paraphrasing and quoting from *Practical Criticism*, pp. 281–82.

61   **whole of the literature of Europe:** From Eliot's "Tradition and the Individual Talent," *Selected Essays.*

a scuffle in fourteenth-century Siena: There are no references to fourteenth-century Siena in *A Draft of XXX Cantos* (London: Faber and Faber, 1933). Lewis is probably making a loose general reference to Cantos 8–11 which are about the career of Sigismondo Malatesta (1417–1468) of Rimini.

fait-divers: News item.

les cocotiers absents: Baudelaire's "Le Cygne" ("The Swan") contains the lines

> Je pense à la négresse, amaigrie et phtisique,
> Piétinant dans la boue, et cherchant, l'oeil hagard,
> Les cocotiers absents de la superbe Afrique
> Derrière la muraille immense du brouillard.

("I think of the Negress, thin and consumptive, trudging through the mud and searching with haggard eyes for the absent palm trees of proud Africa behind the huge wall of the fog.")

Paul Morand: (1888–1976) French poet, novelist, travel writer, and diplomat, author of impressionistic studies mainly of night life in various European countries.

61   **Ronald Firbank:**   (1886–1926) Homosexual, dandyish, aesthete-novelist, author of such highly mannered, exotic works as *Valmouth* (1919) and *Prancing Nigger* (1924).

Stevenson: Robert Louis Stevenson (1850–1894). Scottish novelist, now chiefly remembered for his boys' romances, *Treasure Island* (1883) and *Kidnapped* (1886).

through a glass darkly: See 1 Corinthians 13:11.

62   **Bertrand Russell's account of the psyche:**   See Russell's *The Analysis of Mind* (London: Allen and Unwin, 1922), in which he concludes that "the ultimate data of psychology are only sensations and images, and their relations. Beliefs, desires, volitions, and so on, [appear] . . . to be complex phenomena consisting of sensations and images variously interrelated" (pp. 299–300).

the Behaviorist: J. B. Watson's *Behaviorism* (revised edition) was published in London in 1931. Lewis discussed it in *The Art of Being Ruled*, pt. 12, ch. 4, and satirized it in *Snooty Baronet* (1932).

L'ouvrage eust été moins mien: ". . . but then the worke had beene lesse mine: whose principall drift and perfection, is to be exactly mine; I could mend an accidentall errour, . . . but it were a kinde of treason to remove the imperfections from me, which in me are ordinary and constant" (Florio's translation). A longer extract, of which these lines form part, is used as the epigraph to *Tarr* (1918, rev. 1928).

63   **the "destructive element":**   "In the destructive element immerse!" – Conrad, *Lord Jim* (1900).

64   **Cyrano:**   Cyrano de Bergerac (1619–1655), French poet and fantasist, whose large nose embroiled him in many duels. He is perhaps best known through the play of Edmond Rostand, whereby he has come to embody the qualities of panache and bravura.

***un peu de Cocteau, quoi!*:**   A little bit of Cocteau, say. For Cocteau, see note to p. 109, below.

the *Criterion*:   Launched under the editorship of T. S. Eliot in 1922 (*The Waste Land* appeared in its first issue), this quarterly journal continued publication until 1939.

***la vieille France*:**   Old France (that is, royalist and conservative French politics).

super-real: Lewis always used this literal translation of "surréal" in place of the more common "surrealist."

exhibited himself as "a royalist":   Cf. Eliot's remark in the Preface to *For Lancelot Andrews* (London: Faber and Faber, 1928) that he was "a classicist in literature, a royalist in politics, and an anglo-catholic in religion."

67   ***The Decay of Lying*:**   A dialogue first published in 1889, revised and collected in *Intentions*, 1891. It protests against realism and naturalism and argues that "lying, the telling of beautiful untrue things, is the proper aim of Art."

67 **She was poor, but she was honest:** Anonymous World War I song. Lewis's publisher wanted him to bowdlerize this innocuous bit of folk poetry by substituting the word "whim" for the sexually inflammatory "crime," but Lewis refused. (See *Letters*, ed. Rose, p. 220, and "Afterword," p. 305, below.)

agonisant: Dying person; one suffering the death-throes.

72 **specifics for more enterprising virility:** This is Lewis's substitution for an original that evidently seemed too risqué to his publisher: "As to the 'rubber shop'," Lewis wrote to him, "I will find a less robustious simile than that certainly" (*Letters*, ed. Rose, p. 220).

Pelmanism: A commercial self-improvement system, focussing particularly on memory training.

Chung Yung: The Confucian text known in English as (in Ezra Pound's translation) *The Unwobbling Pivot*.

73 **men are mischievous and disagreeable little animals:** Cf. the King of Brobdingnag's conclusions in Book II, chapter 6, of *Gulliver's Travels*: ". . . I cannot but conclude the Bulk of your Natives, to be the most pernicious Race of little odious Vermin that Nature ever suffered to crawl upon the Surface of the Earth."

74 **Rousseau, with his "noble savage":** See above, note to p. 20.

Wainewrights and Wildes in the making: Thomas Griffiths Wainewright (1794–1852), art critic, forger, and poisoner, subject of an essay by Oscar Wilde ("Pen, Pencil, and Poison").

74 **Vilhjàlmar Stefànsson:** American Arctic explorer (1879–1962), author of *My Life with the Esquimo* (1913) and *The Friendly Arctic* (1921).

Franklin: Sir John Franklin (1786–1847), British Arctic explorer lost while seeking the Northwest Passage.

the anonymous, "impersonal," catalytic: See T. S. Eliot's famous analogy of the catalyst — the shred of platinum whose presence allows two gases to combine — in his essay "Tradition and the Individual Talent": "The mind of the poet is the shred of platinum. It may partly or exclusively operate upon the experience of the man himself; but, the more perfect the artist, the more completely separate in him will be the man who suffers and the mind which creates; the more perfectly will the mind digest and transmute the passions which are its material" (*Selected Essays*).

76 *sending to Coventry*: Subjecting a person to ostracism by refusing to talk with him.

Maritain: Jacques Maritain (1882–1973) Catholic neo-Thomist philosopher; author of *Art et scolastique* (1927; trans. *Art and Scholasticism*, 1930), *Creative Intuition in Art and Poetry* (1953), etc.

Middleton Murry: (1889–1957) Editor, critic (*Countries of the Mind*, 1922), and writer on religion (*Life of Jesus*, 1926; *God*, 1929). Husband of Katherine Mansfield.

77 **sex-dissector of William Wordsworth:** See Herbert Read's *Wordsworth* (London: Jonathan Cape, 1931), which took a Freudian approach to the understanding of the poet's life and work. For an interesting account by Read of his close association with Eliot during the *Criterion*

years (he was a frequent contributor from the start), see "T. S. Eliot: A Memoir," in *The Cult of Sincerity* (New York: Horizon Press, 1969).

77   **Remarque . . . Feuchtwanger . . . Wassermann:** Three celebrated middle-brow novelists. Remarque (1898–1970) is best known for *All Quiet on the Western Front* (1929), Feuchtwanger (1884–1958) for *Jüd Süss* (1925; Eng. trans. *Power*, 1926), and Jakob Wassermann (1873–1934) for *Caspar Hauser* (1908; Eng. trans. 1928). For Lewis's criticism of Remarque, see further *The Old Gang and the New Gang* (1932) or the excerpts from it in *Enemy Salvoes*, ed. C. J. Fox.

78   **spurious verbal algebra:** This sardonic formulation evokes — no doubt deliberately — Eliot's famous pronouncement about the "objective correlative" ("Hamlet," 1919, in *Selected Essays*), itself an echo of Ezra Pound's remark that poetry "is a sort of inspired mathematics, which gives us equations . . . for the human emotions" (*The Spirit of Romance*, 1910 [rpt. New Directions, 1952, p. 14]).

"She bathed her feet in soda water": From *The Waste Land*, line 201.

81   **Kant:** German idealist philosopher, 1724–1804.

Hobbes: English nominalist philosopher, 1588–1679.

Spinoza: Dutch Jewish philosopher, 1632–1677.

Spencer: Herbert Spencer (1820–1903), English evolutionary philosopher.

Maimonides: Spanish Jewish philosopher, 1135–1204.

Rochester: John Wilmot, Earl of Rochester (1647–1680), Restoration libertine wit and poet.

Sedley: Sir Charles Sedley (?1639–1701), like his friend Rochester, a rake and poet.

85   **Saintsbury:** I do not find the exact words in Saintsbury's *Dryden* (1881; rpt. London: Macmillan, 1930), but if Lewis is paraphrasing rather than quoting exactly, the following (from pp. 76–77) is probably his source: "It never does for the political satirist to lose his temper and to rave and rant and denounce with the air of an inspired prophet. Dryden, and perhaps Dryden alone, has observed this rule. . . . [H]is manner towards his subjects is that of a cool and not ill-humoured scorn. . . . [T]his attitude . . . in its turn explains the frantic rage which Dryden's satire produced in his opponents."

coup de main: Surprise attack.

our Hogarth's face, in a nightcap: Lewis is probably thinking either of the Self Portrait in oil of 1745 in the National Gallery (engraved as *Guglielmus Hogarth*, 1748/9), which shows Hogarth with a dog, or of the bust of Hogarth by Roubiliac in the National Portrait Gallery, in which the expression is rather more bulldog-like. In both portraits, Hogarth is wearing an odd-looking piece of headgear.

Satyricon: The Latin novel of low life by Petronius Arbiter (d. 65 A.D.)

Volpone: The play by Ben Jonson (1572/3–1637).

the Médicin malgré lui: The play by Molière (1622–1673).

Taine: Hippolyte Taine (1828–1893), French critic and philosopher.

85   **Brunetière:**   French literary critic (1849–1906), opponent of the art-for-art's-sake school.

Au plus bas degré: "At the bottom of the scale are the types of persons preferred by realist literature and the comic theatre — that is, characters who are limited, flat, foolish, egotistical, weak, and ordinary . . ."

Il n'y a ni beaux: "There are neither beautiful nor ugly subjects . . . one might almost set it down as an axiom, considering the matter from the point of view of pure Art, that there are no subjects at all, style by itself alone being an absolute manner of seeing things." Letter to Louise Colet, 16 January 1852 (*Correspondance*, 9 vols. [Paris: Conard, 1926–1933], 2:345–46).

Nietzsche on the Mahomet of Voltaire: *Mahomet*, a tragedy by Voltaire, produced in 1742 (published as *Le Fanatisme, ou Mahomet*), represents Mahomet as an unscrupulous and cruel charlatan. Nietzsche's expression of admiration for it is found in section 221 of his *Menschliches, Allzumenschliches* (1878), vol. 1 (*Human, All Too Human*):

> One need only read Voltaire's *Mahomet* from time to time in order clearly to perceive what European culture has lost, once and for all, through that breakdown of tradition. Voltaire was the last of the great dramatists who controlled his multiform soul, equal to the greatest tragic storms, through the use of Greek proportion. . . .

He also refers to it in a letter of 13 February 1881.

86   **La faute de Flaubert:**   "Flaubert's fault is a grave one too. To have substituted art for God sets him on a dangerous road."

puisqu'il ne pouvait: "Since he could no longer avoid the study of the modern Prudhomme, very well, then: he would take the bull by the horns; the enormous stupidity of the bourgeois would become the subject of his book, he would give it flesh, it would be his masterpiece. . . . The Bourgeois . . . sits down at his table, sleeps in his bed, fills his days and nights, and at last seizes him by the throat. The Bourgeois in the end has had his hide; he has quite literally assassinated Flaubert. The alchemist of Croisset died a victim to the experiments which he undertook on the human creature: he filtered out the soul from the human mixture in order to get stupidity in the pure state — and it asphyxiated him."

86   **Albalat:**   Antoine Albalat (1856–1935), French literary critic, author of several popular books on style (e.g., *Le Mal d'écrire*, 1895) and of *Gustave Flaubert et ses amis, avec des lettres inédites* . . . (Paris: Plon, 1927).

Gautier: French Romantic poet, novelist, and critic (1811–1872).

87   **Blake's "prolonged vindication":**   Raleigh's remark, quoted above, p. 13.

hommes-plumes: Pen-men, human pens.

mots justes: Exact words (Flaubert's ideal in writing).

"burgess-gentleman":   Cp. *Le Bourgeois gentilhomme*, the title of a play by Molière, often translated as "The would-be gentleman."

87   **Capone:**   Al Capone (1899–1947), celebrated Chicago gangster of the Prohibition era.

88   **Mrs. Grundy:**   A character from Thomas Morton's *Speed the Plough* (1798)
who became a popular symbol of extreme moral severity and self-
righteousness.

Dr. Bowdler: Dr. Thomas Bowdler (1754–1825) published an expurgated
Family Shakespeare, with profanity and indecency excised to make
the works suitable for family readings.

the Geneva Bible: Also popularly known as the "Breeches" Bible (because
of its translation of Genesis 3:7), it was prepared in Geneva by English
exiles fleeing persecution under the Catholic Queen Mary. It appeared
in 1560 with marginal commentaries that made it the favorite of the
Puritans.

89   **Bunyan:**   John Bunyan (1628–1688), Puritan preacher and author of *The
Pilgrim's Progress* (1678, 1684).

cheerfulness . . . will keep breaking in: Boswell's *Life of Johnson*, ch.
41 (17 April 1778) quotes Johnson's old school friend Oliver Edwards:
"You are a philosopher, Dr. Johnson. I have tried too in my time to
be a philosopher; but, I don't know how, cheerfulness was always
breaking in."

Addison: Joseph Addison (1672–1719), poet, playwright, and essayist (*The
Spectator*, 1711–1712). For his use of the word "genius," see *The Spectator*, no. 160 (1711): "There is no Character more frequently given
to a writer, than that of being a Genius. I have heard many a little
Sonnetteer called a *fine Genius*" (cited in OED). Note that Addison
is recording a shift in usage, not recommending it.

90   **Pantagruel:**   Rabelais's comic tale of 1532.

pots de chambre: Chamber pots.

Smollett: Tobias Smollett (1721–1771), picaresque novelist, author of
The Expedition of Humphry Clinker.

91   **Hazlitt:**   William Hazlitt (1778–1830), English political and literary essayist. His *Lectures on the English Comic Writers* appeared in 1819. The
passage quoted is found on p. 42 of the World's Classics edition of 1920.

92   **pity and terror:**   Aristotle's *Poetics* specifies pity and terror as the emotions proper to tragedy.

93   **It is, as you say . . . :**   This passage is not to be found in the four volumes
of Edel's edition of *The Letters of Henry James,* nor have I succeeded
in finding it in James's tales.

95   **Montagu Slater:**   Lewis's attribution of this phrase is in error: it does
not occur in the Slater article. But something very like it occurs in
a review of *Apes of God* published in *The Week End Review* (2:21
[2 August 1930] 168), by L. P. Hartley: "Personal appearance means
a great deal to Mr Wyndham Lewis; but one may safely say it never
draws him on, it always puts him off."

96   **Auguste Rodin:**   French sculptor (1840–1917). "The Kiss" is in the Tate
Gallery.

96   **Bergson:** Cp. ". . . the bergsonian (jameseque, psycho-analytic, wagner-
        ian Venusberg) philosophy of the hot *vitals* — of the blood-stream, of
        vast cosmic emotion, gush and flow — is that of a *blind* organism. There
        are no Eyes in that philosophy" (*The Art of Being Ruled*, p. 403). For
        Lewis's sustained analysis of the time philosophy of Bergson, see *Time
        and Western Man* (1927).

96   **élan vital:** Vital impulse.

        that is all ye know: Keats, "Ode on a Grecian Urn."

        rare Ben Jonson: "O rare Ben Jonson" — the epitaph on Jonson's tomb in
        Westminster Abbey.

97   **"a philosoph of the EYE":** The other book is *Time and Western Man*
        (1927), where in bk. II, pt. 3, ch. 4, we read:

> . . . at the start I intimated that this essay was to be an attempt to provide
> something in the nature of a *philosophy of the eye*. . . . [I]f by "philosophy
> of the eye" is meant that we wish to repose, and materially to repose, in the
> crowning human sense, the visual sense; and if it meant that we *refuse* (closing
> ourselves in with our images and sensa) to retire into the abstraction and darkness
> of an aural and tactile world, then it is true that our philosophy attaches itself
> to the concrete and radiant reality of the optic sense.

        a reader's report: The reader (for a publisher) was Montgomery Belgion,
        a literary critic and contributor to *The Criterion*, author of *The Human
        Parrot* (Oxford Univ. Press, 1931). His report is quoted at length by
        Lewis in *Satire and Fiction*, pp. 30–31.

        visuel: One dominated by the sense of sight.

        de Gourmont: Rémy de Gourmont (1858–1915), French literary critic.
        For the expression, see his *La Culture des idées*, 1901.

98   **Montagu Slater . . . article:** This article, "Satire in the Novel: The Muffled
        Majesty of Irresponsible Authorship," dealing with Lewis's *Apes*,
        Aldington's *Death of a Hero*, and H. G. Wells's *The Autocracy of Mr
        Parham*, appeared in the *Daily Telegraph* of 25 July 1930, p. 10. It
        is quoted in *Satire and Fiction*. Slater was a literary critic who con-
        tributed, for example, to the respected *Calendar of Modern Letters*.

        my criticism of *Ulysses*: See *Time and Western Man*, pt. 1, ch. 16, "An
        Analysis of the Mind of James Joyce."

99   **objections to Mr. D. H. Lawrence:** Lewis's critique of Lawrence's primi-
        tivism is found in *Paleface*, 1929.

        ***Fleurs du mal*:** "Flowers of evil" — the title of Baudelaire's volume of 1857.

100   ***couleur-de-rose*:** Rose-colored.

        ***sub specie aeternitatis*:** From the perspective of eternity (Latin).

101   **Hazlitt:** *Lectures on the English Comic Writers*, World's Classics edition,
        pp. 42–43.

102   **an *Umwertung aller Werte*:** A "revaluation [or transvaluation] of all
        values" — Nietzsche's phrase used as part of the sub-title for his *Der*

Wille zur Macht (*The Will to Power*). It names the effect which Nietzsche believed would follow on a recognition that life has no higher meaning than its own self-aggrandizing energy.

102   **tragedy of blood:**   Also known as the Revenge Tragedy, a type popular in the late Elizabethan and Jacobean theatre.

to *sadify*:   Lewis's coinage, from the Marquis de Sade.

103   **Mr. Roy Campbell:**   South African born poet (1901–1957) whose *Georgiad* (1931) was a satire on the Bloomsbury group.

the "transitionists":   The magazine *transition*, published in Paris by Eugène and Maria Jolas from 1927, printed the later work of James Joyce, as well as contributions by Stein, Beckett, and others. It sponsored what it called "the Revolution of the Word." Lewis carried on a public controversy with the *transition* group following his criticism of Stein and Joyce in *The Art of Being Ruled* and *Time and Western Man*. See *The Enemy* (1927–1929) and *The Diabolical Principle and the Dithyrhambic Spectator* (1931).

104   **Gestalt:**   This German word (literally "shape"), derived from *Gestalt* psychology and referring to whole patterns whose meanings are irreducible to their constituent elements, began to be used in English in the 1920s.

Gauguin . . . Pierre Loti: Gauguin lived and painted for years in Tahiti. Loti (1850–1923), French novelist and travel writer, wrote *Rarahu ou Le Marriage de Loti* (1880) which was set in Tahiti.

107   **Jonathan Swift:**   I have not located this quotation, but if Lewis is paraphrasing from memory rather than transcribing, he may be thinking of "The Digression on Madness" from *A Tale of a Tub* (1704), where, after defining happiness as "a perpetual possession of being well deceived," Swift (or his ironic persona) continues:

> In proportion that credulity is a more peaceful possession of the mind than curiosity, so far preferable is that wisdom which converses about the surface to that pretended philosophy which enters into the depth of things and then comes gravely back with information and discoveries, that in the inside they are good for nothing. . . .
> . . . And therefore, in order to save the charges of all such expensive anatomy for the time to come, I do here think fit to inform the reader, that in such conclusions as these, reason is certainly in the right, and that in most corporeal beings which have fallen under my cognizance the outside hath been infinitely preferable to the in; whereof I have been farther convinced from some late experiments.
> Last week I saw a woman flayed, and you will hardly believe how much it altered her person for the worse. . . .

Toussaint L'Ouverture: François Toussaint L'Ouverture (1743–1803), a Negro revolutionary leader who led a revolt in Haiti and ruled the island until overthrown by Napoleon.

108   *foi de gentilhomme:*   On my honor as a gentleman.

109   ***Dark Night of the Soul:***   A reference to St. John of the Cross, Spanish
       monk, poet, and mystic (1542–1591), author of poems about the soul's
       mystical experience of God, such as *The Ascent of Mount Carmel* and
       The Dark Night.

       badauds: Strollers, gapers (in the street).

       Cocteau: Jean Cocteau (1889–1963), French poet, novelist, and film
       maker. He wrote a book about his drug addiction (*Opium*, 1930) and
       for a brief period became an active Catholic under the influence of
       the philosopher Jacques Maritain. For his "religious *chic*," see, for ex-
       ample, the accusation that Cocteau is writing a kind of religious por-
       nography in Denis Saurat, *Tendances* (Paris, 1928), quoted by Mont-
       gomery Belgion, *The Human Parrot* (Oxford Univ. Press, 1931), p.
       123n.

       Gurdjieff: Georgei Ivanovitch Gurdjieff (?1874–1949), theosophical
       teacher and guru whose doctrines are recorded by Ouspensky in *In
       Search of the Miraculous* (1950). He had an Institute at Fontainebleau
       where, among others, Katherine Mansfield studied (she died there in
       1923).

110   **the Servile State:**   The title of a 1912 book by Hilaire Belloc (1870–1953),
       poet, novelist, and Catholic social critic. A new edition was reviewed
       by T. S. Eliot in *The Criterion* in 1927 (in an issue in which an article
       by Lewis was also printed).

       We who were born free: Echoing the famous line from Rousseau's *Social
       Contract* (1762): "Man is born free, but everywhere he is in chains."

       Epictetus: Roman Stoic philosopher (50–120 A.D.), author of *Discourses*
       and *The Encheiridion.*

111   ***soi-disant:***   Self-styled; so-called.

       Bankers' Olympus: See note to p. 30.

       souffleur: In theatrical usage, a prompter.

       coal-heaver: One who carries sacks of coal, e.g. in delivering them to
       people's homes; thus, a type of the blue collar worker.

112   ***Chansons de geste:***   The romances of chivalry of the late middle ages.

       laboratory . . . lavatory: Similarly accented on the first syllable in British
       pronunciation

       Arthuriad: Not a particular work, but any poem on the subject of the
       knights of King Arthur and the Holy Grail.

115   **"There is surely no principle . . .":**   Henry James, from *Notes and Reviews*
       (Cambridge, Mass.: Dunster House, 1921), p. 19.

       Hemingway . . . accused (by Mr. Eliot):   Neither the Eliot nor Hemingway
       bibliographies have yielded anything that can be identified with cer-
       tainty as Lewis's source. But it is just possible that he is relying on
       his memory of an editor's "Commentary" in *The Criterion* at about

the time he was writing (vol. 12 [1933], no. 48). In it Eliot is attacking the very kind of assumed superiority of the present to the past (even mentioning Strachey) that Lewis here imputes to Eliot himself; he goes on to say: "In America, this pseudo — or not quite good mannered sophistication takes the form of what they call hard boiling. . . . Even Mr. Ernest Hemingway — that writer of tender sentiment, and true sentiment, as in *The Killers* and *A Farewell to Arms* . . . has been taken as the representative of hard boiling. Hard boiling is, of course, only another defence-mechanism adopted by the world's babies. . . ." But Eliot immediately acquits Hemingway of the charge: "He does not belong in the class in which I have placed [Anatole] France, and Gide, and (tentatively) Mr. Aldous Huxley."

115   **Mr. Strachey:** Lytton Strachey's *Eminent Victorians* (1918) was a widely popular book imbued with a complacent sense of superiority to its Victorian subjects.

Tartuffe: Molière's character embodying sanctimonious hypocrisy in the play of the same name.

116   **Bolingbroke:** Henry St. John, first Viscount (1658-1751), Tory politician, friend of Pope and Swift, and political enemy of Marlborough.

Duke of Marlborough: John Churchill, first Duke of Marlborough (1650-1722), successful general at such battles against the French as Blenheim (1704). He had something of a reputation for avarice, though his biographers defend him.

Inigo Jones: The architect and stage designer Inigo Jones (b. 1573) died two years after Marlborough was born. Lewis is thinking of Sir John Vanbrugh (1664-1726), the playwright and architect, who designed Blenheim Palace and had trouble getting paid. He was supposed to be paid, however, not by Marlborough but by the government, Parliament having voted the building as a gift to Marlborough from a grateful nation, but neglecting to vote the funds. Lewis's slip provided his foes with some ammunition: Sir Osbert Sitwell, defending his sister's *Aspects of Modern Poetry* (1934) from an adverse review by G. W. Stonier, wrote "Must every writer be original in his facts; as original, for example, as Mr. Percy Wyndham Lewis . . . ?" and adduced the date of Jones's death and of the building of Blenheim, begun in 1705. Lewis, unabashed, retorted: "I do not know the date of the death of Inigo Jones. But there is one thing about which I am absolutely positive: namely, that it is not 1652 — since a member of the Sitwell family gives it as such! That, I think we can now all agree, is conclusive. The same of course applies to the building of Blenheim." (See *Letters*, ed. Rose, pp. 229-30.)

Cibber, Budgell, and Settle: Minor writers now chiefly remembered only because they were attacked and satirized by Pope and Dryden. Colley Cibber (1671-1757) was a playwright and poet who became laureate in 1730. Like Eustace Budgell (1686-1737), he is satirized in Pope's *Dunciad*. Elkanah Settle (1648-1724) appears as Doeg in Dryden's satire *Absalom and Achitophel.*

118   **the *Book of Snobs*:** An 1848 collection of sketches by Thackeray.

119   **These "high" and "low" values (identified by Nietzsche with "good" and "bad"):** See *The Genealogy of Morals*, first essay, section 4: "The signpost to the *right* road was for me the question: what was the real etymological significance of the designations for 'good' coined in the various languages? I found they all led back to the *same conceptual transformation* — that everywhere 'noble,' 'aristocratic' in the social sense, is the basic concept from which 'good' . . . necessarily developed: a development which always runs parallel with that other in which 'common,' 'plebian,' 'low' are finally transformed into the concept 'bad.' " (Trans. Walter Kaufmann [New York: Vintage Books, 1967], pp. 27-28.)

120   **To be "dogmatically for the great *Without*":** Paraphrasing his own reason no. 9 (p. 105 above) justifying "the *external* approach."

       Proust: Marcel Proust (1871-1922), whose multi-volume novel entitled *À la Recherche du temps perdu* (1913-1927) was published in English translation as *Remembrance of Things Past* (1922-1931).

121   **the beau idéal:** The beautiful ideal, the ideal type.

123   **finicks:** Finickal persons (OED Supp.).

126   **a sort of "Barrens":** "Barrens," a stretch of infertile or waste sandy ground: in quotation marks because an American usage. Lewis wanted to change the title of *Men Without Art* to *Literary Barrens* (letter to Desmond Flower, 19 July 1934, *Letters*, ed. Rose, no. 211), but the book was in production and it was too late.

       an algebraic expression: Cp. "spurious verbal algebra" applied to *The Waste Land* above, p. 78 and note.

127   ***Nacktkultur:*** Nudism (German).

128   **Queen Elizabeth:** See, for example, the "Ditchley Portrait" of Queen Elizabeth, ca. 1592, by Marcus Gheeraerts the Younger (National Portrait Gallery).

       Frobisher: Sir Martin Frobisher (?1535-1594), English navigator and explorer.

129   **a good little Camelot du Roi:** A seller of the Royalist newspaper, hence a royalist militant, specifically one of the young members of the *Action Française*.

       L'Isle des pingouins: Anatole France's novel of 1908, translated as *Penguin Island*.

       IT: Slang: sex appeal.

131   **"We must reconcile ourselves":** From Virginia Woolf, *Mr. Bennett and Mrs. Brown* (London: Hogarth Press, 1928), p. 22.

132   **Mr. and Mrs. Leavis:** Q. D. Leavis cited Mrs. Woolf as the type of the highbrow novelist in *Fiction and the Reading Public*, and in general the Leavises took her seriously enough to review several of her books in *Scrutiny*, but they were also highly critical of both her criticism and her fiction.

132   **the "new signatures":**   *New Signatures* was an anthology of the younger English poets, especially Auden, Day Lewis, and Spender, edited by Michael Roberts and published by Hogarth Press in 1932. Lewis reviewed the group in a two-part article entitled "Shropshire Lads or Robots?" in 1934 (see Morrow and Lafourcade's Lewis *Bibliography*, D197 and D198).

       ***Georgiad*:**   See note to p. 103, above.

133   **the eternal feminine:**   Goethe's phrase ("das Ewig-Weibliche") from the last line of *Faust*, pt. 2.

       "If we try to formulate":   From "Modern Fiction," *The Common Reader* (London: Hogarth Press, 1925), pp. 208–209.

134   **"to stomach these ferocious companions":**   The phrase is from Van Wyck Brooks, *The Pilgrimage of Henry James*, p. 60.

       de Goncourts: Edmond (1822–1896) and Jules (1830–1870) de Goncourt, brothers and authors in collaboration of realist novels, as well as of a notable *Journal* recording Paris literary life.

       Turgenev found: Ivan Turgenev (1818–1883), Russian novelist, author of *Fathers and Sons* (1862). "I do not think my stories," James wrote, "struck him as quite meat for men. The manner was more apparent than the matter; they were too *tarabiscote*, as I once heard him say of the style of a book — had on the surface too many little flowers and knots of ribbon." ("Ivan Turgenieff" [1884] in *Partial Portraits* [New York, 1888].)

       d'outre Manche: From the other side of the English Channel.

       the "creeping Saxon":   In *The Lion and the Fox* (1927), p. 302, Lewis cites Matthew Arnold's essay on Celtic Literature where this phrase occurs, and explains: " 'For dullness, the creeping Saxon,' is a line in an old Irish poem." Arnold, in part 4 of his *On the Study of Celtic Literature*, quotes the quatrain:

>   For acuteness and valour, the Greeks,
>   For excessive pride, the Romans,
>   For dulness, the creeping Saxons;
>   For beauty and amorousness, the Gaedhils.

       baby "polly":   Apollinaris water, similar to seltzer water.

135   **"I should doubt if she was an educated woman":**   The actual text is "I doubt whether she was what you call an educated woman."

       (1910 is the date implied):   Lewis misrepresents some of Woolf's details. The incident in the railway carriage occurred "One night some weeks ago," she tells us. The date 1910 comes from the famous formulation, ". . . on or about December 1910 human character changed." Woolf does say "I was tempted to manufacture a three-volume novel" about her fellow travellers, but she seems to mean this humorously and fantastically, not literally.

136   **eminent Fivetowner:**   That is, Arnold Bennett (1867–1931), author of —among other titles—*Anna of the Five Towns* (1902).

136 **the instinctive outcry of the war-time Sitwells:** Edith Sitwell (1887–1964) edited the magazine *Wheels* from 1916 to 1921, where she published poetry by Wilfred Owen. Lewis is thinking equally of her brother Osbert (1892–1969), whose early verse (*The Winstonburg Line*, 1919) is pacifist in tone. In *The Apes of God*, Lewis had already attacked this attitude, thinly disguising the Sitwells as Lord Osmund and Lady Harriet Finnian Shaw:

> "You must always bear in mind" said Blackshirt quickly "that it is always *the War* that in fact they are talking about. The child-parent-war-game was manufactured in the War-time. Harriet and Osmund took up the cry – they did not invent it – that it was the *Old Colonels*, in league with the *Old Politicians* (and all the sheltered Elders too old to be soldiers, in the decline of their days, who thirsted for their children's blood) who were responsible for the European War. There would be no harm in that if it did not serve to screen the actual villain" (555).

Sassoons: Siegfried Sassoon (1886–1967), author of pacifist verse during World War I and after a spell in the trenches, organizer of an anti-war protest.

The Great Blank of the Missing Generation: See Part II of Lewis's *The Old Gang and the New Gang* (1932), in which he discusses a newspaper article of that title. He attacks the "self-advertising-by-self-pitying rage" of "the recent War Literature" of writers like Sassoon and Remarque. Lewis maintained such slogans as "the missing generation" belonged to advertising and were part of an inter-generational conflict encouraged by the press as a distraction from serious analysis of the causes of war. "The pillorying of the simple *foreground* figures in the English War-poet (. . . and in the Sitwells, after Sassoon) of necessity has tended to occult and to mask more and more the prime movers in the *background*" (*The Old Gang and the New Gang*, p. 61; rep. in *Enemy Salvoes*, ed. C. J. Fox).

"the difference perhaps is": *Mr. Bennett and Mrs. Brown*, p. 12.

no "Passion flowers at the gate: Cf. *A Room of One's Own* (London: Hogarth Press, 1929), pp. 20–22, where Woolf quotes Tennyson's lines "There has fallen a splendid tear / From the passion flower at the gate." Lewis refers again to the lines in *The Revenge for Love* (1937), where he depicts Margot Stamp speaking them to herself "as she imagined that great queen among women (that great weary queen, as she romantically pictured her), her adored Virginia, would have spoken them" (p. 261).

137 **Clayhanger . . . Forsyte . . . Britling:** Cf. Arnold Bennett, *Clayhanger* (1910) and other books in the same series; John Galsworthy, *The Forsyte Saga* (1906–1922); H. G. Wells, *Mr. Britling Sees It Through* (1916).

her Plain Reader: Virginia Woolf published two collections of literary essays under the title *The Common Reader* (1925 and 1932). In "How It Strikes a Contemporary" from the former collection, Woolf writes: "*Ulysses* was a memorable catastrophe – immense in daring, terrific in disaster."

137   **far from being "pale":**   An echo of Lewis's criticism of Lawrence in *Paleface.*

      Sturm und Drang: Storm and stress (German) — a phrase applied to the late 18th century German Romantic writers such as Herder and Schiller.

138   **Venusberg:**   An environment given over to sensual pleasure, from Wagner's *Tannhäuser.*

      "I saw pale kings":   From Keats's "La Belle Dame Sans Merci."

      "unreal city":   Eliot, *The Waste Land*, line 207.

139   **made easy by his natural Epicureanism:**   From Pater's *Marius the Epicurean* (1885), vol. 1, pp. 124–25.

      the fleshly school: From the title of Buchanan's article in the *Contemporary Review* of October, 1871, attacking the Pre-Raphaelites, especially Dante Gabriel Rossetti.

140   **At this time, by his poetic:**   From *Marius the Epicurean*, vol. 1, p. 124.

141   **Pater:**   As cited by Mario Praz in the passage quoted below, p. 144. From Pater's "Duke Carl of Rosenmold."

      Slough of Despond: One of the pitfalls awaiting the journeying Christian in Bunyan's *Pilgrim's Progress.* This whole passage is Bunyanesque in its allegorical landscape.

142   **Rapa Nui:**   Easter Island, the Pacific island noted for its stone monoliths.

143   **Huysmans:**   J-K. Huysmans (1848–1907), now chiefly remembered for his novel *À Rebours* (1884), much admired by Oscar Wilde. Its main character is the aesthete nobleman Des Esseintes, mentioned by Lewis farther on.

      De Lautréamont: Isidore Ducasse (1846–1870) adopted the pseudonym of the comte de Lautréamont; he is the author of the byronic and sadistic prose poems published as the *Chants de Maldoror* (1868), for which he is honored as a forerunner by the Surrealists. Lewis quotes and attacks Lautréamont at length in *The Diabolical Principle and the Dithyrhambic Spectator.*

      homme fatal: Fatal man.

      Byron—in his pageant: Cf. Byron's *Childe Harold* (1812–1818) and Matthew Arnold's lines in "The Grand Chartreuse":

> What helps it now, that Byron bore,
> With haughty scorn which mock'd the smart,
> Through Europe to the Aetolian shore
> The pageant of his bleeding heart?
> That thousands counted every groan,
> And Europe made his woe her own?

      Pen, Pencil and Poison: See note to page 73, above.

      De Quincey: Thomas De Quincey (1785–1859), author of *Confessions of an English Opium Eater* and many essays, among them the one alluded to here, "On Murder Considered as One of the Fine Arts."

      Dorian Gray: Oscar Wilde's *The Picture of Dorian Gray* (1891).

      The Diabolical Principle: Lewis's polemic against *transition*, first published in *The Enemy*, no. 3 (1929) and reprinted in book form as *The Diabolical Principle and the Dithyrhambic Spectator* in 1931.

143   *The Lion and the Fox*: Lewis's book—subtitled *The Rôle of the Hero in the Plays of Shakespeare*—on the political ideas of Shakespeare, published in 1927.

assembled, under my directions: How far this claim to have "directed" Praz's study is a serious one may be doubted. (In his article, " 'Classical Revival' in England," published in *The Bookman* in October 1934, the same month *Men Without Art* appeared, Lewis phrases the relationship more modestly, calling Praz's book "a volume that is, as it were, the *historical dossier* for my 'Diabolical Principle.' ") But Praz himself, at least, took the claim seriously enough to write a letter of rebuttal to the *Times Literary Supplement* (8 August 1935) and to mention the matter again in his "Note" prefacing the second edition of his book in 1951.

The Girl who took the Wrong Turning: A drama by Walter Melville, with music by Edward Reeves, first performed in London in 1906.

144   *De Profundis*: ("Out of the depths") Oscar Wilde's work written from prison as a letter of reproach to Lord Alfred Douglas.

145   *Orlando*: A fantasy (published 1928) by Virginia Woolf which traces its eponymous main character through several centuries of both male and female incarnations.

fond noir à contenter: Black depths to satisfy. (The phrase is from the *Journal* of the painter Delacroix, quoted earlier by Mario Praz, *The Romantic Agony*, p. 140).

Être ondayant et divers: a fluctuating and varying being.

146   *Si le grain ne meurt*: An autobiographical work published in 1926 (translated as *If It Die . . .* , 1935).

ricanement intérieur: Inward sneer.

société des pires gens: Company of the worst people.

savoureux bonheur: Savory happiness.

"Ah! quels regards après . . .": "Afterwards, ah! what looks and kisses we exchanged . . ." (In the first edition, "après" was plausibly misprinted as "âpres," giving the sense "bitter looks.")

avec des rudes favoris: With uncouth favorites of his own age.

violente, voluptueuse et débridée: Violent, voluptuous, and unbridled.

une espèce d'entêtement: A sort of stubbornness in doing the worst.

"Et savez-vous ce que . . .": "And do you know what's the most horrible thing God has done? . . . Sacrificing his own son in order to save us. His son! his son! . . . cruelty—that's the first attribute of God."

pouvoir se dire: To be able to tell himself, when they start taking care of him, "It's too late!"

147   **s'avance vers le lit**: "Approaches the bed where his sister and Bernard are lying. A sheet half covers their intertwined limbs. How beautiful they are! Armand contemplates them for a long time. He would like to be their sleep, their kiss. At first he smiles, then suddenly falls on his knees at the foot of the bed, among the discarded bedclothes. What god can he pray to thus, with his hands folded? An inexpressible emotion seizes him. His lips tremble . . . He notices under the pillow a bloodstained handkerchief; he gets up, seizes it, carries it off, and with a sob, presses his lips to the little amber stain."

147 **Armand avait une main:** "Armand had one hand on the doorknob; with the cane in his other hand he held up the door curtain. The cane caught in a hole in the curtain and made it bigger.

" 'Explain it however you can,' he said, and his face took on a very serious expression. 'Rachel, I truly believe, is the only person in this world whom I love and respect. I respect her because she is virtuous. And I always act in such a way as to shock her virtue. As regards Bernard and Sarah, she suspected nothing. It was I who told her everything. . . . And to think that the eye doctor told her to avoid crying! It's farcical!' "

Ses sacrifiées religieuses: "Gide treats his religious sacrificial victims *con amore* [lovingly], and yet, cruel tormentor that he is, he goes so far as to refuse to the latest and most significant of his heroines (Gertrude of *The Pastoral Symphony*) even the joy of daylight; it is a blind woman whom Love wishes to cradle in his adorable arms. Gide imagines that, when an operation restores her sight, this soul, strangely undone, is thereby naturally committed to suicide."

148 **Point Counter Point:** A novel by Aldous Huxley (1894–1963), popular novelist and essayist, published in 1928, two years after *Si le grain ne meurt.*

Only Yesterday: A widely read journalistic history of the nineteen-twenties by Frederick Lewis Allen, published in 1931.

G. D. H. Cole: (1889–1959) Socialist journalist and historian and author (with his wife) of many detective novels.

Desmond MacCarthy: Literary journalist on the fringe of the Bloomsbury coterie; edited *Life and Letters* from 1928 to 1933.

Edgar Wallace: (1875–1932) Author of many popular thrillers, including *The Four Just Men* (1905).

the Yellow Book: A literary periodical, 1894–1897, which published art by Aubrey Beardsley and writing by Henry James, Dowson, and others.

Sogno di Polifilo: Wainewright's fondness for this work is mentioned by Mario Praz, *The Romantic Agony*, p. 343. It is another name for *Hypnerotomachia* of Francesco Colonna (?1433–1527), an allegorical work in a mixture of Italian and Latin.

149 **Adelphi:** A London theatre.

the Gem Library: *The Gem* was a weekly boys' paper, 1907–1939.

pompes funèbres: Funeral.

the destructive element: See note to p. 63, above.

Croce: Benedetto Croce (1866–1952), Italian philosopher and critic.

mal du siècle: World weariness, melancholy caused by the condition of the world.

151 **Classisch ist das Gesunde:** The classical is the healthy, the romantic the diseased. Quoted by Herbert Grierson in *Classical and Romantic* (rpt. in his *The Background of English Literature* [London: Chatto and Windus, 1934, 1950], p. 277).

151   **The world has declared:** Grierson, ibid. p. 284.

T. E. Hulme: (1883–1917) Poet and anti-romantic theorist and essayist; friend of Lewis and Pound; translator of Bergson and Sorel. The quotation is taken from "Romanticism and Classicism," *Speculations* (London: Routledge and Kegan Paul, 1924; 2nd ed. 1936), p. 127.

Heine: The passage from Heinrich Heine (German Romantic poet, 1797–1856) is quoted by Grierson, op. cit., pp. 257–58.

De Musset: Alfred de Musset (1818–1857), French Romantic poet and playwright.

152   **the Nietzsche criticism of Christianity:** See, for example, Nietzsche's *Jenseits von Gut und Böse* (*Beyond Good and Evil*), 1886.

the mithraic cult: The cult of Mithras, the Persian god of light and truth, later of the sun, a cult which features ritual combat with bulls. That Lewis had read Franz Cumont's *Les Mystères de Mithra* (Brussels, 1900; English trans. 1903) is clear from *Snooty Baronet*, his novel of 1932. He was probably first interested in the cult through conversations with Roy Campbell. (See Lafourcade, ed., *Snooty Baronet*, ch. 4, "Mithras," and notes.) In the novel too (p. 70), just as in the first edition of the present book, Lewis confuses "mithraic" with "mithridatic" (which he further misspells as "mithraditic"—see Table of Emendations).

Marquis de Sade: (1740–1814) Bloody-minded French pornographer.

153   **a sensation I share:** Grierson (ibid., p. 262) quotes Goethe on the "solidity" of classical art.

What we start from: The first edition prints a garbled construction here: "From what we start—in any attempt to place before us these two things—is from . . ." etc.

soupir étouffé de Weber: "A smothered sigh of Weber's." The phrase is from Baudelaire's "Les Phares," quoted by Praz, *Romantic Agony*, p. 142.

the "Fire, Light and Speed," of J. M. W. Turner: Turner is the English Romantic landscape painter (1775–1851); Lewis is most likely thinking of his famous painting of a railway train in a rainstorm, "Rain, Steam and Speed" (1844), which now hangs in the National Gallery, London.

Grierson: Ibid., pp. 272–73.

154   **Literature at such a period:** Grierson, ibid., p. 266.

155   **Cimabue to Magnasco:** Cimabue (c. 1240–?1302), the teacher of Giotto, is perhaps the first great Italian painter of the early Renaissance. Magnasco (1677–1749) painted melodramatic landscapes in a Romantic style.

"Le paganisme," says Brunetière: "Paganism is not this or that thing . . . but rather, in a phrase, the adoration of the energy of nature." Ferdinand Brunetière (1849–1906), leading French literary critic of the 19th century.

Ben Jonson: Jonson's *Timber, or Discoveries* collects the poet's notebook entries on writing.

156 **"the more it advances":** From Hazlitt, "Shakespeare and Ben Jonson," in *Lectures on the English Comic Writers.* Speaking of an implausibility in the plot of *Volpone*, Hazlitt remarks: "the poet does not seem in the least to boggle at the incongruity of it: but the more it is in keeping with the absurdity of the rest of the fable, and the more it advances it to an incredible catastrophe, the more he seems to dwell upon it" etc. In the first edition, Lewis omitted an "it" from his quotation (indicated here with ellipses).

"The Church has no place": Grierson, ibid., pp. 279–80.

157 **"[The classical artist's] preoccupation":** Grierson, ibid., pp. 266–67. Lewis's italics.

Sir John Simon: (1873–1954) Liberal Member of Parliament, Foreign Secretary in the National Government at the time Lewis was writing (1931–1935). However the remark is usually attributed to the Prince of Wales, later Edward VII, speaking in 1885 ("We are all Socialists nowadays" — see H. L. Mencken's *A New Dictionary of Quotations* [New York: Knopf, 1942, rpt. 1966]).

158 **das Gesunde:** Health (German).

159 **Boileau:** (1636–1711) French neo-classic critic and poet.

Bossuet: (1627–1704) French preacher, celebrated for his style.

cris de coeur: Cries from the heart.

Irving Babbitt: Babbitt (1865–1933) was a professor at Harvard where T. S. Eliot was one of his students. With Paul Elmer More (1864–1937), mentioned by Lewis just below, he was a leader of the so-called New Humanism, an attempt to revive classical, anti-Romantic standards of reason and restraint. See his *Rousseau and Romanticism* (1919).

L'art est pour eux: "Art for them is an ornament of everyday life, just like literature; both the artist and the poet are men who partake, each in his way, in the diversity of existence and consequently in its embellishment. They are in no way masters who from the height of their superiority give lessons to their own time."

"tout artiste": "Any artist who sets himself any goal other than beauty is no artist at all."

Emaux et camées: The most famous book of poems of Théophile Gautier (1811–1872), published in 1852. It was admired and imitated by Ezra Pound and T. S. Eliot in their quatrain poems of circa 1912.

160 **Ce que La Fontaine et Molière:** "The moral teaching of La Fontaine and Molière at its most elevated is the art of governing our lives to serve our own best interests and tranquility. In the advice they give us there is no place to be seen for either sacrifice or devotion. Nor perhaps is there enough place for duty. Whoever followed religiously the advice of Molière and the moral maxims of La Fontaine would risk greatly becoming a model of the perfect egoist. Note that I am not reproaching them as artists. On the contrary! For I firmly believe that it is a mistake to want to preach morality in art or in literature. Or rather, above and before all else, the artist has need of freedom, that is, to see himself as confronting no principles other than those which govern his art itself."

161 **Ce que leurs oeuvres:** "What the works of all of them teach us is action, and their prose or poetry is for us a source of energy. They did not

write for the sake of writing, nor to realize a dream of solitary beauty, but for the sake of action. . . . They believed that language was given to us to express ideas, and ideas to enlighten us or to guide our conduct."

162   **Humbert Wolfe:** (1885–1940), Georgian poet and literary journalist.

"I want to maintain": From Hulme, "Romanticism and Classicism," in *Speculations* (see note to p. 151, above), p. 113.

163   **Action Française:** A right wing nationalist and monarchist political movement in pre–World War II France, led by the poet, essayist, and reactionary journalist, Charles Maurras (1868–1952). The movement was founded in 1899, and condemned by Rome in 1926.

"It has become a party symbol.": From Hulme, *Speculations*, pp. 114–15.

165   **"When it . . . does come":** From Hulme, *Speculations*, p. 125.

economic and political nationalism: The first edition prints "naturalism," presumably a printer's error.

Erse names: The revival of the Irish language was official policy of the Irish Free State. Street names were (and are) posted bilingually, and some people changed their names to the Irish form (John Whelan, for instance, became Seán O'Faoláin). Cf. "I would, if I were able to, suppress all out-of-date discrepancies of *tongue*, as well as of skin and pocket" (*Paleface*, p. 68).

Danegelt: A tax levied by the Danish invaders of England in the 9th century. Properly, Lewis should write "Danelaw," i.e., the northeast portion of England where the Danes settled.

166   **there "is always the bitter contrast":** Hulme, *Speculations*, p. 119; Lewis's italics.

"I object even to the best of the romantics": From Hulme, *Speculations*, p. 126.

John Webster: (c.1578–c.1632), Jacobean dramatist, author of *The Duchess of Malfi*, from which (act 4, scene 2) comes the song Hulme is thinking of. It ends with the line "End your groan and come away."

"But the particular verse": From Hulme, *Speculations*, p. 137.

Racine: (1639–1699) French tragic playwright.

Nicolas Poussin: (1593–1665) French classical landscape painter.

Le premier trait: "The primary characteristic of this new spirit is the development of individualism. Before all else, people will now want to be 'themselves'; they will want it 'to the greatest extent possible'; and consequently they will want it 'at all costs.' "

not my pidgin: Defined by Partridge as "Business, concern, duty, task" (*A Dictionary of Slang and Unconventional English*, 8th ed. [New York: Macmillan, 1984]), and usually spelled "pigeon."

168   **Allen Tate:** The American poet (1889–1979), member of the Southern "Fugitives" group; later of help to Lewis during the latter's visits to New York. The source is the book mentioned in the next note.

169   *muchedumbre*: Multitude (Spanish).

"A patriot and a royalist": From Kenneth Burke, "The Allies of Humanism Abroad," in *The Critique of Humanism: A Symposium*, ed. C. Hartley

Grattan (1930; rpt. Freeport, New York: Books for Libraries, 1968), p. 175.

169 **tabula rasa:** Blank slate (i.e., a complete obliteration).

170 **conspué:** Decried, run down, hooted at.

il ne croyait pas: "He did not believe in life. He considered it fundamentally evil and painful."

171 **Croyons fermement:** "Let us hold firmly to the belief . . . that life is evil. . . . Let us hold to the belief that man is evil; and therefore let us make the chief goal of our activity the effort to destroy in ourselves, if we can — or at least to mortify — this 'will to live' whose egoistic manifestations comprise fully half of the ills that make life so burdensome."

173 **Vasari:** Lewis appears to be quoting from the translation by A. B. Hinds (Everyman edition, vol. 2, p. 160), except for using the common spelling of the name instead of Hinds's "Lionardo."

Suffer all fools: Cf. the words of Jesus: "Suffer the little children to come unto me" (Mark 10:114).

Gibbon: The "famous passage" is probably the following remark from chapter 3 of Gibbon's *Decline and Fall of the Roman Empire* (1776) on a little-known Roman emperor: "His reign is marked by the rare advantage of furnishing very few materials for history; which is, indeed, little more than the register of the crimes, follies, and misfortunes of mankind."

Arthur Balfour: (1848–1930) Philosopher and Conservative politician; Prime Minister, 1902–1905 and Foreign Secretary 1916–1919.

175 **Maritain and Fernandez:** For Maritain, see note to p. 76, above. Ramon Fernandez (1894–1944), French author of "philosophic criticism," e.g. in *Messages* (1926; English trans. 1927), contributor to *The Criterion, The Dial.*

176 **closed down the theatres:** The theatres of London were closed during the Puritan rule by Parliament from 1642 to 1660.

their pidgin: See note to p. 166, above.

177 **the five points of Calvinism:** The formulation familiar to Calvinists in present-day Michigan is remembered with the help of the mnemonic "TULIP": Total depravity; Unconditional election; Limited atonement; Irresistible grace; and Perseverance of the saints.

178 **Chatterley gamekeeper:** Cf. D. H. Lawrence's *Lady Chatterley's Lover* (1928; expurgated version published in London, 1932).

179 **"machine-gun" Kelly . . . Dion O'Bannion:** Gangsters familiar to newspaper readers of the Prohibition era.

Sicilian Vespers: The massacre of the French in Sicily on Easter Monday 1282, which began on the stroke of the bell for Vespers. It was a protest against the tyranny of Charles of Anjou.

stumer cheques: Forged or worthless checks.

the "mad house," as it is preferred by Mr. Shaw: George Bernard Shaw (1856–1950), prolific dramatist and polemicist.

180 **middle-west unitarian disguised:** Probably referring to T. S. Eliot.

180   **Buchman "Group Movement":** Frank Buchman (1878–1961) was the founder of the evangelical Oxford Group, which developed into the Moral Rearmament movement.

journalese of the war: The phrase is "Roman steam-roller," which echoes a journalistic cliché of World War I, "the Russian steam-roller," referring to the expected decisive effect of Russian manpower on the speedy outcome of the war.

183   **Ingres:** Jean-Auguste-Dominique Ingres (1780–1867), classical French painter of portraits and scenes from history.

Giotto: (1266/7–1337), often called the founder of modern painting.

Hokusai . . . The old man mad about drawing: After 1833, the Japanese woodblock Ukiyo-e artist Hokusai signed his work "Gwakyō Rōjin," or "Old Man Mad about Drawing."

184   **Quelques Fleurs:** The trade name of a perfume, made by Houbigant, Inc. (Literally, some flowers.)

Mr. Frank Rutter: (1876–1937), art critic of the London *Sunday Times*, author of *Evolution in Modern Art* (1932) and other works which deal in part with Lewis as an artist.

more-than-Lenglen heads: A reference to Suzanne Lenglen (1899–1938), a French champion tennis player, retired in 1927.

186   **Diana of the Crossways:** A novel (1885) by George Meredith (1828–1909)

Burlington House: The home of the Royal Academy.

Punch: English comic weekly, founded 1841 and still appearing.

187   **Burne-Jones:** Sir Edward Burne-Jones (1833–1898), painter of the Pre-Raphaelite group, influenced by Morris and D. G. Rossetti.

Miss Sitwell: Edith Sitwell (1887–1964), self-consciously modernist poet and eccentric (see note to p. 136, above). She sat (intermittently) for one of Lewis's most famous and best portrait paintings, now hanging in the Tate Gallery.

Lord Leighton: (1830–1896) Victorian classical artist and president of the Royal Academy.

Frith: William Powell Frith (1819–1909), enormously popular Victorian painter (member of the Royal Academy from 1853), best known for his genre subjects such as *Derby Day*, now in the Tate Gallery. Opposed to the Pre-Raphaelites.

Priestley: J. B. Priestley (1894–1984), successful popular novelist (*The Good Companions*, 1929; *Angel Pavement*, 1930) and playwright.

Hall Caine: (1853–1931) Best-selling novelist, author of *The Shadow of a Crime* (1885) and many other works. The "Hall Caine of paint" is Burne-Jones.

Ruskin . . . Winnington Hall: John Ruskin (1819–1900), the great Victorian art critic, spent time in residence at Miss Bell's school for girls in Winnington, Cheshire. Burne-Jones and his wife visited him there in 1863.

187   *the artist is older than the fish*:   In Lewis's *The Caliph's Design, or Archi-tects, Where Is Your Vortex?* (1919, rpt. Black Sparrow Press, 1985), Part II is entitled "The Artist Older than the Fish" and begins:

> The artist goes back to the fish. The few centuries that separate him from the savage are a mere flea-bite to the distance his memory must stretch if it is to strike the fundamental slime of creation. And it is the condition, the very first gusto of creation in this scale of life in which we are set, that he must reach, before he, in his turn, can create!

friseur: Hairdresser.

petit maître: Small master, master on a small scale.

191   **Pauvre France:**   "Poor France! . . . forever unable to detach herself from the middle ages, forever preoccupied with the gothic notion of the com-munity, which is nothing but the Roman municipality." Letter of 24 April 1871 (*Correspondance*, 9 vols. [Paris: Conard, 1926–1933], 6:224).

George Sand: Pen name of Amandine-Aurore Lucille Dupin, Baronne Dudevant (1804–1876), French novelist, lover of Chopin, friend of Flaubert.

The Lion and the Fox: See note to p. 143, above. The quotation is from p. 14.

sale affaire: A dirty business.

192   *La patrie est en danger*:   The fatherland is in danger.

193   **Stevenson wrote in his letters:**   From *Vailima Letters . . . to Sidney Colvin* (New York: Scribner's, 1896), vol. 1, p. 176.

William Windham: (1750–1810) Statesman and friend of Dr. Johnson and Burke. *The Windham Papers* were edited by the Earl of Rosebery and published in London in 1913. Lewis quoted extensively from *The Windham Papers* in *Snooty Baronet* (1932; see the edition by Bernard Lafourcade [Black Sparrow Press, 1984], pp. 4, 100–102, and notes).

194   **"L'Europe avait en soi":**   "Europe used to have in herself good reason for subduing, ruling, and ordering the rest of the world for her own pur-poses. She had invincible means and the men who had created them. Far beneath these men were those who commanded her. They were raised on the past, and they only knew how to do that which was past. The opportunity too is past. Her history and political traditions, her village quarrels about bell towers and shops, her petty jealousies and resentments of neighbors—in brief, the short sightedness and pet-tiness of spirit inherited from the time when she was just as ignorant and no more powerful than the other regions of the globe—have caused Europe to lose this immense opportunity whose very existence she never suspected in time to make use of it. . . . The poor Europeans preferred to play at being men of Armagnac or of Burgundy rather than to ac-cept over all the earth the great role that the Romans knew how to accept and maintain for centuries in the world of their time. *Their numbers and their means were as nothing compared to ours, but they found in the entrails of their chickens ideas of greater truth and*

consequence than all those contained in our political science. . . .
Europe will be punished for her politics: she will be deprived of wines
and beer and liquors. And of other things. . . ."

194 **"l'occasion est passé":**   The opportunity is past.

195 **those who "set the sign of the cross over their outer doors":**   This refers
to a custom at Oxford of indicating on the outer door of a resident
student's rooms by an affixed cross that the student within is at his
devotions and not to be disturbed. Hence, the meaning is those who
publicly profess their piety or devoutness.

Ford Madox Ford: (1873–1939) Poet, novelist, critic, and editor. The
"autocriticism" is an article by Ford on his own novel, *The Rash Act.*

197 **"Quelle Barbarie!":**   "What barbarism! What a step backward! . . . This
war for the sake of money, these savage civilized men horrify me more
than cannibals." (*Correspondance*, 9 vols. [Paris: Conard, 1926–1933],
6:202–203.)

"security pacts":   For example, the Locarno pact of 1925, which comprised
seven treaties for mutual security signed by Britain, France, Germany,
and other countries.

198 **en attendant:**   While waiting.

"resolved to do good that evil may come":   See Romans, 3:8 ("Let us do
good that evil may come").

Life is but a day, as has been remarked: Cf. Keats, "Sleep and Poetry":
"Stop and consider! life is but a day; / A fragile dew-drop on its perilous
way / From a tree's summit" (lines 85ff.).

Lansbury: George Lansbury (1859–1940), Labour politician and opposition leader in the House of Commons, 1931–1935.

Cripps: Sir Stafford Cripps (1889–1952; knighted 1930), Labour politician and leader of the left wing of his party in the 1930s; later
(1947–1950) became Chancellor of the Exchequer in the Attlee government after World War II.

199 **Montagu Norman:**   (1871–1950) Governor of the Bank of England,
1920–1944. His return to the Gold Standard was blamed by many for
contributing to the Great Depression.

Von Papen: Franz Von Papen (1879–1969), German Chancellor who
arranged the alliance that brought Hitler to power in 1932; Vice-
Chancellor as Lewis was writing (1933–1934).

Neville Chamberlain: (1869–1940) Chancellor of the Exchequer as Lewis
was writing (1931–1937), later Prime Minister (1937–1940).

Zamora: Niceto Alcalá Zamora y Torres (1877–1949), Republican leader
in Spain and President of the Spanish Republic from 1931 to 1936.

Baruch: Bernard Baruch (1870–1965), wealthy stock market speculator
and self-appointed unpaid advisor to U.S. Presidents, including
Franklin Delano Roosevelt.

200 **Corn Laws:**   Early nineteenth century laws designed to protect English
agriculture which imposed a tax on imported corn, thus raising the
price of bread, the staple diet of the urban poor; repealed 1846.

200 **Civil Wars:** The war in England between the forces of Parliament and the King, 1642–1646.

201 **Goya:** Goya (1746–1828) published his series of anti-war etchings, *Los Desastres de la Guerra* (The Disasters of War) in 1810 to 1814.

Desastres de la Paz: The Disasters of Peace.

Bairnsfather: See above, note to page 23.

Miss Lehmann: Rosamund Lehmann (b. 1901), author of *Dusty Answer* (1927), *Invitation to the Waltz* (1932), and other romantic novels.

Sir Philip Gibbs: (1877–1962) Writer and war correspondent, author of *The Soul of War* (1915), *Realities of War* (1920), etc.

202 **Ivor Novello:** (1893–1951) British actor and composer, author of the popular World War I song "Keep the Home Fires Burning."

cheerfulness: See above, note to p. 89.

203 **Mrs. Proudie:** The militantly Evangelical wife of the bishop of Barchester in Trollope's *The Warden, Barchester Towers*, and other novels.

Big Berthas: World War I soldiers' slang for a large calibre German gun, in allusion to Berta Krupp von Bohlen und Halbach, owner of the Krupp steel works.

204 **minor revolution . . . in Belfast:** "As a result of Republican activities in Belfast . . . There was a sensational round-up in the Falls [i.e. the Catholic] area of Belfast as a result of which a number of Republicans were interned . . ." – *The Annual Register*, 1933, p. 106. (See also *The Times*, 14 October 1933, p. 12.)

landing of . . . machine-guns: The *New York Times* reports the landing of arms for the I.R.A. in its issue of 10 June 1933.

de Valera . . . an "Ogpu": Eamon de Valera (1882–1975), Irish political leader. In 1933 his Fianna Fáil party won a majority in the Irish Dáil and formed a government in which he was Taoiseach (prime minister) and foreign minister. At first supported by the more extremist nationalists of the Irish Republican Army, he was soon denounced by them for delaying the declaration of a Republic. He was also threatened from the right by General Eoin O'Duffy's group known first as the Army Comrades Association, then as the National Guard or (from their uniform of blue shirts and black berets) the "Blue Shirts." On August 6, 1933, the *Irish Press* reported that "The Free State Government have decided to create a new armed force to guard Government buildings. . . . General O'Duffy . . . referred to the Government's new force as 'a new Ogpu.' " Two weeks later, the Blue Shirts were banned as "an unlawful body" and O'Duffy was arrested.

Ogpu: The Soviet secret police organization that succeeded the Cheka in 1922 and was succeeded in turn by the NKVD and the KGB.

Bonus Marchers: From May to July, 1932, groups of veterans conducted marches in Washington demanding immediate payment of a veterans' bonus.

205   **"Vous écrasez d'un ineffable dédain":**   "You crush beneath an unutterable disdain every honest businessman who prefers the lyrics of a popular song to a tercet of Dante. . . . Nevertheless it is these middleclass people whose souls—and they do have souls—are rich in poetry, capable of love and devotion, and filled with emotions which you, whose brain has killed your heart, cannot even feel."

William Godwin: (1756–1836) Radical atheist philosopher and political writer. His *Enquiry Concerning Political Justice* appeared in 1793. The passage Lewis is summarizing and referring to runs as follows:

> In a loose and general view I and my neighbour are both of us men; and of consequence entitled to equal attention. But, in reality, it is probable that one of us, is a being of more worth and importance than the other. A man is of more worth than a beast; because, being possessed of higher faculties, he is capable of more refined and genuine happiness. In the same manner the illustrious archbishop of Cambray was of more worth than his valet, and there are few of us that would hesitate to pronounce, if his palace were in flames, and the life of only one of them could be preserved, which of the two ought to be preferred.
>
> But there is another ground for preference, beside the private consideration of one of them being further removed from the state of a mere animal. We are not connected with one or two percipient beings, but with a society, a nation, and in some sense with the whole family of mankind. Of consequence that life ought to be preferred which will be most conducive to the general good. In saving the life of Fénelon, suppose at the moment he conceived the project of his immortal *Telemachus*, I should have been promoting the benefit of thousands, who have been cured by the perusal of that work, of some error, vice and consequent unhappiness. Nay, my benefit would extend further than this; for every individual, thus cured, has become a better member of society, and has contributed in his turn to the happiness, information and improvement of others.
>
> Suppose I had been myself the valet; I ought to have chosen to die, rather than Fénelon should have died. The life of Fénelon was really preferable to that of the valet. But understanding is the faculty that perceives the truth of this and similar propositions; and justice is the principle that regulates my conduct accordingly. It would have been just in the valet to have preferred the archbishop to himself. To have done otherwise would have been a breach of justice.
>
> Suppose the valet had been my brother, my father or my benefactor. This would not alter the truth of the proposition. The life of Fénelon would still be more valuable than that of the valet; and justice, pure, unadulterated justice, would still have preferred that which was most valuable. Justice would have taught me to save the life of Fénelon at the expense of the other. What magic is there in the pronoun "my," that should justify us in overturning the decision of impartial truth? . . .
> (William Godwin, *Enquiry Concerning Political Justice*, ed. K. Codell Carter [Oxford: Clarendon Press, 1971], Bk. II, chap. 2, p. 70.)

Fénelon: François de Salagnac de la Mothe-Fénelon (1651–1715), archbishop of Cambrai from 1695, tutor of the heir presumptive to the French throne for whose edification and instruction in Greek mythology he wrote the pedagogical novel *Télémaque* (published 1699).

206 **Elinor Glynn:** (1865–1943) British author of mildly scandalous novels such as *Three Weeks* (1907).

Vicki Baum: (1888–1960) Austrian-born American author of *Grand Hotel* (1929).

207 **Sir Jack Squire:** J. C. Squire (1884–1958), middlebrow literary journalist whose group, known as the "Squirearchy," was hostile to avant-garde art and literature. He was knighted in 1933.

211 **Plus que jamais:** "More than ever I feel the need to live in a world apart, on top of an ivory tower." Letter to the Princess Mathilde, 5 September 1871 (*Correspondance*, 9 vols. [Paris: Conard, 1926–1933], 6: 280).

What magic is there: Godwin, in the passage quoted above, note to page 205.

visit . . . North Africa.: Lewis had made such a visit in the spring of 1931 and wrote an account of it in his *Filibusters in Barbary*, 1932; the English edition was withdrawn under threat of a libel suit. See *Journey to Barbary*, ed. C. J. Fox (Black Sparrow Press, 1983).

Europe balkanizing itself: The OED Supplement registers this word as current from the 1920s, used by such writers as Arnold Toynbee and A. L. Rowse. The "Douglas" Lewis mentions is probably not Norman Douglas but rather Major C. H. Douglas, the writer on Social Credit mentioned above, p. 19.

212 **Bankers' Republic:** That is, the Third Republic in France (1871–1939), alleged by its critics—especially in the 1930s—to be too much under the influence of a small cabal of bankers, particularly the board of the Bank of France. (The first edition prints "Banker's," here corrected on the authority of the section's first appearance in *Time and Tide*, 25 June 1932.)

Untermensch: German: inferior man; that is, the opposite of the Nietzschean *Übermensch* or superior man.

L.S.D.: That is, money. L. (usually printed £) stands for "libri," S. for "soldi," and D. for "denarii"—pounds, shillings, and pence in the pre-decimalization English currency.

213 **to parody my old chum Jolas:** Jolas, founder and one of the editors of *transition* (see note to p. 103, above). In *The Diabolical Principle* (p. 17) Lewis quotes one of their editorials: ". . . we are entertained intellectually, if not physically, with the idea of (the) destruction (of contemporary society). But . . . our interests are confined to literature and life. . . . It is our *purpose purely and simply to amuse ourselves*."

Thomas Love Peacock: (1785–1866) Author of *Nightmare Abbey* (1818) and other satires. Peacock uses the phrase in *Crotchet Castle* (1831): "The march of mind—has marched in through my back-parlour shutters, and out again with my silver spoons . . . The policeman . . . says my house has been broken open on the most scientific principles" (ch. 17). He is probably making fun of the original use of the phrase by Burke: "The march of the human mind is slow" (Speech on Conciliation with America).

Hoover: President Hoover's optimistic phrase dates from March 1931.

213   **pour nos beaux yeux:**   For (the sake of) our fine eyes.

214   **Franco-Prussian war:**   Napoleon III's ambitious foreign policy brought
       on a war between France and Bismarck's Prussia, 1870–1871.
       Napoleon's defeat and capture led to the establishment of the Third
       Republic.

       Paris Commune: The Revolutionary Socialist government of Paris from
       March to May 1871, when troops of the National Assembly retook
       the city with much loss of life.

       Il y a sous toutes les grandes villes: "Underneath every great city there
       are dens of lions, stoutly barred caverns where savage, stinking,
       venomous beasts are penned — all the insubordinate perversions which
       civilisation has never been able to tame, those who thirst for blood,
       those for whom arson is an amusement like fireworks, those who
       delight in robbery . . . a foul rabble unknown to daylight, swarming
       sinisterly in the depths of subterranean darkness. One day this is what
       happens: the absent-minded beast-tamer forgets to remove his keys
       from the gates of the menagerie, and the wild animals pour out through
       the terrified city with savage howls. Out from the open cages rush
       the hyenas of '93 and the gorillas of the Commune. But it is not the
       fault of Paris." Gautier wrote his *Tableau de siège* in 1871.

       Gardons notre coeur: "Let us keep up our heart and our spirits."

215   **Veillons sur la flamme:**   "Let us keep watch over the flame, for the sacred
       fire still burns. More than ever, I feel the need to live in a world apart,
       on top of an ivory tower, far above the mire where the ordinary run
       of men flounder about." (*Correspondance*, 9 vols., [Paris: Conard,
       1926–1933], 6: 279–80, where the letter is dated 6 September).

       Pourquoi êtes-vous si triste?:   From the letter of 8 September 1871. "Why
       are you so sad? Mankind offers nothing new. Its irremediable misery
       has filled me with bitterness ever since my youth. And so now I feel
       no disillusion. I believe that the crowd, the herd, will always be
       detestable. All that matters is a little group of kindred spirits, always
       the same ones, who pass on the torch from one to the other." Letter
       of 8 September 1871 (*Correspondance*, ed. cited, 6:280–81.)

       Ne t'occupe de rien: "Pay no attention to anything except yourself. Let's
       leave the Empire to carry on, let us shut our door, climb to the top
       of our ivory tower, to the topmost step, the one closest to the heavens.
       It's cold up there sometimes, isn't it?, but what matter. One can see
       the stars shining brightly and one no longer hears the turkeys." Letter
       to Louise Colet, 22 November 1852 (*Correspondance*, ed. cited,
       3:54–55).

       the "ivory Tower":   This image of the artist's aloofness (deriving from
       the Catholic litany of the Blessed Virgin Mary, in which she is ad-
       dressed as "Tower of Ivory") is found earlier in Flaubert's cor-
       respondence, for example in the letter of 24 April 1852 to Louise Colet.
       Prior to that, it had appeared in 1830 used by Sainte-Beuve, who ap-
       plied it to the poet Alfred de Vigny (see citation in Robert's Dictionary).

215   **Les mots république:** "The words republic and monarchy will make them
       [posterity] laugh. . . . For I defy anyone to show me any essential
       difference between these two terms. A modern republic and a con-
       stitutional monarchy are identical" (*Correspondance*, ed. cited,
       6:281–82).

"Pauvre France!": Translated in note to p. 191, above.

Mr. Edmund Wilson: A rephrased version of this passage appears in *The
Triple Thinkers* (New York: Oxford Univ. Press, 1948), p. 81.

216   **the *Zeitgenossen* of Boz:** Boz was Dickens's pseudonym for some of his
       early journalism and for the *Pickwick Papers* (1836–1837).
       Zeitgenossen: contemporaries (German). Lewis is remembering *Oliver
       Twist*, ch. 43, where Fagin preaches his doctrine of "Number One":
       "Some conjurors say that number three is the magic number, and some
       say number seven. It's neither, my friend, neither. It's number one."

Keats said: From Keats's letter to George and Georgiana Keats, 14 October
1818.

217   **politicians de métier:** Professional politicians.

Je trouve qu'on aurait: "It's my view that they should have condemned the
whole Commune to hard labor and compelled those blood-stained imbeciles to clear up the ruins of Paris with chains around their necks
like simple convicts. But that would have offended 'humanity.' People
are very tender-minded towards mad dogs and not at all so towards
those they've bitten." (*Correspondance*, ed. cited, 6:296–97.)

Je comptais revenir directement: "I was planning to come straight back
to Paris. But 'the new Athens' seems to me to surpass Dahomey in
ferocity and stupidity. . . . Will people never have done with futile
metaphysics and received ideas? All evil stems from our enormous
ignorance. What should be studied is believed without discussion. Instead of looking, people assert. The French Revolution has got to stop
being taken as a dogma and return to being an object of Science, like
all other human things." From a letter to George Sand of 31 March
1871; Lewis begins quoting in mid-sentence and ignores paragraphing.
(*Correspondance*, ed. cited, 6:215.)

Nous pataugeons dans l'arrière-faix: "We are floundering in the after-
birth of the Revolution, which was an abortion, a thing that miscar-
ried. . . . And that is because it came out of medievalism and Christianity. The idea of equality (which is the whole of modern democracy)
is an essentially Christian idea and quite opposed to the idea of justice."
From the letter to George Sand of 8 September 1871 (*Correspondance*,
ed. cited, 6:281).

218   **ratée:** Failed.

La politique!!!: "Politics!!! . . . Politics keeps me from working, going out,
thinking, writing. . . . I demand the abolition of the ruling classes:
of this pack of stupid 'fine gentlemen' who frolic in the skirts of that
stupid and devout old train called 'good society.' . . . Well, I now find
that [17]93 was sweet; that the Septembrists were merciful: that Marat
is a lamb, Danton a white rabbit, and Robespierre a turtle-dove. Since

the old ruling classes are just as unintelligent today as they were then, we must abolish the ruling classes of today as was done then, and drown the cretinous fine gentlemen along with the whorish fine ladies." Maupassant, letter to Flaubert, 10 December 1877.

218   **charognerie moderne:**   modern rot, modern swinishness. Flaubert quotes this phrase of Gautier's in the letter to George Sand cited in the next note.

Ce jour-là, en effet: "That day, in fact — the most accursed one in the history of France — inaugurated an order of things in which people like him no longer have any function in the world. . . . He had two hatreds: the hatred of Philistines in his youth — this gave him his talent; and the hatred of scoundrels in his maturity — this latter killed him. . . . I do not pity him, I envy him." From a letter to George Sand of 28 October 1872 (*Correspondance*, ed. cited, 6:440). Lewis takes the opening sentence of his quotation from a letter of the same date to the Princess Mathilde (6:435); Flaubert repeats it only slightly varied in the letter to George Sand.

219   **las de l'ignoble ouvrier:**   " 'Sick of the base working man, of the inept bourgeois, of the stupid peasant, and of the detestable churchman' . . . the Republic seemed to him to have surpassed the Empire in stupidity." The first part of the quotation is from Flaubert's letter to George Sand of 6 September 1871 (*Correspondance*, ed. cited, 6:276).

Louis Bertrand: (1866–1941) French novelist and literary biographer: *Gustave Flaubert* (Paris: Mercure de France, 1912).

E-L. Ferrère: French literary critic and editor: *L'Esthétique de Gustave Flaubert* (Paris: Conard, 1913), etc.

tout court: Pure and simple.

220   **Les nuages:**   "The clouds — the marvellous clouds!" See Baudelaire's prose poem, "L'Etranger," in *Le Spleen de Paris*, where in answer to repeated questions as to what he loves, the interlocutor's final declaration is "J'aime les nuages . . . les nuages qui passent . . . là-bas . . . là-bas . . . les merveilleux nuages!" ("I love the clouds, the passing clouds — there! there! — the marvellous clouds!")

la haine créatrice: Creative hatred.

Jaurès: Jean Jaurès (1859–1914) French politician and orator, founder of the French socialist party and of *L'Humanité* newspaper. Assassinated.

armed Nestorian bishops: Nestorius was a fifth century Patriarch of Constantinople, whose teaching that Jesus had a dual nature and that Mary was therefore not the "Mother of God" but only of his human nature was anathematized as heretical. His followers still maintain their traditions among the Kurds of Turkey and in Syria. Their leader, the Patriarch Mar Shimun XXI was in the news from August to November 1933, petitioning the League of Nations for help against alleged oppression by the government of Iraq and by armed Kurds instigated by that government. (See, for example, *The Times*, 10, 23, and 24 August 1933.)

220 **Calatrava:** The order of Knights of Calatrava was founded in 1158 by a Cistercian (not Benedictine) to guard the town of Calatrava, recaptured from the Moors. It was confirmed as a religious military order under Cistercian rule by Pope Alexander III in 1164.

221 **de cap à pied:** From head to foot.

Flaubert in his Thébaïde at Le Croisset: Flaubert lived a retired life at Le Croisset in Normandy. The region near Thebes in Egypt was a place where many early Christians fled persecution to live an ascetic life in the desert; hence, figuratively, a Thébaïde is a place of solitary retreat.

en tant que religion: As far as religion goes; considered as a religion.

222 **Flaubert . . . engouffre tout:** "Flaubert swallows up all that touches on philosophy, on religion, on history, on mechanics, on the applied arts, not in order to learn anything whatsoever . . . but in order to transform this huge acquisition into nightmares and false ideas. . . . The efforts of the ages culminate in these profound caricatures."

La faute de Flaubert est grave: "Flaubert's fault is a grave one too. To have substituted art for God sets him on a more dangerous road than baffled or despised art could ever have done. It's not by accident that he employs, to paint his life of dedication to literary work, the language of mysticism. With full knowledge of what he is doing, he usurps the place of infinite Being. . . . For if he knows what the painful struggles of a saint are like, he knows even better the sensual delights that tinge the pleasure of the Christian."

J'ai été obligé de me lever: "I was forced to get up and fetch my handkerchief: tears were running down my face. . . . I was taking exquisite pleasure at once in the emotion of my idea, in the sentence which rendered it, and in the satisfaction of having found that sentence." Flaubert's letter to Louise Colet, 4 April 1852 (*Correspondance*, ed. cited, 2:395).

Ici Flaubert nous oblige: "Here Flaubert makes us think of those satisfactions about which Saint Teresa writes that they provoke tears of suffering, which one might imagine born from some passion."

223 **Lucretius:** First century Roman poet, author of *De Rerum Natura*.

225 **Irving Babbitt:** From Babbitt's "True and False Liberals," in *Democracy and Leadership* (Boston: Houghton Mifflin, 1924), p. 202.

Middleton Murry: See note to p. 76, above.

Prince Mirsky: Dmitry Svyatopolk-Mirsky (1890–c.1940), author of *Lenin* (1930), *Literature and Films in Socialist Russia* (1932), etc. He was a lecturer in Russian literature at King's College, University of London. His Marxist critique of Bloomsbury, *The Intelligentsia of Great Britain*, appeared in English translation in 1935 (see *The Diary of Virginia Woolf*, ed. Ann Olivier Bell [New York: Harcourt Brace Jovanovich, 1982], pp. 112n, 288n.)

226 **the best known of these:** Lewis is most probably thinking of Murry.

Thorstein Veblen: (1857–1929) U.S. economist, author of *The Theory of the Leisure Class* (1899).

227   **informed by Mr. Eastman:**   See Max Eastman, *The Literary Mind*, pp.
       36–37 (full citation in note to p. 56, above.)

       Economic and other conditions: See Eastman, ibid., p. 38.

       Genuine justice: This passage is only partly quoted by Eastman; as noted
       above, it comes from Babbitt's *Democracy and Leadership*, p. 202.

229   **"The Jolly Corner":**   A short story by Henry James in which a character
       living in Europe revisits the America of his birth and encounters, in
       the form of an alter ego, a version of what he might have become had
       he stayed in his homeland. Discussed by Van Wyck Brooks as James's
       autobiographical meditation on the career he might have had.

229   ***Daisy:***   Edmund Wilson's novel, *I Thought of Daisy* (1929).

230   **Eastman ... quotes Paul Elmer More:**   See Eastman, ibid., p. 40.

231   **"economic blizzard":**   I.e. the great Depression, in the midst of which
       Lewis was writing.

232   **homo animal ridens:**   Man, the animal that laughs (Latin).

       Henry Moore: The sculptor Henry Moore (1898–1986), whose work Lewis
       admired, was lecturing at the Chelsea School of Art from 1932 on.
       He had his first individual exhibitions in 1928 (Warren Gallery) and
       at the Leicester Galleries in 1931 and 1933.

       Cissy Caffrey: Like Leopold Bloom, a character in *Ulysses*, one of Gertie
       MacDowell's friends in the "Nausicaa" episode.

       Klipstein and Krumpacker: See T. S. Eliot's *Sweeney Agonistes* (1932).

233   **à plus forte raison:**   All the more; a fortiori.

237   **an essay of mine:**   Lewis is referring to *Satire and Fiction*, published in
       1927. "The Taxi Cab Driver Text" is reprinted from it with only a few
       minor changes.

238   **Boileau ... Congreve ... Dryden:**   Boileau (1636–1711), French neo-
       classic critic and poet. Congreve (1670–1729), English Restoration
       playwright. Chapman (?1559–1634), English dramatist and translator
       of Homer.

       Verlaine: French symbolist poet (1844–1896). Jane Austen's dates are
       earlier: 1775–1817.

       article by Mr. Hugh Walpole: Walpole (1884–1941) was a novelist (*Rogue
       Herries*, 1930), literary journalist, friend of Virginia Woolf. Lewis
       quotes from an article entitled "Cheaper Books" on p. 154 of the issue
       cited.

239   **und so weiter:**   And so forth (German).

       Arnold Bennett: Bennett was not only a popular novelist but, through
       his weekly book column in the *Evening Standard* from 1926 on, a
       powerfully influential reviewer. Lewis attacked his "Tipster Techni-
       que in Literary Criticism" in "A Tip from the Augean Stable," *Time
       and Tide*, 19 and 26 March 1931. (See also *Letters*, pp. 207–209.)

       Gerald Gould: Essayist and reviewer (1885–1936), satirized by Lewis as
       Geoffrey Bell in *The Roaring Queen* (completed 1930; published 1973).
       He was the father of Michael Ayrton, the novelist and painter who
       became a close friend and ally of Lewis in his later years.

239   **upon "Mediocre Writers":**   The article is entitled "It's the Mediocre Writers who Make Money" and appears on p. 7 of the issue cited.

245   ***Point Counter Point:***   Aldous Huxley's 1928 novel, mentioned above, p. 148.

245   ***The Ivory Tower:***   Henry James's last novel, left unfinished at his death in 1914.

LIST OF BOOKS

Selected Works by Wyndham Lewis

1914 *Blast*, no. 1 (periodical, edited by W. L.)
1915 *Blast*, no. 2
1918 *Tarr*.
1919 *The Caliph's Design*. (New edition, ed. Paul Edwards. Black Sparrow Press, 1986.)
1926 *The Art of Being Ruled*.
1927 *The Enemy*, no. 1 (periodical, edited by W. L.)
1927 *The Lion and the Fox*.
1927 *The Wild Body* (New edition, with additional material, as *The Complete Wild Body*, ed. Bernard Lafourcade. Black Sparrow Press, 1983.)
1927 *Time and Western Man*.
1928 *Tarr* (revised edition).
1928 *The Childermass*.
1928 *The Enemy*, no. 2
1929 *Paleface*.
1929 *The Enemy*, no. 3
1930 *Satire and Fiction* (pamphlet)
1930 *The Apes of God*. (Reprint, Black Sparrow Press, 1981).
1931 *The Diabolical Principle and the Dithyrhambic Spectator*.
1932 *Filibusters in Barbary*. (New edition, with additional material, as *Journey Into Barbary*, ed. C. J. Fox. Black Sparrow Press, 1983.)
1932 *Snooty Baronet*. (New edition, ed. Bernard Lafourcade, Black Sparrow Press, 1983.)
1932 *The Doom of Youth*.
1934 *Men Without Art*.
1937 *The Revenge for Love*.
1938 *Blasting and Bombardiering*.
1950 *Rude Assignment*. (New edition, ed. Toby Foshay. Black Sparrow Press, 1984.)
1951 *Rotting Hill*. (New edition, ed. Paul Edwards. Black Sparrow Press, 1986.)
1952 *The Writer und the Absolute*.
1954 *Self Condemned*. (New edition, ed. Rowland Smith. Black Sparrow Press, 1983.)
1954 *The Demon of Progress in the Arts*.

1955   *The Human Age.*
1956   *The Red Priest.*
1963   *The Letters of Wyndham Lewis*, ed. W. K. Rose (London: Methuen; Norfolk, Conn.: New Directions).
1969   *Wyndham Lewis: An Anthology of His Prose*, ed. E. W. F. Tomlin (London: Methuen).
1975   *Enemy Salvoes: Selected Literary Criticism*, ed. C. J. Fox (London: Vision).

Selected Books about Wyndham Lewis

Cooney, Seamus, ed. *Blast 3* (Black Sparrow Press, 1984).

Kenner, Hugh. *Wyndham Lewis* (Norfolk, Conn.: New Directions, 1954).

Meyers, Jeffrey. *The Enemy: A Biography of Wyndham Lewis* (London: Routledge & Kegan Paul, 1980).

Michel, Walter. *Wyndham Lewis: Paintings and Drawings.* (London: Thames and Hudson; Berkeley: Univ. of California Press, 1971).

Morrow, Bradford and Bernard Lafourcade, *A Bibliography of the Writings of Wyndham Lewis* (Black Sparrow Press, 1978).

Pritchard, William H. *Wyndham Lewis* (New York: Twayne, 1968).

AFTERWORD

I

Men Without Art is Wyndham Lewis's defense of his second calling, literature. It is also his liveliest and most accessible book of literary criticism. For its sustained analyses of individual major figures alone — the essays on Hemingway, Faulkner, Virginia Woolf, and (above all) T. S. Eliot — it deserves a permanent place in the criticism of modern literature. And yet of these essays, only that on Hemingway is at all widely known. At a time when academic literary studies proliferate, often seeming to be written from no motive other than career-making, Lewis's highly personal comic gusto is a salutary and refreshing reminder of what the criticism of a committed artist can be like.

The book is a plea for the removal of the barriers against art, and a call to artists to resist and overcome art's enemies, whether they come from outside the literary world (moralists; marxists) or from within (Bloomsbury denizens disapproving of satire; journalistic critics disapproving of all that is not "nice" or beautiful in a conventional way). Its burden is another variant of Lewis's long-running anti-romantic campaign, a campaign in defense of satire, classical values, and the external approach: but always in defense of art, even including the art of those whose artistic credo he differs with. He must be understood to be defending art even when attacking rival artists: he at least takes them seriously. The continuity of Lewis's interests comes out when we look at something he wrote a few years earlier about his previous book of criticism, Paleface, and which we can apply equally well to Men Without Art:

> My main object . . . has been to place in the hands of the readers of imaginative literature . . . a sort of key; so that, with its aid, they may be able to read any work of art presented to them, and, resisting the skilful blandishments of the fictionist, reject this plausible "life" that often is not life, and understand the ideologic or philosophical basis of these confusing entertainments, where so many false ideas change hands or change heads.[1]*

This interest in hidden ideological implications — in politics in a more enduring sense than the demand prevalent in the nineteen thirties for social relevance — may help us understand a puzzling feature of Men Without Art: that is, why Lewis "attacks" writers whom he acknowledges to be excellent or at least better than average artists. It is because he perceives their tendencies ("political" tendencies, as he calls them) as working, despite their

* Notes to the Afterword begin on p. 316. Page references in parentheses, unless otherwise indicated, are to the text of the present edition.

intentions, to subvert art in general, whether by too unquestioningly depicting mass man, "those to whom things are done," like Hemingway; by devaluing the currency of sincerity and coherent self-assertion, like Eliot; or by cosily rewriting recent literary history so as to excuse feebleness of scope and debility of grasp on the external world, like Woolf.

Men Without Art was written during the busiest period of Lewis's literary life. His publishing career shows a long period of semi-retirement between the years 1919, when after returning from the trenches of World War I he published the lively pamphlet of art criticism The Caliph's Design, and 1926, when there appeared The Art of Being Ruled, the first of his large scale diagnoses of the condition of civilization. This was followed the next year by Time and Western Man and his first book of exclusively literary criticism, The Lion and the Fox, on Shakespeare's politics. In fiction there was the revision of Tarr and the first volume of The Childermass, both in 1928, and then in 1930 came Lewis's bid to rank with the Joyce of Ulysses, the major work of satirical fiction, The Apes of God, with its defensive appendage, the pamphlet Satire and Fiction, much of which gets reworked into Men Without Art,[2] although no fewer than seven more books appeared before the present one in 1934 (see List of Books, p. 301). This is an astounding record of productivity, especially when we remember that along with all this writing he was continuing to work at drawing and painting — and under difficult and straitened circumstances in his private life.

Both in private life and public, Lewis took a fundamentally grim view of the world. In part 3, chapter 1 of the present work ("The Artist and the New Gothic"), his sense of the contingency of modern life is rendered with unsettling power — threatened by imminent insane war and by spreading depression in a world of plenty. Such passages should dispel any facile sense of Lewis as a comfortable reactionary or conservative; indeed his independence of mind is remarkable. Adopting his favorite stance of outsider "Enemy," he shows a rare combination of passion and detachment from any party line.[3] He is radically pessimistic not only about politics ("All [political systems] are apt to be equally bad") but as a general principle: "Human life [is] a very bad business indeed" (213). Nonetheless, on this perception of the absurdity of life he builds a conception of the usefulness of art: "We are merely talking monkeys . . . [but] enabled . . . to know that we are animals . . ." (231) and to recognize our own ridiculousness. Art may be a game, as he phrases it, but it is essential to civilized life. The barrenness of a world without art is fully restated a few years later in Blasting and Bombardiering (1937): "Yet the artist is, in any society, by no means its least valuable citizen. Without him the world ceases to see itself and to reflect. . . . Deprived of art, the healthy intellectual discipline of well-being is lost. Life instantly becomes so brutalized as to be mechanical and devoid of interest."[4] It is against this brutalized world and in favor of what The Caliph's Design had called "a state of mind of relish, of fullness and exultation" that Men Without Art, like the best of Lewis's writings, so energetically operates.

II

The contemporary critical reactions to *Men Without Art* run the gamut from enthusiastic praise to fury. Probably the first to offer a reaction was Lewis's publisher, Desmond Flower of Cassell's, who had agreed to publish three books by him. It's clear from the abundant misprints that the book did not get much in the way of editing, and some indication of the publisher's concerns comes from Lewis's letter to Flower of July 19, 1934. Not only is the author's wish to change the name of his book (to *Literary Barrens*) not granted—understandably enough, if the book was in production—but evidently what has mainly preoccupied the publisher and printer (printers were legally liable for any material judged obscene that they had printed) is the matter of libel and indecency. Lewis agrees to soften an analogy he had used in reference to I. A. Richards's "ritual for heightening sincerity" in which he had evidently compared it to dubious commercial aphrodisiacs such as were sold in disreputable shops for "rubber goods" (condoms) in Britain at the time (see p. 72 and note); he replaces this lively sounding simile with the innocuous phrase "specifics for more enterprising virility." But when requested to bowdlerize the innocuous popular song which begins "She was poor but she was honest, / victim of a rich man's crime," he draws the line:

As to the "rich man's crime", it has always been *crime* in the mouths of the song-birds I have heard, and "crime" is I think funnier than "whim" a little. So let us leave crime.[5]

Turning from Lewis's publisher to the targets of his satirical criticism, we know something of Hemingway's reaction to the chapter on him. (The story is told by Carlos Baker in his biography.) Hemingway was handed the article to look at in Sylvia Beach's Paris bookshop, and his chagrin on reading it was such that he lashed out in a rage against some nearby potted flowers, smashing both flowers and vase alike.[6] His revenge was delayed several decades, but he took it at last in *A Moveable Feast*, in his spiteful portrayal of Lewis, whom he memorably described as "the nastiest man I've ever seen," having the eyes of "an unsuccessful rapist."[7] But this vignette tells us little about Lewis and much about its author. (Jeffrey Meyers establishes clearly that it is not an account of Hemingway's reaction at the time but the result of retroactive chagrin.[8]) Lewis's account of Hemingway, on the other hand, is wickedly funny but essentially impersonal, directed at the persona created by Hemingway's prose style, a legitimate target. Furthermore it includes several strong statements about Hemingway's stature as an artist, and it is always clear that Lewis ranks him higher than Faulkner. Lewis's regard endured through the years of Hemingway's decline and is still attested to in *Rude Assignment*.[9]

Lewis's critical attack on T. S. Eliot is far more severe and penetrates to a deeper level than that on Hemingway. It is also at least equally funny. But Eliot's public urbanity remained unruffled and his cordial respect — if not affection — for Lewis continued.[10] He sat for the great portrait of 1938, and he continued to pay him tribute throughout Lewis's life — and after. In an obituary comment he wrote, perhaps recalling *Men Without Art*: "His criticism was impartial. He had been a frank and merciless critic even of his friends, to whom indeed he devoted more attention than to his foes — witness his comments, in *Time and Western Man*, on Joyce and Pound, and elsewhere on myself. . . . We have no critic of the contemporary world at once so fearless, so honest, so intelligent, and possessed of so brilliant a prose style."[11]

Our most detailed account of the reactions of one of the authors Lewis criticized in *Men Without Art* comes from the diaries of Virginia Woolf.[12] After the satire of Bloomsbury in *The Apes of God*, Woolf knew to expect an attack as soon as she read the advertisement for the forthcoming book:

> Now I know by reason & instinct that this is an attack; that I am publicly demolished: nothing is left of me in Oxford & Cambridge & places where the young read Wyndham Lewis. My instinct is, not to read it.

And she confronts her motives with honesty: "Why then do I shrink from reading W.L.? Why am I sensitive? I think vanity. I dislike the thought of being laughed at." So she resolves "craftily to gather" the gist of the attack and in a year, perhaps, to read it. But three days later she writes, "This morning I've taken the arrow of W.L. to my heart." She then strikes a not entirely convincing attitude of appreciating the fun while simultaneously managing to read into Lewis's attention a flattering meaning that we are not likely to agree in finding: "[H]e makes tremendous & delightful fun of B. & B. [*Mr. Bennett and Mrs. Brown*]: calls me a peeper, not a looker, a fundamental prude; but one of the 4 or 5 living (so it seems) who is an artist." Of course the only ground for this inference is that the book devotes a chapter to her alongside those on Hemingway, Faulkner, and Eliot. That Woolf's bravado was in part assumed is shown by her entry of two days later: "Quite cured today. So the W.L. illness lasted 2 days." Even in the first reaction of the "illness," however, she had also shown a stoical trust in her own talents: "If there is truth in W.L. well, face it: I've no doubt I am prudish and peeping, well then live more boldly. But for God's sake dont try to bend my writing one way or the other."[13]

If Virginia Woolf's reaction to being attacked is both humanly comprehensible and admirably honest (in the privacy of her diary), her defender Stephen Spender's tactics in a review of the book for *The Spectator* are less disinterested (Spender, himself one of the targets of *The Apes of God*, no doubt having an axe to grind). His repeated imputation to Lewis of "a great deal of malice" provoked the latter to a spirited defence in a letter to the editor:

. . . in *Men Without Art* I have everywhere stressed that my criticisms are rather a writer's than a reader's. It is the internal creative *machinery* that I expose. . . . Criticism of this nature is "destructive," of necessity — especially where a reputation is so flimsy as to be peculiarly susceptible of "destruction."

Lewis repeats in summary his criticisms of Eliot and (from *Time and Western Man*) of Pound and points out that in contrast to Woolf's, their reactions showed "no amateurish touchiness on the score of 'originality.' " Finally he delivers a more scathing judgement than any in *Men Without Art*, consigning Woolf to the company of the author of "The boy stood on the burning deck," as though to hint at what true maliciousness might have wrought:

> Mrs. Woolf is charming, scholarly, intelligent, everything that you will: but here we *have* not a Jane Austen — a Felicia Hemans, rather, as it has been said: for there are some even more "malicious" than I am, I am afraid.[14]

Other reviews of *Men Without Art* were more favorable. G. K. Chesterton (whose book on St. Thomas Aquinas probably suggested to Lewis his satirical sobriquet for Hemingway, "The Dumb Ox") gave it a favorable brief mention in the widely read *Listener*, which also printed a full and favorable account by Lewis's admirer and expositor Hugh Gordon Porteus.[15] The reviewer for the *Times Literary Supplement* complained that Lewis was "bogged" in a "negative view of art," comparing him unfavorably in this regard to Middleton Murry, "one who has found his way from intellectual bankruptcy to something at least positive" — i.e., in his " 'conversion' to Communism." This provoked lively letters of rebuttal and comment from Lewis (and from Murry, too, insisting he was a "democratic Socialist," not a Communist). In one of them (to Herbert Read, who he at first thought might have written the review in question), Lewis writes, "tell me what you mean by my 'negative' attitude," and he goes on to ask scathingly,

> Was the typical artist of the anti-religionist Renaissance "negative" (say da Vinci?) Are the Chinese, because they have at all times shown themselves less prone to fanatical emotionality, of a religious order, than have the Semites and the Anglo-Saxons — have they been "negative" always, because on the whole laodicean, philosophic, and preoccupied with external beauty?[16]

The Criterion, despite the book's attack on Eliot, gave it a favorable review by D. G. Bridson, later to be a close friend and to produce Lewis's work on the B.B.C. Bridson's praise comes with a qualification that most readers will still echo:

> *Men Without Art*, in fact, is not to be taken too seriously as a reasoned study in general principles. The best things in it, as in so much of Mr. Lewis's critical writing, are those which stand out as most obviously unrelated to what he is attempting to demonstrate in general. His chapters on Hemingway and Faulkner, for instance, as critical analyses, are brilliant. As a piece of ingenious

reading-by-letter, his chapter on Mr. Eliot as Critic is brilliant again. So are his chapters on Satire, Henry James and himself. It is only when trying to square these self-contained particularities to his general theme, that he ceases to be impressive.[17]

Bonamy Dobrée, who had reviewed *The Lion and the Fox* very favorably in *The Criterion* in 1927, did the same for *Men Without Art* in *The London Mercury*. He calls the book "extremely exhilarating" and declares that "it has a style of its own . . . an explosive, compulsive, subduing style; you have to read whether you want to or not; and you will not be quite the same man when you have finished." He agrees, in effect, with Bridson's finding of a lack of overall coherence but is more tolerant than complaining: Lewis, he writes,

> leads one such a breathless scramble over hill and dale, up mountains, defiant of rocks; but it is not the business of an artist to have clear little docketed views on every mortal subject; the attitude is all, and Mr. Lewis's is clear enough. He hates the second-rate, the muddle-headed, the un-individual, and has no very exalted opinion of humanity. . . .

Praising, like almost all reviewers, as "brilliant" the opening "monolith" essays, he is nevertheless concerned to defend T. S. Eliot:

> The two earlier ones are more purely literary, though they connect the writers with the ethos that produced them; the one on Mr. Eliot, as witty as could be wished, is, rather, an examination of points of view. He is a little hard on Mr. Eliot, who might well complain that remarks thrown out in journals (one with which Mr. Lewis makes much play appeared originally in No. 1 of *The Enemy*) are not to be taken as *ex cathedra* statements, and that after all he has a right to progress and change his mind. . . .

(Lewis as editor had printed Eliot's "A Note on Poetry and Belief" in *The Enemy*, but that hardly required him to refrain from disagreeing with it.) But Dobrée, whatever his reservations, concludes resoundingly:

> In such an age as ours there is nothing for Mr. Lewis to do but to occupy, though without arrogance, the position of Enemy No. 1. He sustains the position with an irresistible drive, and the careless supremacy of a giant. Few of us after reading this book will feel ourselves unscathed, if we are at all honest, or fail to see more clearly and accurately what is happening. What a tonic it is, too, not only to stiffen the sinews and summon up the blood, but to make the grey-matter more alert and responsive: it is profoundly exciting.[18]

That Lewis himself remained pleased with the book is suggested by his (fruitless) interest in republishing it in 1946[19] and by a fragment found in his papers at Cornell. In this, probably from the same time, he has jotted the note:

MEN WITHOUT ART

Up to p. 232. The book, up to this point, consists of (1) the three essays on Hemingway, Eliot, and Virginia Woolf: (2) a long, muscular, argument in favour of the objective as against the subjective = against the romantic, specially in its diabolic form.

Of these 232 pages all that need be [altered *crossed out*] touched is the eight pages ("Introduction") at the beginning. A new Introduction would have to be substituted.[20]

May it perhaps be because the Faulkner essay provoked none of the defensive reactions the other three elicited that Lewis forgets to mention it and gives its place among the "monoliths" to the piece on Woolf? In any case, he clearly remained pleased with the book and would doubtless be glad to find it back in circulation, knowing it had lost little of timeliness.

III

If reviewers tended to agree — as will most readers — that overall coherence of argument is not the strong point of *Men Without Art*, swamped as it often is under a positively Swiftian exuberance of digression, nonetheless one of the book's most interesting aspects is its continuation of a running argument with T. S. Eliot on the matters of impersonality and belief. A brief sketch of the main lines of this debate may be useful.

Eliot first adumbrates his notions of the necessary impersonality of the artist in "Tradition and the Individual Talent" (1919).[21] Lewis quotes in his text above many of the most illuminating passages; I shall cite here only a few sentences which highlight a feature of Eliot's criticism perhaps not sufficiently noticed: its tacit appeal to the prestige of the exact sciences. (Lewis, who wrote about the "delusion of impersonality" of the scientist in *The Art of Being Ruled* and elsewhere,[22] alerts us to this tendency in the course of his final diagnosis that Eliot's confused position results from the doctrine of original sin and a consequent recourse to a "strictly inhuman" notion of the self as "an hypostasized intellectual contraption, a super-self" [see pp. 73-74].) After speaking of the "mind of Europe" as something the poet must be aware of, Eliot writes: "The progress of an artist is a continual self-sacrifice, a continual extinction of personality" — a "depersonalization" in which "art may be said to approach the condition of science." Then, after the famous analogy of the filament of platinum as catalyst,[23] we find: "The poet's mind is in fact a receptacle for seizing and storing up numberless feelings, phrases, images, which remain there until all the particles which can unite to form a new compound are present together." And in the following, the term "medium" has a scientific sense: "My meaning is, that the poet has, not a 'personality' to express, but a particular medium . . . in which impressions and experiences combine in peculiar and unexpected ways."

(I digress for a moment to quote also the famous formulation that now takes on some poignancy in the light of our greater knowledge of the difficulties of Eliot's private life and marriage: "Poetry is not a turning loose of emotion, but an escape from emotion; it is not the expression of personality, but an escape from personality." Eliot, we know, had urgent personal reasons for wishing to depersonalize the conception of the poet. Of course Lewis knew the facts of Eliot's private life and may be thought to allude to the personal motivation behind Eliot's theorizing in such remarks as the following:

> I do not believe in the anonymous, "impersonal," catalytic, for the very good reason that I am sure the personality is in that as much as in the other part of this double-headed oddity, however thoroughly disguised, and is more apt to be a corrupting influence in that arrangement than in the more usual one, where the artist is identified with his beliefs. (74)

Such an allusion, however, is not dropped to tittilate the knowing; rather it simply undergirds the confident authority of Lewis's insight, already reached on impersonal grounds.)

Although in *The Lion and the Fox* (1927) Lewis has an introductory chapter on "Shakespeare's 'Impersonality' and its Consequences" and a concluding one on "The Depersonalization of Shakespeare," he makes no *explicit* reference to Eliot's views; but it is hard not to feel their presence in the background. Lewis makes clear that he has no interest in Shakespeare's "personality" in what *Men Without Art* calls "the *Ballyhoo* sense . . . an individualist abortion, bellowing that it wants at all costs to 'express' itself" (62). But it's not *strength* of personality as such that Lewis rejects, as the presence of the same verb in the earlier book indicates: "I am setting out to show . . . how . . . bellowing at you from the windy corner of every scene in the great tragedies is a human personality. . . ." It is the *mind* behind — and in — the texts, then, not any Romantic self seeking "expression," that Lewis is interested in, refusing to believe that Shakespeare, however manifold his nature, lacks personality in the sense that *Men Without Art* later beautifully defines it: "a constancy and consistency in being, as concretely as possible, *one thing* — at peace with itself, if not with the outer world . . ." (62).

Lewis of course takes no simple-minded view of the plays as expressing Shakespeare's direct opinions. In his

> control of these creatures Shakespeare showed all the *sang froid* that we associate with the great technician, the tactical transference of the individual experience into a series of prepared puppets. But such puppets are born, not made, by a most painful gestation. It will be my business here to relate the spasms of these scowling and despairing monsters to a particularly concrete figure, or to a mind experiencing things according to identifiable personal laws. (*The Lion and the Fox*, 14)

Lewis, we see, no less than Eliot, is writing criticism with the eye and mind of a practitioner; still deeply immersed in the creation of *The Childermass* and *The Apes of God*, he speaks of Shakespeare's characters in terms that fit his own; and his birth image is in unemphasized but telling contrast to Eliot's scientific one of the catalyst, carrying with it not the wished-for prestige of science but a fully human burden, and with no pretence that the struggling author is absent. The contrasting quality of his imagery is evident also in this: "Each of the great figures of this *theatre of character* is to be regarded as an organ of an organism that we know as Shakespeare" (*The Lion and the Fox*, 15).

Towards the end of *The Lion and the Fox*, Lewis reiterates his view in terms of Shakespeare's thinking, in a passage that Eliot will quote:

> With the exception of Chapman, Shakespeare is the only "thinker" we meet with among the elizabethan dramatists. By this is meant, of course, that his work contained, apart from poetry, phantasy, rhetoric or observation of manners, a body of matter representing explicitly processes of the intellect which would have furnished a moral philosopher like Montaigne with the natural material for his essays. But the quality of this thinking—as it can be surprised springing naturally in the midst of the consummate movements of his art—is, as must be the case with such a man, of startling force sometimes. And if it is not systematic, at least a recognizable physiognomy is there. (179)

In a lecture of 1927 which is largely devoted to a discussion of Lewis's book,[22] Eliot quotes that last paragraph in full and comments: "It is this general notion of 'thinking' that I would challenge. . . . The poet who 'thinks' is merely the poet who can express the emotional equivalent of thought. But he is not necessarily interested in the thought itself." Here Eliot shows the influence of the idea of pseudo-beliefs and pseudo-statements which I. A. Richards had introduced shortly before[23] and which Lewis has so much fun attacking in *Men Without Art*. Naturally, if the statements of poetry are only pseudo-statements, in response to which neither belief nor disbelief would be appropriate on the reader's part, they cannot be admitted to the status of real thinking, an adequate response to which can hardly rule out entirely considerations of agreement or disagreement. So, having adduced Dante, Eliot continues: "In truth neither Shakespeare nor Dante did any real thinking—that was not their job . . . the essential is that each expresses, in perfect language, some permanent human impulse" (135-37). The confident assumption here as to what constitutes "real thinking" is nothing less than crippling, when contrasted to Lewis's view—and to that of D. H. Lawrence, to whom Lewis is far closer than he is to Eliot in this instance.[24] Moving to the question of belief, Eliot sums up with a new series of analogies in the course of which he gives (can it be an inadvertent recurrence?) the "filament" of 1919 a new organic context: "The poet makes poetry, the metaphysician makes metaphysics, the bee makes honey, the spider secretes a filament; you can hardly say that any of these agents believes: he merely does" (138). Thus Eliot's flight from openly admitting his personal presence in his poetry ends up by, in effect, impugning the sincerity about *his* own beliefs of the greatest poet of Christendom. Dante, it turns out, was—as a poet, anyway—"merely" expressing emotional impulses, not thought or beliefs. If a poem's statements are pseudo-statements and its expressions of belief only pseudo-belief, then the poet who wants to be "invisible" (as Hugh Kenner's calls Eliot[25]) is off the hook and no longer can be called to account for his utterances by inconvenient cross examiners. (Even Lewis admits the *tactical* usefulness of this defence against misguided moralists.) But what has happened meanwhile to the notion of sincerity?

In *Men Without Art*, Lewis diagnoses the problems of "sincerity" and "personality" as central to Eliot's critical positions. He finds Eliot's idea of personality (as applied to the poet) to be infected by the *time-view* which he had dealt with in *Time and Western Man*, here taking the form of a new exoticism which wishes to make all ages contemporaneous. The cost is serious: "And so the *here and now* is diminished too much and we desert the things that after all we stand a chance of learning something concrete about" (73–74). Those who succumb, following Eliot's model, to the labor of recovering a sense of the past "should scarcely expect not to lose coherence—they must expect to 'sacrifice' more and more of the 'self' or 'personality,' which is merely a living adequately at any given moment, to become an 'impersonal' rendezvous . . ." (74). The poet who is a mere rendezvous, an echo chamber, a "medium" (in several senses), naturally suffers a diminution of the strongly defined "personality" that Lewis values. And in fact (says Lewis) this is what has happened to Eliot. Although Richards's claim that *The Waste Land* shows a poet who has "effected a complete severance between his poetry and *all* his beliefs" embarrassed Eliot, Richards's view "is substantially true": Eliot indeed lacks personality in the Lewisian sense; he holds no real beliefs; he's, if not a humbug, a pseudo everything. "[S]incerity is precisely what Mr. Eliot is afraid of—sincerity in the sense of integral belief of any sort." In this sense, he's the latest in the line of the Decadents, holding, like Wilde, that art is beautiful lying. "For as there can be no absolute truth, let us relegate 'truth' to the category of 'mob belief,' and, as artists, have no more to do with it!" (82) As for Richards's sincerity doctrine, Lewis finds it arising from "a sort of *impotence to believe*," an impotence springing from the recent breakdown not so much of religion as of the certainty of *scientific* beliefs. It is ironic that being true to one's self should be the crisis for Richards, since his own "pseudo-belief" system itself "must tend to undermine the vigour of . . . selfhood to a peculiar degree." And Richards's answer, his "ritual for sincerity," merely promotes "successful extroversion."

In his latest book of 1933, Lewis continues, Eliot has disavowed his own self of 1922, thus further surrendering to the time-mind. Eliot does not now *deny*, even implicitly, Richards's view of *The Waste Land*, he merely surrenders his authority to speak of it and becomes just another reader. Simply, he is no longer the man who wrote it. Lewis has great fun imagining Eliot's pose of quizzical puzzlement about this earlier self, "this poet-fellow (an American I believe!) who was responsible for this cross-word puzzle, of synthetic literary chronology, of spurious verbal algebra. Did the author of *The Waste Land* believe in God? 'How can I say?' drawls Mr. Eliot, testily" (96). Like his own Macavity, the mystery cat, he wasn't there.

No one reading the chapter on Eliot will fail, surely, to find it good humored, even affectionate, though trenchantly adversarial. Many will find its comic mode more engagingly convincing than the very different approach F. R. Leavis took in reaching similar conclusions a quarter of a century later.[26] Even today the seduction of Eliot's style in his essays and the prestige of his standing as poet can bewitch one into too reverent an attitude towards his formulations (a response he himself would be the last to desire). Lewis's lively critique — never reprinted, never given the wide currency it deserved — has only to be experienced to arm the reader against losing his critical senses. We can never again fail to notice the weakness of Eliot's continual self-qualifications, his essential evasiveness. And the sheer comedy of Lewis's performance invigorates and awakens. No Philistine, he yet comes across as a welcome voice of common sense.

IV

Men Without Art is still very much alive. Even if its targets are now either forgotten (and surprisingly few of them are: in his critical polemic Lewis did not in this book lay himself open to the reproach he cites as so often made against his satire: that he wastes his efforts on negligible targets[27]) or enshrined — in both cases we can still profit. If forgotten, we can enjoy his gusto and subtlety of argument. If enshrined, all the more do we profit from the challenge to our habits of inert acceptance, or conditioned-response respect. Eliot, Faulkner, Hemingway, Woolf — what is alive in these writers is not threatened by Lewis's cheerful invective, what is dead or pretentious or silly in them deserves his attacks, and the upshot will be to allow what's best in them to stand free of encumbrance, and to challenge us to a fresh and newly authenticated responsiveness.

E. W. F. Tomlin gives a vivid account of what it was like to read Lewis's books in the thirties, an account in which we can recognize the reactions that *Men Without Art* still elicits:

> . . . there was the immediate impression of the distinctive, the personal, the man apart. The banner-headlines, the unconventional subtitles, the eccentric layout, the liberal and often arcane quotations, the teeming and rich vocabulary, the prodigious learning: these became indelibly associated with even the least of his writings. Finally, once the reading began in earnest (and it could begin at any point), the attention was held by the exhibition of free intellect, the wit, the tough fight-talk, and yet at the same time the urbanity,

and the overall style which Eliot, in his Introduction to *One-Way Song*, describes as one of the most original in modern English. Admittedly, the going was not always easy; Lewis rarely wrote smooth, even, *belles-lettres* prose; but all was food for the intelligence, meaty if sometimes gristly, but never synthetic extract.[28]

And an image that Bonamy Dobrée used in his review of *The Lion and the Fox* also seems memorably apt: "Everything is grist which comes to his mill and a miller he is rather than a baker. For he does not give you the loaf ready to swallow; it is not being spoon-fed to read one of his books."[29] Lewis pays his readers the compliment of expecting them to be able and willing to read more than passively. As we do so, we can hardly fail to be impressed by the astonishing rapidity and breadth of his mind and reading. If at times his working methods suggest haste to the point of carelessness,[30] it's always clear that the haste derives from energy and from an eagerness to get his point made *con brio*. He is capable of moments of high comedy and invective. Look for example at the passage where he strikes the pose of a man addressing a jury (107–108), or at the funny portrayal of T. S. Eliot as captain of the good ship *Criterion* (77–78). True, there are moments when his fluid, careless syntax leads to sentences one itches to emend, but far more frequent are the effects that these flaws are the price for — effects of rapidity, fluidity, improvisatory rhetoric, copiousness, verve, gusto. Some words Donald Davie wrote about Hardy seem applicable: "What he does then will fall short of mechanical precision, but his artifact by its very faultiness will have something better, *virtù*, 'the light of the doer as it were cleaving to it.' (the words are Pound's.)"[31] In brief, Lewis's criticism is never less than an invigorating performance.

But the performance would soon pall if we did not feel it to be undergirded by some ultimate seriousness and an interest in arriving at "true judgement." Bruce Powe has written:

> The tendency of most readers of Lewis is to try and decide to what extent he is *right* in his literary judgments — that is, judge the content of his criticism. This is never the point.[32]

Well, yes and no; it's no more nor less the point than it is with any major critic. We don't read Leavis or Dr. Johnson "to try and decide to what extent [they are] *right*" in this or that judgement; we read to participate in the working of a distinguished mind and sensibility. But this is not to say that persuasiveness of judgement isn't finally a relevant criterion. If we found a critic not just consistently wrong, but wrong as the result of holding a frivolous or repugnant view of life, we would not frequent him for long. Lewis's criticism is the work of an artist, the work of a man with an always serious view of life (if never a comfortable one). His critical writings can be read not only for how they illuminate their particular subjects (and they *do*), but also as imaginative experience, an expansion of mind and feelings, a world to be entered and participated in. We value *Men Without Art* finally less for its incidental aperçus (though they are many and stimulating) than for its life-enhancing qualities, its stimulus to a livelier reading and thinking, its energizing of our intellects, our feelings, and our will.

NOTES TO AFTERWORD

[1] *Paleface* (1929; rpt. New York: Haskell House, 1969), p. 109.

[2] Including "The Taxi-Cab Driver Test for 'Fiction,' " that early gesture towards a sort of "new criticism" approach to prose.

[3] A small example of Lewis's keeping critical judgements clear of party feeling may be gathered by comparing his severe and explicit critical condemnation of some of Aldous Huxley's fiction in *Men Without Art* with his citing of Huxley as a fellow sufferer from partisanship in reviewing: ". . . in the European world of art in the last half-decade more than one prominent writer or painter has undoubtedly suffered in consequence of his non-adherence to Communism. I need only mention . . . in the literary field Mr Aldous Huxley, whose 'Brave New World' was an unforgivable offence to Progress and to political uplift of every description" (*Letters*, ed. Rose, p. 226). This is from a letter to the *Times Literary Supplement* complaining that their review of *Men Without Art* suffered from partisan bias.

[4] *Blasting and Bombardiering*, 2nd ed. (Berkeley: Univ. of California, 1967), p. 259.

[5] *Letters*, ed. Rose, p. 220.

[6] See Carlos Baker, *Ernest Hemingway: A Life Story* (New York: Scribner's, 1969), p. 258. The Hemingway chapter was published six months earlier than the book in the April issue of *Life & Letters*; Baker places the incident in March.

[7] Ernest Hemingway, *A Moveable Feast* (New York: Scribner's, 1964), p. 109.

[8] See Jeffrey Meyers, *Hemingway: A Biography* (New York: Harper and Row, 1985), pp. 87–88.

[9] *Rude Assignment*, p. 218 (the passage is quoted in the Explanatory Note to p. 19).

[10] Herbert Read (not an entirely disinterested witness, however) reports Eliot as saying that Lewis was one of the few people he had ever found it impossible to like (*The Cult of Sincerity* [New York: Horizon Press, 1969], p. 111).

[11] *Hudson Review*, Summer 1957, pp. 169–70; quoted in *Enemy Salvoes*, p. 184.

[12] Her reactions, and the entire relationship between her and Lewis, are discussed by Jean Guiget in "Jeu de miroirs: jeu de massacre (Virginia Woolf et Wyndham Lewis)," *Blast 3*, pp. 135–40.

[13] *The Diary of Virginia Woolf, Volume Four: 1931-1935*, ed. Anne Olivier Bell (New York: Harcourt Brace Jovanovich, 1982), pp. 251–52

[14] *Letters*, ed. Rose, pp. 224–25.

[15] The Porteus review appeared in the issue of 10 October 1934, the Chesterton in that of 28 November. Porteus was the author of *Wyndham Lewis: A Discursive Exposition*, published in 1932.

[16] The *TLS* review appeared in the issue of 22 November 1934. For the resulting correspondence, see *Letters*, ed. Rose, pp. 225–32.

[17] *The Criterion*, 14:55 (January 1935), 335–37.

[18] *London Mercury*, 31:181 (Nov. 1934), 76–77.

[19] See Morrow and Lafourcade's *Bibliography*, p. 79.

[20] Manuscript at Cornell. Published by kind permission of Cornell University Library.

[21] Eliot's essay was first collected in *The Sacred Wood*, 1920. Since Eliot had, only the previous year, in reviewing *Tarr* for *The Egoist* (5:8 [September 1918], 105–106) defined its author as "the most fascinating personality of our time," his views in this essay must have struck Lewis as a peculiarly direct challenge.

[22] See *The Art of Being Ruled*, pt. 1, ch. 6, "The Non-Impersonality of Science": "The popular notion that science is 'impersonal' is one of the first errors we are called on to dispel. . . . A simple belief in the 'detachment' and 'objectivity' of science, the anxiety of a disillusioned person to escape from his self and merge his personality in *things*; verging often on the worship of *things* — of the non-human, feelingless, and thoughtless — of such experiences and tendencies is this delusion composed" (pp. 26–27). Lewis makes the same point in an article published at the time of *Men Without Art*: "Let us admit at once how very relative all 'detachment' or 'impersonality' must be. . . . Even in scientific investigation, the intellect of a Faraday or an Einstein works of necessity in a very biased fashion. . . . That the handling of the material of art or of science — of *fact*, in other words — does 'detach' a man from his personality (composed as the latter is of race, class, period and the rest) is obvious. . . . Bias is *not*, clearly, the ideal. But it is after all something to do with the business; for a god would not be particularly interested in 'discovery' at all . . ." (" 'Detachment' and the Fictionist," *The English Review*, 59 (November 1934), 564–73; the quotation is from p. 570).

[23] See the Explanatory Note to p. 74 for the passage in full.

[24] *Shakespeare and the Stoicism of Seneca*, published for the Shakespeare Association by the Oxford University Press in 1927 and later collected in *Selected Essays*, to which the page numbers refer.

[25] Richards's account was published in the previous year in his book, *Science and Poetry* (1926), but Eliot had already printed the relevant chapter as an article in *The Criterion* in 1925.

[26] For Lawrence's idea of "real thinking" — thinking by the whole man, "man alive" — and its embodiment supremely in the work of art, see his "Why the Novel Matters," and "Introduction to These Paintings" (*Phoenix* [New York: Viking, 1968], pp. 533–38 and 551–84, esp. 573–75). See also John Remsbury, " 'Real Thinking': Lawrence and Cézanne," in *The Cambridge Quarterly*, 2:2 (Spring 1967), 117–47.

[27] See Hugh Kenner, *The Invisible Poet* (New York: McDowell Obolensky, 1959).

[28] See Leavis's "T. S. Eliot as Critic," first published in *Commentary* in November 1958 and reprinted in *'Anna Karenina' and Other Essays* (London: Chatto and Windus, 1967).

[29] Eliot, for one, had made this reproach in a 1931 essay: "Mr. Wyndham Lewis, the most brilliant journalist of my generation (in addition to his other gifts) often squanders his genius for invective upon objects which to everyone by himself seem unworthy of his artillery, and arrays howitzers against card houses . . ." ("Charles Whibley," in *Selected Essays*, 3rd ed. [London: Faber, 1951], p. 499).

[30] E. W. F. Tomlin, ed., *Wyndham Lewis: An Anthology of his Prose* (London: Methuen, 1969), p. 4.

[31] Bonamy Dobrée in *The Criterion*, 5:3 (June 1927), 339–43.

[32] For example, his misrepresentations of Woolf's *Mr. Bennett and Mrs. Brown* — see Explanatory Note to p. 135.

[33] Donald Davie, *Thomas Hardy and British Poetry* (London: Routledge & Kegan Paul, 1973), p. 25.

[34] *Blast 3*, p. 121.

ALPHABETICAL INDEX OF AUTHORS AND TITLES

The letter "q" following a page number indicates a quotation.

Printed in March 1987 in Santa Barbara & Ann Arbor
for the Black Sparrow Press by Graham Mackintosh
& Edwards Brothers Inc. Design by Barbara Martin.
This edition is printed in paper wrappers; there
are 400 cloth trade copies; & 176 numbered deluxe
copies have been handbound in boards by Earle Gray.

WYNDHAM LEWIS (1882–1957) was a novelist, painter, essayist, poet, critic, polemicist and one of the truly dynamic forces in literature and art in the twentieth century. He was the founder of Vorticism, the only original movement in twentieth-century English painting. The author of *Tarr* (1918), *The Lion and the Fox* (1927), *Time and Western Man* (1927), *The Apes of God* (1930), *The Revenge for Love* (1937), and *Self Condemned* (1954), Lewis was ranked highly by his important contemporaries: "the most fascinating personality of our time . . . the most distinguished living novelist" (T. S. Eliot), "the only English writer who can be compared to Dostoievsky" (Ezra Pound).

SEAMUS COONEY was educated at University College Dublin and at Berkeley. Now Professor of English at Western Michigan University, he has published articles on Scott, Byron, Henry James, and Austin Clarke, among others. He has edited the poems of Charles Reznikoff, co-authored the Black Sparrow Press *Bibliography*, and edited *Blast 3*.